NEB

The Wordsworth Dictionary of
Synonyms and Antonyms

D0325335

The Wordsworth Dictionary of

Synonyms and Antonyms

Edited by
Martin H. Manser

Wordsworth Reference

The edition published 1998 by Wordsworth Editions Ltd
Cumberland House, Crib, Street, Ware, Hertfordshire SG12 9ET

Text copyright © Martin H. Manser and
Wordsworth Editions Limited 1998

Wordsworth® is a registered trade mark of
Wordsworth Editions Ltd

All rights reserved. This publication may
not be reproduced, stored in a retrieval system,
or transmitted, in any form or by any means,
electronic, mechanical, photocopying, recording
or otherwise, without the prior permission
of the publishers.

ISBN 1 85326 757 0

Printed and bound in Great Britain by
Mackays of Chatham plc, Chatham, Kent

● 423.1 Wor
02/21/00   NEB

3 1260 01349 0738

The Wordsworth
dictionary of synonyms

KG

LeRoy Collins
Leon County Public Lib
200 W. Park Avenue
Tallahassee, FL 32301

HOW TO USE THIS BOOK

A synonym is a word with a meaning that is similar to the meaning of another word. *The Wordsworth Dictionary of Synonyms and Antonyms* is a concise guide to the synonyms of English. It is designed in particular for students, those writing reports, letters and speeches, and crossword solvers.

Suppose you have already used the word *beginning* in a letter, essay or report. You do not want to use *beginning* again. So you can look up *beginning* as an entry word in this dictionary and find a list of alternative words that you could use instead:

> **beginning** *n.* opening, commencement, start,
> source, spring, origin, initiation, arising, outset,
> rise, inception, inauguration

So in place of *beginning* you could write or say *opening*, *commencement*, etc.

Some words have more than one meaning. In such cases the synonyms are listed in numbered senses:

> **funny** *adj.* **1** humorous, ludicrous, ridiculous,
> droll, comical, farcical, amusing, laughable,
> diverting, jocose **2** odd, strange, weird,
> peculiar, curious

This means that *funny* with the meaning 'humorous' has the synonyms *ludicrous*, *ridiculous*, etc. *Funny* with the meaning 'odd' has the synonyms *strange*, *weird*, etc.

Some entry words with the same spelling have different histories, in which case a small raised number is placed after the entry word:

> **grave[1]** *adj.* **1** important, serious, weighty, cogent,
> momentous **2** sober, sedate, thoughtful, staid,
> solemn, serious, sad, pressing, demure, sombre,
> somber (*N. Am.*), heavy
> **grave[2]** *n.* tomb, vault, crypt

British and American spellings are shown:

guilt *n.* **1** blame, responsibility, fault, guiltiness, culpability, criminality **2** wrong, offensiveness, wickedness, iniquity, sin, offence, offense (*N. Am.*)

Synonyms that can be used in informal or colloquial writing or speech are marked as such:

cowardly *adj.* scared, fearful, faint-hearted, spineless, chicken (*informal*), yellow (*informal*)

Antonyms – words opposite in meaning to the main entry word – are also included at the end of many of the entries:

generous *adj.* charitable, liberal, noble, unselfish, big (*informal*), magnanimous, bountiful, free, munificent, open-handed, disinterested, open-hearted, chivalrous
ANT. mean, miserly, stingy

Not all the words listed as synonyms have exactly the same meaning as the main entry word. So if you are unsure of the meaning of a synonym – or want to check up on how to use it – look it up in a good dictionary.

The Wordsworth Dictionary of Synonyms and Antonyms will help you to find the most appropriate word to use on a wide range of occasions. It is hoped that everyone who refers to this book will discover and enjoy more of the richness and diversity of the English language.

ABBREVIATIONS

adj.	adjective
adv.	adverb
ANT.	antonym(s)
conj.	conjunction
interj.	interjection
n.	noun
N. Am.	North American
pl.	plural
prep.	preposition
pron.	pronoun
v.	verb

ACKNOWLEDGMENT

The editor wishes to thank
Gloria Wren for her meticulous typing
and checking of the manuscript.

A

abandon *v.* **1** leave, forsake, desert, depart from, give up, relinquish, renounce, withdraw from **2** surrender, give up, yield, forgo, renounce, retract, recant
ANT. 1 keep, retain **2** adopt, uphold, maintain

abandoned *adj.* **1** deserted, lonely, unfrequented, forsaken, cast away, rejected **2** unrestrained, wild, uninhibited, shameless
ANT. 1 visited, frequented **2** restrained, controlled

abase *v.* degrade, humiliate, reduce, lower, discredit, disgrace, dishonour, dishonor (*N. Am.*), humble, sink, bring low, cast down, stoop, debase, depress, drop, take down, demean
ANT. elevate, exalt, honour, honor (*N. Am.*), dignify

abashed *adj.* embarrassed, ashamed, bewildered, disconcerted, confused
ANT. encouraged, cheered

abate *v.* lessen, lower, reduce, diminish, moderate, decrease, decline, ebb, mitigate, subside, suppress, terminate, temper, assuage, alleviate, appease, pacify, remit, allow, relax, slacken, soothe, soften, qualify, allay, mollify, compose, tranquillize, quiet, quell, calm, dull
ANT. increase, prolong, magnify, enlarge, extend, aggravate, continue, develop, revive, raise, enhance, amplify

abbey *n.* church, minster, monastery, priory, friary, nunnery, convent

abbreviate *v.* shorten, contract, curtail, cut (down), reduce, abridge, condense, epitomize, compress
ANT. lengthen, extend, dilate, expand, simplify, enlarge, produce, stretch, prolong, elongate, expatiate

abbreviation *n.* contraction, abridgment, condensation, abstract, epitome, reduction, summary, curtailment, compression
ANT. expansion, amplification, extension, production, enlargement, dilation, expatiation

abdicate *v.* resign, relinquish, give up, surrender, abandon, vacate, forgo, renounce, cede
ANT. retain, claim, occupy, maintain, usurp, seize, grasp

abduct *v.* take away, kidnap, seize, run away with, carry off, withdraw, spirit away, drag away, draw away
ANT. restore, reinstate

aberrant *adj.* irregular, abnormal, unusual, exceptional, wandering, rambling, divergent, deviant, deviating, devious, erratic
ANT. regular, normal, natural

aberration *n.* divergence, wandering, irregularity, rambling, disconnectedness, hallucination, illusion, delusion, eccentricity, peculiarity
ANT. regularity, norm

abeyance *n.* **in abeyance** suspended, suppressed, out of operation
ANT. in operation, in action

abhor *v.* hate, detest, loathe, shrink from, recoil from, shudder at, abominate, despise, dislike
ANT. desire, enjoy, covet, like, love, relish, admire, approve of, esteem

abhorrent *adj.* detestable, odious, offensive, shocking, repugnant, loathsome, revolting, horrible, repulsive, nauseating
ANT. lovely, admirable, enjoyable, desirable

abide by keep, accept, obey, observe, comply with, conform to, honour, honor (*N. Am.*), pay attention to
ANT. break, disobey

abiding *adj.* lasting, continuing, permanent, unchanging, durable, constant, stable, immutable, changeless
ANT. fickle, changeable, ephemeral

ability *n.* **1** skill, capability, competence, expertise, proficiency, training, skilfulness, skillfulness (*N. Am.*), dexterity, expertness, genius, gift **2** power, means, resources
ANT. **1** inability, incompetence **2** weakness

abject *adj.* wretched, base, vile, mean, low, despicable, contemptible, worthless, degraded
ANT. dignified, exalted, worthy

able *adj.* **1** skilful, skillful (*N. Am.*), competent, expert, proficient, accomplished, capable, experienced, masterly, talented, gifted **2** authorized, permitted, allowed, capable, prepared, willing
ANT. **1** unable, incompetent, incapable, unqualified, weak **2** unauthorized, forbidden, incapable

abnormal *adj.* unnatural, unusual, irregular, peculiar, exceptional, aberrant, erratic, monstrous, singular
ANT. normal, regular, usual, natural, typical, customary, ordinary, common

abolish *v.* annul, destroy, do away with, get rid of, end, set aside, repeal, revoke, suppress, terminate, rescind, abrogate, cancel, nullify, suppress, overthrow, remove, prohibit, stamp out
ANT. keep, maintain, confirm, continue, restore, reinstate, institute, promote

abominable *adj.* awful, appalling, dreadful, horrible, loathsome, abhorrent, foul, odious, offensive, detestable
ANT. desirable, admirable, enjoyable, pleasing

abortive *adj.* unsuccessful, ineffective, futile, vain, disappointing
ANT. successful, effective

abound *v.* be plentiful, team, swarm, multiply, swell, increase, flow, flourish, prevail, revel, exuberate
ANT. lessen, decrease, die, decay, fall

about *prep.* **1** concerning, regarding, relative to, with reference to, in regard to **2** near, surrounding, around, almost, nearly, well-nigh

above *prep.* on top of, higher than, over, beyond, before
ANT. below, beneath, within, lower, less

above board openly, candidly, frankly, sincerely, fairly, unreservedly, guilelessly
ANT. deceitfully, secretly, elusively, underhand

above-named *adj.* named before, above-mentioned, above-described, mentioned above, aforesaid
ANT. named below, described below, hereinafter named

abrasion *n.* rubbing, friction, wearing away, disintegration, attrition

abreast *adv.* alongside, beside, side by side, aligned
ANT. ahead, astern, behind

abridge *v.* shorten, abbreviate, condense, diminish, reduce, contract, cut down, précis, compress, summarize
ANT. extend, lengthen, amplify, expand, spread out, dilate

abridgment *n.* summary, synopsis, précis, abstract, abbreviation, epitome, outline, compendium, digest
ANT. expansion, lengthening, amplification, exposition

abroad *adv.* overseas, far away, in distant parts, in foreign parts, out of the country
ANT. near, close, at home

abrogate *v.* repeal, abolish, cancel, set aside, annul, make void, invalidate, nullify
ANT. enact, confirm, enforce, establish, continue

abrupt *adj.* **1** sudden, unexpected, hasty, ill-timed, precipitate **2** curt, impolite, rude, short, blunt, unceremonious **3** steep, precipitous, craggy, rough, rugged, jagged
ANT. **1** expected, unrushed, leisurely, gradual **2** courteous, polite **3** gradual

abscond *v.* depart, steal away, decamp, bolt, disappear, run off, hide, retreat, escape, elope, sneak off, absent oneself
ANT. show, appear, emerge, present oneself

absence *n.* 1 non-attendance, non-appearance, non-existence 2 lack, non-existence, defect, privation, deficiency
ANT. 1 attendance, presence 2 existence, supply

absent *adj.* 1 away, gone, missing, out, off, playing truant 2 lacking, missing, non-existent
ANT. 1 present, here, in attendance 2 present

absolute *adj.* 1 complete, downright, perfect, pure, categorical, utter, unconditional, unqualified 2 despotic, arbitrary, autocratic, domineering, tyrannical, imperious, dictatorial
ANT. 1 conditioned, limited, qualified, restricted 2 humble, lenient, meek, mild, yielding, compliant, complaisant

absolutely *adv.* completely, perfectly, entirely, totally, wholly, utterly, positively, unconditionally, categorically, unreservedly
ANT. partially, incompletely, possibly, doubtfully

absolve *v.* acquit, clear, exonerate, forgive, free, liberate, release, pardon, set free, discharge, exempt, exculpate
ANT. accuse, condemn, convict, impeach, charge

absorb *v.* 1 take in, consume, imbibe, swallow, suck up, exhaust 2 engross, engage, immerse, occupy, arrest, rivet
ANT. 1 give up, disgorge, send out, radiate, throw off, eject 2 dissipate, distract, disperse

absorption *n.* 1 assimilation, imbibing, consumption, exhaustion 2 occupation, engrossment, engagement, immersion
ANT. 1 ejection, rejection, expulsion, discharge 2 inattention, disregard

abstain *v.* deny oneself, avoid, cease, stop, withhold, give up, relinquish, refrain, resist, forbear, desist
ANT. indulge, yield to, gratify

abstinence *n.* temperance, abstemiousness, self-control, self-restraint, self-denial, sobriety, fasting, moderation, frugality
ANT. excess, intoxication, self-indulgence, sensuality, wantonness, intemperance, greed, gluttony, revelry, dissipation

abstinent *adj.* abstaining, fasting, abstemious, sober, temperate, self-restraining, self-denying, continent
ANT. sensual, self-indulgent, intemperate, dissipated, debauched

abstract *adj.* theoretical, hypothetical, conceptual, unreal, insubstantial, intangible, metaphysical
ANT. concrete, real, substantial, tangible

abstract *n.* summary, abridgment, synopsis, précis, résumé, outline, digest, brief, compendium
ANT. amplification, expansion

abstract *v.* appropriate, withdraw, remove, separate, take away, detach, part, eliminate, distract, discriminate, abridge
ANT. add, complete, increase, unite, fill up, strengthen, combine

abstruse *adj.* hidden, difficult, complex, cryptic, profound, deep, curious, occult, dark, obscure, mystical, hard, vague, indefinite, enigmatic, esoteric, recondite, mysterious, abstract, transcendental
ANT. simple, obvious, intelligible, clear, easy, plain

absurd *adj.* ridiculous, ludicrous, nonsensical, preposterous, senseless, foolish, farcical, irrational, wild, stupid, silly, unreasonable
ANT. sensible, rational, reasonable, logical

abundance *n.* plenty, wealth, profusion, affluence, copiousness, flow, flood, overflow, richness, store, exuberance, plenteousness
ANT. scarcity, deficiency, rarity, scantiness, dearth, poverty

abundant *adj.* plentiful, abounding, flowing, liberal, bountiful, sufficient, lavish, plenteous, much, copious, full, teeming, replete
ANT. scarce, scant, deficient, insufficient, short, bare, niggardly, sparing, impoverished

abuse v. harm, ill-treat, ill-use, injure, wrong, maltreat, exploit, oppress, molest, malign, impose on, ruin, victimize, slander, violate, ravish, defile, disparage, damage, defame, misuse
ANT. cherish, protect, regard, shield, respect, look after, care for, tend,

abuse n. misuse, dishonour, dishonor (N. Am.), maltreatment, outrage, reviling, defamation, insult, disparagement, reproach
ANT. kindness, praise, deference, respect, honour, honor (N. Am.), good treatment, good usage

abusive adj. insulting, rude, censorious, slanderous, reproachful, injurious, offensive, reviling, insolent
ANT. respectful, attentive, kind, flattering, courteous, complimentary

abut v. border, be adjacent, extend, impinge, project, be continuous, adjoin
ANT. diverge, recede

abyss n. chasm, gulf, gorge, deep, the pit

academic adj. 1 scholarly, intellectual, scholastic, studious, clever 2 abstract, theoretical, hypothetical
ANT. 1 illiterate

academic n. intellectual, thinker, lecturer, scholar, teacher, don

academy n. school, institute, college, seminary, association of artists

accede v. agree, consent, assent, acquiesce, comply, accept, concur, approve
ANT. decline, oppose, refuse, dissent, reject

accelerate v. go faster, hurry, quicken, speed, expedite, urge, push forward, press on, forward, advance, further, hasten
ANT. delay, impede, hinder, drag, obstruct

accent n. stress, beat, emphasis, rhythm, pulsation, intonation, cadence, tone, modulation
ANT. monotony, babble, flow, smoothness

accentuate v. emphasize, lay stress upon, highlight, mark, make prominent
ANT. make light of, make insignificant, underestimate, ignore, play down

accept v. 1 take, receive, acquire, obtain 2 allow, admit, agree (to), consent (to) 3 believe, think, hold, credit, regard 4 tolerate, put up with, bear, come to terms with
ANT. 1 refuse, decline, reject 3 repudiate

acceptable adj. 1 adequate, satisfactory, passable, tolerable 2 welcome, pleasing, gratifying, pleasant, agreeable, desirable
ANT. 1 inadequate, unsatisfactory 2 unpleasant, disagreeable, annoying, grievous, ungrateful, unwelcome

acceptance n. reception, taking, acknowledgment, approval, satisfaction, gratification
ANT. rejection, refusal, exclusion

access n. entrance, approach, passage, way, way in, entry, admission, admittance, audience, interview
ANT. exit, way out, departure

accessible adj. approachable, available, to hand, at hand, within reach, clear, attainable, convenient
ANT. unapproachable, difficult

accession n. addition, increase, enlargement, extension, arrival, attainment
ANT. abandonment, decrease, ebb, drain, subsidence, departure

accessory adj. additional, supplemental, accompanying, contributory, auxiliary, helping, subsidiary, subordinate, conducive, subservient

academic n. assistant, helper, associate, accomplice, companion, partner, confederate
ANT. enemy, foe, rival, adversary, antagonist, opponent

accident n. disaster, incident, misfortune, calamity, collision, crash, pile-up, adventure, casualty, mishap, possibility, chance, happening, hazard

accidental adj. casual, unintended, unexpected, random, fortuitous, chance, unlucky, incidental, inadvertent, unplanned, immaterial, non-essential
ANT. intended, purposed, prepared, appointed, certain

acclaim v. applaud, praise, cheer, congratulate, honour, honor (N. Am.), welcome
ANT. criticize, denounce, censure

acclamation *n.* applause, cheer, homage, congratulation, welcome
ANT. criticism, censure, denunciation

accommodate *v.* **1** serve, furnish, supply, contain, hold **2** adapt, reconcile, adjust, harmonize, suit, conform, arrange
ANT. **1** inconvenience, disturb, disoblige

accommodating *adj.* kind, obliging, considerate, unselfish, polite, yielding, conciliatory
ANT. rude, disobliging, inconsiderate

accommodation *n.* housing, home, house, room(s), lodgings, shelter, digs

accompany *v.* follow, attend, go with, escort, convoy
ANT. abandon, leave, quit, avoid, discard, desert

accomplice *n.* partner, collaborator, helper, confederate, accessory, abetter, associate, ally, aid, assistant, promoter
ANT. enemy, foe, adversary, rival

accomplish *v.* complete, finish, achieve, perform, carry out, attain, realize, execute, perfect, fulfil, do, effect, consummate

accomplished *adj.* experienced, practised, practiced (*N. Am.*), finished, versed, consummate, adroit, expert, apt, skilful, skillful (*N. Am.*), talented, fine, qualified, proficient
ANT. unskilled, ignorant, unpolished, uncouth, incapable, inexpert, incompetent

accomplishment *n.* feat, action, achievement, performance, completion; attainment, proficiency
ANT. failure, blunder, folly, stupidity, incompetence, mismanagement, bungling

accord *v.* agree, correspond, harmonize, grant, concede, give, yield
ANT. differ, disagree, withhold, deny, refuse

accord *n.* agreement, concord, acceptance, approval, compliance
ANT. disagreement, protest, difference

accordingly *adv.* **1** suitably, conformably, agreeably **2** consequently, therefore, hence
ANT. **1** inconsistently **2** conversely

accost *v.* approach, address, greet, confront, speak to
ANT. rebuff, check, repulse, shun, elude, pass, ignore

account *n.* **1** statement, description, explanation, narration, relation, narrative, recital, chronicle, history, exposition **2** record, register, inventory, bill, charge, count, calculation, enumeration **3** consideration, regard, reason, importance, worth, dignity, profit, advantage, benefit

account *v.* explain, solve, regard, deem, judge, think, hold, believe, consider, view, estimate, reckon, rate, esteem

accountable *adj.* responsible, answerable, liable, amenable
ANT. independent, absolute, supreme, despotic, autocratic

accredited *adj.* authorized, commissioned, sanctioned, trusted, believed
ANT. unauthorized, discredited

accretion *n.* growth, accumulation, increase
ANT. disintegration, diminution

accrue *v.* accumulate, increase, arise, issue, ensue, follow, proceed, come
ANT. reduce, weaken, cause, occasion

accumulate *v.* pile, collect, gather up, bring, store, amass, garner, treasure, husband, lay by, hoard, aggregate
ANT. separate, dissipate, disperse, scatter, waste, expend

accumulation *n.* collection, heap, mass, hoard, store, accretion
ANT. separation, segregation, unit, individual

accuracy *n.* exactness, precision, nicety, truth, carefulness, correctness, exactitude, faithfulness
ANT. incorrectness, imprecision, error, fallacy, misconception, misstatement, looseness, slovenliness

accurate *adj.* careful, exact, faithful, precise, truthful, correct, rigorous, close, severe, just, unerring
ANT. careless, inexact, faulty, inaccurate, imprecise, defective, loose

accusation *n.* charge, indictment, arraignment, impeachment, imputation, censure
ANT. discharge, acquittal, vindication, absolution

accuse *v.* charge, indict, arraign, incriminate, impeach, cite, summon, censure, taunt, blame, reproach
ANT. discharge, acquit, defend, vindicate, pardon, absolve, condone, exonerate, release

accustomed *adj.* used, wont, familiar, trained
ANT. estranged, alienated

ache *n.* pain, discomfort, throbbing, anguish, suffering, agony
ANT. pleasure, relief, ease, refreshment, delight

ache *v.* hurt, throb, suffer, agonize, smart, sting

achieve *v.* 1 accomplish, perform, complete, finish, realize, bring to pass, work out, conclude 2 obtain, acquire, gain, win, get
ANT. 1 neglect, spoil, undo, mar 2 omit, fail, lose

achievement *n.* accomplishment, performance, attainment, completion, exploit, deed, feat, consummation
ANT. failure, negligence, frustration, blunder

acknowledge *v.* 1 recognize, be aware of, admit, concede, allow, accept, agree to, confess, avow 2 express thanks for, own, profess
ANT. disclaim, disown, deny, repudiate, ignore

acquaintance *n.* 1 friend, colleague, companion, associate 2 association, familiarity, intimacy, companionship, experience, knowledge, friendship, fellowship
ANT. 2 ignorance, inexperience, unfamiliarity

acquiesce *v.* agree, consent, assent, concur, yield, comply, submit
ANT. object, protest, dissent

acquire *v.* gain, earn, win, reap obtain, attain, achieve, get, secure
ANT. lose, surrender, miss, forgo, forfeit

acquit *v.* discharge, release, absolve, excuse, pardon, exonerate, exculpate
ANT. charge, condemn, sentence, compel, indict, imprison

acquittal *n.* discharge, release, deliverance, liberation, absolution
ANT. judgment, punishment, penalty, trial, retribution, correction

acrimony *n.* bitterness, sharpness, sourness, tartness, severity, hardness, rancour, rancor (*N. Am.*), ill-temper, spite, unkindness
ANT. gentleness, good nature, kindness, sweetness, courtesy

act *n.* 1 deed, exploit, accomplishment, achievement, effect, movement, transaction, work, performance 2 law, bill, decree, regulation, statute
ANT. 1 cessation, inertia, inaction, rest

act *v.* 1 work, do, operate, perform, execute, behave 2 operate, have effect, be, realize 3 play, feign, pretend, dissemble
ANT. 1 rest, cease, stop, stay

action *n.* exercise, motion, movement, step, deed, performance, agency, force, operation 2 battle, war, conflict 3 gesture, representation 4 lawsuit, case
ANT. 1 inertia, torpor, languor, rest, passiveness 2 harmony, truce, peace, ceasefire

active *adj.* 1 agile, brisk, alert, lively, quick, prompt, ready, spry 2 industrious, energetic, busy, diligent, occupied, engaged, committed
ANT. 2 idle, lazy, slow

activity *n.* 1 action, motion, movement 2 undertaking, act, deed, work, enterprise, pursuit
ANT. 1 idleness, slowness

actor *n.* player, performer, entertainer

actual *adj.* real, true, genuine, authentic, certain, absolute, positive, veritable, substantial, present, sensible, perceptible
ANT. possible, fictitious, virtual, theoretical, hypothetical, conjectural

actually *adv.* in fact, really, truly

acumen *n.* discernment, penetration, keenness, shrewdness, insight, sharpness, sagacity
ANT. dullness, obtuseness, stupidity, bluntness

acute *adj.* **1** sharp, intense, piercing, severe, violent **2** perceptive, keen, sharp, quick, discerning
ANT. **1** dull, heavy **2** stupid, dull

adapt *v.* **1** modify, alter, change, revise, amend, correct **2** adjust, harmonize, fit, attune, suit, conform

adaptation *n.* adjustment, fitness, conformity, harmony
ANT. incompatibility, incongruity, misfit, discord

add *v.* total, sum up, increase, append, attach, enlarge, amplify, annex, affix
ANT. deduct, subtract, lessen, reduce, remove, diminish

addicted *adj.* dependent, hooked, inclined, attached, devoted, given over, wedded
ANT. averse, disinclined, unaccustomed, indisposed, divorced

addition *n.* accession, enlargement, increase, extension, accretion, augmentation, adjunct
ANT. subtraction, decrease, diminution

additional *adj.* extra, new, further, supplementary, more

address *n.* **1** speech, lecture, discourse, harangue, oration **2** appeal, request, suit, solicitation

address *v.* speak, accost, approach, greet, hail, salute, court
ANT. avoid, elude, ignore, shun, cut, pass, overlook

adept *adj.* expert, proficient, accomplished, clever, skilful, skillful (*N. Am.*), talented
ANT. inexpert

adept *n.* expert, master, genius, veteran, professor
ANT. novice, tyro, blunderer

adequate *adj.* **1** competent, qualified, suitable, sufficient, acceptable, capable, adapted, satisfactory **2** enough, sufficient
ANT. **1** inferior, poor, useless, worthless, unfit, incompetent

adhere *v.* **1** stick, cling, cohere **2** support, be attached, be devoted

adherent *n.* devotee, follower, supporter, admirer, fan, buff

adjacent *adj.* near, close, bordering, adjoining, beside, contiguous
ANT. distant, remote, detached

adjourn *v.* postpone, delay, defer, suspend, interrupt, close, end, dissolve
ANT. complete, terminate

adjust *v.* **1** set, regulate, mend, repair, fix, change, alter **2** arrange, settle, determine, range, plan **3** acclimatize, accustom, accommodate, adapt
ANT. **2** disturb, confuse

adjustment *n.* **1** regulation, setting, accommodation **2** arrangement, disposal, settlement, agreement, fitting, adaptation, conformity
ANT. **2** disturbance, disorder, confusion

administer *v.* **1** direct, manage, control, superintend, conduct **2** dispense, distribute, supply
ANT. **1** mismanage **2** withhold, refuse

admirable *adj.* excellent, fine, splendid, marvellous, superb
ANT. contemptible, despicable

admiration *n.* high regard, wonder, approval, love, surprise, astonishment, appreciation, reverence
ANT. disapproval, contempt, dislike

admire *v.* honour, honor (*N. Am.*), respect, approve, adore, wonder at, venerate, extol, marvel at, applaud, revere, esteem
ANT. despise, dislike, hate, abhor, scorn, detest

admissible *adj.* allowable, lawful, permissible, possible, probable
ANT. improper, wrong, unlawful

admission *n.* **1** admittance, entrance, access **2** acknowledgment, avowal, concession, allowance, concurrence

admit *v.* **1** receive, accept **2** acknowledge, own, confess, reveal
ANT. **1** exclude, debar **2** deny

adopt *v.* take (up), assume, approve, accept, choose, support, maintain
ANT. reject, abandon

adoration *n.* worship, devotion, praise. homage, reverence, veneration, idolatry
ANT. hatred, detestation

adore *v.* revere, venerate, praise, love, worship, pay homage to, idolize

adorn v. beautify, decorate, embellish, ornament, garnish, illustrate, grace, dignify, exalt
ANT. spoil, mar, deface, disfigure, deform, denude, strip

adroit adj. dexterous, expert, skilful, skillful (N. Am.), apt, handy, quick, clever, ready, deft, ingenious, cunning
ANT. clumsy, awkward

adult adj. developed, fully-developed, mature, grown-up, of age

adult n. mature person, grown-up, man, woman

adulterate v. pollute, contaminate, debase, corrupt, taint

advance v. 1 proceed, progress, push forward(s), send forward(s), propel, promote, elevate, dignify, exalt
2 improve, strengthen, benefit
3 propose, offer 4 raise, augment, increase, thrive, prosper, accelerate
ANT. 1 regress, move backward(s)
2 worsen 4 decrease

advance n. 1 progress, improvement, growth 2 offer, proposal, overture, tender, proposition 3 rise, increase, appreciation
ANT. 1 regress 3 decrease

advantage n. 1 benefit, good, favour, profit, expediency, blessing 2 privilege, convenience, assistance, utility, service
ANT. 1 loss, disappointment, frustration, difficulty, dilemma

advantageous adj. helpful, profitable, useful, valuable, favourable, favorable (N. Am.)

adventure n. venture, experiment, trial, chance, hazard, risk, event, incident, occurrence
ANT. monotony, routine

adventurous adj. bold, daring, venturesome, rash, reckless, headlong dangerous, perilous, fearless, enterprising
ANT. timid, nervous, hesitating, cautious, cowardly

adversary n. enemy, foe, antagonist, opponent, rival, assailant
ANT. ally, helper, assistant, accomplice

adverse adj. opposite, contrary, conflicting, hostile, injurious, harmful, unlucky, unfortunate, disastrous
ANT. favourable, favorable (N. Am.), fortunate, lucky

adversity n. calamity, affliction, trouble, disaster, woe, distress, suffering
ANT. success, prosperity, good luck

advertise v. announce, publish, proclaim, declare, circulate, broadcast, offer for sale, inform, notify
ANT. suppress, conceal, mislead, misinform

advice n. counsel, suggestion, admonition, instruction, guidance, intelligence, notice, recommendation, exhortation, information

advisable adj. judicious, expedient, politic, prudent, desirable, beneficial, profitable, proper, fitting
ANT. imprudent, undesirable, inexpedient, improper, detrimental

advise v. suggest, counsel, guide, advocate, recommend, urge

advocate n. counsel, lawyer, attorney, defender, friend, patron, supporter, pleader, maintainer
ANT. accuser, impugner, adversary, opponent

advocate v. support, suggest, counsel, recommend, urge

affable adj. open, free, frank, unreserved, familiar, cordial, social, polite, gracious, mild, well-bred
ANT. distant, unapproachable

affair n. 1 matter, business, concern, function, circumstance, question, subject 2 event, incident, occurrence, performance 3 romance, relationship, liaison, intrigue

affect v. 1 influence, change, transform, modify, alter, have an effect on
2 concern, interest, touch, move, impress 3 assume, adopt, feign, pretend

affectation n. airs, mannerism, pretension, pretence, pretense (N. Am.), display, show
ANT. simplicity, naturalness, genuineness

affection n. feeling, passion, attachment, fondness, tenderness, love, endearment, devotion, partiality
ANT. repulsion, disaffection, repugnance

affectionate *adj.* fond, tender, loving, caring, kind, devoted, passionate
ANT. unkind, cruel

affiliate *v.* associate, adopt, join, connect, incorporate
ANT. separate, dissociate

affinity *n.* relationship, kin, consanguinity, likeness, resemblance, relation, analogy, connection, closeness, correspondence, sympathy, attraction

affirm *v.* state, declare, maintain, assert, swear, allege, protest, confirm, ratify, approve, endorse, assure, establish
ANT. deny, doubt, contradict

affirmation *n.* declaration, statement, assertion, avowal, testimony, confirmation, ratification, approval, endorsement
ANT. doubt, denial, contradiction

afflict *v.* distress, trouble, hurt, disturb, torment, oppress

affliction *n.* adversity, misfortune, grief, sorrow, distress, tribulation, trial, misery, calamity, pain, anguish, trouble, hardship
ANT. relief, blessing

affluence *n.* wealth, fortune, riches, abundance, plenty, profusion, opulence
ANT. want, scarcity, poverty, penury, lack, indigence

affluent *adj.* rich, wealthy, prosperous, well-off, moneyed

afford *v.* supply, furnish, give, contribute, offer, impart, administer
ANT. withhold, deny, retain

affront *n.* insult, abuse, annoyance, displeasure, outrage, offence, offense (*N. Am.*), provocation, wrong, vexation, wound, exasperation, irritation
ANT. courtesy, compliment

afraid *adj.* **1** fearful, timid, apprehensive, anxious, alarmed, terrified, frightened, scared **2** regretful, sorry, apologetic
ANT. **1** fearless, bold, confident

afresh *adv.* anew, again, newly, frequently, repeatedly, once more

after *prep.* subsequent, later, following, behind, rear, back
ANT. before, preceding, introducing, in front of

again *adv.* anew, afresh, repeatedly, further, moreover, besides, on the contrary, once more
ANT. once, continuously, uninterruptedly, uniformly

against *prep.* opposite, across, adverse to, counter to, facing, fronting, close up to, in contact with

age *n.* **1** duration, period, date, epoch, time, generation, era, century **2** maturity, seniority
ANT. **2** infancy, youth, childhood

age *v.* grow older, get on, mature, mellow

agent *n.* **1** doer, operator, promoter, performer, cause, force, power **2** deputy, factor, attorney, representative, substitute, broker, intermediary, middleman, means, instrument

agglomeration *n.* cluster, accumulation, heap, pile, mass, conglomeration

aggrandize *v.* exalt, honour, honor (*N. Am.*), elevate, dignify, promote, advance
ANT. degrade, impoverish

aggravate *v.* exasperate, provoke, wound, make worse, intensify, embitter, heighten
ANT. diminish

aggregation *n.* collection, accumulation, mass, heap, pile, amount, total, sum, result, whole, agglomeration
ANT. dispersion, division

aggression *n.* attack, invasion, encroachment, assault, injury, offence, offense (*N. Am.*), onslaught, provocation, intrusion
ANT. retaliation, repulsion, retreat, resistance, evacuation

aggressive *adj.* hostile, antagonistic, quarrelsome, belligerent, truculent
ANT. friendly, amicable, peaceful

aghast *adj.* dismayed, horrified, terrified, frightened, dumbfounded
ANT. fearless, unmoved

agile *adj.* nimble, active, lively, smart, alert, supple, brisk, quick, ready, sprightly, spry
ANT. slow, heavy, clumsy, awkward

agitate *v.* **1** disturb, trouble, shake, jar, excite, rouse, ferment **2** fluster, disconcert
ANT. **1** calm, pacify

ago *adv.* in the past, gone, since
ANT. future, coming

agonize *v.* torment, distress, trouble, afflict, torture

agony *n.* anguish, torture, torment, distress, pangs, pain, suffering, woe
ANT. comfort, relief

agree *v.* accept, approve, comply, consent, concur, admit, accede, be of one mind
ANT. disagree, contend, dissent, dispute, protest, oppose

agreeable *adj.* suitable, proper, appropriate, welcome, amiable, pleasing, gratifying
ANT. unpleasant, disagreeable

agreement *n.* 1 unison, unity, conformity, accord, concord 2 arrangement, contract, compact, bond, bargain, covenant, obligation, undertaking, treaty
ANT. 1 discord, dissension

ahead *adv.* in front, forward, onward, in advance
ANT. back, behind

aid *v.* help, support, assist, serve, minister to, relieve, succour, succor (*N. Am.*), supply, give alms to, foster, protect, encourage, favour, favor (*N. Am.*)
ANT. oppose, discourage, deter

aid *n.* help, support, assistance, relief, encouragement, favour, favor (*N. Am.*)

ailing *adj.* sick, ill, indisposed, unwell, feeble, infirm, weakly delicate, unhealthy, pining
ANT. well, healthy

ailment *n.* disease, malady, indisposition, complaint
ANT. health

aim *n.* 1 intention, purpose, goal, target, design, scheme, reason 2 direction, course, tendency, bent, bearing, sight, sighting

aim *v.* point, direct, turn, level, train

air *n.* 1 atmosphere, heavens, sky, gas, breeze, vapour, vapor (*N. Am.*), zephyr, wind, weather 2 appearance, aspect, manner, sort, style, way, behaviour, behavior (*N. Am.*), carriage, bearing, expression, look, demeanour, demeanor (*N. Am.*), mien, fashion

air *v.* 1 freshen, ventilate, cool, fan 2 show, display, reveal, expose, publicize
ANT. 2 hide, conceal

airy *adj.* 1 aerial, thin, breezy, draughty, drafty (*N. Am.*), rare, ethereal, light, subtle, sublimated 2 sprightly, buoyant, vivacious, volatile, jolly, jovial, light-hearted, graceful, lithe, pliant, flexible, showy, jaunty, flaunting, garish
ANT. 1 thick, ponderous, heavy, inert

aisle *n.* passage, gangway, corridor, path, opening

alarm *n.* 1 fear, fright, terror, apprehension, consternation, dismay, dread 2 tocsin, distress signal, war-cry
ANT. 1 confidence, courage

alarm *v.* frighten, scare, terrorize, dismay, startle
ANT. quieten, compose

alarming *adj.* frightening, terrifying, shocking, appalling, daunting, distressing
ANT. comforting, reassuring

album *n.* scrapbook, notebook, book, collection, file, folder

alcohol *n.* liquor, spirits, intoxicant, drink, strong drink, booze (*informal*)

alert *adj.* 1 watchful, attentive, vigilant, wide-awake 2 lively, prompt, ready, prepared, bustling, active, brisk, nimble, sprightly, agile
ANT. 2 slow, lazy, absent, oblivious, sluggish, dilatory

alert *v.* warn, notify, tell, inform, signal

alien *n.* foreigner, stranger
ANT. citizen, native, naturalized person

alien *adj.* strange, foreign, hostile, remote, distant, contrasted, contrary, unlike, unconnected

alienate *v.* estrange, separate, turn away, break off, disaffect
ANT. conciliate, bring together

alienation *n.* estrangement, disaffection, variance, rupture, breach
ANT. conciliation

alight *v.* settle, drop, lodge, perch, dismount, descend
ANT. soar, spring, ascend, start, mount

alike *adj.* similar, kindred, same, resembling, equivalent, homogeneous, identical, analogous, uniform, akin, allied
ANT. different, unequal, dissimilar, unlike, heterogeneous, distinct, various

alive *adj.* living, live, existing, animate, alert, lively, active, breathing
ANT. dead, defunct, lifeless, deceased

all *adj.* whole, entire, complete, total, each, every
ANT. some, part

all *n.* whole, totality, entirety, aggregate
ANT. part, piece, share, portion

allay *v.* quiet, restrain, check, subdue, silence, still, hush, soothe, compose, calm, appease, lull, alleviate, mitigate, relieve, palliate
ANT. aggravate, arouse, excite, stir, kindle, fan, provoke

allege *v.* declare, affirm, claim, maintain, state, advance, introduce, profess, cite
ANT. contradict, refute, deny, disprove, quash

allegiance *n.* loyalty, devotion, faithfulness, obedience, homage
ANT. treason, rebellion, disloyalty, disaffection

allegory *n.* parable, fable, myth, story, tale, metaphor, illustration, simile
ANT. history, fact

alleviate *v.* abate, mitigate, reduce, relieve, lessen, assuage, remove, soften, moderate, lighten
ANT. increase, heighten, intensify, magnify, aggravate, enhance, embitter

alley *n.* way, passage, lane, path, footpath, walk

alliance *n.* 1 agreement, treaty, confederacy, league, union, pact, copartnership, coalition 2 connection, relationship, affinity, affiliation, similarity
ANT. 2 separation, disunion, estrangement, divorce

allocate *v.* assign, allot, distribute, deal out, divide, dispense

allot *v.* divide, apportion, distribute, deal out, dispense, assign, grant, give, appoint
ANT. refuse, retain, withhold, deny, confiscate

allow *v.* 1 let, permit, authorize, approve 2 concede, grant, acknowledge, confess, admit
ANT. 1 forbid, prohibit, disapprove, disallow, reject 2 deny, refuse, protest

allowance *n.* 1 permission, sanction, approval, leave, authorization 2 ration, share, allocation, grant, concession
ANT. 1 refusal, disapproval, denial

alloy *n.* compound, blend, mixture, combination, amalgam, admixture

allude *v.* intimate, insinuate, point, refer, suggest, signify, hint, imply, indicate, mention, touch upon

allure *v.* entice, coax, attract, tempt, lure, seduce
ANT. repel, dissuade, warn, drive away

allusion *n.* hint, suggestion, intimation, reference, implication, insinuation, mention

ally *n.* assistant, helper, friend, associate, colleague, partner, accessory, accomplice
ANT. foe, enemy, opponent, adversary, antagonist

ally *v.* unite, join, combine, unify, connect, associate

almost *adv.* nearly, somewhat, well-nigh, all but, to all intents and purposes

alone *adj.* solitary, sole, single, isolated, deserted, lone, only
ANT. accompanied, associated

along *adv.* onward, forward, ahead, lengthwise, together, beside, simultaneously
ANT. across, sidewise, sideways, lateral, apart, tandem

aloof *adj.* apart, distant, detached, remote, unapproachable, away, off
ANT. close, near, friendly, approachable

aloud *adv.* distinctly, audibly, clearly, out loud, vociferously, clamorously, sonorously
ANT. softly, silently, inaudibly

already *adv.* by now, by this time, up to now, before now, yet

also *adv.* as well, likewise, too, similarly, besides, in addition, further, moreover
ANT. nevertheless, on the contrary, but, yet, in spite of, on the other hand

alter *v.* change, turn, vary, modify, adjust, shift, substitute, remodel, transform, convert
ANT. conserve, preserve

alteration *n.* change, variation, modification, adjustment, conversion, amendment, adaptation, shifting, mutation
ANT. changelessness, preservation, permanence

altercation *n.* dispute, contention, controversy, difference, quarrel, wrangle, dissension
ANT. agreement, compromise, reconciliation, unanimity, harmony

alternate *v.* substitute, interchange, take turns, rotate

alternate *adj.* reciprocal, every other one, one after another, in turn, interchangeable, in rotation
ANT. continuous, successive, consequent

alternative *n.* choice, option, preference, election, pick, resource

alternative *adj.* different, other, distinct, spare

although *conj.* even if, supposing, granting that, albeit
ANT. yet, notwithstanding

altitude *n.* height, elevation, loftiness, ascent, eminence
ANT. depth

altogether *adv.* wholly, quite, completely, totally, utterly, entirely, thoroughly, fully, in the mass, jointly
ANT. partially, piecemeal, by instalments, partly, incompletely, by halves, individually, separately

altruistic *adj.* philanthropic, unselfish, public-spirited, devoted to others, self-sacrificing, self-forgetful, generous
ANT. selfish, self-indulgent, worldly, mean, egotistic

always *adv.* ever, for ever, eternally, everlastingly, perpetually, ever more, uniformly, invariably, generally, habitually
ANT. never, rarely, occasionally, now, momentarily, instantly, suddenly

amalgamate *v.* mix, unite, combine, blend, compound, incorporate, join, fuse, consolidate
ANT. disintegrate, decompose, disperse, separate, dissipate, analyse, analyze (*N. Am.*)

amass *v.* accumulate, heap up, collect, gather, hoard, store
ANT. disperse, divide, scatter, spend, squander, waste, dissipate

amateur *n.* nonprofessional, lay person, learner, novice, beginner, tyro

amaze *v.* astonish, astound, surprise, startle, stupefy
ANT. tire, bore

amazement *n.* astonishment, bewilderment, wonder, marvel, stupefaction, confusion, perplexity, awe
ANT. familiarity, boredom

amazing *adj.* astonishing, astounding, wonderful, surprising, marvellous, marvelous (*N. Am.*), prodigious, strange, miraculous, stupendous, extraordinary
ANT. common, familiar, hackneyed, usual, customary

ambassador *n.* envoy, legate, minister, deputy, plenipotentiary

ambiguous *adj.* doubtful, dubious, unclear, uncertain, indefinite, vague, obscure, indistinct, equivocal, enigmatic
ANT. obvious, plain, clear, lucid, unmistakable

ambition *n.* aspiration, drive, yearning, eagerness, enthusiasm, zeal, competition

ambitious *adj.* aspiring, yearning, eager, enthusiastic, zealous, enterprising
ANT. lethargic, dull

ambush *v.* trap, ensnare, lure, trick, surprise, lurk, waylay, lie in wait for

ambush *n.* surprise attack, trap, snare, pitfall, lure

amenable *adj.* agreeable, open, liable, responsible, answerable, accountable
ANT. obstinate

amend *v.* improve, better, mend, repair, reform, correct, rectify, ameliorate
ANT. harm, corrupt, spoil, debase, aggravate

amendment *n.* improvement, correction, change, alteration, modification, reform, revision

amends *n.* compensation, atonement, recompense, indemnity
ANT. insult, injury, fault

amenity *n.* **1** facility, service, convenience, resource, means
2 softness, mildness, suavity, gentleness, refinement, amiability
ANT. **2** austerity, ungraciousness, discourtesy, moroseness

amiable *adj.* agreeable, gentle, good-natured, pleasant, pleasing, winsome, attractive, charming, lovable
ANT. surly, gruff, disagreeable, ill-tempered

amicable *adj.* kind, friendly, cordial, harmonious, peaceable, propitious, favourable, favorable (*N. Am.*), sociable, amiable
ANT. unkind, hostile, unfriendly

amid *prep.* among, between, in the midst of, surrounded by
ANT. outside, beyond, far from, away from

amiss *adj.* wrong, improper, faulty, incorrect, inaccurate
ANT. correct, right

amount *n.* sum, total, aggregate, whole, measure, quantity
ANT. portion, part

amount *v.* total, count, add up, equal, reach

ample *adj.* generous, abundant, sufficient, liberal, large, spacious, plentiful, copious, lavish, exuberant, bountiful
ANT. scant, insufficient

amplify *v.* enlarge, expand, increase, develop, extend, widen, dilate, augment
ANT. abbreviate, reduce, abridge

amuse *v.* entertain, divert, interest, please, delight, charm

amusement *n.* diversion, sport, play, fun, entertainment, pastime, game, relaxation, merriment

analogy *n.* likeness, similarity, relation, resemblance, comparison, similitude
ANT. unlikeness, incongruity, disproportion, disagreement

analyse, analyze (*N. Am.*) *v.* study, scrutinize, examine, investigate, explain, dissect, anatomize

analysis *n.* study, examination, investigation, partition, separation, dissection
ANT. synthesis, composition, aggregation, combination

analyze (*N. Am.*) See **analyse**

anarchy *n.* misrule, disorder, lawlessness, violence, confusion
ANT. law, order, government

anatomy *n.* analysis, dissection, skeleton, structure, framework

ancestor *n.* forebear, predecessor, parent, forerunner
ANT. descendant

ancestral *adj.* inherited, hereditary

ancestry *n.* descent, lineage, family, line, house, stock, race

anchor *n.* stay, mainstay, mooring, defence, security

anchor *v.* secure, fix, fasten, attach, tie
ANT. loosen, detach, free

ancient *adj.* old, antique, antiquated, obsolete, aged, old-fashioned, primeval
ANT. modern, fresh, new

ancillary *adj.* auxiliary, helping, instrumental, subsidiary, subordinate, subservient
ANT. essential

anecdote *n.* story, tale, narrative, illustration, incident

angel *n.* seraph, cherub, archangel, spirit
ANT. devil

angelic *adj.* seraphic, celestial, pure, ethereal, adorable, rapturous, heavenly, divine, spiritual
ANT. diabolical, devilish, hellish

anger *n.* fury, indignation, rage, temper, vexation, displeasure, animosity, wrath, resentment, ire, passion
ANT. patience, self-control, self-restraint, forbearance, forgiveness, love

anger *v.* enrage, exasperate, infuriate, incense, annoy, irritate, vex
ANT. please, appease, satisfy

angle *n.* **1** corner, bend, edge **2** point of view, viewpoint, standpoint, position, perspective

angry *adj.* furious, indignant, exasperated, irritated, wrathful, resentful, mad (*informal*), passionate, provoked, sulky, piqued, galled
ANT. calm, unresentful, peaceful

anguish *n.* agony, torture, torment, pang, acute distress, pain, misery, extreme suffering
ANT. ease, pleasure

animal *n.* creature, beast, living organism, brute

animate *v.* enliven, vivify, quicken, invigorate, revive, stimulate, waken, rouse, excite, provoke, encourage, inspire, elate
ANT. deaden, discourage, deter, depress, dishearten, stifle

animate *adj.* lively, vital, spirited, vivacious, energetic

animation *n.* life, vitality, spirit, vivacity, energy, exhilaration, sprightliness, courage, force, buoyancy, vigour, vigor (*N. Am.*), liveliness
ANT. dullness, deadness, spiritlessness

animosity *n.* hatred, enmity, aversion, acrimony, strife, bitterness, hostility, dissension, malignity, antipathy, malice, anger
ANT. friendship, harmony, kindness, sympathy

annals *n.* archives, chronicles, records, registers, rolls

annex *v.* add, affix, attach, append, tag, join, unite, connect
ANT. detach, disconnect, separate, remove

annihilate *v.* exterminate, obliterate, eradicate, destroy

annihilation *n.* extermination, obliteration, eradication, destruction, non-existence, oblivion, non-being

annotate *v.* note, comment, remark, observe, explain, illustrate, elucidate

annotation *n.* note, comment, remark, observation, gloss, explanation, illustration, elucidation

announce *v.* tell, declare, communicate, proclaim, publish, report, herald, make known, state, reveal, circulate, enunciate, promulgate
ANT. suppress, hide, cover up, conceal

announcement *n.* notice, proclamation, declaration, advertisement, notification, manifesto, promulgation
ANT. concealment, secrecy

annoy *v.* trouble, irritate, bother, discomfort, vex, torment, disturb
ANT. comfort, relieve

annoyance *n.* trouble, irritation, discomfort, vexation, torment, infliction, nuisance
ANT. delight, relief

annual *adj.* yearly, every year, once a year

annual *n.* yearly publication, yearbook, annals

annul *v.* cancel, abrogate, recall, repeal, revoke, countermand, reverse, abolish, nullify, supersede, invalidate, rescind
ANT. confirm, establish

anomalous *adj.* abnormal, unnatural, irregular, peculiar, exceptional, aberrant, unusual, singular, eccentric, erratic
ANT. normal, regular, usual

anonymous *adj.* nameless, unacknowledged, of unknown authorship
ANT. named, identified

answer *v.* 1 reply, rejoin, respond, acknowledge 2 be accountable, be responsible, be liable
ANT. 1 question, interrogate, query, summon

answer *n.* reply, response, acknowledgment, retort, rejoinder
ANT. question, interrogation

answerable *adj.* responsible, amenable, liable, accountable, refutable
ANT. independent, irresponsible

antagonism *n.* opposition, contradiction, hostility, animosity, enmity
ANT. amity, alliance, association

antagonist *n.* enemy, opponent, foe, adversary, rival

antagonistic *adj.* hostile, opposed, unfriendly, rival
ANT. friendly

antecedent *adj.* preceding, previous, prior, foregoing, anterior, precursory
ANT. following, subsequent

antedate *v.* predate, anticipate, forestall, foretaste
ANT. postdate, follow, succeed

anticipate *v.* 1 expect, foresee, forecast, hope for, look forward to 2 forestall, provide against, intercept

anticipation *n.* expectation, prospect, hope, trust, contemplation

antipathy *n.* repugnance, repulsion, aversion, detestation, abhorrence, hatred, hostility, loathing
ANT. attraction, affinity, congeniality, sympathy, harmony

antiquated *adj.* obsolete, bygone, ancient, archaic, old-fashioned, quaint
ANT. modern, new, fashionable

antiquity *n.* ancient times, old, early days

anxiety *n.* worry, dread, trouble, foreboding, misgiving, eagerness, diffidence, perplexity, apprehension, care, concern, solicitude
ANT. confidence, contentment

anxious *adj.* worried, troubled, apprehension, concerned, uneasy, fearful
ANT. calm, confident

apathetic *adj.* unconcerned, indifferent, uncaring, unfeeling, cold, dull
ANT. enthusiastic, concerned, caring

apathy *n.* unconcern, indifference, stoicism, calmness, composure, lethargy, insensibility, immobility, quietude, phlegm, stillness
ANT. sensitiveness, feeling, passion, vehemence, emotion

ape *v.* mimic, imitate, counterfeit, copy, affect, impersonate, represent

aperture *n.* opening, hole, gap, rift, chasm, loophole, orifice, cleft
ANT. closure, blank wall

apocryphal *adj.* unauthentic, uncanonical, legendary, fictitious, false, equivocal, doubtful, spurious
ANT. authorized

apologetic *adj.* sorry, regretful, penitent, remorseful
ANT. unrepentant

apologize *v.* say sorry, be sorry, confess, regret

apology *n.* plea, excuse, defence, defense (*N. Am.*), confession, acknowledgment, justification, vindication, explanation

apostate *n.* renegade, turncoat, backslider, deserter, pervert, traitor
ANT. adherent, supporter

appal *v.* horrify, terrify, frighten, dismay, shock, daunt, alarm
ANT. reassure, embolden

appalling *adj.* terrifying, shocking, frightful, awful, dreadful

apparatus *n.* machinery, device, instrument, mechanism, equipment, tools, utensils

apparel *n.* clothes, clothing, dress, costume, habit, guise, garments, robes, raiment, attire, wardrobe, equipment, trappings

apparent *adj.* obvious, conspicuous, clear, manifest, patent, evident, plain, seeming, probable, likely, legible, specious
ANT. actual, real

appeal *n.* 1 entreaty, plea, petition, request 2 attractiveness, charm, glamour, fascination
ANT. 2 unattractiveness

appeal *v.* 1 address, invoke, entreat, implore, supplicate, sue, petition 2 attract, interest, captivate, engage, fascinate
ANT. 1 protest

appear *v.* 1 seem, look 2 arise, emerge, come into view, arrive, turn up
ANT. 2 disappear

appearance *n.* 1 look, show, semblance, manner, condition, attitude, fashion 2 arrival, advent, presence
ANT. 2 disappearance, departure

appease *v.* calm, pacify, soothe, quell, mollify, mitigate, lull, propitiate, placate, satisfy, reconcile
ANT. aggravate, exasperate

append *v.* attach, add, supplement, attach, fasten
ANT. detach

appendage *n.* attachment, addition, adjunct, supplement

appetite *n.* hunger, thirst, longing, craving, desire, relish, zest, liking
ANT. loathing

applaud *v.* praise, approve of, clap, cheer, acclaim

applause *n*. praise, approval, commendation, compliment, plaudit, acclamation, clapping of hands
ANT. criticism, denunciation

appliance *n*. device, machine, instrument, tool, contrivance, apparatus, appointment, appurtenance, equipment

applicable *adj*. fit, appropriate, suitable, apt, proper, relevant, germane, pertinent
ANT. irrelevant, inappropriate

applicant *n*. candidate, aspirant, petitioner, solicitor, suitor

application *n*. 1 use, employment, utilization, purpose, value, function 2 form, claim, request, inquiry

apply *v*. 1 use, employ, exercise, utilize, put to use, appropriate, execute, carry out, practice 2 request, appeal, inquire, petition 3 devote, engage, commit, dedicate
ANT. 1 misuse 3 divert

appoint *v*. 1 assign, allot, designate, determine, establish, fix, direct, command, decree, enjoin, impose, require, ordain 2 nominate, name, create 3 equip, supply, furnish, provide
ANT. 1 cancel, withhold

appointment *n*. assignation, assignment, agreement, arrangement, meeting, tryst 2 position, office, place, station 3 decree, command, order, edict, ordinance, mandate, requirement, law

apportion *v*. appoint, allot, appropriate, divide, distribute, share, grant, dispense, assign, deal
ANT. retain

apposite *adj*. suitable, seasonable, fit, applicable, adapted, apt, pertinent, apropos
ANT. irrelevant

appraisal *n*. assessment, evaluation, survey, judgment, estimate

appraise *v*. assess, evaluate, survey, estimate, value, rate, fix a price for, assize
ANT. undervalue, discard, misprize

appreciate *v*. value highly, esteem, prize, recognize, respect
ANT. undervalue, misjudge, depreciate

apprehend *v*. 1 arrest, seize, take, catch, capture 2 imagine, conceive, regard, perceive, realize, understand, appreciate

apprehension *n*. 1 fear, anxiety, uneasiness, disquiet, dread, misgiving 2 arrest, capture, seizure 3 understanding, intelligence, mind, reason, notice, cognizance
ANT. 1 confidence, nonchalance 2 escape, non-detection

apprehensive *adj*. fearful, anxious, uneasy, troubled, worried
ANT. calm, composed

apprentice *n*. learner, beginner, novice, tyro, amateur
ANT. master, expert

apprise *v*. give notice, inform, tell, publish, advise, acquaint

approach *v*. 1 advance, draw near, come near, bring near, go near, near, push 2 resemble closely, be like, similar, or equal
ANT. 1 go back 2 be unlike

approach *n*. 1 coming, nearing, advance, arrival 2 passage, way, road, drive, path 3 method, technique, procedure, means, way
ANT. 2 exit

approbation *n*. approval, liking, praise, commendation, support, endorsement
ANT. disapproval

appropriate *adj*. fitting, suitable, proper, apt, apposite, relevant, pertinent
ANT. irrelevant

appropriate *v*. take, seize, confiscate, take over

approve *v*. praise, commend, support, encourage, favour, favor (*N. Am.*), authorize, sanction
ANT. condemn, repudiate, dislike

approximate *adj*. rough, loose, close, inexact, imprecise
ANT. exact

approximately *adv*. roughly, loosely, inexactly, imprecisely
ANT. exactly

approximation *n*. approach, nearness, similarity, likeness, resemblance
ANT. remoteness, distance

apt *adj*. **1** appropriate, fitting, suitable, proper, apposite, relevant, pertinent **2** likely, prone, disposed, inclined, liable
ANT. **1** inappropriate **2** unlikely

aptitude *n*. gift, talent, disposition, knack, endowment, tendency, inclination, fitness, suitability, bias, propensity

arbiter *n*. umpire, judge, referee, controller

arbitrary *adj*. **1** random, chance, subjective, capricious, fanciful **2** despotic, imperious, dictatorial, autocratic, tyrannical, overbearing, peremptory
ANT. **1** reasoned **2** considerate

arbitrate *v*. mediate, intercede, intervene, interpose, decide, determine, settle, adjudicate

arbitration *n*. mediation, intercession, intervention, interposition, trial, judgment, decision

arch *n*. vault, curve, bend, bow, archway

archaic *adj*. ancient, obsolete, outdated, old, old-fashioned, antiquated
ANT. modern, contemporary

architect *n*. designer, planner, constructor, maker, builder, author

ardent *adj*. passionate, fervent, intense, zealous, enthusiastic, vehement, fierce, fiery hot, burning
ANT. indifferent, apathetic

argue *v*. **1** discuss, debate, reason, contend, plead **2** disagree, quarrel, bicker, wrangle, squabble, row

argument *n*. **1** reasoning, proof, evidence, controversy, discussion, debate **2** disagreement, quarrel, fight, row, squabble **3** subject, topic, theme, thesis, summary, abstract, outline
ANT. **2** agreement

arid *adj*. dry, parched, sterile, infertile, barren
ANT. moist, fertile

arise *v*. **1** originate, spring, issue, flow, proceed **2** rise, ascend, go up, mount, soar
ANT. **1** end **2** sink, fall

aristocrat *n*. noble, peer, lord

arm *v*. equip, furnish, gird, provide, prepare, array, cover, protect, guard, fortify

army *n*. soldiers, troops, forces, legion, armament

aromatic *adj*. fragrant, spicy, balmy, redolent
ANT. offensive, rank

around *prep*. round, about, surrounding

arouse *v*. excite, provoke, instigate, stimulate, warm, whet, summon, awaken, animate, kindle
ANT. quiet

arraign *v*. accuse, charge, summon, indict, impeach, denounce, prosecute
ANT. condone, release

arrange *v*. **1** group, rank, range, distribute, place, order, dispose, marshal **2** plan, project, devise, construct, organize, contrive, settle, determine, adjust
ANT. **1** disorder

arrangement *n*. **1** plan, preparation, measure **2** order, organization, disposition, grouping

array *v*. **1** clothe, dress, adorn, attire **2** order, arrange, line up

array *n*. order, parade, show, exhibition, collection, arrangement
ANT. confusion

arrest *v*. **1** capture, seize, detain, hold, take prisoner, apprehend **2** stop, restrain, delay, hinder, slow **3** attract, captivate, engage, rivet, engross
ANT. **1** liberate, free

arrival *n*. coming, advent, appearance
ANT. departure, going

arrive *v*. **1** reach, get to, come, appear **2** happen, occur
ANT. **1** depart

arrogant *adj*. haughty, insolent, proud, lordly, disdainful, supercilious, self-important, egoistic, overbearing, dogmatic, imperious
ANT. humble, diffident

arrow *n*. **1** shaft, dart, bolt, missile **2** sign, pointer, marker

art *n*. **1** skill, dexterity, aptitude, cleverness, ingenuity **2** craft, practical knowledge, business, calling, employment, trade **3** cunning, artifice, deceit, guile

article *n.* **1** thing, object, substance, commodity, part, portion, particular, point, item, member **2** essay, paper, feature, review, column, monograph, brochure

articulate *v.* enunciate, utter distinctly, pronounce
ANT. whisper

artificial *adj.* **1** unnatural, manufactured, synthetic, unreal **2** feigned, counterfeit, fictitious, spurious, sham, affected, forced, strained
ANT. **1** natural, genuine **2** spontaneous

artist *n.* **1** painter, designer, sculptor, carver **2** designer, contriver, skilled worker, artisan, mechanic, operative

artistic *adj.* creative, imaginative, decorative, sensitive, stylish

ascend *v.* rise, mount, soar, aspire, go up, tower
ANT. descend, fall, sink

ascendancy *n.* power, authority, sway, dominion, rule, mastery, control, government, influence

ascent *n.* rise, climb, slope, ramp
ANT. descent

ascertain *v.* discover, find out, get at, determine, establish, settle, fix, define, verify
ANT. guess, surmise

ascetic *adj.* austere, rigid, severe, self-denying, abstinent, stern, puritanical
ANT. indulgent

ascribe *v.* impute, attribute, assign, refer, charge, set down

ashamed *adj.* humiliated, embarrassed, sorry, guilty, shame-faced, remorseful
ANT. proud, haughty

ask *v.* request, petition, entreat, beg, beseech, supplicate, inquire of, crave, demand, solicit
ANT. refuse, reject, deny

asleep *adj.* sleeping, resting, dozing, slumbering, napping
ANT. awake

aspect *n.* **1** air, look, appearance, expression, feature, bearing, countenance, mien, state, attitude, posture, condition **2** angle, side, feature, viewpoint, view, direction, outlook, prospect

asperity *n.* harshness, acrimony, sourness, sharpness, sternness, severity, bitterness, sullenness, ill-temper, roughness, unevenness
ANT. gentleness, mildness

aspiration *n.* yearning, longing, hope, wish, ardent desire, craving, ambition
ANT. apathy

aspire *v.* yearn, long, desire, hope, wish, crave

assail *v.* attack, invade, charge, set upon

assault *n.* attack, invasion, charge, onset, onslaught, aggression
ANT. resistance

assemble *v.* **1** gather, collect, convene, congregate, meet, come together **2** put together, join, manufacture, build, make, connect
ANT. **1** disperse, scatter **2** dismantle

assembly *n.* **1** gathering, congregation, meeting, convocation, throng, concourse, company **2** congress, parliament, legislature, synod, diet, council, convention
ANT. **1** dispersion

assent *v.* agree, acquiesce, approve, consent, comply, go along with
ANT. disagree, dissent

assent *n.* consent, agreement, acquiescence, acknowledgment, approval, concurrence, approbation, accord, compliance
ANT. disagreement, dissent

assert *v.* declare, affirm, state, maintain, emphasize, insist upon

assertion *n.* declaration, affirmation, position, statement, word, emphasis
ANT. denial, contradiction

assess *v.* value, estimate, compute, fix, assign, determine, impose, tax, appraise

assiduous *adj.* diligent, industrious, untiring, indefatigable, devoted, constant, attentive, painstaking, laborious, persistent, active
ANT. lazy

assign *v.* appoint, allot, apportion, specify, designate, determine, arrange

assignment *n.* appointment, allotment, specification, fixing, determination, offer, presentation

assimilate *v.* take in, digest, appropriate, incorporate, absorb
ANT. separate, segregate

assist *v.* help, aid, relieve, support, befriend, serve, sustain, promote, further, cooperate with
ANT. oppose, antagonize

assistance *n.* help, aid, support, service, cooperation
ANT. opposition

assistant *n.* helper, supporter, aide, partner, colleague, ally
ANT. opponent

associate *v.* join, link, connect, relate, combine

associate *n.* companion, comrade, friend, partner, colleague, accomplice, ally, consort, confederate, peer
ANT. enemy, opponent

association *n.* **1** society, union, partnership, company, confederacy, corporation, federation, alliance **2** fellowship, alliance, companionship
ANT. **2** solitude

assorted *adj.* mixed, varied, various, miscellaneous
ANT. same

assortment *n.* variety, mixture, miscellany

assuage *v.* soothe, pacify, mitigate, ease, alleviate, abate, calm
ANT. excite, inflame

assume *v.* **1** suppose, presume, postulate, surmise **2** undertake, take on, adopt, acquire **3** arrogate, feign, pretend, take, usurp

assumption *n.* presumption, supposition, hypothesis, theory, postulate, conjecture
ANT. truth, fact

assurance *n.* **1** confidence, self-reliance, boldness, assertion, self- confidence, presumption, assumption, arrogance, impudence **2** pledge, guarantee, promise, warranty
ANT. **1** doubt, distrust

assure *v.* pledge, guarantee, promise, warrant
ANT. deny, doubt

astonish *v.* amaze, startle, surprise, astound, stupefy, stagger
ANT. bore

astonishment *n.* amazement, surprise, wonder, awe, bewilderment

astute *adj.* keen, discerning, perceptive, acute, shrewd, sharp, cunning, subtle, discriminating, knowing, perspicacious, crafty
ANT. stupid, unintelligent

atmosphere *n.* **1** climate, air, wind **2** mood, feeling, tone, setting, environment, impression, ambience

atrocious *adj.* infamous, outrageous, villainous, diabolical, heinous, flagrant, horrible
ANT. noble

attach *v.* **1** fix, fasten, tie, bind, connect, join **2** ascribe, attribute, impute
ANT. **1** detach

attachment *n.* **1** adherence, friendship, regard, tenderness, love, esteem, affection, devotion, inclination, union **2** accessory, extra, extension, fastening, joint
ANT. **1** alienation, aversion

attack *v.* **1** assault, storm, assail, invade, charge, rush upon, spring upon **2** censure, criticize, blame
ANT. **1** defend, resist

attack *n.* assault, invasion, charge, rush, onslaught, raid, incursion
ANT. defence, defense (*N. Am.*), resistance

attain *v.* achieve, accomplish, gain, master, secure, earn, obtain, win, acquire, accomplish
ANT. lose, fail

attainment *n.* accomplishing, accomplishment, achievement, securing, winning, getting

attempt *v.* try, undertake, seek, endeavour, endeavor (*N. Am.*), essay, attack, strive

attempt *n.* try, effort, undertaking, endeavour, endeavor (*N. Am.*), trial, go (*informal*), stab (*informal*), crack (*informal*)

attend *v.* **1** go to, be present at, frequent, visit **2** pay attention, heed, observe, note, mark, listen **3** serve, wait on, minister to
ANT. **2** ignore

attendance *n.* **1** presence, appearance, train, retinue **2** service, waiting on, ministration
ANT. **1** absence

attendant *n.* waiter, servant, escort, companion, steward, aide

attention *n.* **1** care, notice, observation, consideration, watchfulness, alertness, study, reflection, application **2** respect, courtesy, politeness, civility, regard, courtship, devotion, wooing
ANT. **1** indifference, carelessness, neglect

attentive *adj.* careful, observant, alert, watchful, heedful, considerate

attenuate *v.* rarefy, thin, reduce, diminish, make slender, make slim, lessen
ANT. amplify, dilate

attest *v.* bear witness, certify, endorse, corroborate, support, authenticate, invoke, adjure
ANT. contradict, disprove

attire *n.* dress, apparel, robes, garments, habit, raiment, uniform, costume, livery, habiliments

attire *v.* dress, apparel, clothe, robe

attitude *n.* position, posture, situation, standing, aspect, regard

attract *v.* draw, allure, fascinate, charm, entice, captivate
ANT. repel

attraction *n.* drawing, allurement, lure, fascination, charm, enticement
ANT. repulsion, aversion

attractive *adj.* appealing, good-looking, beautiful, charming, pleasing, lovely
ANT. unattractive, ugly

attribute *n.* feature, characteristic, quality, property, mark

attribute *v.* ascribe, assign, impute, refer, charge, connect, associate

audacious *adj.* bold, daring, fearless, courageous, intrepid, dauntless
ANT. timid, cowardly, cautious

audible *adj.* perceptible, clear, distinct, discernible
ANT. inaudible

audience *n.* viewers, listeners, spectators, crowd, patrons, public

augur *v.* foretell, portend, predict, presage, prophesy, divine, prognosticate, betoken

auspicious *adj.* successful, fortunate, lucky, happy, prosperous, propitious, promising, opportune, favourable, favorable (*N. Am.*)
ANT. hopeless, unpromising, unsatisfactory, discouraging

austere *adj.* severe, hard, harsh, stiff, stern, uncompromising, unrelenting, ascetic, rigid, formal
ANT. indulgent

austerity *n.* severity, harshness, self-denial, asceticism, hardship
ANT. luxury, comfort

authentic *adj.* genuine, trustworthy, real, accepted, authorized, certain, accredited, sure, true, reliable, original, legitimate
ANT. false, fictitious

author *n.* writer, creator, maker, originator, poet, composer, inventor

authority *n.* **1** power, government, dominion, command, rule, order, supremacy, control, influence, interest **2** authorization, jurisdiction, power, permission, sanction, permit
ANT. **1** anarchy

authorize *v.* empower, commission, sanction, entrust, charge, license, legalize, permit, allow
ANT. ban, prohibit

autocratic *adj.* absolute, unlimited, tyrannical, oppressive, disdainful, overbearing, arrogant
ANT. democratic

automatic *adj.* self-moving, mechanical, mechanized, computerized, electronic
ANT. manual

auxiliary *n.* assistant, helper, confederate, aid, ally, accessory, promoter, subordinate

auxiliary *adj.* supplementary, secondary, subordinate, additional, extra
ANT. essential

avail *v.* help, benefit, profit, be of advantage, be of use

available *adj.* accessible, obtainable, at hand, ready, serviceable, useful, profitable, beneficial, advantageous
ANT. unavailable

avaricious *adj.* greedy, covetous, miserly, stingy, grasping, sordid
ANT. liberal, bountiful

avenge *v.* punish, retaliate, revenge, vindicate
ANT. forgive, pardon

avenue *n.* entrance, entry, approach, passage, way, alley, walk, street, road, route, channel

average *adj.* ordinary, common, typical, normal, medium, medial, middling, tolerable, moderate, mediocre, passable
ANT. abnormal

aversion *n.* dislike, hatred, repugnance, disgust, loathing, antipathy, abhorrence, detestation
ANT. love, desire, affection

avoid *v.* evade, shun, abandon, escape, elude, withdraw, forsake, dodge, quit
ANT. meet, confront, face up to

awake *v.* wake up, arouse, rouse, kindle, excite, provoke
ANT. quiet, subdue

awake *adj.* conscious, aware, alert, vigilant, attentive, watchful
ANT. asleep

award *v.* bestow, give, grant, allot, accord, distribute, assign, decree, determine
ANT. withhold

aware *adj.* conscious, informed, sensible, knowing, apprised, mindful, cognizant
ANT. unconscious, ignorant

away *adj.* absent, gone, out
ANT. present

away *adv.* off, apart, at a distance
ANT. near

awe *n.* reverence, respect, veneration, terror, wonder, fear, dread
ANT. contempt, familiarity, irreverence

awful *adj.* dreadful, appalling, alarming, horrible, frightful, shocking, terrible
ANT. wonderful

awkward *adj.* clumsy, bungling, uncouth, rough, ungainly, uncomfortable
ANT. clever, handy

awry *adj.* oblique, slanting, twisted, crooked, distorted
ANT. straight, direct

axiom *n.* truism, proposition, necessary truth
ANT. contradiction

babble *v.* chatter, prattle, gibber, prate, gossip, tattle, tell secrets, blab, blurt out, murmur

babble *n.* chatter, prattle, gossip, tattle

babel *n.* tumult, disorder, clamour, clamor (*N. Am.*), confusion, discord, din
ANT. silence

baby *n.* babe, infant, child, toddler, tot
ANT. adult

back *adj.* rear, last, end, hind, hindmost
ANT. front

back *v.* **1** support, aid, help, sustain, assist, encourage, endorse **2** reverse, move backward, go backward, retire, retreat, withdraw
ANT. **2** advance, push

back out withdraw, retreat, abandon, give up

backbiting *n.* slander, defamation, denigration, malice, calumny, bitchiness (*informal*)

backbone *n.* **1** spine, vertebral column **2** courage, determination, persistence, resolution, tenacity
ANT. **2** weakness

background *n.* setting, context, circumstance, situation, environment, preparation, education

backslider *n.* apostate, renegade, deserter, recreant
ANT. adherent

backward *adj.* slow, indisposed, reluctant, loath, unwilling, hesitating, wavering
ANT. forward, eager

bad *adj.* **1** evil, wicked, depraved, abandoned, corrupt, immoral, unfair, unprincipled, villainous **2** harmful, hurtful, injurious, detrimental, unwholesome **3** poor, imperfect, defective, imperfect, inferior **4** rotten, mouldy, spoiled, contaminated, putrid,

off **5** mischievous, naughty, disobedient
ANT. **1, 2** good **3** excellent **4** obedient

badge *n.* emblem, symbol, crest, shield

bad-tempered *adj.* cross, annoyed, angry, irritable, ill-natured
ANT. cheerful, good-tempered

baffle *v.* bewilder, mystify, perplex, confound, disconcert, frustrate, thwart, defeat, checkmate, undermine
ANT. enlighten

bag *n.* sack, basket, pouch, container, receptacle

baggage *n.* luggage, suitcases, trunks, bags, belongings, things (*informal*)

bait *n.* lure, enticement, snare, decoy, inducement, temptation

bait *v.* **1** lure, entice, induce, seduce, tempt **2** tease, vex, annoy, bother, badger

bake *v.* cook, toast, roast, harden, dry, parch

balance *v.* **1** weigh, compare, estimate **2** poise, hold in equilibrium, neutralize, counteract, compensate, make up for, offset, counterbalance, equalize, square, adjust

bald *adj.* **1** bare, hairless **2** treeless, unsheltered, naked **3** unadorned, prosaic, dull, vapid, tame, inelegant

baleful *adj.* harmful, hurtful, injurious, baneful, pernicious, deadly, ruinous
ANT. beneficial

balk *v.* **1** hesitate, stop, flinch, shrink from **2** frustrate, defeat, foil

ball[1] *n.* globe, sphere, drop, globule

ball[2] *n.* dance, social, party

balmy *adj.* gentle, mild, pleasant, soothing, sweet, healing
ANT. harsh

ban *v.* forbid, prohibit, outlaw, exclude
ANT. allow, permit

band¹ *n.* group, society, association, company, crowd

band² *n.* belt, strip, ribbon, girdle

bang *n.* explosion, boom, crash, blast, shot, burst

bang *v.* **1** explode, boom, crash, blast **2** hit, strike, bump, bash (*informal*), pound

banish *v.* dismiss, drive out, eject, expel, exile, ostracize, evict, expatriate
ANT. welcome, admit

bank *n.* pile, mound, heap, ridge, embankment

banquet *n.* feast, treat, regalement, entertainment, festivity, carousal, cheer

banter *n.* badinage, irony, raillery, ridicule, satire, mockery, jeering, derision

bar *n.* **1** barrier, obstacle, obstruction, hindrance, impediment **2** counter, saloon, lounge, café

bar *v.* prohibit, obstruct, hinder, forbid, stop, prevent, restrain, deter
ANT. allow, welcome

barbarian *n.* savage, brute

barbarian *adj.* primitive, savage, uncivilized, cruel
ANT. civilized

barbarous *adj.* brutal, atrocious, cruel, inhuman, merciless, savage, barbaric, barbarian
ANT. civilized, humane

bare *adj.* **1** nude, naked, unclothed, exposed **2** bald, unadorned, meagre, meager (*N. Am.*) **3** sheer, simple, mere
ANT. **1** dressed, protected **2** rich, luxurious, costly

barely *adv.* hardly, scarcely, just

bargain *n.* **1** agreement, contract, stipulation, transaction **2** purchase, speculation, haggling, getting, proceeds **3** cheap purchase, good buy, snip (*informal*)

bargain *v.* haggle, trade, barter

barren *adj.* sterile, unprolific, unfertile, unproductive, childless
ANT. productive

barrier *n.* obstruction, hindrance, obstacle, bar, barricade, rampart, restraint, restriction
ANT. encouragement

barter *v.* trade, exchange, traffic

base¹ *n.* bottom, foundation, support, rest, stand
ANT. top

base *v.* establish, found, build, depend, rest

base² *adj.* **1** cheap, worthless, inferior, poor **2** vulgar, humble, low, unknown, mean, contemptible, shameful, scandalous, vile
ANT. **1, 2** noble

bashful *adj.* modest, shy, timid, retiring, reserved, diffident
ANT. bold, forward

basic *adj.* fundamental, chief, main, essential

basis *n.* base, foundation, ground, grounds, justification, reason

bathe *v.* wash, cover, flood, immerse, suffuse
ANT. dry, expose

battle *n.* fight, war, contest, skirmish, combat, encounter, bout, engagement, strife, action, conflict
ANT. armistice, truce

battle *v.* fight, struggle, strive

bauble *n.* trifle, toy, plaything, trinket, gimcrack, knick-knack
ANT. ornament, decoration

bay *n.* cove, gulf, sound, inlet

be *v.* **1** exist, breathe, live, continue, remain, stay, endure, last **2** occur, take place, happen, come about

beach *n.* shore, strand, sands, coast, seashore, rim

beacon *n.* signal, flare, light, flame, mark, sign, guide, warning

bead *n.* drop, ball, blob, pellet, globule

beam *n.* **1** rafter, support, girder, plank, board **2** ray, gleam, streak, shaft, flash

beam *v.* shine, emit, gleam, glitter, radiate

bear *v.* **1** support, sustain, hold up, carry, have, hold, possess **2** suffer, undergo, endure, tolerate, submit to, permit, allow **3** produce, yield, give birth to, generate
ANT. **1** drop

bear out substantiate, confirm, prove, justify

bearing *n.* 1 behaviour, behavior (*N. Am.*), deportment, demeanour, demeanor (*N. Am.*), appearance, aspect, position, carriage, mien, air 2 relation, connection, reference, relevance 3 direction, course, aim, position, location

beast *n.* animal, brute, creature, monster

beat *v.* 1 hit, strike, thrash, flog, cudgel, pound, scourge, whip, batter, spank 2 overcome, conquer, defeat, vanquish

beat *n.* 1 stroke, blow, pulse, pulsation 2 rounds, route, way, path, course, journey

beautiful *adj.* lovely, charming, fair, attractive, pretty, graceful, exquisite, bewitching, picturesque, handsome, comely
ANT. hideous, repulsive, ugly

beauty *n.* attractiveness, loveliness, prettiness, charm
ANT. hideousness, ugliness

because *conj.* since, for, as

beckon *v.* signal, sign, call, call by a gesture, nod
ANT. ignore

become *v.* 1 get, grow, turn, change, come to be 2 suit, befit, set off, be appropriate to

becoming *adj.* attractive, pleasing, pretty, fit, graceful, befitting, seemly, proper, neat, suitable
ANT. unseemly, indecent

before *prep.* preceding, in front of, prior to, previous, in advance of, ahead of
ANT. behind, after

before *adv.* earlier, previously, above, in a former place, formerly, of old, already
ANT. subsequently, later

beg *v.* ask, request, beseech, pray, supplicate, solicit, sue, implore, importune
ANT. demand, extort

beggar *n.* pauper, mendicant, supplicant, suitor, applicant
ANT. giver

begin *v.* start, commence, arise, originate, bring into being, come into being

beginner *n.* novice, apprentice, learner, trainee, amateur

beginning *n.* opening, commencement, start, source, spring, origin, initiation, arising, outset, rise, inception, inauguration
ANT. end, finish

beguile *v.* cheat, deceive, fool, delude, trick, hoodwink

behalf *n.* part, sake, side, interest, benefit

behave *v.* conduct, bear, deport, act
ANT. misbehave

behaviour, behavior (*N. Am.*) *n.* conduct, manners, breeding, carriage, deportment, bearing, action, demeanour, demeanor (*N. Am.*), life
ANT. misconduct, misdemeanour, misdemeanor (*N. Am.*)

behind *prep.* at the back of, at the rear of
ANT. before, in front of

being *n.* 1 reality, existence, actuality, presence 2 essence, inmost nature, substance, life, vital principle, root, heart 3 creature, individual, animal, thing

beleaguer *v.* besiege, beset, blockade, compass, surround

belief *n.* 1 opinion, view, conviction, theory, impression 2 faith, trust, confidence, assurance, conviction, credence, persuasion, reliance, assurance
ANT. 2 distrust

believe *v.* 1 be convinced, accept, have faith, have confidence 2 think, reckon, hold, maintain, suppose, assume

belligerent *adj.* warlike, conflicting, hostile, rival, opposed, adverse, antagonistic, contentious, quarrelsome
ANT. peaceful, friendly

belong *v.* 1 be owned by, be the property of, be possessed by 2 be a member of, be associated with, be a part of

belonging *n.* possession, property, goods, estate, chattel

below *prep.* under, beneath, underneath
ANT. above

belt *n.* band, girdle, sash, strap, stripe

bench *n.* table, trestle, board, counter

bend *v.* 1 curve, twist, crook, bow, deflect, deviate, diverge, twine 2 stoop, squat, kneel, crouch, bow 3 influence, persuade, incline, submit, yield
ANT. 1 straighten, stiffen, direct

beneath *prep*. below, under, underneath
ANT. above

benediction *n*. blessing, gratitude, thanks, praise, benefit, grace, boon
ANT. curse, censure, execration, ingratitude

benefactor *n*. patron, supporter, upholder, friend, contributor
ANT. enemy

beneficial *adj*. good, advantageous, helpful, useful, favourable, favorable (*N. Am.*), valuable, profitable, wholesome
ANT. unwholesome

benefit *n*. good, advantage, profit, favour, favor (*N. Am.*), boon, service, blessing
ANT. loss, damage

benevolence *n*. kindness, humaneness, charitableness, goodwill, altruism, liberality, philanthropy, humanity, sympathy, munificence, generosity, unselfishness, kind-heartedness
ANT. malevolence, selfishness

benign *adj*. kind, gracious, amiable, gentle, friendly, benevolent, humane, obliging, good
ANT. harsh

bent *adj*. 1 crooked, curved, twisted, arched 2 determined, resolved, inclined, set, firm
ANT. 1 straight

bequeath *v*. will, leave, give, grant, hand down, transmit, impart
ANT. disinherit

bereavement *n*. loss, destitution, affliction, deprivation, desolation

bereft *adj*. deprived, stripped, devoid
ANT. endowed, blessed

beseech *v*. beg, implore, pray, ask, solicit, entreat, petition
ANT. grant

beset *v*. surround, circle, hem in, besiege, beleaguer

beside *prep*. near, close together
ANT. far, away from

besides *adv*. moreover, furthermore, further, in addition, beyond that

besiege *v*. lay siege to, blockade, surround, encompass
ANT. relieve, defend

best *adj*. finest, supreme, excellent, outstanding, leading, first-rate, highest
ANT. worse

bestow *v*. give, present, award, grant, confer
ANT. withhold

bet *n*. wager, stake, pledge

bet *v*. wager, gamble

betray *v*. 1 inform on, be treacherous, be disloyal, sell out (*informal*) 2 reveal, expose, divulge, deliver up, deceive, manifest, show, indicate
ANT. 1 protect 2 conceal, suppress

betrothal *n*. engagement, plighting, troth, promise, vow, pledge

better *adj*. 1 finer, greater, preferable 2 healthy, well, recovering, improving
ANT. 1 worse 2 ill

better *v*. improve, correct, advance, reform, amend, ameliorate
ANT. make worse

between *prep*. amid, among
ANT. outside, beyond

bewail *v*. bemoan, lament, sorrow, grieve
ANT. rejoice

beware *v*. take care, be cautious, be wary, look out, mind
ANT. be reckless, careless

bewilder *v*. confuse, perplex, puzzle, mystify, baffle, embarrass

bewilderment *n*. confusion, embarrassment, daze, maze, perplexity, mystification
ANT. enlightenment

bewitch *v*. charm, enchant, fascinate, captivate
ANT. avoid

beyond *prep*. over, across, farther than, before
ANT. beside, near, at hand, close

bias *n*. inclination, prejudice, tendency, leaning, bent, proneness, propensity, partiality

bias *v*. influence, prejudice, predispose, tend, lean

bicker *v*. argue, fight, row, wrangle, quarrel, dispute, squabble
ANT. agree

bid *v*. 1 command, order, direct 2 offer, propose, tender

bidding *n.* 1 command, order, direction, appointment, mandate 2 offer, bid, proposal

big *adj.* 1 large, great, wide, bulky, huge, vast, immense, enormous, massive, colossal 2 important, significant, notable, influential
ANT. 1 small, little 2 humble

bigot *n.* zealot, fanatic, dogmatist, devotee
ANT. sceptic

bigoted *adj.* intolerant, opinionated, prejudiced, dogmatic, narrow-minded, one-sided
ANT. liberal, broad-minded

bill *n.* 1 invoice, account, statement, charge, score, amount due, reckoning 2 poster, placard, advertisement

bind *v.* 1 tie, fasten, shackle, restrict, restrain, secure, fetter 2 compel, oblige, require, engage
ANT. 1 free, loose, set free, untie

birth *n.* family, parentage, creation, origin, start, beginning, appearance, source, lineage, nativity, descent, extraction, race
ANT. death

bit *n.* scrap, part, piece, fragment, particle, morsel
ANT. whole, mass

bite *v.* gnaw, pierce, nip, chew

biting *adj.* gnawing, sharp, severe, sardonic, censorious, piercing, sarcastic, trenchant
ANT. pleasant, gentle, soothing

bitter *adj.* harsh, caustic, cutting, savage, acrimonious, irate, sharp, sour, stinging, pungent
ANT. sweet, honeyed

black *adj.* 1 dark, sooty, inky 2 dirty, filthy, soiled, stained, grubby 3 gloomy, sombre, somber (*N. Am.*), dismal, depressing
ANT. 1 white 2 clean 3 bright, cheerful

blacken *v.* 1 daub, befoul 2 slander, malign, defame, vilify, decry, calumniate
ANT. 1 whiten, whitewash 2 clear, vindicate

blame *v.* censure, rebuke, chide, reprove, reproach, criticize, condemn reprehend
ANT. approve, praise

blame *n.* responsibility, guilt, fault, culpability

blameless *adj.* pure, innocent, irresponsible, without fault
ANT. guilty, blameworthy, faulty

blanch *v.* bleach, whiten, whitewash
ANT. blacken

bland *adj.* soft, gentle, mild, affable, gracious, tender
ANT. harsh

blandishment *n.* flattery, coaxing, wheedling, attraction, charm, fawning, cajolery

blank *adj.* 1 bare, bleak, void, empty 2 expressionless, uninterested, deadpan, poker-faced (*informal*) 3 utter, pure, simple, mere, unqualified, unmitigated
ANT. 1 full 2 alert

blasphemy *n.* profanity, sacrilege, impiety, swearing
ANT. reverence, godliness

blast *n.* explosion, bang, detonation, noise

blast *v.* explode, blow up, burst, shatter, ruin

blaze *n.* fire, flame, inferno, conflagration

blaze *v.* burn, flare, flare up, shine, gleam

blazon *v.* blare, proclaim, publish, publicize, herald
ANT. conceal

bleach *v.* blanch, whiten, pale
ANT. blacken, darken

bleak *adj.* 1 windy, exposed, bare, cold, chill, raw 2 desolate, comfortless, cheerless, depressing
ANT. 1 sheltered, protected 2 cheerful

bleed *v.* 1 lose blood, flow, gush, spurt 2 draw blood, extract, extort, milk

blemish *n.* blot, spot, flaw, fault, imperfection, stain, defacement, tarnish, disfigurement, disgrace, defect, dishonour, dishonor (*N. Am.*), stigma, taint
ANT. purity

blend *v.* mix, unite, combine, fuse, merge, mingle, amalgamate, coalesce, harmonize
ANT. separate

blend *n*. mixture, combination, fusion, merger, amalgamation

bless *v*. delight, gladden, make happy, thank, glorify, exalt, praise, extol, cheer
ANT. curse

blessing *n*. 1 good, benefit, happiness, profit, boon, gain 2 glory, praise, gratitude, benediction

blight *n*. epidemic, sickness, disease, affliction, pestilence, withering

blight *v*. damage, spoil, harm, ruin, destroy, mar

blind *adj*. 1 sightless, unseeing, eyeless, purblind 2 undiscerning, ignorant, unconscious, uninformed, unknowing, unthinking
ANT. 1 sighted 2 discerning

blink *v*. wink, flutter, twinkle, glimmer

bliss *n*. blessedness, happiness, gladness, joy, ecstasy, rapture
ANT. misery

block *v*. obstruct, stop, blockade, impede, hinder, check
ANT. clear

block *n*. obstacle, obstruction, blockade, impediment, hindrance
ANT. aid

blood *n*. 1 gore, plasma, lifeblood 2 ancestry, stock, lineage, heritage, family, extraction

bloodthirsty *adj*. cruel, savage, ferocious, murderous, bloody, gory, barbarous, inhuman, ruthless
ANT. kind, merciful

bloody *adj*. 1 gory, bleeding, sanguinary 2 bloodthirsty, cruel, savage, ferocious, murderous

bloom *n*. 1 blossom, flower, flowering 2 flush, freshness, prime, vigour, vigor (*N. Am.*), glow

bloom *v*. blossom, bud, flower, germinate, sprout, blow, develop
ANT. wither

blooming *adj*. flourishing, flowering, budding, developing
ANT. fading, waning

blot *n*. stain, spot, blur, blotch, smear, taint, blemish, disgrace

blot *v*. sully, spot, tarnish, spoil, discolour, discolor (*N. Am.*), pollute, stain, erase, blur, blotch, smear, obliterate
ANT. cleanse

blot out erase, cancel, expunge, obliterate, destroy, eliminate, wipe out, rub out
ANT. restore, replace

blow¹ *n*. 1 knock, thump, hit, stroke, box, buffet, calamity, cuff, cut, concussion, rap, shock, stroke, wound, affliction, blast, gale, gust 2 disappointment, disaster, misfortune, calamity, tragedy
ANT. 2 relief, comfort, blessing

blow² *v*. breathe, puff, exhale, expel, pant, waft, fan, move, sweep

blow up 1 explode, go off, detonate, burst 2 inflate, enlarge, swell

bluff¹ *v*. deceive, mislead, pretend, fool

bluff *n*. deceit, sham, pretence, pretense (*N. Am.*), show, bluster

bluff² *adj*. abrupt, blunt, inconsiderate, open, rough, unmannerly, uncivil, blustering
ANT. courteous, polite

blunder *n*. error, mistake, misunderstanding, fault, slip, oversight, inaccuracy
ANT. accuracy, correctness

blunt *adj*. 1 dull, worn, unsharpened 2 abrupt, curt, brusque, informal
ANT. 1 sharp 2 tactful

blunt *v*. harden, dull, make dull, deaden
ANT. sharpen

blur *v*. obscure, dim, dull, confuse, stain, smear
ANT. clarify, clear

blush *v*. flush, redden, glow, go red, colour, color (*N. Am.*)

blush *n*. flush, bloom, colour, color (*N. Am.*), reddening
ANT. pallor

bluster *v*. storm, rage, insult, roar, swagger, boast

board *n*. 1 plank, timber, slat, panel 2 food, meals, provisions 3 committee, council, group, body, panel

boast v. brag, swagger, vaunt, magnify, make much of, swell, bluster, triumph
ANT. cringe

boast n. bragging, vaunting, bluster
ANT. modesty

boat n. ship, craft, vessel, yacht, canoe, dinghy, launch

bodily adj. physical, material, tangible
ANT. spiritually

body n. 1 carcass, corpse, cadaver
2 trunk, torso, stem, bulk, main part
3 person, individual, mortal, creature, being 4 group, party, band, company, society, corporation 5 consistency, substance, density

boil v. bubble, rage, fume, seethe, simmer, effervesce, explode
ANT. calm

boisterous adj. loud, unrestrained, stormy, noisy, lively, furious, violent, clamorous
ANT. quiet, calm

bold adj. courageous, brave, adventurous, intrepid, dauntless, fearless, audacious, daring, valiant
ANT. afraid, fearful, retiring, shy, bashful

bolster v. support, prop, help, sustain, buoy, defend, maintain

bolt n. bar, rod, latch, lock, fastening

bolt v. 1 lock, fasten, latch, bar 2 run, fly, dash, rush
ANT. 1 unlock

bomb n. explosive, mine, shell, torpedo, grenade, incendiary

bombast n. bluster, pomposity, braggadocio, rodomontade
ANT. modesty

bond n. 1 tie, rope, cord, fastening, manacle, fetter 2 link, connection, tie, attachment 3 promise, obligation, security

bondage n. servitude, slavery, imprisonment, captivity, incarceration, subjection, confinement
ANT. liberty, freedom

bonus n. premium, gift, reward, bounty, boon, benefit
ANT. fine, penalty

book n. publication, volume, work, hardback, paperback, text, tome

bookish adj. pedantic, studious, learned, erudite, educated
ANT. illiterate, ignorant

boom v. 1 reverberate, resound, roar, thunder 2 prosper, flourish, thrive, develop
ANT. 2 decline

boom n. 1 roar, reverberation 2 rise, boost, development, increase
ANT. 2 decline

boon n. blessing, benefit, gift, favour, favor (N. Am.)
ANT. disadvantage

boor n. rustic, lout, peasant, countryman, bumpkin

boorish adj. rude, rustic, loutish, awkward, coarse, rough
ANT. polite

boost v. encourage, increase, expand, improve, support, further

boost n. encouragement, support, help, increase, improvement

booty n. plunder, prey, spoil, pillage, loot

border n. 1 frontier, boundary, limit 2 edge, brink, rim, verge
ANT. 2 centre, center (N. Am.)

bore v. 1 weary, tire, trouble, vex, worry, annoy 2 drill, pierce, perforate, penetrate
ANT. 1 delight, please

boring adj. dull, monotonous, tedious, routine, tiresome
ANT. exciting, interesting

borrow v. take, adopt, hire, receive, appropriate
ANT. lend

bosom n. breast, chest, heart, feelings, affections

boss n. supervisor, overseer, manager, director, chief, head
ANT. employee

botch v. bungle, spoil, mismanage, mess up, mishandle

bother v. worry, irritate, pester, annoy, harass, plague, tease, vex
ANT. calm

bother n. fuss, inconvenience, trouble, upset
ANT. comfort

bottle *n.* jug, jar, vase, flask, pitcher

bottom *n.* **1** base, foot, depths, ground, foundation, basis, underside **2** seat, rear, behind, buttocks, posterior
ANT. **1** top

bough *n.* branch, limb, stem, twig

bounce *v.* rebound, spring back, recoil, jump, leap, bound

bound¹ *v.* jump, spring, leap, skip, frisk

bound² *adj.* **1** tied, confined, limited, restricted, restrained **2** sure, certain, destined, required, compelled

boundary *n.* limit, confines, border, bound, frontier, line, barrier, edge

boundless *adj.* unlimited, illimitable, unbounded, measureless, infinite
ANT. restricted

bountiful *adj.* liberal, generous, benevolent, unselfish
ANT. mean, miserly

bounty *n.* liberality, gift, generosity, charity, benefaction, benevolence, donation, reward, bonus

bouquet *n.* bunch, posy, spray, corsage, nosegay

bourgeois *adj.* middle-class, conventional, traditional
ANT. aristocratic

bout *n.* **1** fight, conflict, match, contest **2** spell, period, season, session

bow *v.* **1** bend, stoop, curve, curtsy, kneel, kowtow **2** submit, yield, give in, surrender

bowl *n.* basin, plate, dish, vessel

box *n.* container, carton, package, case

boy *n.* lad, youth, youngster
ANT. man

brace *v.* support, prop, strengthen, fasten, tie

brace *n.* support, prop, truss

brag *v.* boast, vaunt, swagger

braid *v.* bind, weave, plait, tie, wreathe, twine
ANT. unbind, dishevel

brain *n.* intellect, intelligent, mind, sense, reason, understanding
ANT. stupidity

brake *n.* restraint, control, check, curb

brake *v.* slow down, decelerate, curb, stop
ANT. accelerate

branch *n.* **1** bough, limb, shoot, arm, twig, scion, offshoot **2** section, department, division, subdivision, tributary

brand *n.* **1** make, kind, sort, type **2** mark, stamp, emblem, symbol

brand *v.* **1** mark, stamp, label, burn **2** denounce, mark, stigmatize, disgrace

brandish *v.* flourish, wield, wave, swing, flaunt

bravado *n.* boasting, bragging, bluster
ANT. modesty

brave *adj.* bold, courageous, daring, dauntless, fearless, heroic, undaunted, undismayed, adventurous, gallant, intrepid, valiant, venturesome, chivalrous
ANT. afraid, fearful, timid, frightened, cowardly

bravery *n.* courage, gallantry, boldness, fearlessness, heroism, mettle, pluck
ANT. fearfulness, timidity, cowardliness

brawl *n.* fight, fray, affray, row, tumult, fracas, disagreement, disturbance, dispute

brawny *adj.* muscular, strong, powerful, athletic, sinewy
ANT. weak, delicate

brazen *adj.* bold, forward, shameless, brash, saucy, rude
ANT. modest

breach *n.* **1** break, rupture, rift, opening, fracture, flaw, fissure, rent **2** violation, infringement, non-observance **3** quarrel, difference, variance, dissension, schism, alienation
ANT. **1** wholeness **2** keeping, observance **3** reconciliation

break *v.* **1** fracture, crack, snap, part, sever, shatter, smash, shiver **2** violate, infringe, disobey **3** destroy, sunder, burst, rive, crack, crush, demolish, rupture, split **4** weaken, impair, enfeeble, enervate **5** interrupt, discontinue, stop, cut short, halt
ANT. **1** mend **2** observe, keep, obey **4** strengthen **5** continue

break down fail, stop, falter **break in** train, prepare, initiate, educate **break out** begin, start, commence **break through** penetrate, succeed, pass **break up** divide, separate, split, dismantle

break *n.* fracture, crack, split, gap, opening

breast *n.* chest, front, bust, bosom, heart, affection

breath *n.* respiration, inhalation, exhalation, breathing, air, gasp, pant, puff, wheeze

breathe *v.* respire, inhale, exhale, gasp, pant, puff, sigh

breathless *adj.* exhausted, out of breath, lifeless, dead
ANT. cool, composed

breed *v.* 1 bear, conceive, produce, bring forth 2 nurture, foster, nourish, raise, discipline, educate, instruct, train, teach, school 3 occasion, originate, generate, propagate, cause, evolve

breed *n.* lineage, race, pedigree, progeny, stock, line, family, extraction, strain

breeding *n.* discipline, instruction, education, nurture, training, schooling

breeze *n.* wind, flurry, gust, waft, puff, draught, draft (*N. Am.*)

brevity *n.* shortness, conciseness, compression, pithiness, succinctness, abbreviation, abridgment
ANT. verbosity, length

brew *v.* boil, ferment, stew, steep, concoct, compound, mix, collect, gather, grow, impend

bribe *v.* corrupt, tempt, lure, entice, influence, induce, suborn

bribe *n.* inducement, graft, enticement, backhander (*informal*), hush money

bridge *n.* span, arch, flyover, viaduct

bridle *v.* restrain, curb, control, govern, check
ANT. relax, loosen

bridle *n.* restraint, curb, control, check

brief *adj.* 1 short, concise, succinct, condensed, abridged, compact 2 short, fleeting, temporary, transient, ephemeral
ANT. 1 long 2 exhaustive

bright *adj.* 1 shining, glowing, lustrous, beaming, gleaming, glistening, blazing, flaming, flashing, radiant, ruddy, refulgent, brilliant, dazzling, sparkling, resplendent, luminous 2 cheerful, happy, lively, animated 3 intense, vivid, brilliant 4 intelligent, clever, discerning, keen, ingenious 5 encouraging, promising, propitious, favourable, favorable (*N. Am.*), inspiring, auspicious 6 lucid, clear, transparent, pellucid, fine, cloudless
ANT. 1 dull, dark 2 gloomy 3 dark 4 ignorant 5 discouraging 6 sunless, murky, cloudy, overcast

brilliant *adj.* 1 bright, radiant, flashing, lustrous, glorious, luminous, beaming, sparkling 2 clever, intelligent, gifted, talented
ANT. 1 dark, dull 2 stupid

brim *n.* rim, lip, edge, limit, margin

bring *v.* 1 fetch, take, convey, bear 2 usher, take, conduct, guide, lead, attend, accompany, convoy
ANT. 1 remove, send

bring about cause, produce, occasion, accomplish, effect **bring in** yield, earn, produce, profit **bring up** 1 rear, raise, nurture, train, teach, educate 2 propose, raise, introduce, mention

brink *n.* edge, border, verge, limit, boundary

brisk *adj.* lively, quick, vivacious, active, alert, animated, prompt, sprightly, nimble, spry, agile
ANT. slow, heavy, dull

bristling *adj.* full, crowded, swarming
ANT. empty

brittle *adj.* fragile, crumbling, shivery, frail, easily broken, weak
ANT. strong, hardy

broach *v.* 1 suggest, hint, approach, introduce 2 open, pierce, tap

broad *adj.* wide, large, extensive, vast, spacious, capacious, ample, full
ANT. narrow, restricted, limited

broadcast *v.* transmit, relay, air, announce, publish, spread, disseminate, distribute

broadcast *n.* programme, program (*N. Am.*), show, transmission

broaden *v.* widen, enlarge, extend, expand, increase, grow, develop
ANT. narrow, constrict

broad-minded *adj.* tolerant, liberal, open-minded, permissive, indulgent
ANT. narrow, prejudiced

brood *v.* ponder, reflect, deliberate, meditate, dwell on, ruminate

brood *n.* offspring, family, litter, young

brook¹ *n.* stream, beck, rivulet, rill, creek

brook² *v.* tolerate, bear, suffer, endure, abide

brow *n.* forehead, front, face

browbeat *v.* bully, intimidate, bulldoze, overbear

browse *v.* glance, scan, skim, read lightly, leaf, dip

bruise *v.* hurt, injure, wound, contuse, crush, squeeze, break, pound, batter, deface

bruise *n.* injury, abrasion, wound, contusion, mark, blemish

brunt *n.* shock, force, impulse, onslaught, onset, assault

brush *n.* 1 broom, besom, hairbrush, paintbrush 2 scrub, bush, thicket, undergrowth

brutal *adj.* cruel, savage, ferocious, harsh
ANT. mild, kind

brute *n.* beast, monster, savage, animal

bubble *n.* froth, foam, lather, blob, effervescence

bucket *n.* pail, container

buckle *n.* fastener, clasp, clip

buckle *v.* 1 fasten, secure, close 2 collapse, yield, bend, warp

budge *v.* move, go, stir

buffet¹ *v.* beat, strike, batter, pound, thump

buffet *n.* blow, strike, hit, slap, thump

buffet² *n.* meal, snack

buffoon *n.* clown, jester, fool, wag

build *v.* make, construct, erect, raise, form, shape, figure, model
ANT. demolish, overthrow, destroy

build up increase, develop, strengthen, intensify

build-up *n.* body, form, figure, physique

building *n.* structure, edifice, architecture, erection

bulge *v.* swell, expand, stick out, protrude

bulge *n.* swelling, bump, lump, protrusion

bulk *n.* 1 magnitude, size, volume, dimension, mass, greatness, amplitude, massiveness 2 majority, major part, most, principal part

bulky *adj.* big, large, huge, massive, awkward, unwieldy
ANT. small, delicate

bully *n.* ruffian, tough, intimidator, rascal

bully *v.* intimidate, browbeat, harass, torment

bulwark *n.* rampart, fortress, fortification, stronghold, bastion

bump *v.* bang, knock, crash, strike, collide

bump *n.* blow, bang, collision

bunch *n.* group, cluster, clump, collection, batch

bundle *n.* bunch, collection, package, packet

bungle *v.* spoil, blunder, mess up, mismanage, screw up (*informal*), fumble
ANT. accomplish

bungler *n.* botcher, fumbler, incompetent

buoy *n.* float, marker

buoy *v.* float, support, sustain, elevate, inspire, assure, animate, cheer
ANT. sink

buoyant *adj.* 1 light, floating, weightless 2 cheerful, hopeful, joyous, jubilant
ANT. 1 heavy 2 depressed, moody, cheerless

burden *n.* 1 load, weight, cargo, freight 2 worry, trouble, affliction, sorrow, impediment, grievance, trial

bureau *n.* office, agency, department

burglar *n.* thief, housebreaker, robber

burial *n.* funeral, burying, interment, entombment
ANT. exhumation, disinterment

burlesque *n.* parody, travesty, caricature, ridicule, farce

burn *v.* **1** flame, blaze, glow, smoulder **2** char, consume, cremate, scorch, set on fire, singe, ignite, incinerate, kindle

burnish *v.* brighten, polish, glaze, gloss

burrow *n.* tunnel, hole, den, lair

burst *v.* explode, blow up, break, open, split, crack, discharge, shatter, disrupt
ANT. cohere, hold, stand, stick together

bury *v.* **1** inter, cover up, entomb **2** hide, conceal, shroud, secrete, confine, immure
ANT. **1** resurrect, exhume, disinter

bush *n.* shrub, hedge, thicket, scrub, undergrowth

business *n.* **1** occupation, trade, job, profession, employment, craft, commerce, vocation, calling, duty, office **2** firm, company, corporation, organization, partnership **3** concern, affair, matter

bustle *n.* hurry, activity, stir, commotion, excitement, haste, hurry, energy
ANT. idleness, inactivity

busy *adj.* engaged, employed, occupied, active, diligent, industrious, working
ANT. lazy, idle

but *conj.* however, nevertheless, yet, still, on the other hand

but *prep.* except, save, notwithstanding

buy *v.* **1** purchase, obtain, acquire, get **2** bribe, corrupt, pervert, suborn
ANT. **1** sell

by *prep.* **1** through, with, by means of, via **2** near, close by, next to, beside, at

C

cab *n.* taxi, taxicab, minibus

cabal *n.* conspiracy, conclave, faction, gang, coterie, plot, political intrigue, league

cabin *n.* **1** compartment, room, apartment, berth **2** hut, shack, shed, cottage, lodge

cabinet *n.* **1** cupboard, wardrobe, chest, dresser **2** council, assembly, ministry, committee, administration

cable *n.* wire, line, rope, cord

cackle *v.* cluck, crow, quack, squawk, chuckle, laugh

cadaverous *adj.* deathlike, deathly, bloodless, pallid, pale, wan, ghastly, ashy
ANT. rosy, blushing

café *n.* cafeteria, snack bar, restaurant, bistro, coffee bar, buffet, tea-room

cage *n.* enclosure, pound, pen, aviary

cage *v.* imprison, confine, incarcerate, immure
ANT. liberate, free

cagey *adj.* secretive, evasive, cautious, guarded
ANT. frank, open

cajole *v.* coax, persuade, wheedle, flatter, deceive, entrap, beguile

cake *n.* pastry, bun, tart, gateau, biscuit, patisserie

calamitous *adj.* disastrous, unfortunate, unlucky, adverse, ruinous, wretched, distressing, grievous, hapless, ill-omened
ANT. fortunate

calamity *n.* disaster, misfortune, catastrophe, mishap, trial, trouble, affliction, adversity, distress, hardship, ill luck
ANT. blessing, advantage

calculate *v.* work out, number, reckon, sum up, count, compute, account, estimate, measure, enumerate, rate, consider, deem, apportion, investigate
ANT. guess

calculating *adj.* scheming, crafty, cunning, wary, cautious
ANT. direct, guileless

calculation *n.* working out, reckoning, computation
ANT. guess

calibre, caliber (*N. Am.*) *n.* **1** diameter, gauge, capacity **2** gifts, faculty, scope, talent, ability, parts, endowment

call *v.* **1** cry, scream, roar, shout, shriek, bawl, yell, exclaim, bellow, clamour, clamor (*N. Am.*), vociferate **2** name, label, designate, dub **3** phone, ring, telephone, buzz (*informal*) **4** invite, summon, send for, bid **5** assemble, gather, convene, muster **6** elect, ordain, appoint **7** invoke, appeal to
ANT. **1** be silent, hush **5** disperse

call off cancel, abandon, postpone **call on** visit, drop in on, look up **call off** *n.* **1** cry, scream, shout, shriek, exclamation, yell **2** demand, need, cause, occasion, claim

callous *adj.* hard, hard-hearted, cruel, insensitive, unfeeling
ANT. kind, tender

calm *adj.* composed, peaceful, placid, quiet, still, tranquil, self-possessed, serene, undisturbed, dispassionate, collected, imperturbable, unruffled
ANT. frantic, frenzied

calm *v.* pacify, soothe, mollify, relax, hush, assuage
ANT. upset, disturb, excite

camouflage *n.* disguise, covering, mask, cloak, veil, blind, screen, guise

camp *n.* encampment, tent, cabin, bivouac

campaign *n.* exercise, operation, drive, task, crusade, struggle

campaign *v.* fight, struggle, battle, work

cancel *v.* 1 abolish, call off, nullify, annul, set aside, revoke, rescind, make void, repeal 2 obliterate, cross off, rub out, scratch out, erase, efface, expunge
ANT. 1 confirm, maintain

candid *adj.* honest, open, straightforward, transparent, unbiased, frank, guileless, ingenuous, naive, sincere, impartial, unprejudiced, simple, artless, truthful, unsophisticated, fair
ANT. deceitful, artful, sly, cunning, insincere

candidate *n.* nominee, applicant, competitor, aspirant, petitioner, canvasser, claimant

canvass *v.* 1 solicit votes from, apply for, electioneer, campaign for 2 debate, discuss, dispute

capability *n.* capacity, ability, skill, power, competency, efficiency, force, faculty, scope, brains, talent
ANT. inability

capable *adj.* able, skilled, skilful, skillful (*N. Am.*), accomplished
ANT. incompetent, inept

capacity *n.* 1 space, magnitude, volume, dimensions, extent, size, content 2 faculty, gift, talent, genius, competence, capability, discernment, cleverness, skill, aptitude 3 sphere, office, character, function

capital *n.* cash, assets, funds, finance, investment, principal, stock, property

capital *adj.* 1 chief, major, principal, essential, leading, first 2 excellent, prime, first-class, first-rate, fine, splendid
ANT. 1 subordinate, unimportant, minor

capitulate *v.* surrender, yield, submit, give in
ANT. resist

caprice *n.* vagary, whim, fancy

capricious *adj.* fanciful, whimsical, inconstant, uncertain, fitful, fickle, changeable
ANT. firm, inflexible

captain *n.* 1 commander, leader, chief, head, director 2 skipper, master, commanding officer

captious *adj.* carping, hypercritical, censorious, fault-finding, nit-picking (*informal*)
ANT. appreciative

captivate *v.* charm, enchant, fascinate, delight, bewitch, please highly, win, catch
ANT. disenchant, disillusion, disgust

captive *n.* prisoner, hostage, convict, slave

captivity *n.* confinement, imprisonment, custody, detention, bondage, subjection, slavery, servitude, duress
ANT. freedom, liberty

capture *v.* seize, catch, arrest, take prisoner, apprehend, make captive
ANT. liberate, free

capture *n.* seizure, arrest, catching, apprehension
ANT. release

car *n.* automobile, vehicle, motorcar, motor

carcass *n.* body, corpse, cadaver, remains

card *n.* cardboard, paper, sheet, board, poster

cardinal *adj.* chief, main, principal, important, primary, prime, capital

care *n.* 1 anxiety, trouble, concern, vigilance, worry 2 attention, carefulness, heed, forethought, watchfulness 3 protection, custody, charge, supervision, guardianship
ANT. 2 neglect, carelessness

care *v.* 1 mind, be concerned, bother, consider 2 look after, tend, watch, attend to

career *n.* profession, calling, vocation, occupation, job

careful *adj.* 1 cautious, wary, watchful, mindful, guarded 2 thorough, meticulous, scrupulous, precise, painstaking
ANT. 1 incautious 2 careless

careless *adj.* thoughtless, negligent, reckless, sloppy, disorganized, casual
ANT. careful

caress v. embrace, stroke, touch, fondle, kiss, pet, pamper

caress n. embrace, kiss, touch, fondling

cargo n. freight, load, goods, baggage, consignment, merchandise

caricature n. imitation, mimicry, parody, travesty, burlesque, exaggeration, extravaganza, take-off, farce
ANT. portraiture

carnage n. massacre, bloodshed, slaughter, havoc, butchery

carnal adj. sensual, fleshly, lustful, lascivious
ANT. pure

carnival n. festival, revel, masquerade

carol n. song, hymn, noel

carol v. sing, chant, warble, chirp

carousal n. revel, debauch, orgy, binge (informal), feast, festival, banquet

carp v. cavil, find fault, object to, pick holes (informal), challenge, censure
ANT. compliment, approve

carry v. 1 move, transport, lift, bring, bear, transmit, support, sustain, take, convey 2 impel, urge, push forward
ANT. 1 drop, let go 2 impede

carry off seize, kidnap, abduct **carry on** continue, proceed, go on **carry out** complete, fulfil, perform, do, implement, accomplish

cart n. barrow, wagon, handcart, carriage

carton n. box, container, case

carve v. cut, chisel, sculpt, hew, shape, fashion

case¹ n. 1 instance, example, occurrence, happening, circumstance, event, contingency 2 lawsuit, suit, action, process, trial, claim

case² n. box, container, crate, chest, carton, package, receptacle, suitcase

cash n. money, coin, banknotes, change, currency

cast v. 1 throw, hurl, pitch, fling, drive, thrust, sling, toss 2 impart, shed, direct, communicate 3 found, form, shape, fashion, mould, mold (N. Am.) 4 direct, turn

caste n. grade, rank, order

castigate v. rebuke, chastise, reprimand, censure, discipline, punish, whip, flagellate, cane

castle n. citadel, fort, fortress, chateau, mansion, palace

casual adj. 1 accidental, incidental, fortuitous, chance 2 informal, sporty, relaxed
ANT. 1 certain, fixed 2 formal

casuistry n. sophistry, sophism, fallacy, quibbling

catalogue, catalog (N. Am.) n. list, register, index, enrolment, entry, record, roll, inventory, schedule

catastrophe n. disaster, mishap, misfortune, calamity, cataclysm, blow
ANT. success, blessing

catch v. 1 grasp, seize, clutch, capture, clasp, secure, snatch, grip, lay hold, take, arrest 2 trap, ensnare, entrap 3 contract, develop, go down with, succumb to 4 grasp, comprehend, apprehend, understand
ANT. 1 drop

catch on become fashionable, become popular **catch out** trick, trap **catch up** pass, reach, overtake

catch n. 1 take, bag, capture, seizure 2 bolt, latch, fastening, clip, hook

categorical adj. plain, absolute, distinct, positive, affirmative
ANT. obscure, ambiguous

category n. class, division, order, rank, section, group, grouping, kind, sort

cattle n. pl. animals, herd, stock, cows, bulls

cause n. reason, agent, origin, source, root, spring, ground
ANT. effect, result

cause v. occasion, bring about, give rise to, produce, provoke

caution n. 1 care, heed, wariness, vigilance, watchfulness, circumspection, forethought, discretion 2 warning, advice, counsel, admonition

caution v. warn, advise, urge, forewarn

cautious adj. careful, watchful, vigilant, wary
ANT. foolish

cavalier *adj.* arrogant, haughty, overbearing, insolent, disdainful
ANT. courteous

cave *n.* cavern, hole, hollow, grotto

cavil *v.* carp, object, censure, quibble, complain
ANT. approve

cavity *n.* opening, gap, aperture, hole, fissure
ANT. filling

cease *v.* end, stop, finish, desist, leave off, quit, refrain, abstain, discontinue, terminate
ANT. begin, commence, start

celebrate *v.* commemorate, honour, honor (*N. Am.*), mark, remember, keep, observe
ANT. ignore

celebrated *adj.* famous, well-known, renowned, distinguished, famed, illustrious, eminent, glorious, notable, exalted
ANT. obscure, unknown

celebration *n.* 1 party, festivity, carnival 2 observance, commemoration, solemnization, praise, commendation

celebrity *n.* 1 star, notable, dignitary, hero, heroine, VIP, person of note, lion 2 fame, renown, reputation, glory, honour, honor (*N. Am.*), repute, eminence, distinction
ANT. 2 obscurity

celerity *n.* speed, rapidity, haste, velocity, swiftness
ANT. slowness

celestial *adj.* heavenly, angelic, atmospheric, immortal, seraphic, divine, godlike
ANT. earthly, terrestrial

cell *n.* room, cubicle, compartment, chamber, recess

cellar *n.* basement, crypt, vault, storeroom

censor *n.* inspector, examiner, reviewer, critic, inquisitor

censure *n.* blame, disapproval, reproach, reprimand, condemnation, remonstrance, rebuke
ANT. praise, approval

censure *v.* disapprove, condemn, blame, criticize, reproach, reprimand, rebuke
ANT. praise, approve

centre, center (*N. Am.*) *n.* middle, midst, inside, midpoint, focus, heart, nub, core
ANT. perimeter, circumference

central *adj.* 1 middle, mid, inner, halfway, focal 2 chief, key, main, essential, basic, fundamental
ANT. 1 extreme 2 peripheral, incidental

centralize *v.* concentrate, converge, collect, localize
ANT. decentralize

ceremonial *adj.* ritual, ritualistic, formal, official, ministerial, pompous, sumptuous
ANT. casual

ceremonial *n.* ceremony, ritual, rites, formalities, etiquette

ceremonious *adj.* formal, studied, punctilious, exact, precise, prim
ANT. plain, simple

ceremony *n.* service, rite, ritual, observance

certain *adj.* 1 sure, positive, convinced, assured, undoubted 2 particular, definite, settled, fixed, determined
ANT. 1 doubtful

certainly *adv.* undoubtedly, unquestionably, without doubt, positively

certainty *n.* assurance, conviction, confidence, positiveness
ANT. hesitation, doubt, misgiving

certificate *n.* document, credential, declaration, warrant, authorization

certify *v.* acknowledge, declare, prove, inform, assure, attest, avow

cessation *n.* stop, pause, suspension, lull, respite, abeyance
ANT. continuity

chafe *v.* irritate, rub, tease, worry, harass, annoy, fret, vex, gall, chagrin
ANT. soothe

chaff *n.* 1 husks, dregs, remains 2 banter, badinage, nonsense, frivolity

chagrin *n.* annoyance, irritation, vexation, humiliation, shame, mortification, confusion, dismay, disappointment
ANT. delight

chain *n.* bond, link, restraint, shackle, manacle, fetter

chair *n.* **1** seat, stool, bench **2** chairperson, chairman, chairwoman, moderator, convenor, leader, head, director

challenge *v.* dare, brave, defy, threaten, demand, require, claim, object to, take exceptions
ANT. pass

challenge *n.* dare, defiance, provocation, test, trial, objection

champion *n.* hero, winner, chief, victor, combatant, defender, protector, vindicator
ANT. traitor

champion *v.* support, promote, back, defend, protect, vindicate
ANT. oppose, attack

chance *n.* **1** accident, luck, fortune **2** opportunity, opening, possibility, prospect
ANT. **1** purpose, design

change *v.* alter, transform, vary, turn, shift, qualify, modify, exchange, substitute, diversify, convert, veer, metamorphose
ANT. continue, endure

change *n.* modification, alteration, variation, transformation, conversion, transition, variety, vicissitude, transmutation
ANT. constancy

changeless *adj.* constant, steadfast, immutable, unchanging, undeviating, immovable, reliable, consistent
ANT. changeable, fluctuating

channel *n.* **1** passage, duct, conduit, groove **2** way, approach, route, means

chant *n.* song, cantata, canticle, hymn, intonation

chant *v.* sing, recite, chorus, carol

chaos *n.* disorder, turmoil, confusion, havoc
ANT. order

chaotic *adj.* disordered, disorganized, confused, messy
ANT. well-ordered, organized

character *n.* **1** constitution, nature, disposition, qualities, features, characteristics, turn, cast, bent **2** personality, temperament, moral qualities, traits, habits **3** person, individual, role **4** reputation, repute, name, integrity **5** letter, mark, figure, sign, symbol, emblem
ANT. **4** disrepute

characteristic *n.* attribute, quality, peculiarity, trait, sign, indication, mark, feature, distinction, singularity, property, idiosyncrasy
ANT. generality

characteristic *adj.* distinctive, typical, distinguishing, special, individual
ANT. general

charge *v.* **1** demand, ask, price **2** attack, assault, assail, storm **3** accuse, blame, impeach, incriminate, arraign, indict **4** entrust, commit, consign
ANT. **2** retreat **3** acquit

charge *n.* **1** price, cost, payment **2** accusation, blame, impeachment, incrimination, indictment **3** attack, assault, raid, onslaught **4** trust, responsibility, safekeeping

charitable *adj.* kind, generous, benevolent, benign, bountiful, liberal, mild, considerate
ANT. mean

charity *n.* **1** kindness, benevolence, liberality, bounty, generosity, philanthropy **2** donation, gift, contribution, assistance, benefaction

charlatan *n.* quack, conman (*informal*), impostor, pretender, humbug, cheat, mountebank

charm *n.* **1** fascination, attraction, attractiveness, allurement **2** spell, incantation, enchantment, witchery, sorcery, magic, necromancy **3** amulet, talisman
ANT. **1** repulsion

charm *v.* attract, fascinate, allure, captivate

chart *n.* diagram, plan, map, table

chary *adj.* **1** careful, cautious, wary, prudent **2** frugal, sparing, saving, reluctant
ANT. **1** reckless

chase v. pursue, run after, track, hunt, follow, prosecute
ANT. flee

chase n. pursuit, hunt, race

chaste adj. pure, spotless, immaculate, modest, virtuous, simple
ANT. corrupt, impure

chasten v. discipline, chastise, rebuke, reprove, subdue, afflict, punish, try
ANT. pamper, spoil

chat v. talk, chatter, converse, natter (informal), gossip

chat n. talk, conversation, natter

chattels n. pl. goods, belongings, property, wares, effects, furniture

chatter v. talk, chat, converse, natter, gossip

cheap adj. 1 inexpensive, low-priced, low-cost, cut-price, reduced 2 common, mean, worthless, shoddy, paltry, poor, inferior, indifferent
ANT. 1 costly, expensive, dear 2 good-quality

cheat n. 1 deceiver, fraudster, trickster, swindler, impostor, fraud, conman (informal) 2 fraud, trick, artifice, swindle, deceit, fiction, imposture

cheat v. deceit, trick, swindle, fool, hoodwink, defraud, rip off (informal)

check v. 1 examine, investigate, review, look over, scrutinize 2 restrain, curb, stop, control, bridle, hinder, impede, inhibit 3 reprove, chide, reprimand, rebuke.
ANT. 2 indulge, allow

check n. 1 examination, investigation, review, inspection, test 2 restraint, restriction, curb, control, bridle, hindrance

cheer n. 1 cry, shout, hurrah, applause, approval 2 cheerfulness, happiness, hope, gladness, joy, mirth, merriment, conviviality

cheer v. 1 applaud, clap, shout 2 encourage, hearten, comfort
ANT. 1 boo 2 depress

cheerful adj. happy, joyful, glad, lively, animated, jolly, buoyant, merry, joyous
ANT. sad, gloomy

cherish v. foster, nurture, protect, shelter, comfort, treasure, hold dear, value, prize
ANT. abandon, discourage

chest n. 1 breast, bosom, bust 2 box, container, case, trunk, coffer, cabinet

chew v. bite, crunch, munch, champ, gnaw, grind, nibble

chide v. reprimand, rebuke, scold, punish, reprove
ANT. praise

chief n. leader, head, boss, ruler, commander, captain
ANT. subordinate, minor, inferior

chief adj. head, important, excellent, high, principal, leading
ANT. subordinate, minor, inferior

chiefly adv. mainly, mostly, especially, predominantly, primarily, principally, on the whole

chieftain n. captain, commander, general, leader, chief

child n. infant, toddler, youngster, boy, girl, youth, kid (informal)
ANT. adult

childish adj. immature, puerile, weak, silly, foolish
ANT. mature

chill n. coldness, cold, coolness, rawness

chilly adj. cold, cool, bleak, raw, fresh, wintry
ANT. warm

chimerical adj. illusory, visionary, imaginary, unreal, dreamy, fanciful
ANT. real, actual

chip n. piece, bit, scrap, fragment, flake, sliver, splinter, slice, wedge

chip in interrupt, break in

chivalrous adj. brave, noble, courteous, knightly, gallant, heroic, valiant

chivalry n. bravery, nobility, courtesy, knighthood, gallantry

choice n. option, preference, alternative, selection, pick

choice adj. select, fine, rare, valuable, precious
ANT. common, ordinary

choke v. strangle, suffocate, stifle, smother, asphyxiate

choose *v.* select, pick out, decide, settle, opt for, prefer, elect
ANT. reject, refuse

chop *v.* cut, hew, fell, axe, lop

chorus *n.* refrain, response, song, melody

chronic *adj.* persistent, ingrained, continuous, constant, permanent, unending, lingering
ANT. temporary

chronicle *n.* diary, journal, annals, record, register, memorials, archives, history

chronicle *v.* record, set down, narrate

chuckle *v.* giggle, chortle, laugh, titter

church *n.* **1** congregation, parish, denomination **2** chapel, cathedral, abbey, meeting-house, sanctuary

cipher *n.* **1** code, character, symbol, device, monogram **2** zero, nothing, nought

circle *n.* **1** ring, loop, disc, disk (*N. Am.*), globe, sphere, revolution **2** realm, province, domain, sphere, orbit

circuit *n.* revolution, lap, orbit, tour, course

circular *adj.* round, spherical, ring-shaped

circular *n.* advertisement, placard, handbill, notice, leaflet

circulate *v.* distribute, pass round, diffuse, spread, propagate, publish, notify, disseminate, promulgate

circumference *n.* periphery, circuit, boundary, outline, perimeter, edge

circumlocution *n.* wordiness, verbosity, prolixity, diffuseness, periphrasis, redundancy, tautology
ANT. brevity, compression

circumscribe *v.* surround, encircle, define, limit, delineate, enclose, confine, restrict

circumspect *adj.* cautious, wary, heedful, careful, attentive, prudent, watchful, vigilant
ANT. careless, reckless

circumstance *n.* event, situation, occurrence, position, detail, fact, incident, feature, factor, accompaniment, particular, point, item, condition

cite *v.* refer to, quote, mention, call, summon, name, select

citizen *n.* inhabitant, resident, subject, dweller, native, national, burgher, denizen
ANT. foreigner, alien

city *n.* town, metropolis, conurbation, municipality

civil *adj.* **1** municipal, domestic, home **2** polite, courteous, well-mannered, respectful
ANT. **2** impolite, rude

civilization *n.* **1** culture, society **2** cultivation, refinement, sophistication

civilize *v.* refine, cultivate, enlighten, sophisticate

claim *v.* **1** demand, ask, require, call for **2** assert, insist, request, maintain
ANT. **1** repudiate, waive

claim *n.* **1** demand, call, request, requirement, assertion, requisition **2** title, privilege, right, interest

clairvoyance *n.* premonition, foreknowledge, extrasensory perception, telepathy, intuition

clamour, clamor (*N. Am.*) *n.* noise, uproar, hubbub, outcry, din, exclamation
ANT. silence

clan *n.* family, tribe, race, house

clandestine *adj.* secret, private, hidden, furtive, stealthy, underhand, sly, surreptitious
ANT. open

clang *v.* ring, resound, jangle, jingle

clap *v.* applaud, cheer, praise, acclaim
ANT. hiss, boo

clarify *v.* make clear, explain, define, elucidate
ANT. muddle, confuse

clarity *n.* clearness, lucidity, definition, precision, intelligibility
ANT. obscurity

clash *n.* **1** crash, clank, clatter, clang **2** conflict, discord, opposition, disagreement
ANT. **2** harmony

clash *v.* **1** crash, clank, clatter **2** disagree, jar, collide, differ
ANT. agree

clasp v. hold, grip, squeeze, hug, grasp, clutch

clasp n. hook, fastener, catch, pin, buckle, brooch

class n. 1 group, grade, order, rank, division, sort, kind, type, circle, association, club, clique, coterie, set 2 form, year, group, set

classic adj. excellent, outstanding, superior, first-rate, model

classic n. masterpiece, model, standard, exemplar, paradigm

classical adj. refined, elegant, polished, chaste, pure
ANT. corrupt

classification n. 1 category, type, designation, order, species, nature, character, genus 2 grouping, arrangement, distribution, disposition

classify v. order, arrange, sort, organize, group

clause n. portion, section, passage, paragraph, stipulation, article, chapter, provision

claw n. talon, nail, hook

clean adj. 1 spotless, immaculate, unsullied, washed, dusted, cleansed 2 pure, neat, clear, untarnished
ANT. 1 dirty 2 impure

clean v. wash, rinse, mop, wipe, disinfect, scrub, sponge, scour, sweep, dust, vacuum
ANT. dirty, soil

cleanse v. purify, wash, clean, disinfect, scour, sponge, scrub, sweep, wipe, rinse, dust
ANT. pollute

clear adj. 1 plain, intelligible, understandable, obvious, evident, apparent 2 sure, certain, positive, doubtless 3 bright, unclouded, light, sunny 4 transparent, see-through, pellucid, limpid
ANT. 1 indistinct, unclear 2 unsure 3 cloudy, dull 4 opaque

clear v. 1 empty, evacuate, extricate, remove, free 2 acquit, exonerate, free, liberate, release, let go, emancipate
ANT. 1 fill 2 condemn

cleave[1] v. split, divide, separate, part, crack, chop
ANT. unite

cleave[2] v. stick, cling, adhere, hold, stand by
ANT. leave

clergyman n. cleric, member of the clergy, spiritual leader, minister, rabbi, priest, vicar, parson, pastor, preacher

clerical adj. 1 priestly, ecclesiastical, pastoral 2 secretarial, office, white-collar

clerk n. office worker, typist, junior

clever adj. gifted, capable, apt, bright, ingenious, quick-witted, skilful, skillful (N. Am.), smart, talented, keen, knowing, intelligent, quick, sharp
ANT. foolish, slow, stupid

client n. customer, patron, regular, consumer

cliff n. precipice, crag, bluff, scar, escarpment

climax n. culmination, height, consummation, acme, top, summit, zenith, head
ANT. base

climb v. mount, ascend, go up, scale, rise, soar
ANT. descend

cling v. stick, adhere, fasten, hold

clinic n. hospital, infirmary, sickbay

clip[1] v. cut, trim, snip, pare, crop, shear

clip[2] n. fastener, pin, paper clip

clique n. set, gang, coterie, faction, group, party

cloak n. wrap, shawl, coat, cape, mantle

cloak v. conceal, hide, shroud, veil, mask
ANT. show, reveal

close[1] v. 1 shut, fasten, lock, bolt 2 end, stop, complete, terminate, conclude
ANT. 1 open 2 begin

close[2] adj. 1 near, nearby, adjacent, neighbouring, neighboring (N. Am.) 2 unventilated, stuffy, muggy, oppressive 3 stingy, mean, tight, niggardly 4 packed, condensed, compressed, restricted
ANT. 1 distant 2 fresh 3 generous 4 spacious

cloth *n.* material, fabric, textile

clothe *v.* dress, garb, apparel

clothes *n. pl.* clothing, garments, dress, apparel, attire

cloud *n.* vapour, vapor (*N. Am.*), haze, mist, fog

cloudy *adj.* **1** overcast, dark, murky, gloomy, sunless **2** obscure, dim, confused, vague

clown *n.* jester, joker, comic, fool, buffoon, harlequin

clownish *adj.* foolish, awkward, clumsy, rustic, boorish

club *n.* association, society, group, organization, company, circle

clue *n.* suggestion, hint, indication, tip-off, inkling, trace, suspicion

clumsy *adj.* awkward, inexpert, bungling, unskilful, unskillful (*N. Am.*), unwieldy
ANT. graceful

cluster *n.* group, collection, gathering, bunch

cluster *v.* group, collect, gather, assemble

clutch *v.* grasp, grip, hold, clasp, seize, grab

coach *n.* **1** bus, vehicle, carriage **2** instructor, tutor, trainer, teacher, manager

coach *v.* instruct, train, teach, educate

coalesce *v.* blend, mix, harmonize, unite, consolidate, combine, adhere

coalition *n.* league, union, alliance, confederacy, combination, amalgamation

coarse *adj.* **1** crude, rough, gross, unrefined **2** indecent, rude, crude, rough, indelicate, unrefined, unpolished, vulgar, common, ordinary
ANT. **1** fine **2** polite

coast *n.* beach, shore, seashore, strand, seaboard

coast *v.* glide, sail, ride, drift, cruise

coat *n.* jacket, raincoat, mackintosh, overcoat

coat *v.* cover, apply, spread, paint

coax *v.* persuade, wheedle, flatter, cajole, fawn, allure, seduce
ANT. coerce

coerce *v.* impel, restrain, use force, compel, drive, check, intimidate
ANT. persuade, coax

cogent *adj.* forcible, powerful, effective, irresistible, convincing, conclusive, persuasive, potent, urgent
ANT. weak, feeble

cogitate *v.* meditate, think, reflect, consider, ponder, contemplate

cognizance *n.* knowledge, observation, notice, recognition, experience

coherent *adj.* compact, consecutive, close, logical, consistent
ANT. rambling, loose

coil *v.* twist, wind, ring, loop, spiral
ANT. uncoil

coincide *v.* agree, harmonize, match, correspond
ANT. clash

coincidence *n.* chance, accident, fluke (*informal*), fortuity

cold *adj.* **1** cool, chilly, frosty, icy, polar, wintry, frigid **2** unemotional, unfriendly, unimpassioned, apathetic, indifferent, spiritless
ANT. **1** hot, warm **2** friendly, passionate

cold-blooded *adj.* cruel, brutal, savage, ruthless, callous, pitiless
ANT. sensitive, feeling

collaborate *v.* work together, cooperate, team up

collapse *v.* fall, subside, fail, break down
ANT. recover

collapse *n.* fall, failure, downfall, overthrow, destruction, breakdown
ANT. recovery

colleague *n.* associate, co-worker, collaborator, helper, companion, partner, assistant, ally, confederate
ANT. opponent, competitor

collect *v.* gather, assemble, convoke, accumulate, glean, amass, garner, muster, congregate
ANT. distribute, dispense

collection *n.* gathering, assembly, cluster, group, hoard, accumulation, store, heap, pile

college *n.* school, university, polytechnic, institute, institution, academy, faculty

collide v. crash, hit, bump, smash, strike, conflict

collision n. clash, shock, impact, crash, smash, pile-up, contact, opposition, conflict
ANT. divergence

colloquial adj. informal, popular, familiar, casual, conversational, everyday, idiomatic, vernacular

colour, color (N. Am.) n. hue, tint, tinge, shade, complexion, tone, pigment, paint

colloquial v. paint, stain, dye, tint, tinge, decorate

colossal adj. immense, huge, vast, enormous, gigantic
ANT. tiny, minuscule

column n. 1 pillar, post, prop, shaft, support, upright 2 article, feature, review

combat n. conflict, fight, battle, struggle, contest, contention
ANT. surrender

combat v. fight, battle, struggle, contend, oppose

combination n. 1 mixture, compound, blend, synthesis 2 association, connection, union, alliance , league

combine v. mix, blend, associate, unite, join, connect, compound, amalgamate

come v. 1 near, advance, approach, move towards, reach, arrive 2 happen, occur, take place

come about happen, occur, take place
come across find, discover, meet, stumble upon **come to** regain consciousness, revive, recover, recuperate **come up with** suggest, propose, put forward, produce

comeback n. revival, recovery, return

comedy n. farce, satire, slapstick, pantomime, revue

comfort v. console, encourage, cheer, hearten, reassure, relieve, calm
ANT. discourage, trouble

comfort n. 1 consolation, solace, encouragement, reassurance 2 luxury, ease, contentment, plenty
ANT. 1 distress, trouble 2 need

comfortable adj. 1 relaxed, at ease, satisfied, contented 2 snug, cosy, cozy (N. Am.), comfy (informal)
ANT. 1 awkward, uneasy 2 uncomfortable

comical adj. funny, farcical, ludicrous, ridiculous, humorous, laughable, droll
ANT. serious, solemn

command v. order, direct, bid, instruct, charge, enjoin, demand, rule, decree, govern
ANT. beg

command n. order, direction, instruction, charge, demand, decree, authority

commemorate v. celebrate, observe, remember, mark, perpetuate
ANT. forget, ignore

commence v. begin, start, open, initiate, inaugurate, undertake
ANT. finish, conclude, terminate

commend v. approve, encourage, applaud, praise, recommend
ANT. blame, condemn, censure, denounce

commendable adj. admirable, praiseworthy, noble
ANT. deplorable

commendation n. praise, approval, applause, approbation
ANT. criticism

comment n. remark, observation, explanation, note, illustration, commentary, review, report

comment v. remark, observe, explain, note, expound, interpret, illustrate

commerce n. trade, traffic, business, exchange

commercial adj. financial, economic, business, trade, trading, entrepreneurial

commiserate v. sympathize, feel sorry for, feel for, comfort, console

commission n. 1 duty, task, assignment, job, charge 2 committee, board, council, delegation 3 dividend, percentage, share, fee, royalty, rake-off (informal)

commission v. authorize, entrust, commit, appoint, assign

commit v. 1 assign, entrust, consign, trust 2 perform, carry out, do, execute

commitment n. undertaking, promise, vow, pledge, duty, responsibility

committee n. council, board, commission, delegation

commodious adj. ample, spacious, roomy, convenient, comfortable, suitable
ANT. narrow, cramped

commodity n. article, produce, stock, staple, ware

common adj. **1** general, public, joint, shared, communal **2** usual, ordinary, regular, average, customary, everyday, conventional **3** vulgar, cheap, low, commonplace, coarse
ANT. **1** private **2** unusual, distinctive, exceptional **3** refined

commonplace adj. ordinary, everyday, undistinguished, unexceptional, hackneyed, trite, dull
ANT. distinctive, exceptional

commotion n. disturbance, agitation, turmoil, tumult, disorder, fuss
ANT. quiet

communal adj. common, public, shared, collective
ANT. private

communicate v. impart, disclose, tell, announce, notify, publish, transmit, convey, divulge
ANT. conceal, withhold

communication n. **1** announcement, message, report, account, statement, news, information, communiqué **2** transmission, declaration, notification, spreading, dissemination

communion n. exchange, rapport, dialogue, fellowship, participation

communist n. Marxist, Bolshevik, socialist, radical, red (informal)

community n. **1** town, city, neighbourhood, neighborhood (N. Am.), village, parish, area **2** society, public, nation, people

commute v. **1** travel, drive, go by train/bus **2** exchange, replace, barter **3** reduce, shorten, lessen, diminish

commuter n. driver, motorist, traveller, passenger

compact¹ adj. compressed, dense, close, solid, firm, concise, short, brief, terse, pithy, succinct
ANT. diffuse, wordy

compact² n. agreement, contract, pact, bond, treaty, covenant

companion n. friend, associate, partner, comrade, colleague, mate
ANT. adversary, enemy

companionable adj. friendly, agreeable, sociable, pleasant, affable, genial
ANT. distant, cold, unfriendly

company n. **1** firm, business, partnership, corporation, association, syndicate **2** gathering, crowd, meeting, multitude, assembly, conference, congregation, convention, convocation

comparable adj. like, relative, alike, related, resembling, corresponding, equivalent

compare v. **1** liken, parallel, equate, relate, match, equal, correspond, contrast **2** rival, vie, compete

comparison n. resemblance, likening, equation, relation, match, correspondence, contrast

compartment n. section, department, space, division, partition, part

compassion n. pity, sympathy, kindness, tenderness, mercy, condolence, clemency
ANT. cruelty, harshness

compassionate adj. sympathetic, kind, merciful, tender, soft-hearted
ANT. cruel, harsh

compatible adj. consistent, congruous, harmonious
ANT. contradictory

compel v. force, drive, coerce, constrain, necessitate

compensate v. **1** recompense, reimburse, repay, make amends, indemnify, requite, satisfy **2** offset, balance, counterbalance

compensation n. recompense, reparation, amends, indemnification, reward, damages, requital, satisfaction
ANT. harm, hurt, injury

compete v. contest, rival, vie, oppose, strive, struggle
ANT. share, participate

competence *n.* ability, skill, capability, expertise, proficiency
ANT. inability, incompetence

competent *adj.* able, skilful, skillful (*N. Am.*), capable, expert, proficient, qualified
ANT. unable, incompetent

competition *n.* contest, match, tournament, championship, race, rivalry
ANT. alliance

competitor *n.* contestant, rival, opponent, challenger, adversary, candidate, entrant
ANT. friend, partner

compile *v.* put together, collect, prepare, arrange, organize, compose, assemble, gather

complacent *adj.* pleased, self-satisfied, contented, smug, unconcerned

complain *v.* grumble, moan, groan, protest, murmur, find fault, remonstrate
ANT. approve, commend

complement *v.* complete, add to, round off, set off
ANT. clash, conflict

complement *n.* **1** companion, supplement, counterpart, finishing touch **2** total, totality, quota, whole

complementary *adj.* completing, integral, matched, corresponding, reciprocal, harmonious
ANT. conflicting, clashing

complete *adj.* **1** total, whole, entire, full, perfect **2** ended, finished, concluded, consummated **3** absolute, thorough, utter, downright, out and out (*informal*)
ANT. **1** partial **2** unfinished

complex *adj.* complicated, intricate, involved, mixed, confused, entangled
ANT. simple

complexion *n.* skin, face, feature(s), appearance, look, character, indication

compliance *n.* yielding, submission, obedience, acquiescence
ANT. resistance, disobedience

complicated *adj.* difficult, involved, complex, intricate, elaborate, confused

compliment *n.* flattery, praise, commendation, honour, honor (*N. Am.*), approval, appreciation, admiration
ANT. insult

compliment *v.* praise, flatter, commend, honour, honor (*N. Am.*), approve, appreciate, admire

complimentary *adj.* commendatory, flattering, appreciative, approving
ANT. insulting, abusive

comply *v.* obey, agree to, fulfil, conform to, yield, submit, observe, perform
ANT. disobey

component *n.* constituent, factor, element, ingredient, part
ANT. entirety

compose *v.* **1** make, form, create, produce, compile, construct **2** constitute, comprise, make up

composed *adj.* calm, relaxed, quiet, at ease, tranquil, serene, self-possession, untroubled
ANT. excited, agitated, restless

composition *n.* **1** making, creation, production, formation **2** arrangement, structure, make-up, form **3** essay, work, article, piece

composure *n.* tranquillity, calm, self-possession, serenity
ANT. restlessness, excitement, agitation

compound *n.* mixture, combination, aggregate, amalgamation, synthesis, coalescence

compound *adj.* multiple, composite, complicated, compound, intricate

comprehend *v.* **1** understand, conceive, grasp, perceive **2** include, enclose, comprise, embrace
ANT. **1** misunderstand, misconstrue **2** except, exclude

comprehension *n.* understanding, conception, awareness, perception, knowledge, apprehension, capacity, intellect, reason, mind, intelligence

comprehensive *adj.* wide, broad, extensive, complete, full, exhaustive, sweeping, compendious
ANT. narrow, partial, fragmentary, limited

compress *v.* condense, squeeze, contract, press, pack, squash
ANT. expand, diffuse, stretch

comprise *v.* include, consist of, constitute, involve, contain, comprehend
ANT. exclude

compromise *n.* settlement, agreement, arbitration, concession, negotiation, give-and-take (*informal*)

compromise *v.* adjust, arbitrate, settle, agree, concede, accommodate, give-and-take (*informal*)

compulsion *n.* force, coercion, constraint, pressure, control
ANT. coaxing, persuasion

compulsive *adj.* obsessive, inveterate, habitual, compelling, overwhelming

compulsory *adj.* necessary, obligatory, binding, imperative, unavoidable
ANT. optional, voluntary

compunction *n.* regret, remorse, contrition, penitence

compute *v.* calculate, reckon, work out, count, number
ANT. guess

comrade *n.* friend, companion, colleague, associate, partner
ANT. opponent

concave *adj.* hollow, sunken, depressed, excavated
ANT. convex

conceal *v.* hide, obscure, cover, suppress, secrete, disguise
ANT. reveal, expose, show

concede *v.* admit, resign, yield, allow, acknowledge, surrender
ANT. refuse, contradict, deny

conceit *n.* pride, self-esteem, vanity, egotism, boastfulness, arrogance, affectation
ANT. humility

conceited *adj.* egotistical, opinionated, vain, proud, arrogant, boastful
ANT. unassuming, unaffected, humble

conceive *v.* imagine, picture, believe, design, think, apprehend, understand, perceive, grasp

concentrate *v.* **1** think (hard), meditate, ponder, pay (close) attention **2** centralize, focus, convene, assemble, congregate, muster
ANT. **2** disperse

concentration *n.* **1** study, application, attention, thought **2** focus, centralization, collection, assembly
ANT. **1** distraction **2** dispersal

concept *n.* idea, notion, thought, theory

concern *v.* **1** interest, relate to, regard, affect, involve **2** disturb, worry, trouble, distress, bother
ANT. **2** calm

concern *n.* affair, matter, business, duty **2** anxiety, worry, care, solicitude

concerned *adj.* worried, anxious, troubled, disturbed, distressed, bothered

concerning *prep.* about, regarding, in relation to, respecting, in respect to

concert *n.* **1** performance, recital, entertainment, presentation **2** agreement, harmony, concord, union
ANT. **2** opposition, discord

concerted *adj.* joint, combined, united, cooperative, collaborative
ANT. individual

concession *n.* surrender, yielding, acknowledgment, admission, granting

conciliate *v.* pacify, placate, reconcile, win, gain, propitiate
ANT. alienate

concise *adj.* brief, short, succinct, condensed, compact, terse, pointed, laconic
ANT. long, wordy, rambling

conclave *n.* assembly, synod, cabinet, council, bureau

conclude *v.* **1** finish, close, end, terminate **2** assume, presume, gather, infer, deduce, surmise **3** decide, determine, settle, arrange
ANT. **1** begin, commence

conclusion *n.* **1** end, finish, close, termination, finale, finis **2** inference, deduction, assumption, presumption
ANT. **1** beginning, commencement

conclusive *adj.* final, decisive, positive, definitive, ultimate, indisputable
ANT. inconclusive, vague, uncertain

concoct *v.* contrive, prepare, compound, mix, brew

concoction *n.* compound, mixture, blend, brew

concomitant *adj.* attending, accompanying, attendant, synchronous
ANT. unconnected, independent

concord *n.* harmony, agreement, friendship, unanimity, accord
ANT. animosity, discord

concourse *n.* meeting, assembly, throng, crowd, mob, assemblage, gathering, multitude

concrete *adj.* solid, firm, definite, real, specific, particular, precise
ANT. abstract, general

concur *v.* approve, agree, acquiesce, coincide, combine
ANT. disagree, dissent

concussion *n.* collision, crash, impact, blow, shock

condemn *v.* 1 criticize, blame, disapprove, denounce, censure 2 blame, convict, sentence, reprove, doom
ANT. 1 praise, approve 2 acquit, pardon

condense *v.* abridge, shorten, reduce, digest, compress
ANT. expand, amplify, enlarge

condescend *v.* deign, stoop, lower oneself, humble oneself

condescension *n.* deigning, stooping, humbling oneself

condiment *n.* seasoning, preserve, sauce, pickle, relish, appetizer

condition *n.* 1 situation, position, state, case, circumstances 2 requirement, provision, proviso, consideration, stipulation 3 rank, standing, station, estate, grade

conditional *adj.* provisional, dependent, restricted, relative, contingent
ANT. absolute, categorical

condolence *n.* sympathy, comfort, commiseration, consolation, fellow feeling, pity

condone *v.* pardon, overlook, disregard, forgive, excuse, ignore, turn a blind eye to (*informal*)
ANT. punish

conducive *adj.* leading, helpful, useful, contributory, advantageous, instrumental

conduct *n.* 1 behaviour, behavior (*N. Am.*), manners, ways, actions, bearing, deportment, demeanour, demeanor (*N. Am.*) 2 leadership, direction, guidance, management, administration

conduct *v.* 1 lead, direct, guide, convoy, escort 2 manage, command, govern, regulate, rule, superintend 3 act, behave, carry oneself

confection *n.* sweet, candy, cake, condiment, sweetmeat, confectionery

confederation *n.* alliance, league, treaty, union, coalition, federation

confer *v.* 1 give, bestow, award, grant 2 consult, talk, converse, discuss, deliberate

conference *n.* meeting, consultation, interview, convention, conversation, talk, discourse, convocation, colloquy

confess *v.* acknowledge, admit, disclose, allow, grant, concede, avow
ANT. deny, conceal

confession *n.* admission, avowal, acknowledgment, disclosure

confide *v.* 1 reveal, disclose, divulge, tell, confess 2 trust, rely, hope, depend, believe, put confidence, lean
ANT. 2 doubt, mistrust

confidence *n.* 1 trust, reliance, dependence, assurance, hope, belief, faith, conviction 2 self-assurance, courage, boldness, self-reliance, self-confidence

confident *adj.* sure, certain, positive, assured, self-assured, self-reliant, self-confident, bold
ANT. timid, shy, hesitant

confidential *adj.* intimate, secret, private, personal
ANT. public

configuration *n.* form, figure, outline, shape, contour

confine *v.* limit, enclose, restrict, bound, imprison, circumscribe
ANT. release, free

confirm *v.* verify, substantiate, corroborate, establish, settle, uphold, strengthen, assure, approve, sanction
ANT. cancel, deny

confirmed *adj.* established, habitual, seasoned, inveterate, chronic, hardened

confiscate *v.* seize, take, impound, appropriate, sequestrate
ANT. release

conflict *v.* clash, oppose, contend, collide, disagree, differ

conflict *n.* 1 fight, contest, battle, struggle, encounter 2 clashing, disagreement, interference, discord
ANT. 2 agreement

conform *v.* **1** comply, submit, obey, yield **2** agree, consent, harmonize, correspond
ANT. **1** antagonize **2** dissent, disagree

confound *v.* **1** confuse, perplex, bewilder, mystify, surprise, astonish, astound, startle **2** defeat, destroy, ruin, overwhelm

confront *v.* oppose, threaten, encounter, challenge, meet, face, defy, intimidate

confuse *v.* **1** bewilder, puzzle, perplex, mystify, baffle **2** jumble (up), mix up, disarrange, disorder
ANT. **1** enlighten, clarify **2** arrange

confusion *n.* **1** bewilderment, puzzlement, perplexity **2** jumble, disorder, muddle, mess, turmoil
ANT. **1** enlightenment **2** order

congeal *v.* freeze, convert to ice
ANT. melt, thaw, dissolve

congenial *adj.* friendly, pleasant, sympathetic, agreeable, affable
ANT. unfriendly, disagreeable, unsympathetic

congenital *adj.* innate, inherent, inborn, inbred

congested *adj.* full, crowded overcrowded, blocked, clogged, jammed
ANT. empty, clear

congratulate *v.* compliment, praise, acclaim, honour, honor (*N. Am.*)

congregate *v.* meet, gather, collect, assemble, convene, throng
ANT. disperse, separate, scatter

congregation *n.* meeting, audience, conference, crowd, assembly

congress *n.* council, assembly, parliament, cabinet, legislature, convention, meeting, conference, synod

congruous *adj.* consistent, harmonious, coherent, agreeing, suitable, proper, appropriate, accordant
ANT. inconsistent, inharmonious

conjecture *n.* guess, hypothesis, theory, notion, supposition, surmise
ANT. proof, fact

conjecture *v.* guess, surmise, suppose, assume, infer, theorize, hypothesize
ANT. prove

conjuncture *n.* combination, juncture, point, concurrence, juncture

conjuror *n.* magician, wizard, juggler, sorcerer

connect *v.* join, link, unite, combine, couple, associate, relate
ANT. separate, divide

connection *n.* relationship, junction, link, tie, bond, union, combination, association
ANT. dissociation

conquer *v.* overcome, beat, defeat, overpower, overthrow, prevail over, win, surmount, master, vanquish, subdue, rout, worst, crush
ANT. surrender, capitulate, yield, withdraw

conquest *n.* victory, triumph, mastery, rout, subjugation
ANT. defeat, failure, surrender

conscience *n.* sense of morality, sense of right and wrong, inner voice, moral sense, principles

conscientious *adj.* scrupulous, exact, meticulous, painstaking, diligent, thorough
ANT. careless, slovenly

conscious *adj.* **1** aware, alert, awake, cognizant, sentient, thinking, reflecting, rational, intellectual **2** intentional, deliberate, planned, calculated, premeditated
ANT. **1** unconscious **2** unintentional

consecrate *v.* dedicate, ordain, sanctify, hallow
ANT. desecrate, defile

consecutive *adj.* successive, continuous, serial, orderly, following
ANT. discontinuous

consent *v.* **1** allow, permit, let, assent, approve, agree, yield, comply, acquiesce
ANT. refuse, decline

consent *n.* permission, approval, agreement, assent
ANT. refusal

consequence *n.* **1** result, issue, effect, outcome, end, upshot, sequel **2** importance, significance, value, moment
ANT. **1** cause, occasion, origin **2** insignificance

consequential *adj.* 1 important, following, significant, resulting, connected 2 pompous, conceited, arrogant, self-important, vain

conservation *n.* protection, preservation, maintenance, perpetuation
ANT. neglect, destruction

conservative *adj.* traditional, opposed to change, conventional, cautious, careful, right-wing
ANT. radical, progressive

conserve *v.* keep, retain, protect, preserve, maintain, perpetuate
ANT. neglect, destroy

consider *v.* think, study, ponder, meditate, reflect, contemplate, investigate, weigh, deliberate, observe, attend, regard
ANT. ignore

considerable *adj.* substantial, sizeable, appreciable, marked, great, a lot of, much, important, significant, noteworthy
ANT. little, insignificant, trifling

considerate *adj.* kindly, thoughtful, polite, courteous, unselfish, concerned, sympathetic, charitable
ANT. inconsiderate, thoughtless, rude, selfish

consideration *n.* 1 thought, reflection, attention, study, deliberation 2 kindness, thoughtfulness, unselfishness, politeness, concern, courtesy, sympathy

consign *v.* commit, entrust, hand over, convey, send, deliver, dispatch, ship

consignment *n.* 1 commitment, delivery, handing over, conveyance, dispatch 2 shipment, load, batch

consist *v.* be made up, be composed of, comprise, include, contain, embody

consistency *n.* 1 density, firmness, thickness, solidity, compactness, coherence 2 agreement, correspondence, uniformity, harmony, congruity

consistent *adj.* 1 agreeing, harmonious, corresponding, compatible, congruous 2 constant, faithful, unchanging, regular
ANT. 1 inconsistent, incompatible 2 irregular, erratic

consolation *n.* comfort, condolence(s), sympathy, encouragement, solace
ANT. discouragement

console *v.* comfort, condole with, sympathize, encourage, soothe, solace
ANT. distress, hurt

consolidate *v.* 1 combine, unite, join, amalgamate 2 solidify, thicken, strengthen, harden, condense, compress
ANT. 1 dissect 2 weaken

conspicuous *adj.* 1 plain, clear, perceptible, noticeable, visible, apparent, discernible 2 famous, noted, eminent, distinguished, prominent
ANT. 1 hidden, imperceptible 2 ordinary, mediocre

conspiracy *n.* intrigue, scheme, plot, machination

conspire *v.* plot, intrigue, scheme, plan

constant *adj.* 1 fixed, invariable, unchanging, immutable, permanent, incessant, unbroken, continuous, perpetual, firm, steady, persevering 2 faithful, true, loyal, steady, staunch, committed, devoted
ANT. 1 irregular 2 fickle, untrustworthy, false

consternation *n.* amazement, terror, alarm, dismay, panic, bewilderment
ANT. fearlessness, boldness

constituent *n.* 1 ingredient, component, element 2 elector, voter, supporter

constitute *v.* 1 make up, form, compose 2 establish, found, set up, organize, appoint

constitution *n.* 1 organization, structure, composition, make-up, quality, character, temperament, peculiarity, characteristic 2 law, code, rules, charter

constrain *v.* force, compel, coerce, oblige, drive, urge, pressurize

construct *v.* build, erect, raise, form, shape
ANT. demolish, destroy

construction *n.* 1 building, erection, composition, fabrication, structure, formation, form, figure 2 explanation, version, rendering, interpretation

constructive *adj.* helpful, valuable, useful, positive, productive
ANT. destructive

consult *v.* discuss, deliberate, take counsel, confer, canvass, question, consider

consume *v.* **1** use (up), eat up, devour, spend, exhaust, lavish, dissipate, waste **2** destroy, devastate, ravage, demolish

consumer *n.* buyer, purchaser, user, shopper, customer

consummate *adj.* perfect, excellent, superb, accomplished, masterly, supreme, finished, complete, absolute

consummation *n.* completion, achievement, attainment, termination, accomplishment, fulfilment, realization, close, finish, finale

consumption *n.* use, expenditure, dissipation, exhaustion, waste, extinction, destruction

contact *n.* touch, touching, connection, juxtaposition, junction, contiguity, closeness, union
ANT. separation, isolation

contact *v.* get hold of, communicate with, call, ring, telephone, phone, write to

contagious *adj.* infectious, catching, spreading, contaminating

contain *v.* hold, include, comprise, consist of, embody, comprehend, embrace, restrain
ANT. exclude

container *n.* receptacle, holder, case, box, jar, tin, can, bowl, pot

contaminate *v.* pollute, soil, dirty, taint, defile, corrupt, sully
ANT. cleanse, purify

contemplate *v.* **1** think about, meditate, study, ponder, reflect, deliberate **2** intend, design, plan, propose, have in mind **3** look at, view, survey, observe, watch

contemplating *adj.* meditative, thoughtful, studious, reflective, pensive, lost in thought

contemporary *adj.* **1** modern, fashionable, up-to-date, latest, recent, present-day **2** co-existent, concurrent, synchronous
ANT. **1** ancient, old-fashioned

contempt *n.* disrespect, disdain, scorn, malice, mockery
ANT. respect, admiration

contemptible *adj.* mean, low, despicable, detestable, abject, base, worthless
ANT. respectable, admirable

contemptuous *adj.* disrespectful, disdainful, scornful, malicious, insulting, sneering, mocking
ANT. polite, flattering

contend *v.* **1** fight, strive, struggle, combat, argue, dispute **2** affirm, assert, maintain, claim, debate, argue

content *adj.* happy, satisfied, pleased, comfortable, contented
ANT. dissatisfied

content *n.* substance, matter, essence, themes, gist, drift, subject matter

contention *n.* strife, dissension, fighting, quarrel, dispute, debate, controversy, altercation
ANT. peace, harmony

contentious *adj.* **1** quarrelsome, argumentative, belligerent **2** disputed, controversial, debatable
ANT. **1** obliging **2** undisputed

contest *n.* **1** competition, match, tournament, game, race **2** fight, struggle, battle, conflict

contest *v.* oppose, dispute, fight, struggle, challenge, contend, compete

contestant *n.* competitor, entrant, participant, opponent, rival

contingent *adj.* dependent, provisional, conditional, uncertain

continual *adj.* constant, regular, perpetual, repeated, frequent, continuous
ANT. occasional

continue *v.* **1** remain, endure, persist, carry on, stay, last, persevere **2** resume, proceed, recommence, carry on
ANT. **1** stop, cease **2** interrupt

continuous *adj.* uninterrupted, unbroken, unremitting, ceaseless, constant

contract *n.* agreement, arrangement, bargain, covenant, pact, obligation, pledge, engagement, bond

contract *v.* **1** narrow, abbreviate, abridge, lessen, reduce, compress, shrivel, shrink **2** agree, pledge, undertake, commit oneself, stipulate, bargain

contradict *v.* deny, oppose, counteract, annul, thwart, abrogate, object to, dispute, impugn
ANT. agree, affirm

contrary *adj.* 1 opposite, opposed, adverse, counter, conflicting, contradictory, antagonistic, repugnant 2 perverse, obstinate, stubborn, headstrong
ANT. 1 similar 2 obliging

contrast *v.* differentiate, distinguish, discriminate, oppose, contradict, compare
ANT. resemble, be like, be similar

contrast *n.* difference, distinction, opposition
ANT. resemblance, likeness, similarity

contribute *v.* give, donate, assist, subscribe, grant, provide, supply
ANT. refuse, withhold, deny

contribution *n.* donation, offering, gift, subscription, grant, subsidy, aid, assistance

contrite *adj.* sorry, remorseful, repentant, penitent

contrive *v.* 1 plan, design, devise, invent, project, form, frame, scheme, plot, hatch 2 manage, make out, engineer, bring about, arrange

control *v.* 1 direct, manage, rule, command, sway, superintend 2 hinder, repress, restrain, restrict, limit, curb, check

control *n.* 1 direction, management, rule, command, sway, superintendence 2 restraint, curb, check, restriction, limitation

controversial *adj.* contentious, debatable, disputed, disputable, at issue

controversy *n.* dispute, argument, quarrel, contention, disagreement, altercation
ANT. agreement

convalesce *v.* recover, get well, get better, recuperate, improve

convene *v.* meet, congregate, summon, muster, collect, assemble
ANT. dismiss

convenience *n.* 1 suitability, fitness, appropriateness, availability, usefulness 2 advantage, benefit, help, aid, assistance
ANT. 1 inconvenience 2 hindrance

convenient *adj.* 1 suitable, fit, appropriate, proper, adapted 2 advantageous, available, accessible, handy, comfortable, useful, serviceable
ANT. 1 inconvenient, useless, awkward

convent *n.* nunnery, abbey, priory, religious community

convention *n.* 1 conference, meeting, assembly, concourse, session, synod, congress, convocation 2 practice, custom, tradition, rule, law, usage

conventional *adj.* usual, customary, traditional, ordinary, regular, prevalent, social, everyday, habitual, wonted
ANT. unusual, extraordinary

converge *v.* meet, join, concentrate, unite, focus, coincide, come together
ANT. diverge

conversant *adj.* familiar, skilled, acquainted, proficient, versed
ANT. ignorant, unacquainted

conversation *n.* talk, chat, communication, discourse, converse, colloquy, dialogue

converse *adj.* opposite, reverse, contrary, counter, contradictory
ANT. identical, one, same

converse *v.* talk, chat, speak, communicate

conversion *n.* alteration, change, transformation, transmutation

convert *v.* 1 alter, change, transform 2 win over, reform, proselytize

convex *adj.* rounded, bulging
ANT. concave, hollow

convey *v.* take, transfer, move, change, bear, carry, shift, transmit, transport, remove

conveyance *n.* transport, transportation, transfer, vehicle, car, automobile, lorry, truck, van, train, plane

convict *n.* criminal, culprit, felon, prisoner, crook (*informal*)

convict *v.* condemn, sentence
ANT. acquit

conviction *n.* belief, assurance, certainty, persuasion, trust, faith
ANT. doubt, disbelief

convince *v.* persuade, win over, bring round, prove to, satisfy, enlighten, indoctrinate

convivial *adj.* social, festive, jovial, jolly
ANT. inhospitable

convocation *n.* convention, meeting, congress, assembly, council, synod

convolution *n.* coil, spiral, twist, contortion

convoy *n.* escort, guard, protection, attendance

convulse *v.* disturb, shake, agitate, toss, heave
ANT. calm, compose

cook *v.* prepare, heat, boil, fry, grill, roast, toast, bake, poach, boil, stew

cool *adj.* 1 cold, chilling, frigid, freezing, icy, frosty 2 calm, unimpassioned, composed, collected, unruffled, self-possessed, sedate, placid, quiet 3 distant, unfriendly, chilly, apathetic
ANT. 1 hot, warm 2 excitable, ardent, eager 3 friendly, warm

cooperate *v.* work together, collaborate, join forces, assist, help, aid, concur
ANT. oppose

coordinate *v.* arrange, organize, match, harmonize, integrate, synchronize

coordinate *adj.* equal, equivalent, proportionate, commensurate, tantamount

cope *v.* manage, hold one's own, get by, deal with

copious *adj.* plentiful, abundant, ample, lavish, rich
ANT. scanty

copy *n.* facsimile, duplicate, reproduction, imitation, likeness, image, print, transcript, counterfeit
ANT. model, original

copy *v.* duplicate, reproduce, imitate, counterfeit, plagiarize

cordial *adj.* friendly, warm, hearty, ardent, affectionate, sincere, genial, affable, pleasing, grateful
ANT. cool, formal, distant

core *n.* centre, heart, nub, focus, kernel
ANT. exterior

corner *n.* 1 angle, bend, turn 2 nook, recess, niche

corollary *n.* inference, conclusion, deduction, consequence

corporation *n.* association, company, organization, partnership

corps *n.* body, division, squadron, band, company, regiment, unit, detachment

corpse *n.* remains, (dead) body, cadaver, carcass

correct *adj.* true, exact, accurate, proper, faultless, right
ANT. incorrect, false, untrue, wrong, inexact, inaccurate

correct *v.* 1 amend, put right, remedy 2 discipline, punish, warn, caution, admonish

corrective *adj.* regulative, preventive, preservative, rectifying, modifying, improving, reformatory

correlation *n.* interrelation, correspondence, interdependence, mutuality, reciprocation, interchange, reciprocity
ANT. contradiction, independence, opposition

correspond *v.* 1 agree, suit, match, fit, coincide, tally, harmonize, compare, answer 2 communicate, write
ANT. 1 vary, disagree, clash

correspondence *n.* 1 adaptation, agreement, matching, coincidence, congruity 2 writing, letter, communication, mail, post
ANT. 1 incongruity, discord, disagreement

corridor *n.* passageway, passage, aisle, hall, hallway

corroborate *v.* strengthen, establish, sustain, support, confirm, uphold
ANT. rebut, invalidate

corrode *v.* eat away, waste, impair, rust, wear, consume, crumble, canker
ANT. renew, restore

corrupt *adj.* 1 dishonest, unscrupulous, crooked, untrustworthy 2 evil, wicked, depraved, immoral, perverted, base
ANT. 1 honest 2 virtuous

corrupt *v.* defile, pollute, infect, taint, contaminate, debase, spoil, deteriorate
ANT. cleanse, purify

corruption *n.* 1 dishonesty, bribery, unscrupulousness, untrustworthiness 2 evil, wickedness, depravity, immorality 3 decay, decomposition, pollution, defilement, contamination, adulteration

cost *n.* 1 price, value, worth, expenditure, expense, charge, rate, amount, disbursement, outlay 2 loss, sacrifice, penalty, damage, pain

costly *adj.* expensive, dear, valuable, steep (*informal*)
ANT. cheap, inexpensive

costume *n.* dress, clothing, robes, uniform, attire, apparel

cosy, cozy (*N. Am.*) *adj.* comfortable, snug, warm, sheltered
ANT. uncomfortable

council *n.* board, committee, meeting, conference, parliament, cabinet, chamber, convocation, consultation, convention, bureau, conclave, synod

counsel *n.* 1 advice, guidance, consultation, opinion, suggestion, recommendation, instruction, caution 2 lawyer, barrister, attorney, advocate, solicitor

counsel *v.* advise, guide, suggest, recommend, instruct

counsellor, counselor (*N. Am.*) *n.* adviser, guide, helper, confidant(e), mentor

count *v.* add, estimate, number, enumerate, sum, calculate, work out, compute, reckon

countenance *n.* 1 face, features, visage, aspect, appearance 2 approval, support, help, aid, assistance, encouragement

countenance *v.* approve, support, sanction, help, aid, abet, encourage, patronize
ANT. oppose, discourage

counter[1] *n.* 1 board, table, bar 2 disc, disk (*N. Am.*), token, piece

counter[2] *adv.* contrary, opposed, opposite, against

counteract *v.* oppose, foil, baffle, thwart, hinder, rival, resist, defeat, offset, frustrate, neutralize, counterbalance
ANT. promote, advance

counterfeit *n.* forgery, fake, copy, fraudulent copy, cheat, pretence, pretense (*N. Am.*), sham, fabrication

counterfeit *adj.* fake, fraudulent, false, sham, fabricated, spurious

counterfeit *v.* forge, fake, falsify, fabricate, copy, imitate

countermand *v.* abrogate, annul, revoke, rescind, recall, make void
ANT. confirm

counterpart *n.* duplicate, copy, match, equivalent, opposite number, mate, tally, twin, complement, supplement
ANT. contradiction

country *n.* 1 land, nation, state, people, kingdom 2 countryside, farmland, rural districts, backwoods, outback, bush, sticks (*informal*)

countryside *n.* country, farmland, rural districts, backwoods, outback, bush, sticks (*informal*)

couple *n.* pair, two, twosome, duo

couple *v.* join, link, unite, connect, tie, yoke, pair
ANT. separate, detach

courage *n.* bravery, boldness, daring, valour, valor (*N. Am.*), fearlessness, spirit, heroism, fortitude, hardihood, mettle, pluck, resolution, intrepidity
ANT. cowardice, timidity, fear

courageous *adj.* brave, bold, daring, fearless, intrepid
ANT. cowardly, afraid, timid, fearful

course *n.* 1 route, way, path, road, track 2 direction, way, bearing, progress, process, duration, period, conduct 3 series, system, succession, flow 4 method, policy, procedure, plan

court *n.* 1 square, yard, quadrangle, plaza, enclosure 2 law court, tribunal, bar, bench, trial, assize, session

court *v.* woo, flatter, seek, invite, solicit

courteous *adj.* polite, civil, well-mannered, respectful, obliging
ANT. rude, impolite

courtesy *n.* politeness, civility, good manners, graciousness, complaisance, affability, urbanity
ANT. rudeness, incivility

courtly *adj.* polished, elegant, polite, ceremonious, formal, respectful
ANT. undignified, unrefined

covenant *n.* agreement, promise, pledge, bond, contract, bargain, arrangement, pact, treaty

cover *v.* 1 hide, conceal, cloak, veil, screen, mask, shroud, disguise 2 spread,

coat, protect, overlay, clothe, wrap
3 protect, shield, guard, defend, shelter
4 comprise, embrace, comprehend, embody, contain, involve

cover *n.* **1** covering, lid, stopper, cast, envelope **2** protection, guard, defence, defense (*N. Am.*), shelter

covet *v.* desire, long for, wish for, aim after, aspire to
ANT. despise

covetous *adj.* jealous, envious, eager, desirous, greedy, grasping, acquisitive, avaricious, rapacious
ANT. liberal, unselfish, generous, bountiful

coward *n.* sissy, weakling, chicken (*informal*)
ANT. hero

cowardly *adj.* scared, fearful, faint-hearted, spineless, chicken (*informal*), yellow (*informal*)

coy *adj.* bashful, shy, modest, reserved, timid, shrinking
ANT. bold, forward, pert

crack *v.* **1** split, break, chop, snap, rend **2** solve, work out, decode, decipher

craft *n.* **1** skill, ability, power, talent, expertise, aptitude **2** trade, employment, vocation, profession, calling, art, handicraft **3** artifice, shrewdness, guile, deception, cunning, deceit

crafty *adj.* shrewd, cunning, deceitful, sly, double-dealing, clever
ANT. guileless, ingenuous

cramp *v.* restrain, restrict, hinder, check, confine, hamper, clog, fetter, cripple
ANT. free, liberate, loose

cramp *n.* pain, spasm, contraction, convulsion

crank *n.* **1** lever, handle, shaft, arm **2** eccentric, crackpot (*informal*), nut (*informal*), oddball (*informal*)

crash *n.* smash, smash-up, bump, collision, prang, pile-up

crash *v.* collide, hit, bump, bang, smash

crass *adj.* gross, stupid, dense, insensitive

crave *v.* desire, long for, hunger for, yearn, beg, beseech, implore

crazy *adj.* mad, lunatic, insane, delirious, cracked, demented, deranged, potty (*informal*), nuts (*informal*)
ANT. sane, whole

crease *n.* fold, wrinkle, ridge, furrow, groove, line

create *v.* form, produce, make, compose, fashion, design, construct, originate, cause, occasion, generate, appoint, constitute
ANT. demolish

creation *n.* **1** construction, beginning, start, origination, invention, design **2** universe, world, earth, life, nature

creature *n.* being, animal, living thing, human being, person

credence *n.* belief, trust, faith, acceptance, confidence, reliance
ANT. distrust, disbelief, doubt

credentials *n. pl.* diploma, certificate, warrant, voucher, testimonial, authorization

credible *adj.* believable, probable, possible, likely, reliable, trustworthy
ANT. improbable, unlikely

credit *n.* **1** praise, honour, honor (*N. Am.*), acknowledgment, merit, commendation **2** reputation, name, standing, influence, power, esteem, regard **3** trust, belief, faith, confidence, credence, reliance
ANT. **1** shame, disgrace **3** distrust

credit *v.* **1** believe, trust, accept, have faith in **2** attribute, ascribe, assign

creditable *adj.* worthy, praiseworthy, admirable, commendable, respectable
ANT. shameful

credulity *n.* gullibility, credulousness, simplicity
ANT. suspiciousness, incredulity

creed *n.* belief, confession, article(s) of faith, tenet, dogma, doctrine, credo, catechism

creek *n.* **1** inlet, bay, cove, bight, estuary **2** stream, brook

creep *v.* crawl, sneak, slink, slither, wriggle

crestfallen *adj*. downcast, disheartened, depressed, despondent, downhearted, dispirited, dejected

ANT exuberant, elated

crew *n*. team, company, group, squad, gang, set, band, horde, crowd, mob, throng

crime *n*. offence, offense (*N. Am.*), misdeed, wrong, wrongdoing, misconduct, felony, sin, iniquity, misdemeanour, misdemeanor (*N. Am.*), transgression, wickedness, delinquency

criminal *n*. offender, lawbreaker, felon, wrongdoer, malefactor, crook (*informal*)

criminal *adj*. immoral, iniquitous, sinful, unlawful, wicked, wrong, vile, illegal

ANT. lawful, legal, right

cripple *v*. maim, disable, hurt, damage, injure, impair, break down, weaken, cramp, curtail

ANT. strengthen

crisis *n*. emergency, predicament, dilemma, quandary, turning point, climax

criterion *n*. standard, test, rule, principle, guideline, yardstick, touchstone, measure

critic *n*. **1** judge, reviewer, commentator, authority, expert, arbiter **2** faultfinder, censor, carper

critical *adj*. **1** faultfinding, condemning, censorious, disapproving **2** dangerous, hazardous, risky, precarious **3** decisive, crucial, important, all-important, vital, determining

ANT. **1** flattering, praising **2** safe **3** unimportant, inconclusive

criticism *n*. **1** censure, faultfinding, objection **2** review, critique, commentary, evaluation, appraisal

ANT. **1** praise, approval

criticize *v*. **1** censure, find fault with, judge, condemn, disapprove of, rebuke, knock (*informal*), slate (*informal*), pick holes in (*informal*) **2** examine, estimate, discuss, scan

ANT. **1** praise

crooked *adj*. **1** bent, curved, distorted, twisted, wry, askew, deformed, disfigured **2** dishonest, unfair, unscrupulous, fraudulent, deceitful

ANT. **1** straight **2** honest

crop *n*. harvest, fruit, produce, yield, gathering

crop *v*. cut, mow, lop, trim, shorten

cross *adj*. irritable, annoyed, bad-tempered, angry, fretful, petulant, peevish, snappish, touchy, morose, sullen, sour, captious, crabbed, sulky

ANT. good-tempered

cross *v*. **1** go across, traverse, pass over, bridge, intersect **2** interbreed, hybridize, mix, blend **3** oppose, obstruct, frustrate, foil, resist

cross out cancel, delete, strike out

crouch *v*. stoop, bend, hunch, duck, squat

crowd *n*. throng, swarm, pack, horde, herd, host, rabble, mob

crowd *v*. **1** throng, swarm, pack, mob **2** pack, cram, press, squeeze, stuff

crown *n*. **1** diadem, coronet, circlet, tiara, garland, chaplet, wreath, laurel, bays **2** reward, honour, honor (*N. Am.*), distinction **3** summit, top, head, brow, crest, apex

ANT. **3** base, bottom

crown *v*. **1** honour, honor (*N. Am.*), decorate, invest, reward, endow **2** complete, consummate, conclude, seal, round off

crucial *adj*. decisive, critical, momentous, vital, significant, important, all-important

ANT. trivial, unimportant

crude *adj*. **1** rude, coarse, vulgar, indecent, gross, obscene **2** coarse, rough, unrefined, unfinished, unprocessed

ANT. **1** polite **2** refined

cruel *adj*. savage, harsh, inhuman, merciless, unfeeling, ruthless, pitiless, relentless, brutal, ferocious, blood-thirsty

ANT. gentle, merciful

cruelty *n*. savageness, harshness, brutality, inhumanity, ruthlessness

ANT. compassion, kindness

cruise *n*. voyage, journey, tour

cruise *v*. sail, travel, journey, drift, coast

crumb *n*. fragment, bit, scrap, particle

crumble *v.* break up, fall apart, disintegrate

crumple *v.* crease, rumple, collapse, crush, wrinkle, crinkle, pucker

crunch *v.* chew, munch, grind, bite, masticate

crush *v.* pound, crumble, squeeze, compress, shatter, raze, pulverize, demolish, overpower

cry *v.* 1 weep, sob, wail, bawl, blubber 2 shout, yell, exclaim, roar, scream, shriek

cuddle *v.* hug, embrace, clasp, kiss, caress

cue *n.* suggestion, hint, sign, indication, reminder

culminate *v.* conclude, finish, end, come to a head, reach a climax

culmination *n.* conclusion, finish, end, success, climax, consummation, completion, apex

culpable *adj.* faulty, wrong, blameworthy, blamable, censurable, reprehensible
ANT. innocent

culprit *n.* criminal, offender, delinquent, felon, malefactor

cult *n.* sect, faction, group, clique

cultivate *v.* 1 till, farm, seed, plant, work, fertilize 2 educate, improve, refine, train, discipline, develop 3 nourish, foster, cherish, promote, improve

cultural *adj.* edifying, enriching, enlightening, elevating, instructive

culture *n.* 1 civilization, society, way of life, customs 2 refinement, sophistication, breeding

cumulative *adj.* increasing, intensifying, growing, accruing, snowballing

cunning *adj.* crafty, sly, artful, devious, wily, foxy
ANT. guileless

cunning *n.* slyness, artfulness, craftiness, craft, artifice, deceit, intrigue, subtlety, chicanery
ANT. guilelessness, sincerity

cup *n.* mug, beaker, container

cupboard *n.* closet, wardrobe, cabinet, locker, sideboard

curb *v.* restrain, check, control, repress, bridle
ANT. indulge

curb *n.* restraint, check, control, limitation, rein

cure *n.* remedy, treatment, antidote, restorative, corrective, help, healing, medicine, restoration, convalescence, alleviation

cure *v.* remedy, heal, restore, make well, help, alleviate

curiosity *n.* 1 inquisitiveness, prying, snooping, nosiness (*informal*) 2 wonder, marvel, rarity, oddity

curious *adj.* 1 prying, meddling, inquisitive, snooping, nosy (*informal*) 2 strange, rare, odd, unusual, extraordinary, singular
ANT. 1 indifferent, uninterested 2 common, usual

curl *v.* twist, coil, bend, wind, loop

curl *n.* coil, twist, loop, spiral, whorl

current *adj.* present, contemporary, modern, up-to-date, popular, ordinary, general, common, prevalent
ANT. obsolete

current *n.* flow, course, stream, tide

curse *n.* 1 oath, expletive, swear word, obscenity, blasphemy, profanity 2 denunciation, execration, malediction, anathema 3 scourge, plague, torment, affliction, trouble
ANT. 1 benediction 3 success

curse *v.* denounce, condemn, swear
ANT. bless

cursory *adj.* hasty, superficial, careless, slight, rapid, desultory
ANT. elaborate, thorough

curtail *v.* shorten, cut short, cut, decrease, reduce
ANT. lengthen

curtain *n.* drape, hanging, screen, shade, blind

curve *v.* bend, twist, wind, coil

curve *n.* bend, twist, arch, vault, hook

cushion *n.* pillow, bolster, bag, rest, headrest, support

cushion *v.* protect, support, stifle, soften, suppress

custody *n.* 1 care, keeping, safekeeping, charge, protection 2 confinement, imprisonment, arrest, detention, duress

custom *n.* usage, habit, fashion, practice, rule, convention, form, formality, observance

customary *adj.* usual, common, general, regular, habitual
ANT. rare, unusual

customer *n.* client, patron, consumer, shopper

cut *v.* 1 gash, slash, nick, wound, lacerate 2 slice, carve, cut up 3 lop, crop, shear, trim, dock, prune 4 lower, decrease, reduce, lessen, cut down

cut back reduce, decrease, cut down **cut in** push in, interrupt, intervene, interpose **cut off** stop, end, halt, terminate, discontinue

cute *adj.* sweet, delightful, charming, appealing, attractive

cutting *adj.* sharp, keen, sarcastic, cruel, severe, satirical, wounding, piercing, trenchant, stinging, sardonic
ANT. soothing, flattering

cycle *n.* series, circle, revolution, succession

cylinder *n.* barrel, drum, vessel

cynical *adj.* sceptical, skeptical (*N. Am.*), suspicious, distrustful, derisive, contemptuous, scornful, pessimistic, misanthropic

D

dabble *v.* play, trifle, dally, toy, fool

daft *adj.* silly, stupid, crazy, idiotic, foolish
ANT. clever, intelligent

dainty *adj.* **1** delicate, fine, elegant, exquisite, pretty **2** delicious, tasty, savoury, savory (*N. Am.*), choice
ANT. **1** clumsy **2** loathsome

dally *v.* **1** dawdle, linger, loiter, dilly-dally **2** play, toy, trifle, flirt, fool around

dam *n.* barrier, wall, bank, dyke

dam *v.* block, obstruct, stop, slow, restrict, check

damage *n.* hurt, injury, harm, destruction, loss, impairment
ANT. benefit

damage *v.* harm, hurt, spoil, injure, mar, impair, vandalize

damp *adj.* moist, wet, humid, steamy, soggy, dank
ANT. dry, arid

damage *n.* moisture, water, wet, wetness, humidity
ANT. dryness

dampen *v.* **1** moisten, wet, humidify **2** discourage, stifle, deaden, restrain, temper
ANT. **1** dry **2** encourage

dance *n.* **1** step, tango, polka, waltz, ballet **2** ball, disco, party, social

dance *v.* tango, polka, waltz, skip, swing, frolic

danger *n.* peril, risk, hazard, threat, insecurity, uncertainty, liability, jeopardy
ANT. safety, security

dangerous *adj.* risky, perilous, hazardous, precarious, unsafe, insecure, uncertain, treacherous
ANT. safe, secure

dangle *v.* hang, swing, suspend, droop, sway

dare *v.* brave, risk, venture, hazard, challenge, defy, confront

daring *adj.* adventurous, fearless, risky, brave, courageous, dauntless, intrepid
ANT. cautious, timid

dark *adj.* **1** black, unlit, dim, gloomy, shadowy, sunless, murky, cloudy, overcast **2** bleak, gloomy, depressing, dismal, cheerless **3** deep, incomprehensible, unfathomable, unintelligible, obscure, hidden, mysterious, enigmatic **4** wicked, foul, horrible
ANT. **1** white, light **2** bright, clear **3** transparent **4** good

darken *v.* shade, shadow, overshadow, cloud, obscure, dim, eclipse

darkness *n.* dark, gloom, night, dusk, shadows

darling *n.* sweetheart, love, pet, beloved, favourite, favorite (*N. Am.*), idol, dear

darling *adj.* dear, beloved, favourite, favorite (*N. Am.*)

darn *v.* mend, repair, stitch, patch, sew, embroider

dash *v.* **1** rush, run, race, drive, send, speed, dart, bolt **2** throw, smash, strike, hurl, toss **3** disappoint, ruin, frustrate, destroy, spoil

data *n. pl.* facts, information, evidence, figures, statistics

date *n.* **1** time, era, epoch, period, age **2** appointment, meeting, engagement **3** boyfriend, girlfriend, steady (*informal*)

daub *v.* smear, plaster, paint, sully, soil, deface, defile, begrime

daunt *v.* frighten (off), discourage, unnerve, terrify, alarm, intimidate
ANT. encourage

dauntless *adj.* brave, daring, heroic, chivalrous, bold, valiant, fearless, intrepid, indomitable, unconquerable
ANT. cowardly, fearful

dawdle v. lag, dally, lag behind, delay, idle, take one's time
ANT. hurry

dawn n. 1 daybreak, break of day, sunrise, sun-up, first light, morning 2 origin, beginning, start, commencement, birth, appearance, emergence
ANT. 1 sunset 2 end

dawn v. 1 grow light, break, rise 2 appear, begin, open, start

daydream v. fantasize, dream, muse, imagine

daze v. stun, confuse, bewilder, amaze, shock, dumbfound

daze n. stupor, bewilderment, confusion, trance

dazzle v. 1 daze, blind, stun 2 astonish, surprise, overpower, bewilder, confuse.

dead adj. 1 lifeless, breathless, inanimate, deceased, defunct, departed, gone 2 unconscious, spiritless, insensible, heavy, still, inert, motionless, torpid 3 dull, cold, frigid, inert, indifferent, apathetic
ANT. 1 living, alive, animate

deaden v. paralyse, paralyze (N. Am.), anaesthetize, anesthetize (N. Am.), numb, weaken, blunt, muffle, stifle

deadlock n. standstill, impasse, stalemate

deadly adj. 1 mortal, fatal, lethal, destructive, noxious, malignant, pernicious, baneful, venomous 2 ghastly, deathly, ghostly, pale, ashen
ANT. 1 wholesome, life-giving 2 ruddy

deaf adj. 1 hard of hearing, unhearing, stone-deaf 2 dull, unaware, insensible, heedless, oblivious, stubborn
ANT. 1 listening 2 attentive, willing, susceptible

deal v. 1 trade, do business, bargain, traffic 2 distribute, give out, divide, share, apportion, mete out

deal with manage, handle, treat, take care of, see to, cope with

dear adj. 1 costly, high-priced, expensive, precious , pricey 2 beloved, loved, valued, precious, treasured, cherished, prized
ANT. 1 cheap, inexpensive 2 hated

dearth n. shortage, need, lack, want, scarcity, poverty
ANT. plenty, abundance

death n. decease, dying, demise, passing, departure, exit, expiration
ANT. birth, life

debar v. exclude, bar, shut out, stop, prevent, obstruct, prohibit, restrain, hinder
ANT. admit, allow, permit

debase v. degrade, deprave, corrupt, abase, disgrace, alloy, deteriorate, lower, impair
ANT. enhance, exalt, purify

debatable adj. doubtful, dubious, uncertain, unsettled, questionable, disputable, problematical
ANT. sure, certain, incontestable, self-evident

debate n. discussion, dispute, controversy, argument, contention, contest

debate v. discuss, argue, contend, dispute, question

debauchery n. depravity, corruption, immorality, dissoluteness, intemperance, dissipation, licentiousness

debility n. weakness, infirmity, feebleness, languor, exhaustion
ANT. strength, energy, vitality

debt n. liability, obligation, default, claim, bill, account, score
ANT. credit, liquidation, assets

debtor n. borrower, mortgagor
ANT. creditor, lender, mortgagee

debut n. premiere, introduction, first appearance, launch, entrance

decadent adj. degenerate, corrupt, immoral, depraved, self-indulgent

decay v. 1 corrupt, putrefy, decompose, rot, spoil, moulder, molder (N. Am.), wither, perish 2 deteriorate, decline, waste away, decrease
ANT. 1 flourish 2 grow, increase

decay n. 1 corruption, decomposition, rottenness, rotting, spoiling, mould, mold (N. Am.) 2 decline, downfall, collapse

deceased adj. dead, departed, late, former
ANT. living, alive

deceit *n.* fraud, deception, cheating, dishonesty, artifice, guile
ANT. honesty, openness, fair dealing, uprightness, integrity, sincerity, frankness, truth

deceitful *adj.* dishonest, false, fraudulent, cheating, insincere
ANT. honest, open, sincere, fair, frank

deceive *v.* cheat, mislead, swindle, defraud, dupe, delude, beguile, fool, trick, entrap
ANT. enlighten, guide

decent *adj.* 1 proper, fitting, becoming, seemly, respectable, modest, decorous 2 adequate, fair, reasonable, acceptable 3 kind, thoughtful, generous, obliging
ANT. 1 indecent, improper, rude 2 unacceptable 3 cruel

deception *n.* deceitfulness, falsehood, treachery, cunning, lying, fraud, hypocrisy, trickery, craftiness, delusion, duplicity
ANT. honesty, sincerity, truth, openness, guilelessness, frankness, simplicity

decide *v.* determine, settle, choose, go for, make up one's mind, adjudicate, terminate, end, resolve
ANT. hesitate, waver

decipher *v.* solve, decode, unravel, reveal, explain, unfold
ANT. puzzle, mystify

decision *n.* conclusion, judgment, determination, settlement, finding, verdict, sentence
ANT. vacillation, hesitation

decisive *adj.* 1 conclusive, positive, final, definitive, categorical, indisputable 2 resolute, firm, determined
ANT. 1 vague, hypothetical, indeterminate, dubious, problematical 2 indecisive, irresolute, weak, wavering

deck *n.* level, platform, floor, storey, story (*N. Am.*)

deck *v.* decorate, adorn, dress, ornament
ANT. deface

declaim *v.* speak, recite, proclaim, debate, harangue

declamation *n.* harangue, tirade, speech, lecture, address, debate, oratory, recitation, elocution

declaration *n.* statement, pronouncement, publication, proclamation, (official) announcement, assertion, affirmation, avowal
ANT. denial, recantation

declare *v.* state, say, claim, maintain, affirm, assert, announce, publish, advertise, reveal, proclaim
ANT. suppress, withhold, conceal

decline *v.* 1 refuse, say no, reject, forgo 2 decrease, lessen, deteriorate, sink, weaken, fail, degenerate, decay, waste away 3 descend, lower, slope, slope downwards, sink
ANT. 1 accept 2 increase, improve, flourish 3 rise, ascend

decline *n.* 1 decrease, lessening, weakening, deterioration, failing, degeneration 2 downward slope, slope, descent, incline
ANT. 1 increase, growth, improvement 2 ascent, rise

declivity *n.* fall, slope, decline
ANT. ascent, rise

decompose *v.* 1 decay, putrefy, rot, moulder, molder (*N. Am.*), go bad, fall apart, disintegrate, break up 2 analyse, analyze (*N. Am.*), dissolve, break down, atomize, dissect

decorate *v.* ornament, enhance, adorn, colour, color (*N. Am.*), embellish, improve
ANT. spoil, mar, deface

decoration *n.* 1 ornamentation, adornment, embellishment, enhancement, colouring, coloring (*N. Am.*), improvement 2 award, medal, badge, citation, ribbon

decorum *n.* dignity, order, seemliness, propriety, correctness, good manners
ANT. disorder, unseemliness

decrease *v.* lessen, diminish, decline, dwindle, curtail, reduce, lower
ANT. increase, grow, expand

decrease *n.* lessening, decline, dwindling, curtailment, reduction, lowering, diminution
ANT. increase, growth, expanse

decree *n.* law, edict, order, mandate, declaration, proclamation, manifesto, decision, determination

decrepit *adj.* 1 weak, infirm, feeble, frail, tottery, aged 2 dilapidated, tumbledown, broken-down, run-down, ramshackle
ANT. 1 strong, youthful 2 well-built

decry *v.* disapprove, criticize, disparage, detract, denounce
ANT. praise, extol

dedicate *v.* 1 devote, hallow, consecrate, sanctify 2 assign, apply, set apart, set aside, devote 3 address, inscribe
ANT. 1 desecrate

deduce *v.* conclude, reason, infer, draw, derive
ANT. guess

deduct *v.* subtract, take away, take off, remove
ANT. add, increase

deed *n.* 1 performance, act, action, exploit, feat 2 document, certificate, title, instrument

deem *v.* consider, regard, determine, judge, hold

deep *adj.* 1 profound, bottomless, low, extensive 2 difficult, mysterious, incomprehensible, hard, intricate, obscure, arcane 3 intelligent, discerning, learned, intellectual, sagacious, astute 4 intense, thorough, serious, great, grave 5 engrossed, immersed, absorbed, preoccupied, involved
ANT. 1 shallow 2 plain

deface *v.* disfigure, spoil, mar, deform, sully, tarnish, scratch
ANT. beautify, decorate

default *n.* neglect, failure, omission, oversight, want, destitution, lack, lapse, forfeit, absence

defeat *v.* 1 overcome, conquer, beat, overpower, quell, crush, subdue, vanquish 2 thwart, confound, foil, frustrate, spoil
ANT. 1 surrender

defeat *n.* overthrow, conquest, overpowering, crushing, quelling
ANT. success, triumph, victory

defect *n.* fault, flaw, imperfection, weakness, blemish, omission, want, shortcoming
ANT. perfection

defective *adj.* imperfect, faulty, flawed, deficient, broken, inoperative, out of order
ANT. perfect, operative, working, in good order, in working order

defence, defense (*N. Am.*) *n.* 1 shelter, shield, protection, guard, resistance, safeguard, rampart, fort, fortification, fortress, bulwark, trench 2 justification, vindication, excuse, plea, apology
ANT. 1 attack

defend *v.* 1 protect, guard, safeguard, resist, shield, shelter, screen 2 support, uphold, plead, argue for, enclose
ANT. 1 attack 2 accuse

defer *v.* 1 delay, postpone, put off, procrastinate, adjourn 2 comply, submit, give in, yield, respect
ANT. 1 hurry, hasten, quicken

deference *n.* respect, consideration, politeness, courtesy, regard, reverence, esteem, veneration, homage
ANT. disrespect, impudence, defiance, disobedience

defiant *adj.* antagonistic, disobedient, insolent, stubborn, insubordinate, provocative
ANT. compliant

deficiency *n.* shortage, lack, insufficiency, deficit, scarcity, absence, want, dearth
ANT. abundance, plenty, profusion

deficit *n.* shortfall, shortage, loss
ANT. surplus, excess

defile *v.* contaminate, spoil, pollute, corrupt, debase, adulterate, infect, taint
ANT. purify, cleanse, disinfect, wash, sanctify

define *v.* 1 describe, explain, interpret, designate, spell out 2 demarcate, outline, distinguish, mark off, limit, bound

definite *adj.* 1 certain, fixed, settled, determined, positive, decided 2 clear, unambiguous, exact, precise, specific, sharp, distinct, obvious
ANT. 1 possible 2 vague, ambiguous

definition *n.* sense, meaning, description, comment, explanation, interpretation, exposition, rendering, translation
ANT. misstatement

deformed *adj.* disfigured, distorted, misshapen, twisted, warped, ugly, hideous

deformity *n.* malformation, distortion, disfigurement, abnormal, ugliness, hideousness
ANT. beauty

defraud *v.* swindle, cheat, trick, deceive, rip off (*informal*), do (*informal*)

defray *v.* pay, discharge, settle, meet

defrayal *n.* payment, settlement, liquidation, discharge
ANT. insolvency, non-payment

defy *v.* challenge, dare, oppose, provoke, flout, scorn, brave
ANT. cower, shrink

degeneracy *n.* degradation, deterioration, growing worse, decay, decline, inferiority, meanness
ANT. improvement, advancement

degree *n.* **1** grade, rank, class, step, notch, station, stage, quality, standing **2** extent, measure, intensity, scope, level, range, interval, space **3** award, qualification, attainment

dejected *adj.* disheartened, unhappy, sad, discouraged, depressed, downcast, despondent, gloomy, melancholy, low-spirited
ANT. happy, glad, elated, joyful

delay *v.* **1** postpone, put off, defer, hold up, procrastinate **2** obstruct, hold back, hinder, impede, set back, stop, arrest **3** dawdle, linger, hold back, hesitate, wait
ANT. **1** bring forward **2** hasten, further

delay *n.* **1** postponement, deferral, deferment, procrastination **2** obstruction, hindrance, impediment **3** pause, interval, break, lull, breather (*informal*)
ANT. **1** advance **2** furtherance

delegate *n.* substitute, proxy, representative, ambassador, envoy, emissary, legate, deputy

delegate *v.* depute, deputize, commission, appoint, nominate, authorize, empower, constitute, ordain

delete *v.* remove, cancel, erase, cross out, obliterate, edit

deleterious *adj.* destructive, hurtful, harmful, injurious, pernicious, unwholesome, noxious, deadly, poisonous
ANT. wholesome, healthy, beneficial, salubrious

deliberate *adj.* **1** intentional, planned, calculated, premeditated **2** cautious, careful, wary, well-advised, purposed, studied, thoughtful, methodical **3** slow, leisurely
ANT. **1** unintentional, accidental **2** impulsive, rash, hasty

deliberate *v.* consider, reflect, consult, weigh, judge, meditate, ponder, debate, cogitate

delicacy *n.* **1** fineness, daintiness, exquisiteness, slightness **2** refinement, luxury, nicety, elegance **3** frailty, weakness **4** dainty, luxury, morsel, titbit, tidbit (*N. Am.*), relish
ANT. **2** coarseness, robustness **3** strength

delicate *adj.* **1** fine, dainty, exquisite, slender, thin, slight, fragile **2** weak, frail, ailing **3** sensitive, difficult, critical, precarious
ANT. **1** coarse, thick **2** strong, healthy

delicious *adj.* tasty, appetizing, savoury, savory (*N. Am.*), delightful, scrumptious (*informal*), moreish (*informal*), luscious, exquisite.
ANT. horrible, unpleasant, loathsome, unpalatable

delight *n.* joy, gladness, satisfaction, pleasure, ecstasy, happiness, enjoyment, bliss, charm, rapture, transport
ANT. suffering, sorrow, misery, dejection, trouble, distress, depression

delight *v.* **1** please, thrill, cheer, enrapture, charm, enchant **2** enjoy, revel, love, like, relish
ANT. **1** disappoint, revolt, disgust **2** dislike, hate

delightful *adj.* pleasing, attractive, charming, lovely, agreeable, pleasant, refreshing, welcome, satisfying, acceptable, pleasurable
ANT. miserable, depressing, disappointing, horrible, painful

delineate *v.* describe, figure, represent, sketch, draw, portray, depict, paint
ANT. caricature, misrepresent, exaggerate

delinquent *n.* offender, culprit, criminal, miscreant, malefactor
ANT. model, ideal

deliver *v.* 1 give, distribute, hand over, transfer, consign, yield, grant, resign, surrender, discharge, deal 2 send, carry, bring, convey, transmit 3 pronounce, declare, speak, announce 4 free, set free, liberate, rescue, release, save

delivery *n.* 1 giving, distribution, handing over, transferral 2 diction, articulation, enunciation, style, manner

delude *v.* mislead, deceive, dupe, trick, take in, con (*informal*)

deluge *n.* downpour, cloudburst, flood, inundation, overflow, rush

deluge *v.* flood, inundate, overwhelm, swamp, engulf, drown

delusion *n.* illusion, fantasy, trick, snare, fraud, deception, hallucination, error, fallacy

demand *v.* 1 ask for, request, order, claim, solicit 2 need, require, call for, involve, necessitate 3 command, direct, order, rule, bid
ANT. 1 waive, relinquish

demand *n.* 1 request, claim, order, bidding, command, direction, charge 2 obligation, responsibility, duty, onus 3 call, market, requirement, need

demarcation *n.* outline, sketch, limit, boundary, division, enclosure, separation, distinction

demean *v.* humble, lower, stoop, behave, act, conduct

demerit *n.* fault, weakness, blemish, disadvantage, misdeed, failure
ANT. credit, merit, worth, advantage

democratic *adj.* popular, representative, self-governing, egalitarian, republican
ANT. imperial, autocratic, despotic, tyrannical

demolish *v.* overthrow, destroy, overrun, raze, ruin, devastate
ANT. build, construct, make, restore, repair

demolition *n.* destruction, devastation, razing, ruin
ANT. building, construction

demonstrate *v.* 1 show, display, prove, verify, establish, substantiate 2 show, describe, explain, illustrate, exemplify 3 protest, rally, strike, march
ANT. 1 disprove

demonstration *n.* 1 show, exhibition, display, presentation, proof, evidence 2 explanation, illustration, description, example, experiment 3 protest, rally, strike, march
ANT. 1 concealment

demoralize *v.* 1 discourage, dishearten, dispirit, unnerve, deject, weaken 2 corrupt, deprave, undermine, subvert
ANT. 1 stimulate, inspire, encourage, reassure, animate, uplift

demure *adj.* sedate, staid, modest, shy, reserved, diffident, unassuming, prudish, discreet
ANT. lively, wanton

denial *n.* 1 contradiction, negation, repudiation, disagreement, disavowal 2 refusal, rebuff, rejection, prohibition
ANT. 1 confirmation 2 consent

denomination *n.* 1 name, designation, description, style, title, appellation, class, category, group 2 religion, sect, persuasion, creed, faith

denote *v.* mean, signify, indicate, stand for, represent, mark

denounce *v.* 1 condemn, deplore, attack 2 accuse, blame, charge, brand, defame
ANT. 1 praise

dense *adj.* 1 thick, compressed, condensed, compact, solid, packed, crowded, impenetrable, close, thickset 2 stupid, slow, dull, thick (*informal*)
ANT. 1 sparse, thin, scattered 2 intelligent, clever

dent *n.* indentation, mark, depression, dip, hollow, hole, impression, notch

denunciation *n.* condemnation, attack, castigation, censure, accusation, arraignment
ANT. eulogy, praise

deny *v.* 1 contradict, dispute, negate, disprove, disagree, repudiate, gainsay 2 refuse, reject, forbid, prohibit, turn down, withhold 3 renounce, abjure, disown
ANT. 1 admit, yield, concede 2 allow, permit

depart *v.* leave, go, start, set out, disappear, vanish, withdraw
ANT. arrive, come

department *n.* **1** division, subdivision, section, branch, portion **2** province, sphere, realm, branch, line, function, office, duty, station

departure *n.* leaving, going, setting out, exit, withdrawal

depend *v.* rely, trust, count, bank, be dependent, be contingent, be subject, turn, hang, hinge

dependable *adj.* trustworthy, reliable, faithful, loyal, steady, trusty
ANT. unreliable

dependent *adj.* hanging, resting, contingent, conditional, relying, subject, relative
ANT. independent, free

depict *v.* portray, draw, picture, represent, characterize, paint, delineate

depleted *adj.* consumed, used up, exhausted, drained, empty, spent

deplorable *adj.* regrettable, lamentable, pitiable, sad, mournful, disastrous, calamitous, grievous, distressing, melancholy
ANT. acceptable, happy, welcome

deportment *n.* behaviour, behavior (*N. Am.*), demeanour, demeanor (*N. Am.*), character, conduct, carriage
ANT. misbehaviour, misbehavior (*N. Am.*), misconduct

depose *v.* dethrone, debase, degrade, dismiss, oust, displace.
ANT. enthrone, install, initiate, elevate

deposit *v.* **1** place, put, put down, set down **2** save, store, bank, hoard
ANT. **2** withdraw

deposit *n.* **1** layer, sediment, deposition, silt, dregs, lees **2** security, pledge, warranty, guarantee

depot *n.* warehouse, store, storehouse, repository

depraved *adj.* corrupt, perverted, debase, degenerate, dissolute, licentious, evil, wicked, shameless
ANT. virtuous

deprecate *v.* regret, disapprove, condemn, deplore, denounce, frown on
ANT. commend, praise

depreciate *v.* devalue, lose value, lower in value, decline, undervalue, detract, underestimate
ANT. appreciate, value

depredation *n.* robbery, pillage, plunder, spoliation, theft, trespass, havoc, encroachment
ANT. restitution, compensation, restoration, amends, reparation

depress *v.* **1** sadden, discourage, dishearten, cast down **2** depreciate, devalue, cheapen, undervalue, lose value
ANT. **1** cheer **2** increase in value

depressed *adj.* sad, unhappy, discouraged, dejected, despondent, downcast, miserable, gloomy, disheartened, dispirited, melancholy, down (*informal*)
ANT. happy, glad, cheerful

depression *n.* **1** unhappiness, discouragement, dejection, despondency, misery, gloom, melancholy, blues (*informal*), dumps (*informal*) **2** recession, slump, hard times **3** hollow, dip, cavity, valley, decline
ANT. **1** happiness **2** boom **3** elevation, prominence

deprive *v.* bereave, rob, divest, strip, despoil, dispossess
ANT. provide, supply

depth *n.* deepness, profundity, drop, measure
ANT. shallowness

deputy *n.* assistant, lieutenant, agent, representative, aide, co-worker, envoy, legate, substitute, proxy, delegate, right-hand man/woman
ANT. governor, chief, ruler

derangement *n.* disorder, confusion, disarrangement, disturbance, discomposure, madness, lunacy, insanity, mania, delirium, alienation, aberration
ANT. order, calmness, sanity, rationality

derelict *adj.* forsaken, abandoned, deserted, neglected, dilapidated, decrepit

derision *n.* scorn, contempt, ridicule, mockery, scoffing
ANT. admiration, respect

derivation *n.* source, origin, genesis, fountain, descent, root, etymology

derive *v.* obtain, receive, acquire, draw, gain, flow, proceed, originate

derogatory *adj.* pejorative, disparaging, belittling, offensive, insulting, abusive, injurious
ANT. flattering, complimentary

descend *v.* go down, fall, drop, sink, get off
ANT. ascend, climb

descendant *n.* offspring, family, child, children, posterity, stock, lineage, scion, branch, issue, progeny
ANT. ancestor

descent *n.* drop, fall, plunge
ANT. ascent

describe *v.* portray, picture, trace, draw, represent, depict, mark out, relate, recount, narrate, illustrate, define, explain, characterize

description *n.* account, record, report, narration, portrayal, representation, explanation

descry *v.* perceive, discern, recognize, discover, see, detect, find out, make out, espy
ANT. overlook

desecrate *v.* profane, defile, violate, pollute, pervert, abuse, secularize, prostitute
ANT. hallow, sanctify, respect

desert[1] *n.* wilderness, waste, wasteland, solitude, wild

desert[2] *v.* leave, abandon, forsake, renounce, relinquish, quit, jilt

deserter *n.* defector, runaway, fugitive, renegade, turncoat, recanter, backslider, abjurer, traitor, apostate
ANT. adherent, devotee, supporter

deserve *v.* earn, merit, be worthy of, win, be entitled to
ANT. forfeit, lose, miss

design *v.* 1 intend, plan, prepare, project, contrive, scheme, plot, purpose, mean, aim, devise, propose 2 draw, delineate, draft, sketch, outline, plot 3 invent, conceive, originate, create

design *n.* 1 sketch, delineation, drawing, draft, plan, blueprint, pattern 2 form, shape, arrangement, pattern, motif, configuration 3 intention, meaning, purpose, aim, end, scheme, proposal, project, object, objective, plan, purport, drift, scope, mark 4 invention, contrivance, creation

designate *v.* 1 specify, pinpoint, earmark, define, particularize 2 describe, define, term, entitle, name, call, style, christen 3 appoint, allot, assign, choose, nominate

desirable *adj.* eligible, advantageous, beneficial, advisable, valuable, profitable, enviable, sought-after, wished-for, proper, judicious
ANT. disadvantageous, harmful, inadvisable, evil

desire *v.* long for, crave, yearn, wish, hanker, incline, covet
ANT. hate, abhor

desire *n.* appetite, inclination, longing, craving, impulse, hankering, coveting, propensity, wish
ANT. loathing, disgust, aversion, hate

desk *n.* bureau, table, counter

desolate *adj.* 1 uninhabited, deserted, empty, forsaken, unfrequented, waste, dreary, wild 2 wretched, miserable, comfortless, despondent, friendless, bereaved, forlorn, cheerless, lonely, solitary
ANT. 1 peopled, colonized, populous, crowded, frequented 2 happy, cheerful

despair *n.* desperation, discouragement, hopelessness, despondency
ANT. courage, hope, confidence, elation

despair *v.* lose heart, lose hope, give up

desperate *adj.* 1 despondent, hopeless, wretched, forlorn, lost 2 wild, reckless, rash, risky, dangerous, precipitate, headlong, frantic
ANT. 1 hopeful, glad 2 cautious, timid, shy

despicable *adj.* contemptible, mean, low, base, disreputable, pitiful, wretched

despise *v.* scorn, dislike, condemn, slight, disdain, spurn
ANT. respect, regard, revere

despite *prep.* in spite of, notwithstanding, regardless of, even with

despoil *v.* ravage, rob, plunder, loot, pillage, devastate, lay waste, strip, denude
ANT. rehabilitate

despondent *adj.* dejected, depressed, miserable, downhearted, downcast, sad, melancholy
ANT. happy, cheerful, glad

despot *n.* tyrant, dictator, autocrat, oppressor

despotic *adj.* tyrannical, autocratic, arrogant, absolute, imperious
ANT. democratic, representative

dessert *n.* pudding, sweet, afters (*informal*)

destination *n.* 1 aim, end, object, objective, goal, purpose, target, design, ambition 2 terminus, station, harbour, harbor (*N. Am.*)
ANT. 2 initiation, start

destiny *n.* fortune, fate, lot, doom, star(s), end, predestination

destitute *adj.* 1 poor, impoverished, penniless, distressed, hard up (*informal*) 2 lacking, devoid, deprived, deficient
ANT. 1 rich 2 full

destroy *v.* ruin, demolish, wreck, devastate, extinguish, kill
ANT. create, build

destruction *n.* ruin, devastation, wreckage, annihilation, liquidation, demolition, eradication
ANT. creation

destructive *adj.* ruinous, injurious, harmful, pernicious, baneful, detrimental, hurtful, noxious
ANT. constructive, restorative, beneficial

desuetude *adj.* disuse, non-observance, obsolescence, discontinuance
ANT. use, custom, practice

desultory *adj.* rambling, irregular, haphazard, capricious, wandering, roving, discursive, cursory, erratic, spasmodic, unsystematic
ANT. methodical, continuous, diligent, exact

detach *v.* separate, disconnect, divide, sever, uncouple, unfasten, free, isolate
ANT. connect, join

detail *n.* particular, item, element, circumstance, point, component, feature, aspect
ANT. totality, whole

detain *v.* delay, slow up, hinder, impede, restrain, keep back, check, stop
ANT. forward, free

detect *v.* discover, find out, notice, sense, learn, discern, perceive, determine

detective *n.* police officer, investigator, private eye

detention *n.* 1 hindrance, retaining, restraint, stopping 2 custody, confinement, imprisonment
ANT. 1 letting go 2 release, liberation

deter *v.* hinder, discourage, prevent, restrain, withhold, terrify, scare, dishearten, dissuade
ANT. incite, provoke, tempt, prompt, persuade

deteriorate *v.* decline, degenerate, decay, impair, degrade, debase, disintegrate
ANT. improve

determination *n.* resolution, firmness, tenacity, doggedness, conviction
ANT. irresolution

determine *v.* 1 settle, adjust, decide, resolve 2 ascertain, verify, detect, find out, establish 3 influence, affect, shape, lead, incline
ANT. 1 vacillate, waver

determined *adj.* resolute, firm, fixed, intent, set, persistent
ANT. irresolute

detest *v.* hate, abominate, abhor, despise, execrate, loathe, shrink from
ANT. like, approve, appreciate, praise, love

dethrone *v.* depose, drive out of power, cause to abdicate
ANT. crown, enthrone, exalt

detract *v.* depreciate, disparage, lessen, derogate, slander, defame, decry, vilify
ANT. enhance, increase, flatter, compliment

detriment *n.* loss, damage, injury, harm, evil, prejudice, disadvantage, impairment, inconvenience
ANT. enhancement, remedy, improvement

devastate v. 1 lay waste, raze, ruin, ravage, sack, plunder 2 overwhelm, confound, take aback

develop v. 1 grow, mature, advance, expand, enlarge, open 2 evolve, unfold, disclose, unravel, become known
ANT. 1 stunt, dwarf, hinder, prevent

development n. growth, advance, progress, evolution, maturity, unfolding

deviate v. digress, wander, deflect, veer, diverge, turn aside, depart, err, stray, swerve, differ, vary
ANT. adhere, coincide, converge

device n. 1 tool, machine, instrument, utensil, implement, gadget 2 wile, artifice, stratagem, evasion, fraud 3 crest, badge, emblem, symbol, type 4 contrivance, invention, design, project, plan, scheme, expedient, resource

devious adj. 1 misleading, insincere, sly, dishonest, treacherous 2 roundabout, indirect, erratic, wandering, deviating, crooked, circuitous
ANT. 1 straightforward, honest, fair 2 direct

devise v. plan, design, invent, create, make, originate, contrive, imagine, scheme, project, concoct

devoid adj. void, wanting, empty, destitute, vacant, unprovided for
ANT. full, supplied, provided, replete

devolve v. transfer, consign, convey, devise, deliver, place, attach, commission, charge, depute, fall, pass, be transferred
ANT. deprive, withhold, recall, cancel, alienate, miss

devote v. dedicate, consecrate, give, apply, commit
ANT. withhold, withdraw

devotion n. 1 dedication, consecration, commitment, piety, religion, sanctity, holiness, worship, adoration 2 attachment, affection, love, ardour, ardor (N. Am.), earnestness, zeal, eagerness, self-sacrifice
ANT. 1 impiety, profanity, sacrilege, irreverence, irreligion 2 aversion, indifference, apathy

devour v. 1 consume, gorge, gulp, eat ravenously, swallow 2 destroy, annihilate, waste, swallow up, expend
ANT. 1 vomit, disgorge 2 save, conserve

devout adj. 1 religious, pious, godly, devoted, committed, saintly 2 genuine, sincere, heartfelt, earnest, intense, ardent
ANT. 1 irreligious 2 indifferent, apathetic

dexterity n. aptitude, skill, expertness, readiness, adroitness
ANT. inability, weakness, awkwardness, clumsiness

diadem n. crown, chaplet, wreath, tiara, circlet

diagnosis n. investigation, determination, analysis

diagnostic n. symptom, feature, sign, cue, indication, mark, index

diagram n. chart, illustration, drawing, plan, outline, sketch

dialect n. language, phraseology, tongue, speech, provincialism, idiom, accent

dialogue n. conversation, discourse, tête-à-tête, colloquy
ANT. monologue

dictate v. 1 order, direct, ordain, command, prescribe, bid, require, decree 2 speak, say, utter 3 prompt, suggest, enjoin, instruct
ANT. 1 obey

dictate n. order, injunction, precept, command, rule, maxim, direction

dictator n. tyrant, despot, autocrat, oppressor

dictatorial adj. imperious, domineering, arbitrary, absolute, unlimited, authoritative, unrestricted, overbearing
ANT. democratic

diction n. speech, language, phrase, phrasing, phraseology, style, vocabulary, wording

dictionary n. lexicon, wordbook, glossary, vocabulary

didactic adj. instructive, perceptive, moral, directive, educative

die v. 1 expire, decease, depart, go 2 wither, perish, decay, decline, fade, dwindle, sink, faint, fall, subside, decrease, diminish, cease, vanish, disappear
ANT. 1 live, be born, survive, exist 2 flourish

diet *n.* **1** food, nourishment, aliment, nutriment, provision, rations, fare, subsistence **2** assembly, parliament, congress, council

difference *n.* contrast, diversity, variation, variety, discrepancy, disagreement, inequality, disparity, distinction, divergence, unlikeness
ANT. agreement, uniformity, identity, likeness, resemblance

different *adj.* **1** unlike, differing, dissimilar, contrasting, diverse **2** various, miscellaneous, assorted, sundry
ANT. **1** similar, like

differentiate *v.* distinguish, separate, particularize, specify, discriminate, individualize, segregate, identify
ANT. generalize

difficult *adj.* **1** hard, arduous, exhausting, severe, strenuous, onerous, trying, toilsome, laborious **2** complicated, intricate, complex, involved, obscure, enigmatic **3** unmanageable, opposed, unamenable
ANT. **1** easy, slight, trivial, pleasant, light **2** simple, plain, clear **3** amenable, pliant

difficulty *n.* **1** problem, dilemma, predicament, quandary, complication, trouble, fix (*informal*) **2** arduousness, severity, laboriousness, strenuousness, hardship, trouble, trial
ANT. **2** ease

diffident *adj.* modest, doubtful, reluctant, hesitating, bashful, timid, shy
ANT. bold, aggressive, forward, arrogant, self-conceited

diffuse *adj.* wordy, copious, rambling, verbose, long-winded, diluted
ANT. terse, condensed

diffuse *v.* disperse, scatter, spread, circulate

dig *v.* excavate, scoop, burrow, tunnel, mine, quarry, work, till

digest *v.* **1** eat, consume **2** assimilate, absorb, take in, grasp, understand, master **3** study, ponder, consider, contemplate, meditate **4** shorten, abridge, summarize **5** systematize, arrange, classify, codify

digest *n.* abridgment, summary, abstract, synopsis, compendium, précis

dignified *adj.* stately, noble, grand, majestic, elegant, solemn, self-respecting, imposing, decorous, august, lofty, exalted, pompous
ANT. low, lowly, mean, unimposing

dignify *v.* advance, promote, exalt, ennoble, prefer, grace, honour, honor (*N. Am.*), adorn, elevate, aggrandize
ANT. humiliate, debase, degrade

dignity *n.* distinction, stateliness, nobility, grandeur, majesty, loftiness, solemnity
ANT. lowliness, meanness

digress *v.* deviate, ramble, wander, diverge, stray, go off at a tangent

dilapidated *adj.* ruined, decayed, ramshackle, neglected, shabby, tumbledown, crumbling, run-down
ANT. restored

dilapidation *n.* ruin, decay, disintegration, demolition
ANT. restoration, soundness, solidity

dilate *v.* stretch wide, expand, enlarge, widen, distend
ANT. compress, restrict, narrow, condense, concentrate

dilatory *adj.* slow, loitering, tardy, dawdling, lagging, lingering, sluggish, procrastinating
ANT. prompt, eager, earnest

dilemma *n.* predicament, problem, difficulty, quandary, plight, fix (*informal*)

diligence *n.* activity, perseverance, application, attention, care, heed, industry, assiduity
ANT. laziness, neglect, carelessness

diligent *adj.* industrious, hard-working, assiduous, persevering, careful, attentive
ANT. lazy, careless, inattentive

dim *adj.* obscure, dark, covered, hidden, shadowy, dusky, unclear, faint, vague, indistinct, uncertain
ANT. bright, clear, brilliant, light

dim *v.* darken, obscure, cloud, pale, blur, fade
ANT. brighten

dimension *n.* measurement, mass, extent, bulk, size, capacity, amplitude, massiveness, greatness, importance

diminish v. lessen, reduce, decrease, decline, abate, subside, shorten, dwarf, shrink, retrench
ANT. increase, amplify, magnify, expand

diminutive adj. tiny, small, little, minute
ANT. huge, gigantic

din n. racket, clamour, clamor (N. Am.), noise, uproar, tumult
ANT. silent, peace

dine v. eat, feast, sup, banquet, lunch

dingy adj. dark, dirty, dull, soiled, tarnished, dim, drab, murky, gloomy, obscure, sombre, somber (N. Am.)
ANT. bright

dip v. immerse, plunge, inundate, soak, steep, drown, submerge

dip n. swim, plunge, bathe

diploma n. award, certificate

diplomacy n. negotiation, discretion, tact, ministry, ambassadorship

diplomat n. ambassador, representative, envoy

diplomatic adj. prudent, wise, tactful, astute, polite, gracious, politic, sagacious, judicious, discreet
ANT. blundering, tactless, injudicious

direct adj. 1 unswerving, straight, rectilinear, undeviating 2 straightforward, plain, honest, unambiguous
ANT. 1 meandering, indirect, roundabout, circuitous 2 equivocal

direct v. 1 control, manage, run, lead, guide 2 order, command, instruct, bid 3 guide, show, lead 4 aim, point, fix, level, sight

direction n. 1 management, control, guidance, superintendence, oversight, conduct 2 order, command, instruction 3 course, route, tendency, aim, bearing

directly adv. immediately, at once, soon, speedily, instantly, promptly, presently, quickly, straight away
ANT. by-and-by

director n. manager, executive, governor, supervisor, controller, head, boss (informal)

directory n. list, classification, catalogue, catalog (N. Am.), record

dirge n. requiem, elegy, lament, wake, threnody

dirt n. filth, uncleanness, pollution, foulness, meanness, filthiness, defilement
ANT. cleanness, purity, ablution

dirty adj. 1 filthy, soiled, mucky, unwashed, unclean, foul, polluted, defiled 2 obscene, indecent, pornographic
ANT. 1 clean 2 decent

disability n. unfitness, inability, incompetence, incapacity, injury, disqualification
ANT. fitness

disable v. handicap, cripple, incapacitate

disabuse v. undeceive, set right, correct, enlighten, inform, rectify
ANT. deceive, delude, hoodwink

disadvantage n. drawback, difficulty, obstacle, inconvenience
ANT. advantage, benefit

disagree v. 1 quarrel, dissent, contest, object, conflict, contradict, be at variance
ANT. agree, correspond

disagreeable adj. unpleasant, nasty, objectionable, disgusting
ANT. pleasant

disagreement n. argument, quarrel, misunderstanding, squabble, clash, conflict, fight, opposition

disappear v. vanish, fade (away), cease, go, withdraw
ANT. appear

disappoint v. dissatisfy, let down, disillusion, sadden, frustrate, foil, defeat, baffle, mortify
ANT. satisfy

disappointment n. dissatisfaction, failure, discouragement, let-down, misfortune, frustration
ANT. satisfaction

disapprove v. object to, condemn, dislike, criticize
ANT. approve

disaster n. calamity, catastrophe, misfortune, mishap, reverse
ANT. blessing

disastrous *adj.* calamitous, unfortunate, catastrophic, terrible, dreadful, awful

disburse *v.* spend, expend, consume, waste, use, lay out, pay
ANT. save, economize, hoard, husband

discard *v.* reject, throw away, get rid of, cast aside, scrap
ANT. keep, retain

discern *v.* observe, discriminate, distinguish, perceive, see, discover, penetrate, differentiate
ANT. overlook, neglect, miss

discernible *adj.* noticeable, perceptible, visible, apparent, conspicuous, palpable, plain, manifest, evident
ANT. obscure, minute, invisible

discernment *n.* judgment, perception, discrimination, brightness, astuteness, insight, intelligence, perspicacity, penetration, acuteness, sagacity, ingenuity
ANT. blindness, inattention, dullness, density

discharge *v.* 1 unburden, unload, expel, eject 2 shoot, fire, detonate, explode 3 perform, execute, do, carry out, observe 4 release, exonerate, acquit, liberate, free 5 dismiss, let go, expel, fire (*informal*)
ANT. 4 recruit, employ

discharge *n.* 1 firing, shooting, detonation, explosion, blast 2 release, dismissal, sack (*informal*) 3 performance, execution, observance, fulfilment
ANT. 2 recruitment, employment

disciple *n.* follower, student, believer, pupil, learner, scholar, supporter, adherent
ANT. master, teacher, professor, leader, rabbi

discipline *n.* 1 training, teaching, drill, exercise, practice 2 control, regulation, subjection, government 3 punishment, correction, coercion, chastisement
ANT. negligent

discipline *v.* 1 train, teach, drill, exercise 2 control, regulate, govern 3 punish, correct, chastise, reprove, castigate

disclose *v.* show, reveal, uncover, expose
ANT. hide, conceal, mask

discomfit *v.* defeat, overpower, conquer, foil, disconcert
ANT. encourage, aid, assist

disconcert *v.* frustrate, defeat, thwart, baffle, discompose, embarrass, disturb, upset, perplex, abash, confuse, bewilder
ANT. encourage

disconnect *v.* divide, separate, detach, disengage, uncouple, unhook
ANT. join, connect

disconsolate *adj.* inconsolable, sorrowful, heart-broken, comfortless, melancholy, desolate, forlorn, sad
ANT. happy, joyful, cheerful, glad

discontinue *v.* end, stop, cease
ANT. start, begin

discord *n.* disagreement, clash, dissension, dissonance, conflict, opposition
ANT. harmony, concord

discount *n.* allowance, rebate, deduction, concession

discourage *v.* deject, depress, dishearten, unnerve, dissuade
ANT. encourage, inspire, persuade

discourtesy *n.* impoliteness, disrespect, rudeness
ANT. politeness, courtesy

discover *v.* find, detect, discern, learn, invent, expose, ascertain, determine, disclose, betray, indicate, manifest
ANT. hide, conceal, cover, secrete, bury, suppress, withhold

discovery *n.* finding, uncovering, detection, discernment, invention

discreet *adj.* discerning, wise, tactful, prudent, cautious, judicious, considerate, circumspect
ANT. careless, foolish, heedless, reckless, silly, imprudent, undiscerning, unrestrained

discrepancy *n.* dissonance, discord, discordance, difference, variation, disagreement
ANT. agreement, harmony, correspondence

discretion *n.* prudence, tact, diplomacy, wisdom, thoughtfulness, judgment, discernment
ANT. rashness, carelessness

discriminate v. distinguish, tell apart, differentiate

discrimination n. **1** prejudice, bias, bigotry, intolerance, racism, sexism **2** acuteness, penetration, discernment, shrewdness, insight
ANT. **1** tolerance **2** dullness

discursive adj. roving, wandering, rambling, desultory, inconsequent

discuss v. talk about, consider, deliberate upon, debate, argue, reason

discussion n. debate, argument, talk, conversation, consideration

disdain n. contempt, scorn, disregard, haughtiness, arrogance
ANT. reverence, respect, esteem, considerateness, humility

disdain v. scorn, despise, disregard, slight
ANT. respect, admire

disdainful adj. scornful, contemptuous, proud, arrogant, haughty, sneering
ANT. respectful

disease n. illness, sickness, infirmity, ailment, complaint, malady, indisposition, unsoundness
ANT. health, strength, soundness, convalescence

disgrace n. shame, dishonour, dishonor (N. Am.), discredit, humiliation, embarrassment, disrepute, defamation, scandal
ANT. honour, honor (N. Am.)

disgrace v. shame, dishonour, dishonor (N. Am.), discredit, humiliate, embarrass
ANT. honour, honor (N. Am.)

disguise v. hide, conceal, mark, veil, cloak, shroud, camouflage

disguise n. mask, camouflage, cover, façade, screen, blind, front, pretence, pretense (N. Am.)

disgust n. distaste, loathing, dislike, repugnance, aversion, abhorrence, nausea
ANT. desire, liking, fondness

disgust v. revolt, offend, repulse, nauseate, sicken
ANT. please

disgusting adj. revolting, repulsive, repugnant, nauseating, sickening
ANT. pleasing, attractive

dish n. **1** plate, bowl **2** food, serving, helping, meal

dishonest adj. corrupt, fraudulent, deceitful, false, unscrupulous, untrustworthy
ANT. honest

disintegrate v. break down, separate, divide, shatter, crumble, fall apart

dislike v. hate, loathe, detest, abhor, object to, disapprove of
ANT. like

dismal adj. dark, gloomy, cheerless, dull, dreary, melancholy, lonesome, sombre, somber (N. Am.), sad, doleful, funereal
ANT. cheerful, bright

dismay v. frighten, terrify, appal, alarm, intimidate, daunt
ANT. reassure, encourage

dismay n. fear, terror, dread, horror, alarm, consternation
ANT. reassurance, encouragement

dismember v. disintegrate, mutilate, separate, rend asunder, sever
ANT. incorporate

dismiss v. let go, banish, discard, discharge, remove
ANT. recall, welcome

disobey v. break, transgress, disregard, violate, infringe, contravene, neglect, ignore
ANT. keep

disorder n. confusion, chaos, disorganization, tumult, mess
ANT. order, organization

disparage v. depreciate, decry, undervalue, underrate, defame, reproach
ANT. appreciate, underestimate, extol, praise, exaggerate

dispatch v. send away, send off, post, mail, expedite **2** complete, finish, conclude, discharge

dispatch n. **1** message, communication, report, bulletin, communiqué **2** speed, quickness, rapidity, promptness
ANT. **2** slowness

dispel v. drive away, disperse, dissipate, banish, scatter
ANT. collect

dispensation n. **1** apportionment, allotment, distribution **2** system, scheme, plan, regime

disperse *v.* dispel, scatter, separate, diffuse, spread, disseminate
ANT. gather, collect, concentrate

display *v.* **1** exhibit, show, demonstrate, parade **2** reveal, expand, unfold, extend, uncover, show, open, spread
ANT. **2** conceal, hide, wrap, dissemble, suppress

display *n.* show, exhibit, exhibition, presentation, demonstration

dispose *v.* arrange, place, settle, deal with

dispose of throw away, get rid of, discard

disposition *n.* **1** temper, character, nature, personality **2** tendency, inclination, propensity **3** arrangement, location, placing, grouping, management, control, regulation, direction

disputant *n.* litigant, debater, arguer, controversialist, competitor, claimant
ANT. auxiliary, partner

dispute *v.* **1** quarrel, wrangle, debate, argue, discuss **2** deny, contradict, oppose, contest, impugn
ANT. **2** allow, concede, grant, relinquish

dispute *n.* argument, quarrel, debate, discussion

disqualify *v.* debar, exclude, rule out, eliminate, preclude
ANT. qualify

disquisition *n.* treatise, dissertation, discourse, essay, discussion

disregard *v.* neglect, ignore, overlook, take no notice of
ANT. heed

disregard *n.* neglect, inattention, heedlessness
ANT. heed, attention

disrespect *n.* rudeness, impoliteness, discourtesy, disregard, contempt
ANT. respect

disrupt *v.* upset, disturb, break, break up, interrupt, unsettle, interfere with

dissatisfaction *n.* discontent, unhappiness, disappointment, frustration, discouragement
ANT. satisfaction

dissect *v.* anatomize, analyse, analyze (*N. Am.*), explore, investigate, examine, sift
ANT. integrate

dissemble *v.* hide, conceal, disguise, cloak
ANT. reveal, expose

dissent *v.* differ, disagree, decline
ANT. assent, consent, agree

dissent *n.* disagreement, difference, opposition
ANT. agreement, assent

dissertation *n.* thesis, long essay, disquisition, discussion, treatise

dissipate *v.* scatter, vanish, disperse, disappear, waste, squander
ANT. save, hoard, gather, conserve

dissociate *v.* separate, sever, disjoin, divide, part, disconnect
ANT. associate, join, affiliate

dissolute *adj.* abandoned, corrupt, loose, profligate, reprobate, dissipated
ANT. upright, honest, conscientious, self-controlled

dissolve *v.* **1** thaw, melt, liquefy **2** end, terminate, wind up, discontinue
ANT. **1** solidify **2** start, begin

distance *n.* **1** remoteness, space, length, extent, reach, interval **2** reserve, coldness, stiffness
ANT. **1** proximity, contiguity, closeness, nearness, presence, contact **2** warmth

distant *adj.* **1** remote, far, faraway, far-flying, outlying **2** unfriendly, reserved, cold, stiff
ANT. **1** near, close **2** warm, friendly

distend *v.* dilate, extend, spread, stretch
ANT. contract, narrow, constrict, condense

distil *v.* drop, extract, separate

distinct *adj.* separate, individual, definite, different, clear, plain, unmistakable
ANT. blurred, vague, indefinite, obscure

distinction *n.* **1** difference, dissimilarity, contrast, differentiation **2** fame, honour, honor (*N. Am.*), repute, eminence, importance, prominence

distinguish v. 1 discern, perceive, tell, discriminate, make out 2 differentiate, characterize, mark, separate, divide

distinguished adj. illustrious, famous, celebrated, noted, eminent, marked, renowned, important, conspicuous, supreme
ANT. obscure, inconspicuous, notorious

distortion n. deformity, twist, contortion, perversion, falsification, misrepresentation, alteration, misinterpretation, sophistry, corruption
ANT. regularity, symmetry, right, truth

distract v. divert, perplex, confuse, disconcert, bewilder, confound, derange, craze
ANT. fix, compose, concentrate, collect

distraction n. 1 confusion, perplexity, abstraction, disturbance, turmoil, agitation, frenzy, madness, alienation, aberration, delirium, mania, derangement, lunacy 2 amusement, entertainment, pastime, diversion, recitation
ANT. 1 composure, self-possession, tranquillity

distress n. 1 affliction, calamity, disaster, danger, peril, adversity 2 agony, suffering, anguish, trouble, misery, perplexity, misfortune, poverty, privation, destitution
ANT. 1 blessing 2 happiness

distress v. trouble, worry, upset, grieve
ANT. please

distribute v. share, give out, deal, dispense, scatter, allot, apportion, grant, appoint
ANT. retain, collect, gather

district n. region, area, territory, province, circuit, quarter, zone

distrust v. mistrust, doubt, suspect, be wary of
ANT. trust

distrust n. doubt, suspicion, wariness, misgiving
ANT. trust

disturb v. 1 interrupt, hinder, disrupt 2 annoy, plague, trouble, vex, worry, concern, trouble 3 agitate, shake, stir, disorder, confuse, upset
ANT. 2 quiet, compose, pacify 3 arrange, order

disturbance n. 1 disorder, confusion, commotion, agitation 2 fight, riot, commotion
ANT. 1 calm 2 peace

disuse n. neglect, abandonment, decay, discontinuance
ANT. use

ditch n. trench, channel, drain, gully, furrow

dive v. plunge, fall, drop, dip, submerge, plummet

diverge v. split, separate, divide, branch off, fork
ANT. converge, join

diverse adj. various, varied, different, assorted, distinct
ANT. similar

diversion n. 1 detour, deviation, divergence, redirection 2 entertainment, recreation, amusement, enjoyment, pastime, sport

diversify v. vary, change, alter, modify

diversity n. difference, variation, unlikeness, divergence, dissonance, dissimilitude, heterogeneousness, multiformity
ANT. identity, similarity, uniformity

divert v. turn aside, deflect, avert, distract, redirect, deviate

divest v. strip, dismantle, deprive, unclothe, undress, unrobe
ANT. clothe

divide v. 1 part, separate, disunite, split, detach, sever 2 alienate, estrange, split up, disunite 3 distribute, give out, allot, apportion, assign, share, dispense
ANT. 1, 2 unite

divination n. magic, foretelling, augury, prophecy, prediction, presage

divine adj. godly, holy, almighty, heavenly, supernatural, spiritual, transcendent
ANT. human, earthly

division n. 1 separation, parting, split, partition, disunion, severance 2 part, section, sector, portion, class, category, group, branch

divorce v. separate, split up, part, alienate, disunite
ANT. marry

divorce *n.* dissolution, annulment, separation, split, break-up
ANT. marriage

divulge *v.* disclose, reveal, impart, make known, declare, admit
ANT. hide, conceal

dizzy *adj.* giddy, reeling, shaky, unsteady, light-headed, faint, woozy (*informal*)

do *v.* **1** accomplish, achieve, bring to pass, complete, carry out, effect, discharge, perform, commit **2** finish, complete, perform, conclude, fulfil, execute **3** be adequate, suffice, satisfy **4** make, prepare, arrange, organize, create, produce **5** cheat, deceive, swindle, defraud
ANT. **1** neglect, omit **2** fail

do away with abolish, dispense with, eliminate, destroy, kill, murder **do down** belittle, disparage, humiliate **do in 1** tire, weary, exhaust **2** murder, kill, bump off (*informal*) **do up 1** wrap, tie (up), fasten, pack **2** redecorate, modernize, renovate, refurbish

docile *adj.* manageable, amenable, compliant, gentle, meek, tame, submissive, yielding, tractable, pliable, obedient
ANT. obstinate, firm, inflexible, stubborn, self-willed, wilful, willful (*N. Am.*), determined, dogged

dock *n.* wharf, quay, harbour, harbor (*N. Am.*), pier

doctor *n.* physician, surgeon, general practitioner, locum, specialist, consultant

doctrine *n.* teaching, principle, tenet, dogma, opinion, belief, precept, creed

document *n.* certificate, paper, record, form

dodge *v.* evade, avoid, shirk, hedge, duck (*informal*)

dog *n.* hound, bitch, mongrel, pup, whelp, mutt (*informal*)

dogmatic *adj.* arrogant, authoritative, imperious, domineering, positive, self-opinionated, doctrinal, magisterial, dictatorial
ANT. practical, active, modest, diffident, vacillating, considerate

domestic *adj.* private, family, familiar, homelike, native
ANT. public, foreign, alien, strange

domesticate *v.* tame, teach, train, house-train, break in, accustom

domicile *n.* home, house, residence, dwelling, mansion, abode

dominant *adj.* commanding, ruling, predominant, supreme, main, chief, primary, principal
ANT. subordinate, inferior

dominate *v.* **1** rule, control, govern, command, prevail, tyrannize, oppress, crush **2** overlook, look over, tower above

domination *n.* superiority, lordship, mastery, sway, supremacy, command, ascendancy, government
ANT. subjection, inferiority, weakness, minority, subordination

domineer *v.* lord, tyrannize, oppress, dictate, bully, swagger
ANT. submit, yield, bow, defer, resist

dominion *n.* authority, power, control, government, domination, supremacy, sway, dominance, domain, territory, sovereignty
ANT. submission

donation *n.* gift, present, offering, contribution, benefaction

doom *n.* condemnation, fate, sentence, judgment, destiny, verdict

doom *v.* condemn, ordain, destine, sentence, judge

door *n.* entrance, doorway, opening, gate, portal

dormant *adj.* sleeping, latent, inert, quiescent
ANT. awake, active, alert

dot *n.* point, mark, spot, speck

double *adj.* twice, twofold, repeated, coupled, dual

double *v.* duplicate, repeat, multiply

double *n.* twin, copy, duplicate, counterpart, lookalike, clone, dead ringer (*informal*)

doubt *n.* distrust, scepticism, skepticism (*N. Am.*), disbelief, suspicion, suspense, hesitation, incredulity, irresolution, misgiving, unbelief, perplexity, uncertainty
ANT. conviction, certainty, assurance, belief, confidence, determination, resolution, resolve

doubt v. distrust, disbelieve, question, suspect, hesitate, waver, vacillate
ANT. trust, believe, be confident, depend on

doubtful adj. unsure, uncertain, questionable, unsettled, undetermined, debatable
ANT. certain, definite, sure, positive

downcast adj. sad, unhappy, dejected, depressed, discouraged, despondent, downhearted, crestfallen
ANT. happy, glad, cheerful

downfall n. ruin, fall, collapse, destruction
ANT. rise

downgrade v. lower, demote, humble, decrease, reduce
ANT. improve

downhearted adj. gloomy, sad, discouraged, unhappy, dejected, depressed, despondent
ANT. happy, glad, cheerful

downwards adv. below, beneath, down
ANT. upwards, above

doze v. sleep, slumber, nap, drowse, snooze (informal)

drab adj. dull, shabby, dreary, dismal, dark, dingy
ANT. bright

draft n. sketch, outline, drawing, plan, rough

drag v. draw, pull, bring, haul, tow
ANT. carry, push, propel, raise

drain v. empty, exhaust, draw (off), strain, dry, tap
ANT. fill, supply

drain n. 1 channel, pipe, duct, conduit, ditch, gutter 2 strain, depletion, exhaustion, expenditure

draw v. 1 sketch, outline, trace, picture, depict 2 pull, drag, haul, tow 3 attract, pull, lure, entice, influence, persuade
ANT. 2 push 3 repel, alienate, dissuade

draw n. pull, attraction, lure, enticement
ANT. repulsion, rejection, alienation, estrangement

draw back recoil, withdraw, retreat, shrink **draw on** use, employ, exploit, utilize **draw up** 1 compose, draft, prepare, outline 2 stop, halt, pull up, come to a standstill

drawback n. disadvantage, shortcoming, weakness, defect, deficiency, obstacle
ANT. advantage

drawing n. picture, sketch, outline, illustration, diagram, representation

dread n. fear, terror, horror, alarm, awe, apprehension
ANT. confidence, courage

dread v. fear, tremble, quail

dream n. reverie, daydream, fancy, vision, delusion, hallucination, trance, fantasy, wish, hope, vagary

dream v. imagine, daydream, fancy, vision, visualize, conceive, fantasize

dreary adj. dismal, gloomy, dark, cheerless, depressing, uninteresting, routine, humdrum
ANT. cheerful, bright, promising, inviting

dress n. 1 frock, skirt, suit, gown 2 clothing, garments, costume, apparel, garb, array, attire, raiment, habiliments, vesture, robes, habit, vestments
ANT. 2 nakedness

dress v. 1 clothe, wear, don, attire, robe, cover 2 treat, bandage, plaster
ANT. 1 undress, strip

drift n. 1 tendency, trend, aim, purpose, intention, scope, design, meaning 2 heap, mass, bank, mound, pile 3 direction, bearing, course

drift v. 1 accumulate, amass, pile up 2 wander, meander, ramble, stray

drink v. swallow, gulp, sip, imbibe, quaff, drain, absorb, suck in
ANT. pour

drink n. beverage, liquid, refreshment, sip, gulp

drive v. 1 direct, control, guide, handle, operate 2 impel, push, thrust, urge, propel, compel

drive n. 1 ride, journey, outing, trip, run, spin (informal) 2 energy, vigour, vigor (N. Am.), enterprise, effort, force, pressure

drivel v. dribble, slobber, slaver, drool

drivel n. nonsense, rubbish, twaddle, gibberish

drizzle v. spit, rain, spray, spot

droll adj. funny, ridiculous, odd, whimsical, comical, ludicrous, facetious
ANT. serious, solemn

droop *v.* sag, sink, decline, flag, pine, wither, languish, fade, wilt
ANT. rise

drop *v.* 1 sink, fall, decline, lower, go down, descend, decrease, dive, plunge, plummet 2 drip, trickle, dribble
ANT. 1 rise, ascend, climb, go up, increase

drop *n.* 1 bead, droplet, drip, trickle 2 fall, decline, lowering, decrease, reduction, slump
ANT. 2 rise

drown *v.* 1 die, go under, sink 2 drench, immerse, swamp, overwhelm, overflow, inundate, deluge, flood, overcome, overpower
ANT. 2 dry, drain

drowsy *adj.* tired, sleepy, lethargic, sluggish, dull
ANT. alert, awake

drug *n.* 1 medium, medication, cure, remedy 2 narcotic, stimulant, opiate, dope (*informal*)

drug *v.* sedate, numb, stupefy, anaesthetize, anesthetize (*N. Am.*)

drum *v.* drum up summon, attract, round up, canvass

drunk *adj.* intoxicated, inebriated, tipsy, merry, tight (*informal*), boozy (*informal*)
ANT. sober, abstinent, abstemious, teetotal

drunk *n.* drunkard, drinker, inebriate, alcoholic, dipsomaniac, wino (*informal*)

dry *adj.* 1 arid, parched, waterless, dehydrated, thirsty, craving drink 2 dull, boring, dreary, tedious, tiresome 3 witty, droll, sharp, keen, sarcastic
ANT. 1 moist, fresh 2 lively, entertaining

dubious *adj.* doubtful, questionable, debatable, uncertain, suspect
ANT. certain

due *adj.* 1 owing, owed, payable, unpaid 2 proper, fitting, suitable, appropriate, becoming, rightful
ANT. 2 improper

dull *adj.* 1 boring, uninteresting, monotonous, tiring, wearisome, flat 2 gloomy, overcast, murky, grey, cloudy 3 blunt, indistinct 4 stupid, slow, unintelligent 5 unfeeling, insensitive, lethargic, slow, lifeless
ANT. 1 exciting, lively 2 bright, clear, fine 3 sharp 4 intelligent, quick 5 lively, alert

dumb *adj.* speechless, mute, silent, still, inarticulate

dump *v.* drop, throw down, empty, tip, unload, get rid of

dump *n.* tip, rubbish, heap

dungeon *n.* prison, jail, cell

duplicate *n.* copy, counterpart, imitation, likeness, double
ANT. original, pattern, prototype, model

duplicate *v.* copy, reproduce, repeat, replicate, clone

duplicity *n.* deceit, deception, fraud, dishonesty, guile, artifice
ANT. straightforwardness, frankness, sincerity, honesty

durable *adj.* lasting, enduring, long-lasting, strong, sturdy, substantial
ANT. perishable

duration *n.* length, span, continuance, term, period, protraction, prolongation
ANT. brevity, momentariness

duress *n.* compulsion, pressure, force, constraint, coercion

dusk *n.* twilight, evening, darkness, gloom, gloaming
ANT. dawn

dust *n.* dirt, powder, sand, earth, soil

dutiful *adj.* obedient, faithful, devoted, submissive
ANT. disobedient

duty *n.* responsibility, obligation, onus, task, function, office, business, accountability, right

dwell *v.* live, rest, stop, stay, abide, reside, lodge, sojourn
ANT. visit

dwindle *v.* diminish, lessen, decrease, decline, shrink, fade
ANT. grow, increase

eager *adj.* enthusiastic, earnest, keen, anxious, desirous, yearning, ardent, animated, fervent, impetuous, vehement
ANT. uninterested, unenthusiastic

early *adj.* premature, advanced, new, recent
ANT. late

earn *v.* deserve, acquire, merit, win, get, gain, achieve, collect, obtain, realize
ANT. lose, spend, forfeit, waste, squander

earnest *adj.* serious, sincere, determined, eager, zealous, fervent, intent, fixed
ANT. flippant, frivolous, indifferent, jesting

earth *n.* 1 world, globe, planet 2 ground, land, soil, turf, sod, dirt

earthly *adj.* terrestrial, worldly, mundane, temporal, material, physical
ANT. spiritual, heavenly

earthy *adj.* coarse, unrefined, vulgar, rough, crude, ribald, bawdy
ANT. refined, tasteful

ease *n.* 1 facility, naturalness, skilfulness, skillfulness (*N. Am.*), cleverness, knack, readiness, expertness, easiness 2 comfort, rest, satisfaction, contentment, repose, refreshment, relief
ANT. 1 trouble, difficulty 2 disquiet, uneasiness

ease *v.* comfort, alleviate, relieve, soothe, calm, still, lessen, lighten, reduce
ANT. aggravate

easy *adj.* 1 simple, effortless, uncomplicated, straightforward, natural 2 quiet, comfortable, tranquil, leisurely, unhurried
ANT. 1 hard, difficult 2 uncomfortable, disturbed

easy-going *adj.* relaxed, carefree, casual, easy, tolerant, happy-go-lucky
ANT. strict, rigorous

eat *v.* consume, devour, chew, swallow, munch, breakfast, lunch, dine

eavesdrop *v.* listen in, overhear, pry, snoop, bug (*informal*)

ebb *v.* recede, abate, decrease, subside, wane, sink
ANT. flow, swell, increase, flood

eccentric *adj.* odd, strange, peculiar, irregular, abnormal, uncommon, singular, wayward, aberrant, erratic, whimsical
ANT. normal, usual, regular

echo *n.* reverberation, resonance, repetition, reverberation, imitation, answer

echo *v.* reverberate, resonate, repeat, ring

eclipse *n.* obscuration, dimming, obscurity, hiding, shrouding, concealment, vanishing, extinction, obliteration, destruction
ANT. illumination

eclipse *v.* obscure, hide, conceal, shroud, veil, blot out, dim, darken
ANT. illuminate

economical *adj.* thrifty, sparing, careful
ANT. wasteful, extravagant

economize *v.* save, husband, manage frugally, be frugal, be prudent
ANT. waste, misuse, be lavish, be extravagant, squander

economy *n.* thrift, thriftiness, frugality, saving, providence, good husbandry, good management
ANT. wastefulness, extravagance, prodigality

ecstasy *n.* delight, transport, rapture, inspiration, frenzy, emotion, delight, enthusiasm, happiness
ANT. misery, unhappiness

edge *n.* **1** border, margin, brink, rim, brim, verge **2** sharpness, keenness, intensity, animation, zest
ANT. **1** interior, centre, center (*N. Am.*) **2** bluntness, flatness

edge *v.* **1** trim, border, fringe **2** inch, creep, sidle

edgy *adj.* nervous, tense, on edge, keyed up, irritable, touchy
ANT. calm, placid

edible *adj.* eatable, good, palatable, wholesome, culinary
ANT. inedible

edict *n.* order, command, decree, proclamation, mandate, ordinance

edifice *n.* building, construction, fabric, structure
ANT. ruin

edify *v.* build up, enlighten, improve, stimulate, strengthen, nurture
ANT. corrupt, pervert, defile, debase, mislead, misguide

edit *v.* **1** revise, correct, prepare for press, annotate, emend, alter **2** compile, arrange, compose, direct, publish

educate *v.* teach, instruct, train, nurture, breed, discipline, develop

education *n.* **1** training, teaching, tuition, instruction, schooling, discipline, cultivation, breeding, development, nurture **2** information, knowledge, learning, reading, study, culture
ANT. **1** ignorance, illiteracy

educe *v.* draw out, extract, elicit, evolve, produce

eerie *adj.* strange, weird, uncanny, mysterious, frightening, spooky (*informal*)

efface *v.* obliterate, erase, blot out, destroy, cancel, eradicate, expunge
ANT. delineate, imprint

effect *n.* **1** result, consequence, event, outcome, issue **2** force, significance, meaning, validity, purport, drift, tenor, weight, power **3** implementation, operation, action, execution **4** (*pl.*) chattels, goods, commodities, property, movables, belongings
ANT. **1** cause **3** disuse

effect *v.* cause, produce, accomplish, bring about, change, achieve, create, execute, perform, realize, effectuate, consummate, fulfil

effective *adj.* productive, useful, capable, able, efficient, practical, striking, convincing
ANT. ineffective, useless

effectuate *v.* accomplish, bring about, effect, execute, achieve, secure, fulfil
ANT. prevent, hinder

effeminate *adj.* feminine, womanly, womanish, unmanly
ANT. manly, masculine

effervesce *v.* boil, bubble, froth, foam, ferment, sparkle
ANT. subside

effete *adj.* weak, feeble, decayed, spent, exhausted, worn, wasted, barren, unfruitful
ANT. vigorous, fertile, prolific, productive

efficacious *adj.* effectual, effective, active, productive, operative, powerful, adequate, cogent
ANT. insufficient, inadequate

efficacy *n.* power, potency, force, competence, strength, effectiveness, energy, usefulness
ANT. inefficacy, incompetency

efficiency *n.* effectiveness, skill, competence, proficiency, productiveness, expertise, ability, capability
ANT. ineffectiveness, incompetence

efficient *adj.* effective, skilled, competent, proficient, capable, expert, productive, businesslike
ANT. inefficient, incompetent

effigy *n.* image, representation, figure, statue, likeness, dummy
ANT. misrepresentation, distortion

efflorescence *n.* flowering, blooming, blossoming, budding, bloom, luxuriance, outburst
ANT. fading, waning

effluence *n.* emanation, flow, effusion, issue, outpouring, emission, discharge, overflow
ANT. influx, infusion

effort *n.* endeavour, endeavor (*N. Am.*), attempt, go, trial, exertion, struggle, strain, striving, stretch
ANT. inactivity

effrontery *n.* boldness, impudence, insolence, audacity, shamelessness, presumption, brass (*informal*), sauciness (*informal*)
ANT. modesty, shyness, diffidence, shrinking, timidity, bashfulness

effulgence *n.* brilliance, splendour, splendor (*N. Am.*), lustre, luster (*N. Am.*), brightness, radiance, refulgence, glory, flame, luminosity, resplendence
ANT. darkness, gloom, shade

effusion *n.* outpouring, effluence, discharge, emission, abundance, waste, shedding, spilling
ANT. infusion, absorption, influx

effusive *adj.* gushing, lavish, generous, profuse, prodigal, diffused
ANT. sparing, reserved, taciturn, laconic, curt, brief

egoism *n.* selfishness, self-conceit, self-consciousness, self-confidence, self-esteem, conceit, vanity, self-assertion, self-praise, self-admiration, self-love, self-exaltation
ANT. self-forgetfulness, diffidence, bashfulness, humility, modesty, shyness, unobtrusiveness, unostentatiousness

either *pron.* one of two, the other of two, each, both
ANT. neither

ejaculation *n.* exclamation, cry, utterance, expletive
ANT. silence, speechlessness

eject *v.* force out, expel, dismiss, discharge, oust, reject, banish, throw aside, cast away, emit, vomit, void, evacuate
ANT. retain, absorb, take in, accept, receive, introduce, inject, welcome

eke out add to, supply, increase, stretch, help, make last longer

elaborate *adj.* ornate, ornamental, decorated, fancy, complex, intricate, complicated
ANT. simple, unadorned

elaborate *v.* develop, amplify, expand, improve, decorate, embellish

elapse *v.* pass, pass by, go by, transpire, slip, glide away, lapse, intervene

elastic *adj.* flexible, springy, resilient, pliable, buoyant, alterable, modifiable, rebounding
ANT. rigid, tough, inflexible, unchangeable

elated *adj.* excited, exhilarated, animated, flushed, inspired, cheered, inflated
ANT. depressed, dejected, discouraged, dispirited

elder *adj.* senior, older, more ancient, born earlier
ANT. younger, junior

elect *v.* choose, select, vote for, pick, prefer, decide on, go for, opt for

elect *adj.* picked, selected, chosen, choice, elite, accepted, appointed, delegated
ANT. rejected, abandoned

election *n.* selection, preference, choice, voting, ballot, poll, power to choose

electric *adj.* charge, inspiring, stimulating, thrilling, stirring, exciting
ANT. depressing, discouraging

electrify *v.* charge, rouse, excite, thrill, stir, astonish, astound, amaze, startle, galvanize

elegance *n.* grace, beauty, refinement, polish, politeness, gentility, gracefulness, taste, propriety, symmetry
ANT. deformity, awkwardness, disproportion

elegant *adj.* fine, refined, graceful, well-formed, symmetrical, lovely, handsome, refined, tasteful, ornamental, accomplished, polished
ANT. awkward, deformed, ill-proportioned, misshapen, hideous

elegy *n.* dirge, lament, requiem, funeral song
ANT. paean, jubilee, alleluia, anthem

element *n.* **1** constituent, component, ingredient, part, principle **2** (*pl.*) basics, fundamentals, rudiments, outlines, essential parts
ANT. **1** whole, total, totality

elementary *adj.* simple, basic, fundamental, rudimentary, primary, uncomplicated
ANT. complicated, complex, advanced, sophisticated, developed

elevate *v.* raise, lift, lift up, exalt, promote, advance, aggrandize, improve, dignify, ennoble
ANT. lower, degrade, debase

elevation *n.* **1** raising, elevating, promotion, aggrandizement, exaltation, dignity, refinement **2** hill, mountain, height, altitude, superiority, eminence, loftiness, tallness
ANT. **1** degradation, debasement **2** depression, decline, fall, depth

elicit *v.* draw out, evoke. call forth, bring out, deduce, bring to light, express, extract, worm out
ANT. insert, implant, introduce, infuse

eligible *adj.* desirable, preferable, worthy, fit, qualified, capable, suitable, prime, choice
ANT. ineligible, unqualified, worthless, ordinary, indifferent, undesirable

eliminate *v.* expel, exclude, discharge, remove, get rid of, omit, leave out, reject, erase, obliterate

elimination *n.* expulsion, exclusion, discharge, removal, rejection, eradication, omission, obliteration
ANT. inclusion, retention, preservation, conservation

elision *n.* omission, ejection, ellipsis, abridgment

elliptical *adj.* **1** egg-shaped, oval **2** contracted, abbreviated, concise, succinct
ANT. **2** full

elocution *n.* speech, power of expression, utterance, delivery, diction, eloquence

elongation *n.* protraction, extension, drawing out, continuation, distance
ANT. curtailment, abridgment, contraction

elope *v.* run away, abscond, flee, decamp

eloquence *n.* delivery, expressiveness, fluency, way with words

eloquent *adj.* fluent, articulate, expressive, forceful
ANT. inarticulate

elucidate *v.* explain, illustrate, clear, unfold, make plain, expound
ANT. confuse, mystify, obscure, puzzle, bewilder

elucidation *n.* explanation, illustration, demonstration, comment, annotation, commentary, gloss, exposition
ANT. mystification, confusion, obscurity, ambiguity

elude *v.* **1** evade, escape, avoid, shun, dodge (*informal*), slip away **2** baffle, foil, thwart, disappoint, disconcert, frustrate
ANT. **1** face, meet, encounter, confront

elusive *adj.* **1** shadowy, unsubstantial, intangible, indefinable, transient **2** deceptive, fraudulent, deceitful, shuffling, shifting, slippery (*informal*), fugitive
ANT. **1** substantial **2** certain, solid

emaciated *adj.* lean, lank, thin, attenuated, haggard, wasted, gaunt, skinny
ANT. fat

emanate *v.* flow, issue, arise, spring, proceed, originate, emerge

emancipate *v.* free, set free, enfranchise, liberate, rescue, release, unchain
ANT. enslave, bind

embalm *v.* **1** preserve, cherish, enshrine, keep **2** scent, perfume, make fragrant **3** treasure, store, consecrate
ANT. **1** abandon, desecrate **3** violate, profane

embargo *n.* prohibition, ban, restraint, hindrance, restriction, detention, stoppage
ANT. permit, permission, release, discharge

embark on start, begin, commence, set about, launch, enter
ANT. complete

embarrass *v.* shame, abash, disgrace, humiliate, mortify, distress, trouble, confuse, disconcert, confound
ANT. calm, compose

embarrassment *n.* shame, humiliation, awkwardness, discomfort, self-consciousness, distress, trouble
ANT. ease, composure

embellish *v.* adorn, decorate, ornament, beautify
ANT. disfigure, deface, detract, diminish

embezzle *v.* appropriate, steal, pilfer, cheat, defraud, purloin, falsify, forge, counterfeit

embitter v. make bitter, aggravate, exacerbate, exasperate, enrage, anger, madden, provoke
ANT. compose, quiet, pacify, alleviate, soothe

emblem n. figure, image, sign, symbol, device, representation, token, badge, mark, signal, type, attribute

embody v. incorporate, integrate, comprehend, include, embrace, comprise, contain, combine, collect, systematize, codify, concentrate, compact
ANT. exclude

embolden v. encourage, animate, reassure, inspire, incite, urge, stimulate
ANT. discourage. intimidate, frighten, alarm, deter

embrace v. 1 clasp, hug, press, cuddle, kiss 2 comprehend, include, cover, contain, embody, welcome, accept, take in
ANT. 2 reject, exclude

embroider v. embellish, enrich, emboss, adorn

embroil v. involve, implicate, entangle, ensnarl, disturb, perplex, confuse, distract, trouble
ANT. extricate, separate, remove, compose, pacify, calm

embryo n. germ, rudiment, nucleus, origin
ANT. completion, maturity, fulfilment

emendation n. amendment, correction, rectification, reformation, improvement
ANT. error, fault, incorrectness, inaccuracy, defect

emerge v. appear, become visible, come out, surface, rise, issue, emanate, escape
ANT. disappear, depart

emergency n. crisis, difficulty, predicament, extremity, strait, urgency, necessity

emigrate v. leave, migrate, move, depart, relocate
ANT. move into, settle, stay

eminence n. 1 distinction, celebrity, reputation, renown, repute, fame, preferment, note, conspicuousness, superiority 2 prominence, projection, elevation, hill, mountain, high point, protuberance
ANT. 1 shame 2 decline

eminent adj. 1 famous, celebrated, distinguished, prominent, illustrious, remarkable, renowned, reputed, conspicuous 2 high, lofty, elevated
ANT. 1 mediocre, worthless, notorious

emission n. ejection, expulsion, issue
ANT. admission, entrance

emit v. discharge, eject, expel, throw out, issue
ANT. retain, withhold

emollient adj. softening, laxative, soothing, palliative, balsamic
ANT. irritant, irritating

emolument n. wages, salary, income, gain, pay, profit, remuneration, hire, stipend, compensation
ANT. loss

emotion n. feeling, sentiment, passion, excitement, agitation, sensibility
ANT. indifference, insensibility, impassiveness, imperturbability

emotional adj. 1 passionate, enthusiastic, ardent, fervent, demonstrative, stirring, impetuous, overwrought, hysterical 2 sensitive, feeling, tender, warm
ANT. 1 calm, placid

emphasis n. stress, accent, force, weight, significance

emphasize v. stress, accentuate, highlight, underline, affirm, point up
ANT. play down, understate

emphatic adj. significant, expressive, strong, important, special, forcible, positive, energetic, decided, distinct, unequivocal
ANT. ordinary, unimportant, common, unimpassioned, undemonstrative

empire n. dominion, kingdom, supremacy, sovereignty, authority, government, command, control, sway, rule

empirical adj. tentative, observed, experimental, provisional, experiential

employ v. 1 take on, engage, hire, enlist, entrust, occupy 2 use, apply, utilize, exercise
ANT. 1 dismiss, fire (*informal*)

employee n. worker, wage-earner, labourer, laborer (*N. Am.*)

employer *n.* manager, director, proprietor, owner, boss (*informal*)

employment *n.* **1** work, job, occupation, business, vocation, pursuit, calling, profession, craft, trade, position, service, agency, office, employ **2** application, utilization, exercise
ANT. **1** leisure, recreation

empower *v.* commission, authorize, allow, permit, warrant, qualify, sanction, enable, encourage
ANT. prevent, discourage, disqualify, disable

empty *adj.* **1** vacant, unoccupied, void, without contents, bare, blank, destitute, devoid, unfilled, hollow **2** senseless, futile, meaningless, worthless, insubstantial, trivial, idle
ANT. **1** full, occupied **2** significant, important, substantial

empty *v.* clear, void, drain, deplete, evacuate, vacate, unload, discharge, pour out

emulation *n.* imitation, rivalry, competition, jealousy, envy, contention, vying, aspiration, contest

enable *v.* empower, strengthen, authorize, qualify, allow, sanction, make capable, capacitate, invigorate
ANT. disqualify, incapacitate, disable, hinder

enact *v.* **1** decree, establish, ordain, rule **2** perform, act, play, personate, represent, feign, dissimulate
ANT. **1** abolish, abrogate, cancel, repeal

enamour, enamor (*N. Am.*) *v.* charm, captivate, fascinate, enchant, inflame, endear, bewitch
ANT. repel, disgust, disenchant

encamp *v.* camp, pitch, bivouac, settle, quarter
ANT. decamp, retire, retreat, advance, charge

enchain *v.* bind, fetter, manacle, hold, enslave
ANT. loose, free

enchant *v.* charm, fascinate, bewitch, delight, captivate, win, catch, enrapture, ravish
ANT. repel, disgust, horrify

enchantment *n.* **1** incantation, spell, charm, magic, witchery, sorcery **2** delight, fascination, charm, rapture, ravishment, transport, bliss
ANT. **2** disillusionment, repulsion

encircle *v.* surround, encompass, ring, gird, enclose, hem in, beset, circumscribe

enclose *v.* surround, encompass, encircle, shut, include, envelop, wrap, circumscribe

enclosure *n.* yard, compound, pound, pen, ring, limit, park, field, boundary, precinct

encomium *n.* eulogy, praise, tribute, eulogium, panegyric, commendation, laudation, paean, compliment, good word
ANT. slander

encompass *v.* encircle, enclose, ring, gird, hem in, surround, circumscribe

encounter *v.* **1** meet, come across, confront, face, experience, withstand **2** fight, assault, combat, engage, attack, contend, compete with, struggle
ANT. **1** avoid, escape, shun

encounter *n.* **1** meeting, confrontation, experience **2** fight, clash, assault, attack, combat, conflict, engagement

encourage *v.* **1** inspire, cheer up, animate, embolden, hearten, incite, stimulate, comfort, strengthen, console, support, reassure, prompt, urge **2** advance, further, help, aid, foster, abet, patronize
ANT. **1** deter, discourage, dishearten, dissuade **2** hinder, prevent

encouragement *n.* inspiration, comfort, strength, consolation, support, reassurance, stimulus, heartening
ANT. discouragement

encroach *v.* intrude, trespass, infringe, invade, creep, advance stealthily, transgress

encumber *v.* obstruct, hinder, hamper, burden, overload, clog, load, impede, involve, entangle, complicate
ANT. free, liberate, relieve

encumbrance *n.* impediment, hindrance, obstacle, burden, load
ANT. relief

end *n.* 1 finish, conclusion, limit, outcome, extremity, extent, bound, termination, boundary, completion, close, expiration, finale 2 aim, goal, intention, fulfilment, purpose, point, result
ANT. 1 beginning, commencement, origin

end *v.* finish, stop, cease, break off, close, complete, conclude, halt, quit, desist, terminate, expire, wind up
ANT. begin, start, commence, initiate

endanger *v.* hazard, risk, peril, jeopardize, imperil, commit, compromise, expose to danger
ANT. protect, shield, save, defend

endear *v.* make dear, attract, charm, captivate, engage
ANT. embitter, antagonize, estrange, alienate

endeavour, endeavor (*N. Am.*) *v.* attempt, try, strive, undertake, make effort, labour, labor (*N. Am.*), aim, exert oneself, essay
ANT. neglect, omit, abandon

endeavour, endeavor (*N. Am.*) *n.* attempt, effort, struggle, undertaking, enterprise, venture, go (*informal*), shot (*informal*)

endless *adj.* 1 interminable, boundless, limitless, unlimited, infinite, immeasurable, illimitable 2 incessant, ceaseless, uninterrupted, continual, continuous, everlasting, perpetual, eternal, unending, without end, immortal, deathless, undying, imperishable
ANT. 1 limited, brief, temporary, transient, ephemeral, transitory

endorse *v.* 1 approve, sanction, confirm, uphold, support, ratify, back 2 sign, countersign

endow *v.* give, bestow, furnish, enrich, endue, put on, present, supply
ANT. deprive, strip

endowment *n.* 1 grant, gift, bequest, bounty, present, largesse, boon, provision, property, fund, revenue 2 talent, gift, qualification, ability, faculty, power, quality, capability, aptitude, genius

endure *v.* 1 continue, last, remain, persist, be permanent 2 suffer, experience, bear, tolerate, allow, sustain, support, undergo, brook

enemy *n.* adversary, foe, opponent, rival, antagonist, competitor
ANT. friend, accomplice, supporter, helper, associate, abettor, ally

energetic *adj.* vigorous, active, forceful, forcible, powerful, effective, potent, efficient, able, capable
ANT. weak, faint, sluggish, exhausted, feeble, spiritless, inactive

energy *n.* activity, force, power, strength, intensity, vigour, vigor (*N. Am.*), might, potency, agility, spirit, animation, life, zeal
ANT. laziness, slowness, sloth, inactivity, sluggishness, heaviness, inertness

enervate *v.* unnerve, weaken, enfeeble, debilitate, break, paralyse, paralyze (*N. Am.*), incapacitate
ANT. invigorate, strengthen, harden, nerve, brace, empower

enfeeble *v.* enervate, weaken, debilitate, unnerve, incapacitate
ANT. strengthen, nerve, invigorate, brace

enfold *v.* envelop, wrap, enclose, embrace, encircle, encompass
ANT. unwrap, develop, reveal, expose

enforce *v.* urge, compel, constrain, oblige, force, require, insist, exact, exert, strain
ANT. abandon, waive

enforcement *n.* constraint, compulsion, urgency, obligation, force, insistence
ANT. abandonment, remission

enfranchise *v.* free, emancipate, liberate, release, qualify
ANT. disenfranchise, disqualify

engage *v.* 1 employ, hire, take on, appoint, commission, enlist 2 absorb, engross, occupy, involve, busy 3 encounter, attack, fight with, battle with, contend, struggle, contest
ANT. 1 dismiss, fire (*informal*) 2 bore 3 retreat

engaged *adj.* 1 betrothed, spoken for, pledged, affianced 2 busy, occupied, unavailable, in use, tied up (*informal*)

engagement *n.* **1** betrothal, affiancing, promise, stipulation, contract, obligation, assurance, pledge **2** appointment, meeting, arrangement, commitment **3** employment, job, occupation, business, vocation **4** fight, combat, battle, contest, encounter, action, conflict

engaging *adj.* attractive, charming, pleasing, interesting, delightful, enchanting, winning
ANT. repulsive, unattractive

engender *v.* cause, produce, generate, create, breed, occasion, propagate, beget
ANT. suppress, stifle, destroy

engine *n.* motor, machine, mechanism, locomotive, device, contrivance

engrave *v.* carve, cut, chisel, imprint, cut, infix, impress deeply, sculpture
ANT. erase, obliterate, wear out, destroy

engross *v.* absorb, engage, engulf, occupy, involve, consume
ANT. bore, distract

enhance *v.* heighten, swell, intensify, advance, increase, augment, aggrandize
ANT. undervalue, depreciate, disparage, detract, underestimate

enigmatic *adj.* puzzling, perplexing, obscure, hidden, mysterious, unintelligible, ambiguous, incomprehensible, recondite, mystical, occult
ANT. plain, clear, manifest, self-evident, lucid, open, intelligible

enjoin *v.* **1** urge, admonish, advise, order, direct, command, bid, require **2** prohibit, forbid, ban, restrain
ANT. **2** allow

enjoy *v.* delight in, like, be pleased with, have a good time
ANT. dislike, hate

enjoyment *n.* pleasure, delight, happiness, satisfaction, gratification
ANT. displeasure, dissatisfaction, misery, wretchedness, grief, affliction, suffering

enlarge *v.* increase, amplify, extend, expand, magnify, grow, swell, augment, make greater, ennoble
ANT. decrease, contract, narrow, reduce, diminish, restrict, lessen, curtail

enlighten *v.* **1** inform, teach, instruct, edify **2** illuminate, light up
ANT. **1** confuse, perplex, confound **2** darken, obscure

enlist *v.* enrol, sign up, register, incorporate, enter, embody, record, chronicle
ANT. leave, withdraw, dismiss

enliven *v.* amuse, quicken, animate, rouse, invigorate, inspire, cheer, delight, gladden, exhilarate
ANT. depress, subdue, oppress, weary

enmity *n.* hatred, hostility, opposition, bitterness, ill will, hate, malice, rancour, rancor (*N. Am.*), animosity, antagonism, acrimony, malevolence, spite, malignity, maliciousness, asperity, aversion, discord
ANT. friendship, love, affection

ennoble *v.* dignify, elevate, exalt, ameliorate, enlarge, make great
ANT. debase, degrade, deteriorate

enormity *n.* outrageousness, abomination, heinousness, depravity, atrocity, wickedness, villainy, perpetration, sin
ANT. inoffensiveness

enormous *adj.* huge, vast, immense, colossal, gigantic, inordinate, abnormal, exceptional, monstrous, prodigious
ANT. small, tiny, diminutive

enough *adj.* sufficient, adequate, plenty, satisfactory, ample, abundant
ANT. insufficient, short, inadequate, scant, ill-supplied, bare

enquire See inquire

enquiry See inquiry

enrage *v.* anger, infuriate, exasperate, provoke, irritate, madden, incite, incense, inflame, excite, aggravate
ANT. soothe, conciliate, allay

enrapture *v.* charm, fascinate, captivate, attract, enchant, entrance, enravish, delight, transport, satisfy, please, gladden, bewitch, enslave
ANT. disgust, repel, torment, torture, horrify

enrich *v.* **1** enhance, endow, store, supply, augment, aggrandize **2** adorn, decorate, ornament, embellish
ANT. **1** impoverish

enrol *v.* enlist, register, record, sign up, recruit

enrolment *n.* registration, enlisting, signing up, recruitment

enshrine *v.* treasure, preserve, cherish, immortalize, embalm, consecrate
ANT. destroy, desecrate

enslave *v.* captivate, charm, enthral, master, dominate, bewitch, delight, fascinate
ANT. repel, disgust

ensue *v.* follow, result, arise, come, succeed, happen, take place, issue, arise, spring
ANT. precede, introduce, herald

ensure *v.* guarantee, make sure, secure, assure, necessitate, require

entail *v.* transfer, transmit, fix, involve, leave, induce, necessitate
ANT. prevent, nullify

entangle *v.* implicate, involve, entrap, perplex, embarrass, confuse, interweave, intertwine
ANT. straighten, extricate, disentangle, unravel

enter *v.* 1 go into, come into, arrive 2 begin, commence, embark, enlist, join 3 register, record, inscribe, chronicle 4 pierce, penetrate, invade, introduce
ANT. 1 depart, leave, go out 2 finish, end 4 withdraw

enterprise *n.* 1 adventure, undertaking, venture, project, effort, attempt, endeavour, endeavor (*N. Am.*), trial, experiment 2 energy, initiative, activity, readiness, willingness, courage, boldness

enterprising *adj.* resourceful, bold, adventurous, daring, audacious, energetic, eager, zealous, progressive
ANT. unenterprising, timid, cautious, inactive, fearful, wary, prudent, indolent, unready, laggard

entertain *v.* 1 amuse, interest, divert, cheer, delight, recreate, please, occupy, gratify, enliven 2 consider, ponder, cherish, hold, receive
ANT. 1 annoy, tire, bore

entertainment *n.* diversion, amusement, enjoyment, pastime, hobby, fun, pleasure, recreation, sport, hospitality
ANT. work, toil, fatigue

enthrone *v.* crown, install, exalt, elevate, invest with power
ANT. dethrone, depose

enthusiasm *n.* earnestness, zeal, eagerness, excitement, inspiration, frenzy, vehemence, warmth, ecstasy, passion, rapture, devotion, fervency, fanaticism, fervour, fervor (*N. Am.*), intensity
ANT. indifference, coldness

enthusiast *n.* fan, fanatic, supporter, devotee, zealot, fiend (*informal*)

enthusiastic *adj.* earnest, keen, eager, zealous, excited, inspired, passionate, devoted, warm, fanatic
ANT. indifferent, cold

entice *v.* lure, draw, trap, attract, seduce, coax, persuade, wheedle, cajole, delude, entrap, inveigle, lead astray, induce
ANT. deter, repel

entire *adj.* whole, complete, perfect, unimpaired, unbroken, undiminished, undivided, full, integral, thorough, solid, intact, unalloyed
ANT. partial, incomplete, broken

entitle *v.* 1 enable, fit, empower, qualify, allow, authorize 2 name, designate, christen, call, style, characterize, denominate
ANT. 1 disable, disqualify

entity *n.* being, essence, existence
ANT. nonentity, fantasy, hallucination

entomb *v.* bury, inter, inhume
ANT. exhume, disinter

entrance *n.* 1 entry, approach, doorway, opening, door, gate, gateway, portal, access, admission, admittance, entrée, introduction, avenue 2 beginning, commencement, initiation, appearance, arrival
ANT. 1 departure, exit

entreat *v.* beg, supplicate, solicit, beseech, implore, pray, urge, appeal, petition, crave, importune, enjoin, adjure

entry *n.* 1 entrance, access, admission, way in, avenue, passage, door, gate, hall, inlet, opening 2 note, minute, record, item, register, memorandum
ANT. 1 exit, departure, outlet

entwine *v.* interlace, weave, entwist, wreathe together
ANT. disentwine, dissever

enumerate *v.* compute, reckon, calculate, number, tell, cite, estimate, specify, detail

enunciate *v.* **1** announce, proclaim, declare, state, affirm, propound, relate, utter, publish **2** pronounce, articulate

envelop *v.* wrap, surround, enclose, contain, encircle, fold, encompass, cover, hide
ANT. expose, unwrap

envenom *v.* **1** poison, taint, vitiate, infect, pollute **2** embitter, enrage, provoke, exasperate, irritate, madden, inflame
ANT. **1** purify, disinfect **2** delight, please, gratify

envious *adj.* jealous, suspicious, grudging, resentful, covetous
ANT. contented, satisfied

environment *n.* surroundings, milieu, habitat, setting, ambience

envisage *v.* foresee, expect, contemplate, imagine, conceive, anticipate

envoy *n.* messenger, ambassador, minister, legate

envy *n.* malice, ill will, jealousy, hate, spite, hatred, grudging, covetousness, discontentment, chagrin
ANT. goodwill, regard, esteem

ephemeral *adj.* transient, momentary, transitory, fleeting, fugitive, brief, evanescent
ANT. permanent, immortal, eternal, lasting, enduring

epic *n.* saga, story, legend, narrative

epigrammatic *adj.* pointed, terse, laconic, concise, succinct
ANT. wordy, lengthy, diffuse, copious, verbose

episode *n.* incident, event, occurrence, occasion

epitome *n.* **1** personification, embodiment, archetype, representation **2** summary, compendium, abstract, curtailment, reduction
ANT. **2** expansion, extension, amplification

equable *adj.* even, uniform, steady, regular, proportionate, smooth, easy, invariable
ANT. variable, fitful, irregular, disjointed

equal *adj.* **1** like, equivalent, identical, same **2** uniform, regular, even, steady **3** proportionate, commensurate, equivalent, tantamount **4** competent, fit, adequate, sufficient
ANT. **1** dissimilar **2** irregular, unsteady **3** incommensurate, disproportionate **4** incompetent, inadequate

equal *v.* match, correspond, amount to, come up to

equal *n.* match, counterpart, equivalent, opposite number, partner, fellow, mate

equality *n.* likeness, uniformity, sameness, entity, evenness, equableness
ANT. dissimilarity, difference

equanimity *n.* composure, calmness, tranquillity, steadiness, serenity
ANT. impatience, restlessness, disquiet

equip *v.* provide, furnish, fit (out), supply, dress, array, arm, garnish, arrange, invest, clothe
ANT. divest

equipment *n.* material(s), tackle, apparatus, furniture, furnishings, gear, outfit, dress, rigging, trappings, provisions, arms, supplies

equitable *adj.* just, impartial, unbiased, unprejudiced, reasonable, fair, right, proper, honest, upright, even-handed
ANT. unfair, unjust, unreasonable, prejudiced, biased

equity *n.* justice, right, uprightness, fairness, impartiality, fair play, honesty, integrity, rectitude
ANT. injustice, corruption, dishonesty, partiality, unfairness, prejudice

equivalent *adj.* equal, tantamount, commensurate, synonymous, interchangeable
ANT. unequal, incommensurate, uneven, unbalanced

equivalent *n.* counterpart, equal, match, opposite number, partner

equivocal *adj.* ambiguous, indefinite, dubious, uncertain, doubtful, questionable, perplexing, indeterminate, indistinct, suspicious
ANT. clear, plain, direct, obvious, unquestionable, unambiguous, certain, indisputable

equivocate *v.* prevaricate, evade, fudge, fence, dodge, beat about the bush (*informal*)

era *n.* epoch, time, age, period

eradicate *v.* obliterate, abolish, extinguish, exterminate, extirpate, uproot, destroy
ANT. encourage, propagate

erase *v.* rub out, efface, expunge, cancel, obliterate, blot out, scratch out
ANT. imprint, engrave

erect *adj.* upright, straight, vertical, standing, elevated
ANT. leaning, lying

erect *v.* build, construct, raise, uplift, put upright, set up
ANT. lower

erode *v.* wear down, eat away, corrode, consume, devour, destroy
ANT. build up

err *v.* 1 deviate, wander, ramble, rove 2 mistake, misjudge, blunder, stray, stumble, go astray 3 sin, fall, lapse, trip, offend, trespass
ANT. 2 succeed, prosper

errand *n.* message, mandate, commission, mission, charge, task, job, delegation

erratic *adj.* irregular, abnormal, eccentric, variable, unpredictable, desultory, aberrant, flighty, changeful, capricious
ANT. undeviating, steady, regular, normal

erring *adj.* fallible, wandering, misguided, misled, sinful
ANT. good, upright

erroneous *adj.* wrong, mistaken, incorrect, inaccurate, untrue, false
ANT. right, correct, accurate, true

error *n.* blunder, mistake, misapprehension, oversight, inaccuracy, fault, offence, transgression, sin, iniquity, trespass, delinquency, misdeed, shortcoming, wrongdoing, deception, fallacy, untruth, falsity, hallucination
ANT. truth, correctness, accuracy, soundness, exactness, verification

erudite *adj.* learned, knowledgeable, academic, scholarly
ANT. illiterate, ignorant, stupid

erudition *n.* knowledge, learning, scholarship, letters
ANT. illiteracy, ignorance, stupidity

erupt *v.* eject, break out, emit, discharge, emit, burst forth

eruption *n.* explosion, outbreak, outburst, ejection, discharge
ANT. absorption

escalate *v.* increase, intensify, grow, step up
ANT. diminish

escape *v.* 1 run away, get away, flee, fly, abscond 2 avoid, shun, evade, flee from, elude
ANT. 2 meet, confront, encounter

escape *n.* flight, release, departure, breakout

escort *n.* partner, companion, chaperone, bodyguard, guide, protector, convoy

escort *v.* accompany, guide, lead, usher, conduct

esoteric *adj.* private, secret, inner, inmost, profound, abstruse

especially *adv.* particularly, very, chiefly, unusually, notably

essay *n.* composition, dissertation, thesis, paper

essence *n.* nature, quintessence, substance, element, core, basis, nature, vital part

essential *adj.* vital, important, necessary, critical, indispensable, requisite
ANT. dispensable, redundant, superfluous

essential *n.* necessity, requisite, requirement, vital part, must (*informal*)

establish *v.* institute, originate, constitute, found, fix, settle, make steadfast, plant, organize, form, place, secure, set up, confirm, sanction, ratify, approve, verify, prove, substantiate
ANT. unsettle, supplant, uproot, break up

estate *n.* property, land, possessions, effects, assets, domain, freehold, demesne

esteem *n.* favour, favor (*N. Am.*), regard, respect, estimation, honour, honor (*N. Am.*), admiration, consideration
ANT. hatred, dislike, contempt

esteem *v.* revere, honour, honor (*N. Am.*), respect, admire, venerate, love, like, hold, consider, regard, prize, value, think, appreciate, calculate, believe, affect
ANT. disregard, hate, dislike

estimable *adj.* worthy, admirable, respected, excellent, good, deserving, lovable, praiseworthy, meritorious
ANT. unworthy, undeserving

estimate *v.* evaluate, gauge, value, reckon, assess

estimate *n.* reckoning, value, evaluation, assessment, judgment, guesstimate (*informal*)

eternal *adj.* immortal, perpetual, unceasing, timeless, undying, unending, unfading, perennial, unfailing, imperishable, endless, everlasting, ever-living, interminable, never-ending, never-fading
ANT. ephemeral, transient, fleeting, temporary, transitory

etiquette *n.* manners, good manners, breeding, fashion, decorum, conventionality, social graces, propriety
ANT. rudeness

euphonious *adj.* clear, musical, sweet-toned, melodious, harmonious, mellow, euphonic, mellifluous
ANT. harsh, discordant, dissonant

evacuate *v.* **1** leave, forsake, desert, abandon, withdraw from, relinquish, quit (*informal*) **2** empty, expel, excrete, throw out, discharge, void
ANT. **1** seize, occupy **2** fill

evade *v.* avoid, elude, escape, get away from, steer clear of, dodge (*informal*)

evaporate *v.* vaporize, disappear, vanish, melt, liquefy, dissolve, distil
ANT. solidify, crystallize, harden

evasion *n.* shift, quibble, fencing, prevarication, equivocation, quibbling, subterfuge, shuffling
ANT. straightforwardness

evasive *adj.* equivocating, deceitful, devious, slippery (*informal*)
ANT. straightforward

even *adj.* **1** smooth, level, flat, plane **2** equal, uniform, calm, steady, unruffled, balanced, well-balanced **3** fair, just, equitable
ANT. **1** irregular, bumpy **2** unequal **3** unfair, unjust

evening *n.* dusk, nightfall, twilight, sundown
ANT. morning, dawn, sunrise

event *n.* accident, adventure, circumstance, chance, happening, occurrence, incident, result, possibility, sequel, outcome, fact, episode, end, contingency, case, issue, consequence

eventful *adj.* stirring, memorable, momentous, important, signal, remarkable, marked, noted, notable
ANT. ordinary, uninteresting, characterless, trivial

eventual *adj.* consequent, ultimate, final
ANT. present, current

eventually *adv.* ultimately, finally, later, later on

ever *adv.* **1** always, perpetually, continually, evermore, eternally, for ever, forever (*N. Am.*), at all times, constantly, incessantly **2** at any time, at all
ANT. **1, 2** never

everlasting *adj.* endless, unending, perpetual, incessant, ceaseless, continual, uninterrupted, unceasing, interminable, eternal, constant, never-ending, never-ceasing, imperishable, undying, never-dying, deathless, immortal, ever-living
ANT. ephemeral, transient, transitory

every *v.* all, any, both, either, each
ANT. none, no one, not any one

evict *v.* expel, dismiss, remove, dispossess, eject, throw out
ANT. reinstate, admit

evidence *n.* testimony, ground(s), witness, proof, declaration, appearance, sign, token, indication, exemplification, illustration, manifestation
ANT. conjecture, disproof, concealment

evident *adj.* clear, transparent, visible, perceptible, obvious, open, conspicuous, distinct, discernible, indubitable, overt, plain, unmistakable, indisputable, incontrovertible, patent, palpable, manifest
ANT. doubtful, uncertain, questionable, dubious, hidden, concealed, secret, obscure, unseen, unimagined, unknown

evil *adj*. ill, wrong, bad, hurtful, unhappy, adverse, harmful, wicked, mischievous, sinful, corrupt, unfair, notorious, miserable, sorrowful
ANT. wholesome, right, virtuous, pure, good

evince *v*. prove, show, exhibit, manifest, demonstrate, establish, indicate, display
ANT. suppress, disprove, conceal

evoke *v*. summon, call forth, excite, arouse, elicit, rouse, provoke, produce
ANT. stop, silence, prevent

exact *adj*. precise, accurate, correct, strict, nice
ANT. inaccurate, inexact, loose

exactly *adv*. precisely, accurately, strictly, nicely
ANT. loosely, inaccurately, incorrectly

exaggerate *v*. overstate, strain, stretch, amplify, enlarge, magnify, heighten
ANT. understate, minimize, mitigate, qualify, soften, modify

examination *n*. inspection, investigation, test, scrutiny, study, inquiry, discussion, exploration

examine *v*. inspect, observe, investigate, scrutinize, consider, study, test, inquire into, search into, look into, weigh, ponder, discuss, explore
ANT. conjecture, guess

example *n*. instance, model, pattern, ideal, archetype, exemplar, standard, sample, specimen, type, warning, illustration, copy, exemplification, prototype

exasperate *v*. anger, annoy, infuriate, disturb, bother, provoke, madden, aggravate (*informal*)

excavate *v*. hollow, dig, scoop out, cut, trench, disinter
ANT. inter, inhume, bury, fill, level

exceed *v*. beat, outdo, surpass, excel, outstrip, transcend

excel *v*. surpass, outshine, beat, eclipse, top

excellent *adj*. very good, fine, splendid, marvellous, wonderful, superlative
ANT. terrible, awful, bad

except *prep*. excepting, without, saving, exclusive of

except *v*. exclude, leave out, omit, bar
ANT. include, reckon, count

exception *n*. exclusion, omission, rejection
ANT. inclusion

exceptionable *adj*. undesirable, objectionable, offensive
ANT. unobjectionable, desirable, exemplary

exceptional *adj*. irregular, rare, unusual, uncommon, unnatural, different, strange, peculiar, anomalous, abnormal, aberrant
ANT. common, usual, normal, ordinary, regular, unexceptional

excess *n*. surplus, waste, extravagance, wastefulness, superfluity, lavishness, exorbitance, superabundance, dissipation, profusion, prodigality, redundancy
ANT. deficiency, defect, want, lack, need, poverty

excess *adj*. surplus, superfluous, lavish, exorbitant, profuse, extravagant

excessive *adj*. immoderate, intemperate, extreme, exorbitant, overmuch, inordinate, unreasonable, extravagant, superabundant, disproportionate, undue, exuberant, superfluous
ANT. insufficient, scant, inadequate, lacking, wanting, deficient

exchange *v*. swap, transfer, trade, barter, interchange

exchange *n*. trade, barter, transfer, interchange, substitution, replacement

excitability *n*. sensibility, sensitiveness, irritability, irascibility, passionateness
ANT. composure, insensitiveness, imperturbability

excite *v*. stir, stir up, rouse, arouse, stimulate, animate, provoke, inspire
ANT. calm, compose

excited *adj*. stirred, inspired, animated, agitated, disturbed, distracted
ANT. calm, composed

excitement *n*. enthusiasm, animation, stimulation, exhilaration, restlessness
ANT. calmness

exciting *adj*. stirring, inspiring, interesting, intriguing, stimulating, rousing, provocative, disturbing
ANT. boring, dull

exclaim v. shout, cry, yell, call

exclamation n. cry, shout, call, yell, outcry

exclude v. keep out, shut out, prohibit, leave out, rule out, ignore, ban, bar, expel
ANT. include, retain, keep, allow

exclusion n. prohibition, omission, ban, bar, expulsion, rejection
ANT. inclusion, admission

exclusive adj. 1 select, choice, fashionable, elegant 2 restricted, limited, narrow, undivided, full
ANT. 1 common 2 shared

excommunicate v. dismiss, exclude, banish, bar, eject, blackball, expel, denounce, proscribe, anathematize
ANT. admit

excruciating adj. agonizing, painful, intense, acute, severe, unbearable
ANT. soothing

exculpate v. acquit, clear, set right, vindicate, absolve, exonerate, defend, release
ANT. charge

excursion n. trip, ramble, tour, journey, expedition, jaunt

excuse v. pardon, forgive, absolve, acquit, exonerate, exculpate, extenuate, justify, free, exempt, release, let off, overlook, condone, remit, vindicate, defend, mitigate
ANT. charge, accuse, condemn, inculpate, convict, sentence

excuse n. reason, explanation, plea, apology, justification, grounds, pretext

execrable adj. detestable, cursed, loathsome, accursed, hateful, abominable, damnable, diabolical, odious, abhorrent, vile, offensive, disgusting, nauseous, obnoxious, repulsive, revolting
ANT. desirable, respectable

execration n. curse, detestation, abhorrence, horror, loathing, abomination, denunciation, malediction, ban, anathema, imprecation
ANT. benediction, blessing

execute v. 1 perform, enforce, carry out, do, complete, achieve, administer 2 kill, put to death, behead, hang

executive n. manager, administrator, supervisor, official, leader, director

executive adj. administrative, managing, governing

exemplary adj. praiseworthy, excellent, correct, estimable, worthy, virtuous, laudable

exemplify v. illustrate, show, demonstrate, embody, exhibit, represent, manifest
ANT. misrepresent, falsify

exempt v. relieve, set free, release, grant immunity to, excuse, exonerate, except
ANT. subject, render liable, bind, oblige

exempt adj. free, excused, liberated, clear, absolved, privileged, unamenable
ANT. liable, subject, responsible

exemption n. immunity, privilege, exception, release, freedom from liability
ANT. liability, subjection, obligation

exercise n. application, use, drill, employment, exertion, practice, training, occupation, performance, operation, act, activity, action
ANT. inaction, idleness, inactivity

exercise v. apply, use, employ, utilize, act, operate, perform, train, drill, practise, practice (N. Am.)

exertion n. use, exercise, effort, endeavour, endeavor (N. Am.), struggle, trial, attempt, stretch, strain, labour, labor (N. Am.), toil
ANT. relaxation, rest, recreation

exhalation n. breath, expiration, emission, evaporation, vapour, vapor (N. Am.), fume, steam, smoke, fog, mist, damp
ANT. inhalation, absorption

exhale v. emit, breathe out, give out, evaporate, vaporize
ANT. breathe in, inhale

exhaust v. 1 wear out, weary, tire, fatigue, cripple, weaken, debilitate, enervate, disable 2 drain, empty, expend, spend, waste, consume, squander, lavish, destroy
ANT. 1 refresh, invigorate 2 fill, replenish

exhibit v. 1 show, display, demonstrate, illustrate, manifest, express, disclose, indicate, make known, offer, present, propose, betray, reveal
ANT. conceal, mask, hide, suppress

exhibition *n.* display, show, presentation, performance, sight, representation, pageant, manifestation

exhilarate *v.* cheer, enliven, inspire, stimulate, animate, rejoice, delight, please, elate, gladden
ANT. depress, unnerve, dispirit

exhort *v.* urge, stimulate, persuade, incite, encourage, advise, counsel, enjoin
ANT. dissuade, warn

exigency *n.* demand, urgency, need, necessity, requirement, want, pressure, crisis, emergency, juncture, quandary

exile *n.* banishment, separation, isolation, expulsion, expatriation, ostracism, proscription
ANT. welcome, return

exile *v.* banish, expatriate, ostracize, expel, proscribe, relegate
ANT. welcome, reinstate

exist *v.* be, live, breathe, last, continue, survive, endure

existence *n.* being, continuation, duration, life, animation, entity, essence, creature, thing, subsistence
ANT. nonentity, non-existence

exit *n.* way out, door, doorway, gate, outlet
ANT. entrance, way in

expand *v.* spread out, dilate, enlarge, stretch, open, swell, diffuse, extend, increase, develop, unfold, amplify, distend
ANT. contract, curtail

expanse *n.* extent, stretch, area, reach, span, vast, void, space, breadth, expansion, firmament, sky, canopy, vault
ANT. limit, enclosure, confine, bound

expatiate *v.* range, enlarge, be copious, amplify
ANT. contract, summarize

expect *v.* look for, foresee, forecast, forebode, await, look for, anticipate, rely upon, count upon, reckon upon, calculate upon, look forward to

expectation *n.* anticipation, expectancy, prospect, reliance, confidence, assurance, trust, hope, presumption

expedient *adj.* advantageous, profitable, useful, fit, proper, suitable, desirable, advisable
ANT. disadvantageous, inexpedient

expedition *n.* trip, excursion, voyage, trek, march

expel *v.* drive out, drive away, send away, eject, banish, oust, discharge

expend *v.* use, exert, consume, spend, employ, waste, exhaust
ANT. conserve

expense *n.* cost, price, charge, payment, expenditure, outgoings, outlay
ANT. income, gain, proceeds

expensive *adj.* dear, costly, high-priced, valuable, rich, lavish, wasteful, extravagant
ANT. cheap, inexpensive

experience *n.* **1** wisdom, judgment, skill, knowledge, understanding, discernment **2** event, incident, episode, adventure, encounter

experience *v.* feel, undergo, go through, endure, suffer, be subject to, encounter

experienced *adj.* practised, practiced (*N. Am.*), versed, accomplished, able, qualified, familiar, skilled, accustomed, conversant, instructed
ANT. inexperienced, untutored

experiment *n.* trial, test, examination, proof, research, observation, investigation, experimentation, illustration, exemplification

experiment *v.* test, try, prove, examine, research, observe, investigate

expert *n.* authority, specialist, professional, master, dab hand (*informal*), ace (*informal*)
ANT. novice

expert *adj.* knowledgeable, experienced, skilled, proficient
ANT. inexperienced, unskilled

expire *v.* **1** finish, end, stop, run out, cease, terminate **2** die, perish, pass away

explain *v.* **1** interpret, unfold, clarify, define, make sense of, make plain, elucidate, expound **2** account for, give the reasons for, solve, warrant, justify

explanation *n.* 1 interpretation, exposition, illustration, description, sense, explication, elucidation, solution 2 warrant, justification, account, key

explicit *adj.* express, expressed, stated, clear, plain, definite, positive, unambiguous, unreserved, categorical, determinate, detailed, unobscure
ANT. implicit, implied, ambiguous, doubtful, indefinite, uncertain, vague

explode *v.* blow up, go off, set off, burst, detonate, go bang, blast, fire, discharge

exploit *n.* achievement, accomplishment, feat

explore *v.* examine, investigate, study, inspect, analyse, analyze (*N. Am.*), probe

explosion *n.* blast, bang, boom, detonation, discharge, firing

exponent *n.* example, type, representative, illustration, specimen, indication

export *v.* send abroad, sell abroad, ship, produce
ANT. import

expose *v.* bare, reveal, uncover, disclose, show, display, divulge, exhibit
ANT. hide, conceal, cover

exposed *adj.* unprotected, defenceless, defenseless (*N. Am.*), unguarded, endangered
ANT. protected, guarded, defended

express *v.* state, speak, utter, declare, assert, represent, indicate, show, signify, exhibit, denote, intimate
ANT. conceal, suppress, repress

express *adj.* 1 quick, rapid, fast, swift, non-stop 2 explicit, clear, definite, plain, positive, categorical, exact, accurate, faithful, true, close, precise, special, particular, specific, pointed, direct
ANT. 1 slow 2 general, vague, inaccurate, inexact, approximate

expression *n.* 1 assertion, statement, utterance, declaration, phrase, term 2 air, tone, look, representation, feeling, indication

expunge *v.* blot out, delete, erase, efface, obliterate, cancel

exquisite *adj.* fine, nice, accurate, delicate, discriminating, exact, refined, dainty, precious, valuable, select, choice, rare, excellent, perfect, complete, matchless, consummate
ANT. ordinary

extemporaneous *adj.* improvised, off-hand, unpremeditated, extempore, impromptu
ANT. prepared, studied, rehearsed, recited, premeditated

extend *v.* 1 stretch, reach, spread 2 prolong, continue, lengthen, increase, expand, dilate, enlarge, widen, amplify, augment, protract, diffuse 3 impart, give, offer, yield
ANT. 2 contract, curtail, limit, reduce

extension *n.* stretching, lengthening, increase, enlargement, protraction, dilation

extensive *adj.* broad, wide, spacious, large, huge, vast, widespread
ANT. limited, confined, restricted

extent *n.* degree, range, amount, quantity, expanse, amplitude, extension, stretch, reach, compass, length, volume, bulk, magnitude, size, distance
ANT. limitation, diminution, restriction

extenuate *v.* lessen, diminish, reduce, mitigate, excuse, qualify, palliate
ANT. enhance, heighten

exterior *adj.* outside, outward, external, outer, superficial
ANT. inner, internal, inward

exterior *n.* outside, surface, face, appearance, covering

exterminate *v.* wipe out, remove, destroy, eradicate, abolish, overthrow, uproot, expel, banish, root out, extirpate, annihilate

extermination *n.* annihilation, eradication, abolition, destruction, extinction, excision, elimination, extirpation

external *adj.* outward, outer, exterior, outside, superficial
ANT. inner, internal, inside, inmost, hidden

extinction *n.* destruction, annihilation, extermination, abolition, stifling, death, suffocation, cessation, extirpation
ANT. birth, life, survival

extinguish v. put out, quench, destroy, suppress, put down, smother, choke, stifle

extort v. wring out, force, fleece (*informal*), squeeze out, extract, exact, wrest, wrench

extortionate adj. exorbitant, oppressive, exacting, severe, close-fisted, monstrous, preposterous, hard, harsh
ANT. moderate, reasonable

extra adj. additional, reserve, spare, supplementary

extra n. addition, supplement, reserve

extract n. selection, passage, quotation, excerpt, citation

extract v. draw, pull, take out, derive, determine, find, elicit, gather, collect, select, quote, cite
ANT. insert, incorporate

extraneous adj. foreign, unconnected, unrelated, extrinsic, inessential, superfluous
ANT. intrinsic, internal, vital

extraordinary adj. unusual, remarkable, wonderful, unprecedented, marvellous, prodigious, monstrous, preposterous, strange, uncommon, singular, signal, rare, extra
ANT. common, usual, frequent, ordinary, unremarkable, unimportant

extravagance n. excess, exorbitance, unreasonableness, preposterousness, wildness, absurdity, irregularity, prodigality, lavish expenditure, profusion, waste
ANT. carefulness, economy, frugality, saving, provision, prudence, foresight

extravagant adj. excessive, inordinate, unreasonable, preposterous, exorbitant, wild, foolish, absurd, irregular, lavish, profuse, wasteful, spendthrift, prodigal
ANT. economical, frugal, careful, regular, usual

extreme adj. **1** utmost, greatest, highest, last, final, ultimate, farthest, most remote, most distant, uttermost, outermost **2** extravagant, immoderate, excessive, unreasonable
ANT. **1** nearest **2** moderate

extremely adv. very, enormously, greatly, remarkably, exceptionally, excessively, unreasonably

extremity n. end, verge, termination, edge, border, extreme, utmost point
ANT. beginning, commencement, opening, origin

exude v. ooze, drip, percolate, secrete
ANT. absorb

exultant adj. exulting, jubilant, triumphant, elated, joyous, transported
ANT. sad, depressed, mournful, dispirited

exultation n. elation, joy, triumph, delight, transport, ecstasy
ANT. sadness, depression, mourning

fable *n.* **1** story, parable, myth, legend, allegory **2** falsehood, lie, fib, untruth, fabrication, forgery, fiction, invention, figment
ANT. **1** fact **2** truth

fabric *n.* **1** cloth, material, texture, stuff, weave **2** structure, building framework, organization, construction, constitution, make-up

fabricate *v.* **1** make, manufacture, build, frame, construct, assemble, form, produce, devise **2** falsify, misrepresent, forge, invent, coin, feign
ANT. **1** demolish, destroy

fabulous *adj.* fantastic, wonderful, amazing, astonishing, unbelievable, incredible

face *n.* **1** features, countenance, physiognomy, visage, mug (*informal*), phiz (*informal*) **2** expression, appearance, look, aspect, front, surface, façade, exterior, outside, veneer

face *v.* **1** be opposite, overlook, look onto, look out on **2** confront, face up to, deal with, meet, encounter, brave, oppose
ANT. **2** avoid, evade

facetious *adj.* witty, jocose, jocular, humorous, waggish, funny, comical, droll, playful, flippant
ANT. grave, serious

facile *adj.* **1** slick, glib, superficial, shallow **2** simple, easy, effortless, fluent, skilful, skillful (*N. Am.*), expert, adroit
ANT. **2** awkward

facility *n.* **1** easiness, ease, skill, quickness, adroitness, effortlessness, expertise, readiness, dexterity, ability, knack **2** amenity, appliance, convenience, means, advantage, resource, material, equipment
ANT. **1** awkwardness, difficulty

fact *n.* **1** detail, point, particular, factor, item, piece of information **2** reality, truth, certainty, actuality **3** event, occurrence, incident, circumstance, act, deed

faction *n.* group, splinter group, gang, party, clique, camp

factious *adj.* disagreeing, quarrelsome, rebellious, seditious, refractory, turbulent, recalcitrant

factitious *adj.* artificial, false, unnatural, affected, spurious
ANT. natural, unaffected, genuine

factor *n.* element, component, part, point, item, cause

factory *n.* works, plant, shop, mill, foundry

factual *adj.* true, real, genuine, actual, authentic
ANT. false, incorrect

faculty *n.* **1** ability, capability, gift, talent, skill, power **2** department, school

fad *n.* craze, rage, fashion, vogue

fade *v.* **1** pale, grow dim, blanch, bleach, discolour, discolor (*N. Am.*) **2** diminish, decline, languish, droop, decay, wither, vanish, disappear, pass away, fall, sink, dwindle
ANT. **1** flourish, bloom **2** rise, increase, grow

fail *v.* **1** go wrong, be unsuccessful, fall through, misfire, backfire, be frustrated, disappoint, flop (*informal*), fizzle out (*informal*), bomb (*informal*) **2** deteriorate, fade, dwindle, weaken, wane, ebb **3** go bankrupt, go under, crash (*informal*), go bust (*informal*), go broke (*informal*)
ANT. **1** succeed **2** grow

failure *n.* lack of success, defeat, breakdown, collapse, disappointment, disaster, fiasco, flop (*informal*), washout (*informal*)
ANT. success

faint *adj.* weak, feeble, dim, ill-defined, indistinct, exhausted, worn, listless, languid, wearied, fatigued, faint-hearted, faded, faltering, half-hearted, irresolute, purposeless, timid
ANT. strong, clear, prominent, marked, glaring

faint *v.* black out, keel over, collapse, pass out, lose consciousness, swoon

faint-hearted *adj.* cowardly, timid, fearful, chicken (*informal*), yellow (*informal*)
ANT. brave, bold, courageous

fair[1] *adj.* 1 just, reasonable, right, proper, equitable, impartial, lawful 2 moderate, average, reasonable, all right, satisfactory, adequate, OK (*informal*), passable, tolerable 3 light, blond, blonde, pale, fair-haired 4 clear, bright, fine, sunny, cloudless
ANT. 1 unfair, fraudulent 2 excellent, outstanding 3 dark, black 4 dull, cloudy, stormy

fair[2] *n.* show, exhibition, festival, carnival, bazaar, gala

fairy *n.* sprite, elf, pixie, brownie

faith *n.* 1 trust, assurance, belief, confidence, assent, credence, opinion, credit, reliance 2 belief, creed, doctrine
ANT. 1 distrust, disbelief, unbelief, dissent, doubt, scepticism, skepticism (*N. Am.*), suspicion

faithful *adj.* 1 firm, loyal, devoted, staunch, sure, true, trustworthy, trusty, unwavering 2 accurate, precise, close, consistent, exact, equivalent
ANT. 1 faithless, false, fickle, untrue, wavering, untrustworthy 2 inaccurate, inexact, imprecise

fake *adj.* false, counterfeit, bogus, fraudulent, phoney (*informal*)
ANT. genuine, real

fake *n.* counterfeit, imitation, fraud, sham, hoax

fake *v.* counterfeit, forge, pretend, put on, falsify

fall *v.* 1 drop, descend, go down, come down, plunge, plummet, sink 2 collapse, overbalance, stumble, tumble, trip

(over) 3 decrease, decline, diminish, sink, dwindle, slump 4 be defeated, be taken, surrender, yield, give in, submit 5 go astray, lapse, err, sin, transgress
ANT. 1 rise, go up 2 increase, rise

fall *n.* 1 drop, descent, collapse, tumble 2 decrease, drop, decline, slump
ANT. 2 increase

fallacy *n.* error, misconception, illusion, deception, deceit, delusion, mistake, misapprehension
ANT. truth, fact

fallible *adj.* erring, uncertain, imperfect, untrustworthy, ignorant, weak, frail
ANT. infallible, unerring, certain

fallow *adj.* uncultivated, unproductive, untilled, unsowed, neglected, idle, inert, inactive, dormant, quiescent
ANT. cultivated, tilled, productive, worked, sown

false *adj.* 1 untrue, wrong, inaccurate, incorrect, erroneous, mistaken, fictitious 2 deceitful, disloyal, unfaithful, dishonest, lying, treacherous, double-dealing, untrustworthy, insincere, two-faced, double-tongued, perfidious 3 counterfeit, fake, forged, imitation, mock, synthetic, artificial, ersatz, bogus, sham, simulated, phoney (*informal*)

falsehood *n.* story, falsity, lie, fabrication, untruth, fib, counterfeit, cheat, fallacy, error, forgery
ANT. truth, correctness, fact, genuineness, honesty, reality, authenticity

falsify *v.* misrepresent, counterfeit, misstate, mistake, misinterpret, betray, garble, disprove, violate
ANT. correct, check, certify, verify, rectify

falter *v.* hesitate, stumble, quiver, tremble, totter, waver, be undecided, halt, slip, flinch, vacillate, stutter, stammer
ANT. flow, run

fame *n.* renown, reputation, repute, name, honour, honor (*N. Am.*), glory, eminence, credit, celebrity, laurels, distinction

familiar *adj.* **1** well-known, recognizable, common, everyday, usual, customary, traditional, household **2** well-informed, well-versed, aware, conversant, knowledgeable, acquainted, at home **3** disrespectful, presumptuous, bold, forward, overfriendly
ANT. **1** unfamiliar, unknown **2** unaware, ignorant **3** respectful, formal, distant

familiarity *n.* awareness, knowledge, acquaintance, understanding, comprehension
ANT. ignorance

family *n.* **1** relatives, relations, household, flesh and blood, kin, kinsfolk, kindred, kith and kin **2** children, offspring, kids (*informal*), progeny **3** ancestors, forebears, parentage, lineage, forefathers, blood, pedigree, house, dynasty

famine *n.* hunger, starvation, scarcity, want, dearth
ANT. plenty

famished *adj.* starving, empty, hungry, ravenous, voracious

famous *adj.* well-known, celebrated, renowned, distinguished, remarkable, far-famed, eminent, noted, illustrious, glorious
ANT. unknown, obscure

fan *n.* supporter, enthusiast, admirer, fanatic, buff (*informal*), fiend

fanatic *n.* supporter, enthusiast, zealot, admirer, buff (*informal*), crank (*informal*)

fanaticism *n.* enthusiasm, frenzy, intolerance, bigotry
ANT. indifference

fanciful *adj.* capricious, fitful, erratic, whimsical, absurd, fantastic, grotesque, visionary, chimerical, unreal, imaginary, freakish
ANT. ordinary, usual, commonplace

fancy *n.* imagination, whim, vagary, caprice, belief, conception, desire, idea, thought, notion, image, inclination, mood, liking, supposition, predilection

fancy *adj.* ornate, decorative, ornamental, showy, elaborate
ANT. plain, simple

fancy *v.* like, desire, wish, want, desire

fantastic *adj.* **1** wonderful, marvellous, tremendous **2** unbelievable, incredible, imaginary, unreal
ANT. **1** poor **2** realistic

far *adj.* distant, removed, remote, faraway, far-flung, apart, separate, out of the way
ANT. near, close

farce *n.* comedy, humour, humor (*N. Am.*), burlesque, satire

farcical *adj.* comic, funny, nonsensical, droll, absurd, ridiculous, ludicrous
ANT. grave, serious, tragic, solemn

fare *n.* charge, rate, tariff, fee, ticket, cost, price

fare *v.* get along, do, happen, turn out, make out, feed

farewell *n.* adieu, goodbye. valedictory, leave-taking, departure, parting, congé
ANT. welcome, greeting

farm *n.* homestead, ranch, farmstead, grange, plantation, smallholding, croft

fascinate *v.* charm, enchant, delight, attract, bewitch
ANT. bore

fashion *n.* **1** style, mode, look, custom, trend, vogue, fad, **2** way, manner, method, usage, custom, style, mode, conventionality **3** form, shape, figure, cut, make, model, cast, pattern, appearance, configuration

fashion *v.* shape, form, mould, mold (*N. Am.*), make, design

fashionable *adj.* stylish, up to date, trendy, in fashion, in vogue, modish, snazzy (*informal*), swish (*informal*)

fast *adj.* quick, rapid, speedy, swift, brisk, hasty, hurried, expeditious, nippy (*informal*)
ANT. slow

fast *adv.* quickly, rapidly, swiftly, hurriedly, in haste, hastily
ANT. slowly

fasten *v.* attach, secure, bind, tie, fix, attach, join, unite, connect, hold together, hold compact, affix, annex
ANT. unfasten, detach, loosen, undo

fastidious *adj.* particular, punctilious, overnice, over-delicate, critical, dainty, squeamish, over-refined
ANT. uncritical

fat *adj.* **1** overweight, plump, obese, stout, podgy, chubby, portly, rotund, tubby, large, big, heavy, thick, broad, wide **2** greasy, fatty, oily, unctuous **3** rich, profitable, lucrative
ANT. **1** thin, lean, slender, emaciated

fatal *adj.* **1** deadly, mortal, lethal **2** disastrous, crucial, critical, destructive, calamitous, ruinous
ANT. **1** beneficial, revitalizing

fate *n.* destiny, chance, luck, lot, doom, inevitable necessity

father *n.* **1** parent, ancestor, forefather, progenitor, sire, dad (*informal*), daddy (*informal*), papa, pa (*informal*), old man (*informal*), pater **2** creator, originator, designer, founder

fathom *v.* **1** penetrate, reach, understand, comprehend **2** measure, probe, sound

fathomless *adj.* bottomless, profound, unfathomable, immeasurable
ANT. superficial, shallow

fatigue *n.* tiredness, weariness, exhaustion, hardship, toil, languor, enervation
ANT. freshness, vigour, vigor (*N. Am.*), indefatigability

fatigue *v.* weary, tire, harass, jade, exhaust
ANT. inspire, refresh, enliven, animate

fatten *v.* cram, stuff, bloat, swell
ANT. slim

fatuity *n.* folly, madness, absurdity, foolishness, imbecility, idiocy
ANT. sense, soundness

fatuous *adj.* foolish, absurd, silly, inane, idiotic, mad

fault *n.* **1** defect, blemish, imperfection, flaw, weakness, failing, frailty **2** misdeed, misdemeanour, misdemeanor (*N. Am.*), offence, offense (*N. Am.*), trespass, wrong, transgression, delinquency, indiscretion, slip, error, lapse, failure, omission, want, drawback

faultless *adj.* without blemish, perfect, flawless, unblemished, immaculate, complete, innocent, guileless, blameless, sinless, spotless, guiltless, stainless
ANT. imperfect, defective, faulty

faulty *adj.* defective, imperfect, broken, damaged
ANT. complete, perfect

favour, favor (*N. Am.*) *n.* **1** approval, liking, support, backing, kindness, friendliness, goodwill **2** good turn, good deed, kindness, courtesy
ANT. **1** disapproval, rejection

favour, favor (*N. Am.*) *v.* **1** prefer, choose, select, opt for, support, back, side with, incline to **2** facilitate, encourage, benefit, help, aid, assist, promote
ANT. **1** reject, disapprove of

favourable, favorable (*N. Am.*) *adj.* encouraging, promising, beneficial, advantageous, convenient, suitable, fit, conducive, contributing, kind, friendly, willing, auspicious, propitious
ANT. reluctant, unpropitious, unfavourable, unfavorable (*N. Am.*), impartial

favourite, favorite (*N. Am.*) *n.* preferred, chosen, beloved, best-liked, pet

favouritism, favoritism (*N. Am.*) *n.* partiality, invidiousness
ANT. impartiality

fawn *v.* **1** flatter, wheedle, cajole, cringe, slaver
ANT. insult, rebuke, reprimand

fear *n.* **1** panic, alarm, terror, horror, fright, dread, apprehension, trepidation, consternation **2** reverence, awe, wonder, honour, honor (*N. Am.*), respect
ANT. **1** courage, confidence, assurance, fearlessness, trust, boldness, fortitude **2** irreverence, disrespect, sacrilege, blasphemy

fear *v.* **1** be afraid of, dread, be frightened of, be scared by, be alarmed at, be anxious about, be apprehensive about **2** revere, stand in awe before, honour, honor (*N. Am.*), respect

fearful *adj.* **1** afraid, apprehensive, timid, nervous, timorous, fainthearted, cowardly **2** dreadful, terrible, awful, shocking, terrific, horrible, frightful, dire
ANT. **1** bold, confident, audacious **2** attractive, inviting

fearless *adj.* bold, brave, courageous, confident
ANT. fearful, timid, afraid, apprehensive

feasible *adj.* manageable, possible, likely, probable, practicable
ANT. impossible, impracticable

feast *n.* 1 banquet, regalement, entertainment, carousal, spread (*informal*) 2 festival, holiday 3 delight, enjoyment

feature *n.* 1 characteristic, aspect, quality, attribute, peculiarity, part, point, trait, mark, item, component, element 2 face, countenance, visage, physiognomy

feature *v.* emphasize, highlight, spotlight, point up, play up

federation *n.* confederation, union, league, alliance, coalition, confederacy, combination
ANT. secession, disunion

fee *n.* pay, payment, reward, recompense, compensation, remuneration

feeble *adj.* weak, faint, imperfect, dim, wretched, poor, enfeebled, incomplete, fruitless, enervated, debilitated, infirm, languid, sickly, languishing, declining, frail, drooping
ANT. strong, powerful, intense, forceful, forcible

feed *v.* give food to, nourish, nurture, provide for, suckle

feed *n.* fodder, forage, food

feel *v.* 1 touch, handle, manipulate, grasp, grip, finger, stroke, caress, fondle 2 sense, experience, be aware of, be conscious of, perceive, detect, discern 3 think, believe, consider, suppose, be of the opinion that, judge

feeling *n.* emotion, experience, perception, sense, awareness, sensation, impression, idea, opinion, belief, thought, attitude, sentiment

feign *v.* pretend, counterfeit, affect, assume, simulate, invent, imagine, forge, fabricate

felicitous *adj.* fit, appropriate, apt, pertinent, opportune, well-timed, timely, happy, ingenious
ANT. unhappy, unfortunate, inauspicious, untimely, inopportune

felicity *n.* happiness, joy, delight, bliss, blessedness
ANT. bad luck, misfortune, sorrow, unhappiness, sadness

fell *v.* cut down, hew down, demolish, waste, bare, prostrate, level, bring to the ground, hurl down, knock down
ANT. raise, plant, erect, support

fellow *n.* 1 partner, friend, colleague, member, associate, companion, comrade, equal, peer, compeer, mate, match, counterpart, adherent 2 man, chap, boy, person

fellowship *n.* companionship, familiarity, intimacy, acquaintance, participation, partnership, communion, sociability, affability, association, company, membership, society

felon *n.* offender, criminal, convict, culprit, wrongdoer

feminine *adj.* female, womanly, ladylike, girlish

fen *n.* marsh, swamp, bog, moor, morass, quagmire

fence *n.* barrier, hedge, wall, railing, barricade, paling

fence *v.* surround, enclose, shut in, encircle, protect, defend, guard

ferment *v.* 1 excite, agitate, rouse, stir up, inflame, provoke 2 seethe, concoct, brew, heat, warm, effervesce, foam, froth, rankle, fester
ANT. 1 dampen, cool, dissipate, subside, evaporate, disperse

ferment *n.* 1 yeast, leaven, fermentation 2 agitation, commotion, tumult, excitement

ferocious *adj.* savage, fierce, wild, vicious, brutal, cruel, bloodthirsty
ANT. gentle, harmless

fertile *adj.* fruitful, productive, rich, plenteous, exuberant, teeming, luxuriant, prolific, fecund
ANT. unproductive, fruitless, poor, sterile, barren

fervent *adj.* ardent, passionate, zealous, eager, keen, earnest
ANT. apathetic, indifferent

festival *n.* celebration, carnival, gala, fair, fête

festive *adj*. happy, convivial, joyful, joyous, gay, merry
ANT. sad

fetch *v*. go and get, go for, bring, bring back, get, retrieve

fetching *adj*. attractive, charming, enchanting, alluring, fascinating
ANT. unattractive, repulsive, ugly

fetid *adj*. stinking, foul, strong-smelling, offensive, rank, rancid, malodorous, mephitic, noisome
ANT. fresh, perfumed, scented, balmy

fetter *n*. chain, manacle, iron, shackle, imprisonment, bond, handcuff, bondage, custody, duress

fetter *v*. chain, bind, tie, confine, restrain, encumber, manacle, hinder, impede, shackle, hamper, trammel
ANT. free, liberate

feud *n*. contest, dispute, enmity, hostility, quarrel, argument, strife, dissension, affray, animosity, bitterness, contention, brawl, fray
ANT. friendliness, sympathy, reconciliation

fever *n*. 1 disease, sickness, illness, high temperature 2 heat, flush, excitement, agitation, ferment

few *pron*. a small/low number of, not many, not too many, scarcely any, hardly any

fiasco *n*. disaster, catastrophe, calamity, failure
ANT. success

fibre, fiber (*N. Am.*) *n*. 1 thread, strand, pile, filament 2 strength, toughness, stamina, endurance
ANT. 2 laxity, flabbiness

fickle *adj*. wavering, unsteady, unstable, inconstant, variable, vacillating, volatile, mercurial, fitful, changeable, irresolute, unsettled, restless, shifting, capricious, fanciful, unreliable, mutable
ANT. steady, reliable, well-regulated, uniform

fiction *n*. novel, romance, story, tale, fable, falsehood, myth, invention, fabrication, legend, allegory, apologue
ANT. fact

fictitious *adj*. feigned, imaginary, invented, unreal, fanciful, false, counterfeit, spurious
ANT. real, true, historical, genuine, authentic

fidelity *n*. 1 faithfulness, devotion, loyalty, true-heartedness, honesty, allegiance, integrity, adherence 2 accuracy, closeness, exactness, truthfulness, precision
ANT. 1 disloyalty, treachery 2 inaccuracy, inexactness

field *n*. 1 pasture, green, meadow, paddock, ground, pitch, playing field, tract 2 range, scope, province, department, region, realm, domain, ground, arena, room, opportunity

fierce *adj*. 1 violent, cruel, savage, wild, ferocious, vicious, dangerous, barbarous 2 intense, powerful, strong, uncontrollable, wild, passionate, ardent, fervent, earnest
ANT. 1 gentle, peaceful 2 weak, feeble

fiery *adj*. 1 hot, ardent, heated, flaming, glowing 2 impetuous, vehement, fierce, passionate, impassioned, excited, hot-blooded, irritable, irascible, choleric
ANT. 1 cold, icy, frigid, chilly 2 passionless, unimpassioned, mild, tame

fight *n*. combat, conflict, contest, battle, struggle, engagement, encounter, action, affair, fray, affray, brush, broil, riot, resistance, contention, campaign

fight *v*. battle, struggle, strive, wage war, oppose, resist, defy, attack, wrestle, brawl, spar, scrap (*informal*)

figurative *adj*. metaphorical, tropical, symbolic, allegorical, typical, representative, emblematical
ANT. literal

figure *n*. 1 number, numeral, digit, character, symbol, cipher 2 form, shape, configuration, conformation, outline, image, likeness, appearance, representation, effigy 3 pattern, diagram, drawing, picture, illustration

figure *v*. 1 represent, signify, typify, symbolize 2 imagine, conceive, picture 3 calculate, work out, compute, cipher 4 adorn, decorate

file¹ *n.* **1** row, line, column, rank **2** folder, envelope, document holder, portfolio

file¹ *v.* arrange, classify, record, register

file² *v.* rasp, scrape, grind, smooth, finish, polish, perfect, refine, improve
ANT. roughen

fill *v.* **1** fill up, pack, squeeze, cram, stuff, crowd, satiate, glut, swell, sate **2** block, stop, close, plug, cork, bung **3** occupy, hold, perform, do, carry out, fulfil, discharge
ANT. 1 empty, exhaust, drain

fill out fill in, complete, answer

film *n.* **1** movie, motion picture, picture, video, flick (*informal*) **2** coat, coating, covering, layer, sheet, skin, membrane

filter *v.* strain, ooze, percolate, exude, refine, distil, leak, purify, cleanse

filth *n.* **1** dirt, uncleanness, impurity, foulness, pollution **2** obscenity, pornography, grossness, indecency, smut

filthy *adj.* **1** dirty, nasty, foul, defiled, unclean, squalid, impure, corrupt, gross, insanitary, unwholesome **2** obscene, pornographic, indecent, vulgar, lewd, smutty
ANT. 1 clean, pure, sanitary, wholesome

final *adj.* **1** last, ultimate, closing, finishing, terminal, terminating, conclusive, eventual **2** decisive, definitive, conclusive, irrevocable, unalterable
ANT. 1 first

finally *adv.* eventually, lastly, at last, in the end, ultimately

financial *adj.* monetary, economic, fiscal, pecuniary

find *v.* **1** discover, locate, track down, come across, meet, encounter, see, learn, notice, detect, realize, discern, catch, obtain, get, acquire **2** provide, supply, furnish

find out discover, learn, detect, realize, perceive, discern, uncover, unmask

fine *adj.* **1** excellent, supreme, great, very good, marvellous, brilliant, outstanding, splendid, superior **2** thin, delicate, filmy, slender, attenuated, dainty, small,
little, slight **3** bright, clear, dry, fair, sunny, cloudless
ANT. 1 poor, inferior **2** thick, wide, coarse **3** dull, cloudy

fine *n.* penalty, punishment, forfeit

finery *n.* trinkets, ornaments, trimmings, decorations, trappings, tinsel, trash, dressiness

finicky *adj.* fastidious, dainty, over-particular, hard-to-please, choosy (*informal*), overnice, affected, elegant

finish *v.* end, terminate, close, stop, cease, conclude, put an end to, accomplish, execute, discharge, complete, perform, achieve, do, get done, round off
ANT. start, begin, commence

finish *n.* **1** end, ending, close, conclusion, completion, termination **2** surface, gloss, polish, varnish, coating, appearance
ANT. 1 beginning, start, commencement

finite *adj.* bounded, limited, contracted, restricted, terminated
ANT. infinite, unlimited, unbounded

fire *n.* **1** blaze, burning, conflagration, flame, combustion, heat **2** passion, violence, force, impetuosity, fervency, intensity, animation, spirit, enthusiasm, light, radiance, inspiration

firm *n.* business, company, corporation, partnership, concern, establishment

firm *adj.* **1** hard, solid, stiff, inflexible, set, unyielding **2** secure, steady, stable, fixed, immovable, anchored, rooted **3** decisive, determined, fixed, adamant, staunch, steadfast, inflexible, unyielding, unwavering
ANT. 1 soft, flexible **2** unstable, unsteady **3** indecisive, hesitant, wavering

first *adj.* **1** earliest, original, fundamental, basic, elementary, primitive **2** leading, chief, principal, main, head, highest, key, prime
ANT. 1 last, final, complex **2** lowest, unimportant, least important

first *adv.* in the first place, to begin with, at the outset, in the beginning, first and foremost

fit *adj.* **1** suitable, appropriate, apt, apposite, meet, seemly, becoming, befitting, proper, good, decent, convenient, fitting, decorous, adapted, congruous, adequate, calculated, ripe, right, contrived **2** ready, prepared, qualified, suited, competent, fitted **3** healthy, well, sound, strong, sturdy **ANT. 1** inappropriate, unsuitable **2** unprepared, ineligible, unqualified **3** ill, unfit

fit *v.* **1** be comfortable for, suit, go, belong, match, harmonize **2** provide, equip, supply, furnish, rig

fit *n.* convulsion, spasm, attack, seizure, spell, bout

fitful *adj.* variable, irregular, impulsive, spasmodic, unstable, fickle, whimsical, fanciful, capricious, restless, inconstant **ANT.** regular, equable, orderly, systematic, calculable

fitting *adj.* suitable, appropriate, apt, apposite, befitting **ANT.** unsuitable, inappropriate

fix *v.* **1** attach, tie, connect, set, place, establish, plant, fasten, secure, make firm, rivet **2** mend, repair, patch, restore **3** determine, define, appoint, limit, settle, establish, arrange **ANT. 1** displace, unsettle, remove, disarrange, uproot

flabbergasted *adj.* astonished, amazed, astounded, dumbfounded, staggered, stunned

flabby *adj.* weak, loose, limp, drooping, floppy, soft, yielding **ANT.** firm

flaccid *adj.* lax, drooping, flabby, soft, limp, yielding **ANT.** firm, strong, powerful

flag *n.* banner, colours, colors (*N. Am.*), standard, pennon, pennant, ensign, streamer, gonfalon

flag *v.* **1** hang loose, droop, languish, faint, decline, pine, sink, succumb, grow weak, become dejected **2** pall, grow stale, lose interest, weary, tire, give in **ANT. 1** freshen, flourish **2** persevere, hold, brace up, persist

flagrant *adj.* blatant, glaring, shocking, outrageous, scandalous

flake *n.* layer, slice, shaving, chip, wafer

flame *n.* blaze, fire, combustion, light

flap *v.* flutter, swing, wave, fly

flare *n.* flash, blaze, gleam, glare, sparkle

flash *n.* **1** flame, flare, beam, ray, gleam, spark **2** moment, instant, second, split second, twinkling

flash *v.* flare, blaze, beam, gleam, glare, sparkle

flat[1] *adj.* **1** level, horizontal, even, plane, smooth, low, prostrate, laid low **2** dull, uninteresting, pointless, boring, monotonous, lifeless, spiritless, unanimated, tame, prosaic **ANT. 1** uneven, rough, vertical **2** exciting, interesting, thrilling, sensational, melodramatic

flat[2] *n.* apartment, rooms, penthouse

flatter *v.* praise, compliment, adulate, wheedle **ANT.** insult

flaunt *v.* display, vaunt, flourish, boast, flutter, parade, wave ostentatiously **ANT.** hide, conceal, suppress

flavour, flavor (*N. Am.*) *n.* **1** taste, savour, savor (*N. Am.*), relish, tang, zest, aroma, smack, gusto **2** essence, quality, character, characteristic, spirit, soul **ANT. 1** insipidity, tastelessness, flatness

flavour, flavor (*N. Am.*) *v.* spice, season

flaw *n.* blemish, defect, imperfection, fault, spot

flee *v.* run away, fly, escape, decamp, scarper (*informal*)

fleeting *adj.* brief, passing, temporary, ephemeral, swift **ANT.** permanent, lasting, durable

flesh *n.* meat, body, tissue, fat

flexible *adj.* **1** elastic, pliable, pliant, supple **2** yielding, agreeable, easy, affable, tractable, compliant, docile, gentle **ANT. 1** tough, rigid, inelastic, hard, inflexible **2** hard, unyielding

flicker *v.* quiver, flutter, falter, waver, glimmer, twinkle, shimmer, scintillate

flight *n.* **1** flying, take-off, soaring, mounting **2** fleeing, departure, running away, escape, evasion, disappearance, stampede, hegira, exodus **ANT. 2** return

flimsy *adj.* **1** transparent, thin, gauzy, light, weak, shallow, superficial, slight, unsubstantial **2** trifling, trivial, inane, puerile, weak, feeble, frivolous, foolish
ANT. **1** solid, sound, strong, substantial **2** strong

flinch *v.* wince, swerve, recoil, blench, shrink, draw back
ANT. dare, face, meet, endure, challenge, defy

fling *v.* throw, cast, toss, hurl, pitch, chuck (*informal*), overthrow, throw down

flippant *adj.* frivolous, offhand, impertinent, rude, pert, irreverent, disrespectful, forward, bold, superficial, thoughtless, saucy
ANT. considerate, respectful

flirt *v.* make advances, make overtures, ogle, trifle, chat up (*informal*)

flit *v.* dart, fly, dash, hop

float *v.* drift, flow, waft, swim
ANT. sink

flock *n.* group, gathering, collection, company, congregation, brood, bevy, herd, lot, pack, swarm, set, hatch, drove, litter

flock *v.* crowd, congregate, assemble, throng, herd, troop
ANT. disperse, scatter, separate

flog *v.* whip, thrash, beat, strike

flood *n.* deluge, overflow, inundation, abundance
ANT. drought

flood *v.* inundate, overwhelm, overflow, deluge

floor *n.* ground, surface, bottom

flop *v.* **1** fall, slump, collapse, hang, dangle **2** fail, founder
ANT. **2** succeed

florid *adj.* flowery, ornate, decorative, figurative, embellished
ANT. simple, unadorned, bare

flounder *v.* struggle, toss, roll, wallow, tumble

flourish *v.* **1** grow, thrive, prosper, succeed, be successful **2** brandish, wave, wield, swing, shake
ANT. **1** fail, decline, fade

flow *v.* **1** stream, run, pour, roll, sweep, glide, wave, undulate, float, career, progress, course **2** issue, emanate, proceed, come, grow, arise, follow, spring, result
ANT. **1** stop, fail

flower *n.* **1** blossom, bloom **2** best part, perfection, acme, gem, cream

fluctuate *v.* waver, swerve, veer, vacillate, vary, undulate, oscillate, hesitate, falter
ANT. persist, stand fast, stay, stick, hold fast

fluctuation *n.* wavering, oscillation, undulation, unsteadiness, variation, change, shifting, rise and fall, inconstancy, hesitation, vacillation
ANT. steadiness, firmness, constancy, stability, fixedness

fluency *n.* smoothness, flowing quality, eloquence, articulateness, glibness
ANT. awkwardness, slowness

fluent *adj.* smooth, eloquent, articulate, glib

fluid *n.* liquid, solution, gas, vapour, vapor (*N. Am.*)
ANT. solid

fluid *adj.* liquid, flowing, running, liquefied
ANT. solid

flurry *v.* excite, agitate, disconcert, confuse, disturb, hurry, ruffle, worry, fluster, perturb
ANT. quiet, calm, soothe, compose

flush *adj.* **1** flat, level, even, smooth **2** rich, wealthy, well-off, in the money (*informal*), rolling (*informal*)

flutter *v.* hover, flap, flit, quiver, flicker, fluctuate, waver, oscillate, vacillate, be inconstant, be unsteady, palpitate, tremble
ANT. settle, rest

flux *n.* flow, flowing, change, shifting, transition, motion, progression, substitution, transmutation, mutation
ANT. stagnation, stillness, invariableness, immutability

fly *v.* **1** soar, hover, wing, mount, flit **2** escape, flee, run away, decamp, scarper (*informal*)

foam *n.* froth, lather

focus *n.* centre, center (*N. Am.*), convergence, core, nucleus

foe *n.* enemy, opponent, adversary, antagonist
ANT. friend, ally

fog *n.* 1 mist, haze, cloud 2 confusion, daze, muddle, bewilderment

foggy *adj.* 1 misty, hazy 2 confused, dazed, bewildered, muddled
ANT. 1, 2 clear

foible *n.* frailty, weakness, failing, defect, imperfection, infirmity, fault, weak point

foil[1] *n.* 1 contrast, enhancement, setting, background, set-off 2 sheet, leaf, metal

foil[2] *v.* frustrate, hamper, hinder, thwart, baffle

foist *v.* impose, thrust, palm, pass

fold *n.* crease, tuck, pleat, wrinkle

fold *v.* double, enfold, enwrap, envelop, wrap, bend, embrace, enclose

folder *n.* file, envelope, binder, pocket

follow *v.* 1 come next, succeed, ensue, go after 2 obey, observe, heed, note, conform 3 pursue, run after, chase, track
ANT. 1 precede, lead 2 break

follower *n.* supporter, disciple, adherent, pupil, attendant, retainer, dependant, companion, associate
ANT. leader, teacher

following *n.* supporters, disciples, circle, admirers

folly *n.* silliness, foolishness, imbecility, stupidity, shallowness, absurdity, imprudence, nonsense, fatuity
ANT. wisdom, sense, prudence, judgment

foment *v.* excite, instigate, stimulate, encourage, promote, abet, stir up, cherish, propagate, brew
ANT. discourage, allay, extinguish, quench

fond *adj.* 1 doting, affectionate, loving, tender, attached, enamoured, enamored (*N. Am.*), devoted 2 foolish, silly, weak, absurd, empty, vain, senseless, baseless
ANT. 1 unloving, unaffectionate 2 sensible, well-grounded

fondle *v.* caress, pet, pat, stroke

fondness *n.* 1 tenderness, love, affection, doting 2 liking, preference, partiality, predilection, relish, appetite
ANT. 1 repulsion, aversion, dislike, hostility 2 hatred, contempt

food *n.* refreshment, nourishment, sustenance, nutrition, provisions, rations, subsistence, aliment, nutriment, viands, victuals, provender, regimen, fodder, diet, forage, feed, fare

fool *n.* 1 idiot, blockhead, simpleton, dunce, ninny 2 buffoon, harlequin, jester, clown
ANT. 1 expert, scholar, master

fool *v.* mess, play, joke, jest, trick, deceive

foolish *adj.* senseless, idiotic, silly, weak, daft, puerile, idle, trivial, trifling, contemptible, vain, childish, simple, irrational, unwise, unreasonable, absurd, ridiculous, preposterous, imprudent, injudicious, imbecile, nonsensical, brainless, witless
ANT. sensible, sound, wise, prudent, judicious

footing *n.* foothold, foundation, basis, groundwork, grade, status, state, condition, settlement, establishment

foppish *adj.* dandyish, vain, coxcombical, dressy, dandified

foray *n.* inroad, incursion, raid, invasion
ANT. flight, retreat

forbear *v.* stop, abstain, avoid, withhold, refrain, forgo, desist, pause, cease, stay, break off, be tolerant, tolerate, endure, be patient, put up with, shun, decline
ANT. indulge, gratify, yield

forbid *v.* prohibit, ban, outlaw, disallow, deter
ANT. let, allow, permit

forbidding *adj.* repulsive, repellent, unpleasant, odious, abhorrent, disagreeable, offensive
ANT. attractive, alluring, encouraging

force *n.* 1 strength, power, energy, pressure, might, vigour, vigor (*N. Am.*), efficacy, efficiency, potency, validity, virtue, cogency, agency 2 compulsion, violence, constraint, coercion, enforcement 3 army, troop, legion, battalion, host, squadron
ANT. 1 weakness, feebleness

force *v.* compel, make, coerce, oblige

forceful *adj.* intense, strong, powerful, compelling, effective, persuasive, vigorous
ANT. weak, feeble

forecast *v.* predict, foresee, anticipate, plan, project

forecast *n.* prediction, prognosis, anticipation, projection, plan

forefather *n.* ancestor, forebear, progenitor
ANT. descendants, progeny

foreign *adj.* strange, exotic, from abroad, unfamiliar, alien, external, exterior, outward
ANT. domestic, native

foreigner *n.* stranger, alien, newcomer, outsider, immigrant
ANT. native, resident

forerunner *n.* precursor, herald, harbinger, foregoer, predecessor, prognostic, sign, omen, premonition, prelude
ANT. successor, follower

foresee *v.* foreknow, forecast, predict, anticipate, foretell, forebode, divine

foresight *n.* wisdom, prudence, forethought, anticipation, precaution, farsightedness
ANT. hindsight

forest *n.* wood, woods, woodland, grove, copse

foretell *v.* predict, prophesy, forewarn, prognosticate, foreshow, foreshadow, portend, augur, bode, betoken

forethought *n.* foresight, anticipation, precaution, forecast, provision, prudence

forever *adv.* always, eternally, everlastingly, ever, endlessly, evermore, perpetually
ANT. never, at no time

forfeit *v.* lose, surrender, renounce, relinquish, give up
ANT. retain, keep

forfeit *n.* loss, fine, confiscation, penalty, damages

forge *v.* 1 beat, hammer out, fabricate, frame, form, make, shape, work, produce 2 falsify, counterfeit, feign

forgery *n.* counterfeit, falsification, fraudulent imitation
ANT. genuineness, verification, signature

forget *v.* overlook, not remember, neglect, ignore, obliterate
ANT. remember, acquire, learn, recall

forgetful *adj.* negligent, inattentive, careless, heedless, neglectful, mindless
ANT. attentive, careful, mindful

forgetfulness *n.* negligence, inattention, carelessness, heedlessness, oblivion
ANT. remembrance, recollection, recalling

forgive *v.* pardon, excuse, acquit, absolve, overlook
ANT. blame, punish, condemn

forgo *v.* relinquish, resign, renounce, surrender, cede, yield, abandon, give up, part with, let go, waive, drop, abjure
ANT. seize, grasp, retain

forlorn *adj.* wretched, miserable, pitiable, destitute, desolate, helpless, comfortless, disconsolate, deserted, forsaken, solitary, abandoned, lost, friendless, luckless, lone, lonesome
ANT. happy

form *n.* 1 shape, figure, configuration, outline, fashion, cast, cut 2 manner, system, sort, kind, order, style, mode, method, formula, ritual, regularity, arrangement 3 ceremony, formality, ceremonial, conventionality, etiquette 4 paper, blank, document 5 pattern, model, mould, mold (*N. Am.*), frame

form *v.* shape, mould, mold (*N. Am.*), fashion, constitute, arrange, frame, construct, contrive, conceive, make, produce, create, devise, invent, compose, dispose, combine
ANT. deform

formal *adj.* 1 regular, set, conventional, established, methodical, fixed, rigid, stiff 2 ceremonial, dignified, solemn, stately, pompous, precise, correct, punctilious, starched, prim, exact 3 express, explicit, positive, strict, official
ANT. 1 irregular 2 informal

formalism *n.* rigidity, ceremoniousness, pomposity, externalism
ANT. simplicity, unaffectedness, unostentatiousness, unceremoniousness

formality *n.* custom, ceremony, etiquette, conventionality, form, parade, affectation, punctiliousness, stateliness, established mode
ANT. informality, unceremoniousness, unconventionality

formation *n.* arrangement, disposal, combination, disposition, construction, shape, structure, creation, production, composition, constitution

former *adj.* previous, prior, preceding, foregoing, past, bygone, foregone, first-named, first-mentioned, earlier, ancient, anterior, antecedent, late, old-time
ANT. subsequent, succeeding, posterior, latter, coming, future

formidable *adj.* awful, alarming, terrifying, appalling, serious, horrible, dreadful, fearful, shocking, terrible, tremendous
ANT. feeble, harmless, contemptible, powerless, weak, helpless

formula *n.* rule, principle, method, procedure, recipe, equation

forsake *v.* abandon, renounce, give up, leave, desert, quit (*informal*)

fort *n.* castle, stronghold, fortress, citadel

forthcoming *adj.* 1 future, approaching, prospective, imminent
2 communicative, talkative, open, chatty
ANT. 1 previous 2 reticent

forthright *adj.* blunt, direct, candid, frank, outspoken
ANT. evasive

forthwith *adv.* instantly, directly, immediately, without delay, instantaneously

fortification *n.* castle, fort, stronghold, fortress, citadel, bulwark

fortify *v.* reinforce, brace, stiffen, strengthen, protect, surround, confirm, corroborate, garrison
ANT. weaken, dismantle

fortitude *n.* bravery, endurance, resolution, courage, firmness, patience, heroism,

calmness, resignation, composure, stoicism
ANT. timidity, flinching

fortuitous *adj.* accidental, casual., contingent, chance, incidental, undesigned
ANT. purposed, planned, designed, anticipated, foreseen

fortunate *adj.* lucky, successful, prosperous, happy, propitious, auspicious, favourable, favorable (*N. Am.*), advantageous, providential
ANT. unhappy, unlucky, unfortunate, wretched

fortune *n.* 1 chance, accident, luck, fate, destiny, fortuity 2 wealth, affluence, riches, opulence, livelihood, estate, substance, property, possessions
ANT. 1 design, purpose 2 misfortune, ill luck, poverty

forward *adj.* 1 onward, progressive, advancing, front, fore, anterior
2 presumptuous, confident, bold, impertinent, pert, obtrusive, self-assertive, assuming, flippant 3 ready, prompt, eager, willing, zealous, earnest
ANT. 1 backward 2 reluctant, retiring, backward, slow, modest, indifferent

forward *v.* support, foster, advance, promote, further, encourage, aid, favour, favor (*N. Am.*), help, hasten, accelerate, quicken, speed, hurry, dispatch, expedite, transmit, send on
ANT. delay, prevent, hinder, frustrate

foster *v.* support, advance, promote, further, encourage, aid

foul *adj.* 1 impure, nasty, dirty, unclean, squalid, filthy, tarnished, soiled, stained, polluted, sullied, disgusting, loathsome, offensive, noisome 2 evil, base, scandalous, infamous, vile, wicked, dark, abominable, detestable, disgraceful, shameful, vulgar, coarse, low, abusive, insulting, scurrilous, dishonourable, dishonorable (*N. Am.*), unfair, sinister, underhanded 3 stormy, cloudy, rainy, bad, thick, turbid, muddy
ANT. 1 pure, uncorrupt, unstained, undefiled, uncontaminated, unsullied, stainless, fair, unspotted, spotless, unpolluted 2 good, holy 3 clear, bright

found *v.* build, construct, raise, erect, establish, organize, institute, originate, plant, set up, base, set, fix, place, ground, rest, endow, root
ANT. uproot, subvert, supplant, disestablish

foundation *n.* base, establishment, settlement, ground, origin, rudiments, substratum, underlying principle, groundwork, basis, bottom, footing

founder *n.* originator, institutor, establisher, planter, author
ANT. destroyer

fountain *n.* spring, well, jet, stream, source, origin, original cause, first principle

fracas *n.* fight, brawl, dispute, scrap (*informal*)

fraction *n.* part, portion, fragment, piece, bit, scrap, section
ANT. whole, total, amount, sum

fractious *adj.* cross, irritable, bad-tempered, captious, petulant, testy, peevish, fretful, irritable, waspish, snappish, pettish
ANT. good-humoured, good-humored (*N. Am.*), agreeable

fracture *n.* crack, rupture, break, breach, division, split

fracture *v.* crack, break, divide, split, tear, rupture

fragile *adj.* 1 delicate, brittle, breakable, easily broken, frangible 2 infirm, frail, weak, feeble, delicate, slight
ANT. 1 tough, hardy 2 strong

fragment *n.* part, bit, piece, remnant, fraction, scrap, chip, morsel
ANT. bulk, body, whole, mass

fragrance *n.* smell, odour, odor (*N. Am.*), perfume, scent, aroma, balminess, incense

fragrant *adj.* perfumed, sweet-scented, sweet-smelling, aromatic, redolent, spicy, balmy, odoriferous
ANT. smelly, noxious

frail *adj.* weak, feeble, infirm, fragile, brittle, breakable, delicate
ANT. tough, hardy, strong, sturdy

frame *n.* 1 framework, skeleton, carcass, framing, form, structure, system, fabric, constitution, scheme, condition, state, temper, mood 2 border, case, casing, shell

frame *v.* 1 construct, build, put together, form, compose, make. constitute, invent, devise, plan, contrive 2 enclose, border, mount

framework *n.* frame, skeleton, form, structure, system

franchise *n.* right, privilege, licence, license (*N. Am.*), exemption, immunity, freedom
ANT. disqualification, liability

frank *adj.* open, ingenuous, free, sincere, candid, artless, without disguise, unreserved, familiar, honest, outspoken, easy, plain
ANT. close, reserved

frantic *adj.* wild, frenzied, furious, raving, raging, distracted, maniacal
ANT. calm, collected, cool, composed

fraternity *n.* association, circle, society, company, brotherhood, league, clan

fraternize *v.* associate with, cooperate with, harmonize, sympathize, consort, concur

fraud *n.* deceit, deception, dishonesty, treason, artifice, trick, trickery, cheating, imposture, swindle, treachery, duplicity, imposition
ANT. honesty, truth, uprightness, fairness, integrity

fraudulent *adj.* deceitful, dishonest, fake, tricky, crafty, treacherous

fraught *adj.* filled, stored, laden, charged, abounding, loaded, teeming
ANT. empty, wanting, poor, scant, devoid, divested

freak *n.* abnormality, oddity, anomaly, deformity, monstrosity, monster

freakish *adj.* abnormal, anomalous, deformed, monstrous
ANT. normal

free *adj.* 1 independent, at liberty, unrestrained, released, emancipated, delivered, liberated 2 idle, empty, unoccupied, available 3 without charge, complimentary, gratuitous 4 exempt, clear, allowed, permitted, open, unobstructed, unimpeded, unrestricted 5 frank, ingenuous, candid, artless, unreserved, sincere, open, familiar, unconstrained, easy, informal 6 generous, liberal, bountiful, charitable, open-handed, prodigal, lavish, immoderate **7** ready, eager, willing, prompt

ANT. 1 bound **2** busy **4** restricted, obstructed, closed, occupied **6** stingy, niggardly

freedom *n.* independence, liberty, release, scope, range, play, franchise, immunity, privilege, laxity

ANT. slavery, imprisonment, captivity

freeze *v.* ice up, ice over, refrigerate, chill, cool, harden, solidify

freight *n.* cargo, load, consignment, goods, shipment

frenzy *n.* madness, rage, fury, insanity, raving, distraction, excitement, agitation, lunacy, derangement, mania, delirium

ANT. calm, composure, collectedness, sanity, equanimity

frequent *adj.* common, usual, everyday, customary, habitual, oft-repeated, recurrent, general, numerous, continual

ANT. rare

frequent *v.* attend, visit often, go to, haunt

fresh *adj.* **1** new, recent, crisp, blooming, flourishing, unfaded, unwilted, unwithered, well-preserved **2** well, rested, renewed, revived, vigorous, healthy, hardy, strong , unworn, unwearied, unexhausted, unfatigued **3** rosy, ruddy, fair, delicate, fresh-coloured, fresh-colored (*N. Am.*) **4** vivid, lively, keen, unabated **5** inexperienced, raw, uncultivated, untrained, unskilled, young, untried **6** pure, cool, refreshing, sweet, unsalted, health-giving, bracing, brisk, stiff, strong

ANT. 1 old, stale, tarnished, faded, decayed **2** tired, exhausted, weary, jaded **3** pallid, sickly **5** experienced, trained **6** impure, stagnant, putrid, mouldy, moldy (*N. Am.*), musty, fusty

fret *v.* worry, be anxious, grieve, brood, trouble

fretful *adj.* irritable, bad-tempered, fractious, impatient, discontented, touchy, peevish, petulant, testy, snappish, waspish, splenetic, spleeny, captious

ANT. patient, contented, forbearing, meek, resigned, unmurmuring

friction *n.* rubbing, abrasion, resistance, grating, contact, attrition **2** tension, conflict, disagreement

ANT. 1 detachment, isolation **2** peace, harmony

friend *n.* **1** acquaintance, companion, chum, confidant(e), intimate, associate, colleague, ally **2** encourager, well-wisher, advocate, adherent, defender, supporter, patron

ANT. 1 enemy, opponent, foe, adversary, antagonist

friendly *adj.* kind, kindly, loving, well-disposed, companionable, genial, neighbourly, neighborly (*N. Am.*), cordial, affectionate, fond, social, tender, affable, accessible, sociable, amicable, complaisant, hearty, sincere

ANT. unfriendly, antagonistic, unkind, distant, disaffected, hostile, cold, indifferent, ill-disposed

friendship *n.* friendliness, attachment, care, affection, good will, devotion, amity, comity, consideration, favour, favor (*N. Am.*), love, regard, esteem, admiration

ANT. hostility, hatred, enmity, contempt, disdain, antipathy

fright *n.* shock, terror, fear, alarm, panic

frighten *v.* alarm, intimidate, scare, terrify, daunt, browbeat, dismay

ANT. calm, soothe, comfort, ease, reassure, encourage

frightful *adj.* awful, shocking, terrible, fearful, terrific, dire, dread, dreadful, horrid, horrible, hideous, ghastly, grim, grisly, gruesome, alarming, ugly, monstrous

ANT. delightful, attractive

frigid *adj.* **1** cold, dull, cool, uninteresting, lifeless, unanimated, tame, spiritless **2** formal, prim, stiff, forbidding, chilling, rigid, freezing, repulsive, repellent **3** passionless, cold, uncaring, distant

ANT. 1 warm, ardent, impassioned, vehement, zealous **2** passionate

fringe *n.* border, edge, edging, hem, trimming

frisk *v.* leap, play, skip, hop, frolic, jump, romp, gambol, dance, sport

frisky *adj*. lively, sportive, playful, wanton, frolicsome

fritter *v*. waste, squander, dissipate, idle

frivolous *adj*. trivial, worthless, light, trifling, silly, foolish, petty, idle, childish, puerile
ANT. serious, earnest, important, grave

frolic *n*. gambol, lark, caper, escapade, prank, fun, merriment, merrymaking, play, game, festivity, sport, entertainment

frolicsome *adj*. lively, frisky, sportive, playful, merry, joyous, festive
ANT. grave, serious, earnest

front *n*. **1** exterior, face, façade **2** head, start, top, lead
ANT. **1** back, rear

front *v*. face, overlook, look onto, look out on

frontier *n*. border, boundary, edge, limit

froth *n*. lather, foam, suds, bubbles, effervescence

froward *adj*. contrary, fractious, perverse, unyielding, ungovernable, wayward, disobedient, peevish, cross, captious, petulant, refractory
ANT. obedient, docile, amenable

frown *n*. scowl, glare, grimace
ANT. smile

frown *v*. scowl, pout, disapprove of
ANT. smile, approve of

frugal *adj*. provident, economical, careful, choice, saving, chary, thrifty, unwasteful, sparing, parsimonious, abstinent, abstemious, temperate
ANT. wasteful, extravagant, prodigal, intemperate, self-indulgent

frugality *n*. parsimony, thrift, providence, prudence, economy, sparing, miserliness, scrimping, parsimoniousness
ANT. liberality, luxury, waste, extravagance, affluence, abundance, riches

fruit *n*. harvest, crop, product, production, result, effect, consequence, outcome, offspring, issue, young, produce, reward, outgrowth
ANT. seed, cause, origin, operation, growth

fruitful *adj*. productive, prolific, fertile, abundant, rich, plentiful, plenteous, successful, useful, fecund
ANT. unproductive, sterile, barren, fruitless, useless, abortive, ineffectual

fruition *n*. fulfilment, reaping, attainment, use, possession, enjoyment
ANT. loss, disappointment, non-attainment

fruitless *adj*. unproductive, sterile, barren, useless, abortive, ineffectual, futile, vain
ANT. fruitful, productive

frustrate *v*. thwart, check, discourage, prevent, defeat

frustration *n*. disappointment, annoyance, irritation, thwarting, discouragement

fuel *n*. combustible, source of energy, substance, material, oil, petrol, gas, gasoline, oil, wood

fugitive *n*. runaway, refugee, deserter, escapee

fulfil *v*. accomplish, carry out, achieve, realize, execute, consummate, complete, perfect, obey, observe, perform, do, discharge, keep, adhere to, comply with, meet, satisfy, answer, fill, fill out
ANT. neglect, ignore, falsify

full *adj*. **1** filled, packed, saturated, replete **2** complete, whole, entire, unabridged **3** extensive, vast, large, broad, ample **4** resonant, deep, rich
ANT. **1** empty **2** abridged, shorter **3** restricted, limited

fully *adv*. completely, entirely, totally, wholly, absolutely
ANT. partly

fulminate *v*. **1** roar, denounce, condemn, thunder, hurl threats **2** explode, detonate, blow up

fulsome *adj*. excessive, extravagant, gross, offensive, nauseous, disgusting, repulsive, coarse, ribald, loathsome, sickening, fawning
ANT. moderate

fumble *v*. **1** feel for, grope, search **2** bungle, botch, mishandle, muff

fume *v.* **1** smoke, reek, emit vapour, emit vapor (*N. Am.*), exhale **2** rave, rage, chafe, storm, bluster, fret, flare up, be in a rage

fume *n.* smoke, vapour, vapor (*N. Am.*), gas, pollution

fun *n.* amusement, pleasure, enjoyment, entertainment, sport, recreation, diversion

function *n.* **1** purpose, use, role, part, task, duty, operation, performance **2** ceremony, reception, gathering, party

function *v.* operate, work, run, go, perform, act, behave

fund *n.* stock, capital, reserve, supply, store, money, means, resources, investment
ANT. expenditure, outlay

fundamental *adj.* basic, elementary, essential, radical, primary, principal, important
ANT. secondary, unimportant, non-essential

fundamental *n.* principle, element, essential, basic, basis, rudiment

funeral *n.* burial, interment, cremation

funereal *adj.* mournful, sad, gloomy, dismal, solemn, deathlike, lugubrious, woeful, dark, plaintive, sombre, somber (*N. Am.*), melancholy
ANT. happy, joyous

funny *adj.* **1** humorous, ludicrous, ridiculous, droll, comical, farcical, amusing, laughable, diverting, jocose **2** odd, strange, weird, peculiar, curious
ANT. **1** grave, serious, sad **2** normal, usual

fur *n.* coat, hair, skin, hide, pelt

furious *adj.* angry, fuming, infuriated, raging, enraged, wild, fierce
ANT. calm

furnace *n.* boiler, kiln, heater

furnish *v.* provide, supply, fit, equip, fit out, afford, give, contribute, present, yield, bestow
ANT. withhold, withdraw

further *adj.* more, additional, extra, new

further *adv.* furthermore, moreover, in addition, besides, as well, also

further *v.* support, advance, promote, forward, encourage

furthermore *adv.* further, moreover, in addition, besides, as well, also

furtive *adj.* secret, sly, clandestine, stolen, stealthy, surreptitious, secretive
ANT. open, undisguised, unconcealed, unreserved

fury *n.* rage, anger, temper, wildness, fierceness, ferociousness
ANT. calmness, quiet

fuse *v.* **1** join, combine, unite, amalgamate, blend, mix, intermingle, coalesce **2** melt, liquefy, smelt
ANT. disunite

fuss *n.* bother, commotion, to-do, ado, bustle, stir, agitation, excitement, tumult
ANT. quiet, peace, calm

fuss *v.* bother, annoy, pester, worry, fret

fussy *adj.* over-particular, choosy, fastidiousness, hard to please, discriminating

futile *adj.* **1** useless, worthless, valueless, vain, idle, unprofitable, profitless, unavailing, fruitless, ineffective, ineffectual, nugatory **2** trivial, minor, unimportant, trifling
ANT. **1** worthwhile **2** important, useful

future *adj.* forthcoming, coming, approaching, imminent
ANT. past, former, bygone

gabble *v.* jabber, chatter, gibber, gab, gossip, prattle

gabble *n.* jabber, twaddle, chatter, gibberish, babble, gossip, palaver, prattle

gadget *n.* device, contraption, appliance, tool

gag *v.* **1** silence, stifle, muzzle, muffle, hush **2** retch, choke, heave

gain *n.* **1** profits, earnings, addition, winnings, income, proceeds, return **2** blessing, profit, advantage, good, benefit, improvement
ANT. **1** loss

gain *v.* **1** get, acquire, win, earn, obtain, procure, secure, carry, achieve **2** profit, benefit, make, gross, net, clear, bring in, realize, reap **3** reach, attain, arrive at
ANT. **1** lose

gainful *adj.* advantageous, profitable, beneficial, fruitful, rewarding, lucrative, paying, productive, remunerative, winning
ANT. unprofitable, disadvantageous

gallant *adj.* **1** courageous, brave, valiant, valorous, intrepid, heroic, fearless, bold, daring, high-spirited, noble, lofty, magnanimous, high-minded **2** polite, courteous, chivalrous, attentive
ANT. **1** cowardly **2** discourteous

gallop *v.* race, rush, hurry, canter, dash, bolt, fly

gamble *v.* bet, wager, back, punt, stake. speculate, venture, game

gamble *n.* bet, wager, risk, chance, flutter (*informal*), speculation
ANT. certainty

gambol *v.* frisk, frolic, romp, caper, leap, hop, skip, jump, sport

game *n.* **1** sport, play, amusement, entertainment, pastime, recreation, diversion **2** match, competition, contest, fixture, meeting, event **3** plan, scheme, stratagem, strategy

gang *n.* band, group, company, troop, crowd, horde

gangster *n.* criminal, crook, gunman, hit man, hoodlum, hood (*informal*)

gap *n.* break, space, opening, interval

gape *v.* stare, gaze, gawp, wonder

garb *n.* dress, clothing, clothes, garments, vesture, costume, attire, habit, apparel, raiment

garble *v.* mix up, jumble, confuse, falsify, misrepresent, misquote, pervert

garish *adj.* showy, gaudy, ostentatious, flashy, flamboyant, loud, bold, tasteless
ANT. subdued, unassuming, unobtrusive, modest

garnish *v.* decorate, adorn, embellish, deck, grace, beautify, ornament, set off
ANT. strip, bare, denude

garrulity *n.* loquacity, verbosity, chatter, loquaciousness, babble, babbling, talkativeness, prattle, prate
ANT. reticence, taciturnity, reserve, silence

garrulous *adj.* chatty, chattering, talkative, loquacious, verbose
ANT. reserved, reticent, silent, taciturn, laconic

gasp *v.* pant, puff, blow, wheeze

gasp *n.* breath, pant, puff, wheeze

gate *n.* barrier, opening, entrance, door

gather *v.* **1** assemble, collect, congregate, accumulate, amass **2** pick, pluck, reap, harvest, garner **3** understand, conclude, assume, learn
ANT. **1** disperse, scatter

gathering *n.* meeting, assembly, crowd, company, throng

gaudy *adj.* garish, glittering, bright, colourful, colorful (*N. Am.*), tawdry, tinsel, flashy, showy, overdecorated, loud
ANT. simple, subdued

gauge, gage (*N. Am.*) *n.* 1 instrument, measuring instrument, device
2 measure, standard, criterion, mark, norm, guideline, benchmark, yardstick

gauge, gage (*N. Am.*) *v.* measure, estimate, judge, weigh, determine, fathom, probe

gaunt *adj.* lean, lank, thin, skinny, scrawny, emaciated, slender, attenuated, spare
ANT. plump

gawky *adj.* awkward, ungainly, clumsy, boorish, rustic, green, uncouth, loutish
ANT. graceful

gay *adj.* 1 showy, bright, fine, brilliant, colourful, colorful (*N. Am.*), gaudy, flaunting, flashy, garish, tawdry, glittering, tinsel 2 lively, jovial, merry, cheerful, gleeful, blithe, jolly
3 homosexual, lesbian
ANT. 1 dull 2 sad

gaze *v.* stare, look, regard, contemplate, view, scan, behold, glower
ANT. ignore, glance

gear *n.* 1 cog, wheel, gearing, mechanism 2 equipment, apparatus, accessories, instruments, belongings, kit, material 3 clothes, clothing, garments, dress, wear, togs (*informal*)

gem *n.* jewel, precious stone, treasure

general *adj.* 1 broad, extensive, comprehensive, sweeping, overall
2 usual, frequent, ordinary, universal, common, commonplace, customary, everyday, public, prevalent, familiar, normal, popular, habitual
ANT. 1 specific, precise, particular, special
2 uncommon, exceptional, rare, unusual

generality *n.* universality, bulk, mass, body, majority
ANT. minority, individuality

generally *adv.* usually, normally, in general, mainly, mostly, chiefly, on the whole, as a rule, by and large

generate *v.* produce, form, make, cause, bring about, originate, beget, procreate, engender, breed, propagate
ANT. terminate, annihilate

generation *n.* 1 production, formation, creation, origination, procreation
2 period, epoch, age, era, lifetime
3 family, stock, race, breed, offspring, progeny

generic *adj.* general, common, collective, racial, comprehensive
ANT. particular, specific, individual

generous *adj.* charitable, liberal, noble, unselfish, big (*informal*), magnanimous, bountiful, free, munificent, open-handed, disinterested, open-hearted, chivalrous
ANT. mean, miserly, stingy

genial *adj.* cheerful, pleasant, warm, warm-hearted, festive, merry, jovial, joyous, rejuvenating, restorative
ANT. cold, unfriendly

genius *n.* 1 talent, gift, ability, aptitude, faculty, capacity, endowment, ingenuity, invention, sagacity, intellect, brains, parts, wit, inspiration 2 expert, prodigy, virtuoso, adept
ANT. 1 dunce 2 stupidity, folly

genteel *adj.* polite, courteous, civil, refined, polished, well-bred, gentlemanly, ladylike, fashionable, stylish, elegant, graceful, refined, aristocratic, cultivated, cultured
ANT. rude, uncultivated, ill-bred, boorish, uncultured, unpolished

gentle *adj.* 1 mild, bland, moderate, kind, tender, compassionate, indulgent, meek, soft, lenient, humane, merciful, tender-hearted, gentle-hearted 2 tame, docile, meek, tractable, calm, quiet
3 gradual, moderate, slow, light, easy
4 noble, high-born, well-born, cultivated, refined, courteous, well bred, polished, placid
ANT. 1 rough 2 wild, savage 3 harsh

genuine *adj.* real, true, authentic, pure, uncorrupt, unalloyed, unadulterated, unaffected, sincere, natural, sound
ANT. false, artificial, spurious, adulterated, counterfeit

germ *n.* **1** embryo, seed, microbe, bacterium, bug (*informal*) **2** origin, source, nucleus, embryo, seed
ANT. **1** fruit **2** result, development, product

germane *adj.* relevant, appropriate, apposite, fitting, suitable, pertinent, related, akin, cognate, allied
ANT. irrelevant, unconnected, alien

germinate *v.* bud, shoot, vegetate, sprout, push, burst forth, put forth, spring up
ANT. wither, decay

gesture *n.* signal, sign, motion, action, gesticulation

gesture *v.* signal, sign, motion, wave, beckon, gesticulate

get *v.* **1** obtain, acquire, attain, earn, achieve, receive, win, secure, gain, procure **2** grow, become, develop, go, turn **3** take, carry, fetch, bring, collect **4** prepare, make ready **5** persuade, talk into, influence, sway, induce, urge **6** arrive, come, reach
ANT. lose

get by manage, cope, survive **get off** disembark, alight, dismount, leave, depart **get on** board, mount, embark **get over** over overcome, survive, recover **get up** rise, arise, stand

ghastly *adj.* **1** grim, dismal, hideous, terrible, horrible, frightful, shocking, grisly **2** pale, wan, white, deathlike, deathly, pallid
ANT. blooming, fresh

ghost *n.* apparition, spectre, specter (*N. Am.*), spirit, soul, phantom, shade, departed spirit, spook (*informal*), vision

giant *n.* ogre, monster, colossus

giant *adj.* gigantic, colossal, huge, enormous, immense
ANT. tiny, minute

gibberish *n.* rubbish, nonsense, drivel, twaddle
ANT. sense

gibe *v.* jeer, mock, ridicule, deride, sneer, scoff, taunt, flout, jest, rail at
ANT. compliment

giddy *adj.* **1** dizzy, vertiginous, light-headed, woozy (*informal*) **2** inconstant, fickle, changeable, unsteady, unstable, vacillating, irresolute, careless, heedless, wild, reckless, harebrained, flighty
ANT. **2** sensible

gift *n.* **1** present, donation, grant, gratuity, bequest, benediction, boon, largesse, bounty, offering, alms, allowance, contribution, subscription, subsidy, legacy, demise **2** talent, ability, endowment, genius, faculty, strength, power, capacity, capability, turn, forte
ANT. **2** inability, weakness

gigantic *adj.* vast, huge, colossal, enormous, giant, prodigious, herculean, immense, tremendous
ANT. tiny, minute, insignificant, pygmy

gingerly *adj.* hesitant, timid, cautious, gentle

girdle *v.* gird, bind round, belt, hem, surround, encircle, encompass, enclose, embrace

girl *adj.* lass, miss, youngster

gist *n.* substance, main point, essence, pith, core, marrow, kernel, force, ground, foundation

give *v.* **1** grant, present, bestow, award, donate, provide, supply, offer, proffer **2** surrender, yield, give way, give in, relinquish, sacrifice **3** produce, develop, cause, yield **4** communicate, utter, announce, convey, pronounce **5** collapse, break, give way, yield
ANT. **1** withhold, take **2** retain

give away betray, reveal, disclose, divulge, let slip **give in** surrender, yield, submit **give off** emit, exude, discharge, release **give out** distribute, deal out, allocate, hand out, spread **give up** stop, end, discontinue, cease, renounce, surrender, submit, yield

glad *adj.* **1** delighted, happy, pleased, gratified, contented, cheerful, joyous, joyful, gladsome, elated, light-hearted, cheery, animated **2** pleasing, encouraging, delightful, good
ANT. **1** unhappy, sad **2** gloomy, bad

gladden *v.* please, delight, cheer, exhilarate, bless, rejoice, gratify, make glad
ANT. grieve, disappoint, depress, trouble, sadden, displease

glamour *n.* charm, allure, fascination, attraction, excitement

glamorous *adj.* charming, attractive, beautiful, smart, elegant, fascinating, thrilling

glance *v.* glimpse, look, peep, peek

glance *n.* glimpse, look, peep, peek

glare *v.* **1** glitter, glisten, dazzle, flare, gleam, sparkle, beam, shine, glow, ray, radiate **2** glower, look fierce, scowl, frown

glass *n.* beaker, cup, tumbler

glassy *adj.* clear, shiny, smooth, polished, glacial, pellucid, limpid, glossy, silken, crystal, transparent, gleaming, brilliant, shining
ANT. rough, uneven, pliant, rugged, tough, opaque, turbid, muddy, dull, dark

glaze *v.* coat, cover, shine, polish, gloss, burnish, lacquer, varnish

gleam *v.* glimmer, glow, glisten, beam, shine, sparkle, shimmer

glean *v.* gather, collect, reap, harvest

glib *adj.* easy, slick, smooth, ready, fluent
ANT. hesitant

glide *v.* slide, slip, flow, coast, skim, drift, roll

glimpse *n.* glance, glimmering, sight, impression, flash, survey, trace, tinge
ANT. observation, investigation, inspection, exposure, examination

glisten *v.* glitter, shine, glimmer, shimmer, sparkle, twinkle

glitter *v.* sparkle, flash, glisten, twinkle, shimmer, glimmer

glitter *n.* sparkle, twinkle, gleam, brilliance, splendour, splendor (*N. Am.*), glamour, show

global *adj.* worldwide, international, universal

globe *n.* sphere, orb, ball, world, earth

gloom *n.* **1** darkness, obscurity, dimness, gloominess, cloud **2** twilight, gloaming, shadow, obscuration, dullness, cloudiness **3** sadness, dejection, depression, despondency, melancholy
ANT. **1** light **2** daylight **3** happiness

gloomy *adj.* **1** depressing, sad, discouraging, dismal **2** despondent, depressed, glum, sad, melancholy, downhearted, miserable
ANT. **1** encouraging **2** cheerful, happy

glorify *v.* praise, extol, exalt, magnify, bless, honour, honor (*N. Am.*), laud, elevate, ennoble, adorn
ANT. defame, censure, blame, rebuke

glorious *adj.* **1** famous, illustrious, renowned, celebrated, eminent, famed, distinguished, conspicuous **2** splendid, magnificent, resplendent, radiant, bright, brilliant **3** excellent, wonderful, marvellous, enjoyable
ANT. **1** unknown **2** dull **3** awful

glory *n.* **1** fame, honour, honor (*N. Am.*), renown, celebrity, praise **2** splendour, splendor (*N. Am.*), radiance, magnificence, brightness, brilliance, effulgence, gloriousness, nobleness, exaltation, grandeur
ANT. **1** obscurity

glory *v.* boast, triumph, exult, revel

gloss *n.* **1** lustre, luster (*N. Am.*), polish, shine, sheen **2** appearance, façade, front, show **3** interpretation, comment, note, explanation, commentary, annotation

glow *v.* shine, burn, radiate, glimmer, gleam

glow *n.* light, brightness, radiance, gleam, warmth
ANT. darkness

glue *n.* adhesive, gum, paste, cement

glue *v.* stick, fix, gum, paste

glut *n.* repletion, superabundance, surplus, redundancy, overstock, superfluity
ANT. scarcity, want, scantness, dearth

glut *v.* stuff, fill, cloy, sate, satiate, pall, gorge, cram, overfeed
ANT. empty

gluttony *n.* voracity, greed
ANT. abstinence, abstemiousness, temperance, frugality

gnash *v.* grind, bite, snap

gnaw *v.* bite, eat, munch, chew

go 1 depart, set out, leave, withdraw
2 move, travel, pass, proceed, advance,
progress, journey, drive, fly, ride, sail
3 become, turn, grow, get, turn out
4 operate, work, run, function 5 pass,
elapse
ANT. 1 come 2 stop 4 fail, break down

go off explode, blow up, detonate **go on**
1 continue, last, endure, persist,
persevere 2 happen, occur, take place
go through experience, undergo, suffer,
endure

goal *n.* target, aim, objective, purpose

go-between *n.* mediator, intermediary,
agent, middle party

God *n.* deity, supreme being, spirit

good *adj.* 1 enjoyable, pleasant, fine,
satisfactory, favourable, favorable (*N.
Am.*), useful, helpful, beneficial,
profitable 2 fit, skilful, skillful (*N. Am.*),
proficient, gifted, talented, able,
capable, qualified, well-qualified,
suitable 3 kind, friendly, generous,
good-natured, kindly, obliging,
merciful 4 moral, righteous, honest,
upright, well-behaved, obedient
5 healthy, sound, well, robust, vigorous
ANT. 1 bad, unpleasant, unfavourable,
unfavorable (*N. Am.*) 2 incompetent,
unsuitable 3 unkind, cruel,
unfriendly 4 bad, immoral, evil 5 ill,
unhealthy

good *n.* 1 benefit, gain, welfare,
prosperity, interest, advantage, utility,
profit 2 virtue, righteousness,
excellence 3 kindness, benevolence,
generosity, consideration, favour, favor
(*N. Am.*), help, assistance
ANT. 1 disadvantage 2 evil 3 harm, hurt

goodbye *interj.* farewell, adieu, cheerio
(*informal*), so long, au revoir, see you
(later)

good-looking *adj.* attractive, pretty,
beautiful, handsome
ANT. ugly

goodly *adj.* 1 considerable, sizeable,
substantial 2 beautiful, good-looking,
pleasant
ANT. 1 small 2 unattractive

goodness *n.* virtue, good, integrity,
honesty, uprightness, rectitude
ANT. evil, badness, dishonesty

goods *n. pl.* 1 commodities,
merchandise, stock, wares 2
possessions, property, belongings

gorge *v.* stuff, fill, cram, glut, sate,
surfeit

gorge *n.* ravine, canyon, pass

gorgeous *adj.* splendid, shining,
magnificent, grand, fine, rich, superb,
dazzling, showy, glittering
ANT. poor, ugly

gossip *n.* 1 talk, chat, prattle, rumour,
rumor (*N. Am.*), scandal, hearsay
2 scandalmonger, prattler, busybody

gossip *v.* talk, chat, prattle, natter, blab

govern *v.* rule, direct, command,
control, manage, reign over, sway,
influence, guide, supervise, conduct

government *n.* 1 rule, direction,
command, control, authority,
management, sway, influence
2 parliament, council, cabinet, executive

grab *v.* seize, snatch, grasp, take hold of

grace *n.* 1 elegance, polish, refinement,
beauty, symmetry, attractiveness,
gracefulness, ease, excellence, charm
2 favour, favor (*N. Am.*), kindness,
condescension, love, mercy, compassion,
goodwill, pardon, forgiveness
ANT. 1 awkwardness, inelegance
2 unkindness

graceful *adj.* beautiful, comely, elegant,
easy, natural, becoming, flowing,
rounded
ANT. awkward, ugly, ungainly, gawky,
ungraceful

gracious *adj.* kind, favourable, favorable
(*N. Am.*), compassionate, friendly,
benevolent, benign, merciful, tender,
lenient, condescending, mild, gentle,
affable, familiar, civil, polite, courteous
ANT. impolite, haughty, discourteous,
ungracious, ill-disposed, unfriendly

gradation *n.* progress, progression,
succession, graduation, precedence,
arrangement, ordination, standing, rank,
degree, stage, tier
ANT. equality, uniformity

grade *n.* class, position, degree, level,
category, stage, step

grade *v.* sort, arrange, classify, class,
categorize, rank

gradient n. slope, incline, hill, ramp

gradual adj. slow, moderate, continuous, step by step, regular, progressive
ANT. sudden

graft v. join, unite, attach, splice
ANT. separate, divide

grain n. 1 cereal, corn, kernel, seed 2 piece, bit, particle, crumb, scrap, jot

grand adj. 1 impressive, magnificent, splendid, glorious, superb, imposing, large 2 wonderful, marvellous, splendid, magnificent, first-rate
ANT. 1 humble, little 2 poor

grandeur n. magnificence, splendour, splendor (N. Am.), glory, greatness, vastness, loftiness, elevation, majesty, stateliness, pomp
ANT. humility

grandiloquence n. bombast, verbosity, pomposity, stiltedness, turgidity
ANT. simplicity, unaffectedness

grandiose adj. elaborate, impressive, grand, splendid, magnificent, pompous, showy, extravagant, flamboyant

grant v. 1 give, award, bestow, confer, deign 2 yield, admit, agree, concede, allow

grant n. award, allowance, bequest, gift, endowment, concession

graphic adj. vivid, lively, picturesque, striking, telling, impressive, illustrative, pictorial, descriptive, strong, forcible, feeling
ANT. obscure, indefinite, unclear

grapple v. clasp, grasp, grip, seize

grasp v. 1 clasp, hold, seize, grip, grapple, catch, clutch, clinch, lay hold of 2 understand, comprehend, hold, retain
ANT. 1 loose, release 2 misunderstand

grasp n. 1 grip, hold, clasp, clutches, possession 2 understanding, comprehension, capacity

grateful adj. appreciative, thankful, indebted, obliged, beholden
ANT. ungrateful, unappreciative

gratification n. satisfaction, pleasure, indulgence, enjoyment, delight

gratify v. please, satisfy, delight, gladden, indulge, fulfil
ANT. displease, dissatisfy

gratitude n. thankfulness, appreciation, obligation, gratefulness, indebtedness
ANT. thanklessness, ingratitude, ungratefulness, resentment

gratuitous adj. free, voluntary, uncompensated, groundless, unwarranted, unsought, unnecessary, spontaneous, baseless
ANT. compulsory, involuntary, obligatory, necessary, warranted , well-founded

grave[1] adj. 1 important, serious, weighty, cogent, momentous 2 sober, sedate, thoughtful, staid, solemn, serious, sad, pressing, demure, sombre, somber (N. Am.), heavy
ANT. 1 unimportant, trivial, light 2 happy, joyous

grave[2] n. tomb, vault, crypt

gravity n. 1 seriousness, importance, concern, significance 2 pressure, gravitation
ANT. 1 unimportance, triviality

graze[1] v. scrape, scratch, rub, brush, abrade

graze[2] v. feed, pasture, browse, forage

grease n. oil, lubricant, fat

great adj. 1 large, big, vast, huge, bulky, ample, immense, gigantic, enormous 2 excessive, inordinate, considerable 3 famous, renowned, exalted, prominent, important, significant, elevated, celebrated, noted, distinguished, eminent, famed, illustrious 4 chief, principal, main, leading, major 5 wonderful, excellent, fine, marvellous, fantastic
ANT. 1 small, little 2 slight 3 unknown, lowly, insignificant 4 minor 5 awful

greed n. avarice, avidity, hunger, voracity, ravenousness, gluttony, eagerness, longing, greed, intense desire, grasping, rapacity, selfishness
ANT. generosity, selflessness

greedy adj. selfish, grasping, avaricious, hungry, covetous, eager, desirous, voracious, ravenous, insatiable, gluttonous, rapacious
ANT. generous, unselfish, abstemious

greet v. welcome, salute, address, meet

greeting n. welcome, salutation, address

grief *n.* sadness, sorrow, trouble, tribulation, woe, mourning, affliction, distress, regret, melancholy, bitterness, misery, agony, anguish, heartache, heartbreak
ANT. happiness, joy, delight

grievance *n.* hardship, wrong, injury, burden, oppression, affliction, trial, sorrow, grief, distress, woe, complaint, trouble, injustice
ANT. benefit, privilege

grieve *v.* 1 weep, lament, mourn, sorrow 2 sadden, hurt, distress, wound
ANT. 1 rejoice, celebrate 2 please

grievous *adj.* awful, atrocious, heinous, outrageous, intolerable, dreadful, sad, distressing, regrettable, painful, deplorable, lamentable, hurtful, injurious, detrimental, calamitous, sorrowful, baleful, burdensome, unhappy, disastrous
ANT. acceptable, commendable

grim *adj.* 1 frightful, horrible, hideous, dire, horrid, appalling, terrific, dreadful. ghastly 2 harsh, severe, stern
ANT. 1 attractive 2 mild

grime *n.* filth, dirt, muck, soil

grin *n.* smile, smirk, beam

grin *v.* smile, smirk, beam

grind *v.* 1 crush, pound, mill, grate, pulverize 2 smooth, sharpen, sand, file

grip *v.* clasp, hold, seize, grasp, clutch

grip *n.* hold, clasp, grasp, clutches, possession

groan *v.* moan, cry, sigh, sob

groan *n.* moan, cry, sigh, sob

groove *n.* channel, furrow, rut

grope *v.* feel, touch, fumble

gross *adj.* 1 flagrant, shameful, outrageous, extreme, shameful, glaring 2 coarse, rough, rude, crude, vulgar, indecent, improper, indelicate, sensual, impure, vulgar, low, broad 3 large, big, bulky, heavy, dense, thick 4 whole, total, entire, aggregate
ANT. 2 refined, pure 3 slight 4 net

grotesque *adj.* odd, unnatural, strange, bizarre, fantastic, whimsical, fanciful, droll, extravagant, ludicrous, absurd, ridiculous, burlesque
ANT. normal, ordinary

ground *n.* 1 earth, soil, sod, clod, loam, turf 2 land, region, territory, country, domain 3 estate, land, property, acres, field 4 motive, consideration, reason, basis, base, support, foundation, cause, account

ground *v.* 1 found, base, fix, set, root, establish 2 instruct, teach, train, prepare

groundless *adj.* vain, unfounded, false, baseless, fanciful, gratuitous
ANT. well-founded, authoritative, substantial, actual, authentic

group *n.* gathering, collection, assembly, set, order, bunch, cluster, knot, class, clump

group *v.* 1 assemble, collect, gather 2 sort, classify, arrange, organize

grovel *v.* creep, crawl, sneak, fawn, cringe

grow *v.* 1 enlarge, increase, swell, expand, extend 2 flower, develop, vegetate, shout, sprout, germinate, advance, progress, improve 3 raise, produce, cultivate, nurture, propagate, breed 4 become, go, turn
ANT. 1 diminish, recede, shrink, contract 2 fail, stop, die, wane, decline, subside, ebb, decay

growl *v.* snarl, roar, rumble

growth *n.* increase, enlargement, rise, expansion, extension, progress, improvement
ANT. decline, contraction, decay

grudge *n.* 1 resentment, bitterness, spite 2 grievance, dissatisfaction, discontent, refusal 3 hatred, pique, spite, malice, malevolence

gruff *adj.* curt, rough, brusque, abrupt, surly, churlish
ANT. friendly, polite

grumble *v.* complain, moan, carp, gripe (*informal*)

guarantee *n.* warranty, promise, pledge, assurance, bond

guarantee *v.* certify, warrant, promise, pledge

guard *v.* defend, protect, preserve, safeguard, shield, shelter, patrol, police

guard *n.* patrol, sentry, watch, lookout, warden, keeper, protector, defender, preserver, custodian, conservator, protection

guardian *n.* warden, keeper, protector, defender, preserver, custodian, conservator

guess *v.* suppose, think, believe, fancy, imagine, conjecture, find out, solve, penetrate, fathom, divine, surmise
ANT. know

guess *n.* judgment, opinion, belief, conjecture, estimate, reckoning, theory, hypothesis

guest *n.* visitor, caller
ANT. host

guidance *n.* direction, leading, advice, counsel, help, influence

guide *n.* 1 leader, director, conductor, usher, pilot, escort 2 mentor, monitor, adviser, instructor, counsellor 3 clue, key, hint, sign, pointer 4 guidebook, handbook, manual
ANT. 1 follower

guide *v.* 1 lead, direct, conduct, pilot, steer 2 direct, rule, manage, regulate, govern, control 3 superintend, influence, train, advise, counsel
ANT. 1 follow

guile *n.* cunning, craft, subtlety, artifice, artfulness, deceit, deception, treachery, fastidiousness, hypocrisy, fraud, wiles, trickery
ANT. frankness, simplicity, honesty

guilt *n.* 1 blame, responsibility, fault, guiltiness, culpability, criminality 2 wrong, offensiveness, wickedness, iniquity, sin, offence, offense (*N. Am.*)
ANT. 1 innocence

guilty *adj.* to blame, at fault, responsible, blameworthy, culpable
ANT. innocent, blameless

guise *n.* aspect, appearance, form, shape, figure, manner, mode, fashion

gulf *n.* 1 chasm, ravine, abyss, rift 2 bay, inlet, sound

gulp *v.* swallow, bolt, guzzle, eat/drink quickly

gum *n.* adhesive, glue, paste

gumption *n.* sense, good sense, common sense, shrewdness, discernment, skill, cleverness, ability

gun *n.* revolver, pistol, rifle, shotgun

gurgle *v.* babble, burble, ripple

gush *v.* burst, stream, flow, rush, spout, spurt, pour out, flow out

gust *n.* 1 puff, breeze, wind, gale, blast, squall 2 feeling, emotion, fit, outburst, burst

gutter *n.* channel, ditch, drain, trough, trench

habit *n*. **1** custom, practice, use, way, manner, usage, wont, fashion, system, routine, rule, habituation, familiarity, association, inurement **2** addiction, compulsion, dependence, obsession

habitat *n*. environment, surroundings, element, ambience

habitual *adj*. usual, customary, wonted, common, accustomed, regular, ordinary, familiar, everyday, perpetual
ANT. unusual, occasional, irregular, extraordinary

haggard *adj*. gaunt, lean, spare, drawn, worn, wasted, rawboned, attenuated, wrinkled, ghastly, hollow-eyed
ANT. fresh, bright

hail¹ *n*. **1** ice, rain, sleet, snow **2** shower, barrage, onslaught, volley, bombardment

hail² *v*. greet, welcome, address, salute, call, speak, signal
ANT. ignore, avoid, insult, rebuff

hair *n*. locks, growth, beard, moustache, mustache (*N. Am.*), coat, fur

halcyon *adj*. calm, quiet, placid, still, peaceful, tranquil, happy, undisturbed, unruffled, serene
ANT. stormy, tempestuous

hale *adj*. healthy, sound, strong, robust, hearty, hardy, well
ANT. feeble, ill, weak

half-hearted *adj*. unenthusiastic, cool, lukewarm, indifferent, uncaring
ANT. enthusiastic, keen

hall *n*. lobby, foyer, vestibule, passage, corridor

hallow *v*. honour, honor (*N. Am.*), consecrate, dedicate, sanctify, devote, make holy, reverence, venerate, respect, pay homage to
ANT. desecrate, profane, execrate, blaspheme, abominate

halt *v*. stop, hold, stand, pull up, cease, rest, falter, pause, stand still, hesitate
ANT. advance, proceed

hamper¹ *v*. hinder, obstruct, prevent, thwart, restrain, impede, fetter, entangle, shackle, clog, encumber
ANT. assist, expedite, speed, accelerate

hamper² *n*. basket, pannier

hand *n*. **1** palm, fingers, paw (*informal*), mitt (*informal*) **2** help, assistance, aid, support **3** helper, assistant, labourer, laborer (*N. Am.*), worker, operative, artisan, craftsperson, employee **4** agency, share, part, intervention, participation
ANT. 3 employer

at hand near, nearby, close, handy, accessible, available **hand down** pass on, bequeath, will **hand out** distribute, pass out, give out **hand over** transfer, deliver, pass over

handicap *n*. hindrance, disadvantage, obstacle, drawback, disability

handicap *v*. hinder, prevent, thwart, disable

handle *v*. **1** touch, feel, finger **2** tackle, manage, use, wield, control, treat, deal with, operate, manipulate

handle *adj*. knob, grip

handsome *adj*. **1** good-looking, attractive, fine, elegant, becoming **2** generous, liberal, ample, large, considerable
ANT. 1 ugly **2** mean, stingy

handy *adj*. **1** convenient, near, at hand, nearby, close **2** dexterous, adroit, skilful, skillful (*N. Am.*), skilled, ready, clever, expert
ANT. 1 inconvenient, remote **2** awkward, clumsy

hang *v*. **1** rest, lean, suspend, dangle, incline, drop, decline, droop **2** execute, kill, lynch **3** hover, float, waft, drift
ANT. 1 stand

hanker v. long, yearn, desire, crave, covet

haphazard adj. chance, random, arbitrary, accidental
ANT. intended, deliberate

happen v. take place, come to pass, occur, befall, chance, betide

happiness n. delight, joy, pleasure, enjoyment, well-being, light-heartedness, cheerfulness, satisfaction, comfort, bliss, triumph, mirth, gaiety, ecstasy, gladness, rejoicing, rapture, contentment, merriment, blessedness
ANT. grief, sorrow, anguish, trouble, misfortune, affliction, disaster, woe, agony, distress, melancholy

happy adj. 1 glad, joyful, cheerful, contented, pleased, satisfied, blessed, delighted, joyous, jolly, successful, rejoicing, blissful, lucky, merry, fortunate, buoyant, bright, cheery, smiling 2 fortunate, lucky, favourable, favorable (N. Am.), felicitous, seasonable, auspicious, opportune
ANT. 1 unhappy, sad, miserable 2 unlucky, unfortunate, infelicitous

harangue n. speech, address, lecture, sermon, tirade, oration

harangue v. lecture, address, hold forth, declaim, spout (informal)

harass v. vex, plague, worry, distress, trouble, disturb, torment, fatigue, tire, weary, annoy, exhaust
ANT. relieve, refresh, comfort

harbinger n. herald, forerunner, precursor, announcer

harbour, harbor (N. Am.) n. 1 port, haven, destination, home, anchorage 2 asylum, refuge, shelter, cover, retreat, sanctuary, resting-place

harbour, harbor (N. Am.) v. 1 shelter, lodge, house, protect, shield 2 entertain, indulge, foster, cherish
ANT. 1 expose, reject 2 expel, discard, discourage, banish, dismiss

hard adj. 1 firm, solid, compact, impenetrable, rigid, unyielding 2 difficult, complicated, knotty, puzzling, intricate, perplexing 3 laborious, difficult, arduous, toilsome, wearying, fatiguing 4 harsh, unkind, cruel, oppressive, rigorous, severe, exacting, inflexible, obdurate, callous, unfeeling, unsympathetic 5 grievous, distressing, painful, calamitous, unpleasant, disagreeable
ANT. 1 soft, pliable 2 simple, uncomplicated 3 easy, undemanding, simple 4 tender, kind 5 pleasant

hard up poor, needy, poverty-stricken, insolvent, down and out, broke (informal), skint (informal)
ANT. rich

harden v. 1 consolidate, set, compact, solidify, petrify 2 fortify, strengthen, toughen, steel, nerve, brace 3 season, form, train, accustom, habituate, inure
ANT. 1 soften, melt 2 weaken, relax

hardly adv. scarcely, barely, narrowly, just, only just, no sooner

hardship n. difficulty, trial, affliction, trouble, misfortune, calamity, burden

hardy adj. strong, robust, firm, tough, sturdy, stout, healthy, rigorous, hale, sound, hearty
ANT. weak, delicate, tender, fragile, frail, infirm

harm v. injure, hurt, damage, spoil, mar, abuse
ANT. benefit

harm n. injury, hurt, damage, abuse, prejudice, disadvantage, evil, criminality, wrong, wickedness, misfortune, ill, mishap
ANT. benefit, good, improvement

harmful adj. hurtful, injurious, damaging, detrimental, dangerous, cruel, pernicious, destructive
ANT. beneficial

harmless adj. innocuous, innocent, inoffensive, gentle
ANT. harmful, hurtful, noxious, deadly, pernicious, destructive

harmonious adj. 1 melodious, tuneful, musical, concordant, harmonic, consonant, dulcet, mellifluous 2 friendly, cordial, amicable, congenial 3 correspondent, compatible, consistent, symmetrical, congruent
ANT. 1 unmelodious, grating 2 unfriendly, quarrelsome 3 incongruous, inconsistent

harmony *n.* agreement, conformity, consonance, congruity, consistency, concord, amity, unison, unanimity, unity, accord, uniformity, symmetry, union
ANT. conflict, disagreement, antagonism, opposition, incongruity, difference, inconsistency

harness *n.* bridle, yoke, tack, tackle, straps

harness *v.* control, use, utilize, exploit

harrowing *adj.* distressing, disturbing, agonizing, terrifying, tormenting

harsh *adj.* 1 rough, hard, severe, stern, austere, cruel, acrimonious, ill-natured, unkind, unfeeling, rude, uncivil, blunt, ungracious, gruff, brutal 2 grating, coarse, rough, discordant, jarring
ANT. 1 gentle, kind 2 mellow, tuneful, melodious

harvest *n.* fruit, crop, yield, increase, result, return, proceeds, product, growth, ingathering, harvest festival, harvest time, harvest home

harvest *v.* gather, collect, reap, glean

haste *n.* speed, quickness, hurry, swiftness, dispatch, celerity, promptitude
ANT. delay, slowness, tardiness

hasten *v.* 1 accelerate, speed, hurry, expedite, dispatch, quicken, precipitate, press on, urge forward 2 rush, hurry, run, dash, fly
ANT. 1 retard, impede, obstruct 2 dawdle, linger

hasty *adj.* 1 quick, fast, rapid, brisk, swift, speedy 2 cursory, slight, hurried, superficial, rushed 3 rash, impetuous, reckless, precipitate, headlong, indiscreet, thoughtless
ANT. 1 slow, leisurely 2 careful, reflective 3 thoughtful, deliberate

hat *n.* cap, hood, bonnet, beret

hatch *v.* 1 incubate, brood 2 devise, conceive, scheme, plot, plan

hate *v.* detest, loathe, abhor, dislike, abominate, execrate
ANT. like, love

hate *n.* hatred, loathing, abhorrence, dislike, aversion, execration
ANT. like, love

hate *n.* enmity, dislike, hostility, abhorrence, loathing, aversion, spite, revenge, grudge, ill-will, malice, antipathy, resentment, animosity, repugnance, detestation, malevolence
ANT. love

hateful *adj.* abominable, detestable, odious, execrable, abhorrent, horrid, shocking, loathsome, disgusting, nauseous, foul, repulsive, offensive, vile, obnoxious, revolting, repugnant, heinous, accursed, damnable
ANT. lovely, delightful, attractive, enjoyable, pleasant

hatred *n.* enmity, dislike, hostility, abhorrence, loathing, aversion, spite, revenge, grudge, ill-will, malice, antipathy, resentment, animosity, repugnance, detestation, malevolence
ANT. love

haughty *adj.* proud, arrogant, vain, conceited, snobbish, snooty (*informal*)
ANT. humble, modest, lowly

haul *v.* pull, drag, draw, lug
ANT. push

have *v.* 1 hold, occupy, own, possess, be in possession of, regard, consider, esteem 2 obtain, get, acquire, receive, accept, take, gain 3 experience, undergo, feel, suffer, enjoy 4 give birth to, bear, bring forth, beget

have to must, be obliged to, be compelled to

havoc *n.* 1 devastation, destruction, desolation, waste, ruin, ravage 2 chaos, disorder, mayhem

hazard *n.* danger, jeopardy, peril, venture, risk, chance

hazard *v.* risk, venture, chance, stake, gamble, dare

hazardous *adj.* risky, dangerous, perilous, precarious, unsafe
ANT. safe, secure

haze *n.* mist, fog, cloud

hazy *adj.* foggy, misty, cloudy, murky, gloomy, nebulous, filmy, gauzy
ANT. clear, transparent, bright, shining

head *n.* 1 skull, brain, nut (*informal*) 2 understanding, mind, thought, intellect, intelligence 3 top, summit, front, acme

4 chief, leader, commander, superintendent, director **5** source, origin, beginning, start, rise, commencement **6** class, section, department, category, division **7** crown, crisis, culmination
ANT. **3** bottom, foot **4** subordinate **5** end

head *v.* lead, direct, command, guide, control, run, manage, rule, govern

head *adj.* chief, leading, main, first, top, principal

headstrong *adj.* self-willed, stubborn, obstinate, wilful, willful (*N. Am.*), intractable

headway *n.* progress, advance, movement

heal *v.* cure, remedy, restore, make well, recover
ANT. harm, hurt, injure, wound

health *n.* well-being, fitness, strength, wholeness
ANT. illness

healthy *adj.* **1** fit, well, vigorous, strong, sound, robust, wholesome **2** healthful, sanitary, hygienic, hearty, hale, salutary, salubrious, invigorating, bracing
ANT. **1** ill, sickly, weak, diseased, feeble, emaciated, fainting, failing, unsound **2** unhealthy, noxious, insalubrious

heap *n.* pile, stack, mound, mass, collection, abundance, lot, plenty

hear *v.* listen to, catch, perceive

heart *n.* **1** interior, centre, center (*N. Am.*), essence, core, kernel **2** temperament, disposition, mind, will, inclination, feelings, emotion, passion **3** love, affection, feeling, emotion, sympathy **4** courage, bravery, boldness, firmness, spirit, fortitude, resolution
ANT. **1** surface, exterior **3** cruelty, apathy **4** cowardice

heartbroken *adj.* miserable, wretched, desolate, cheerless, comfortless, in despair, broken-hearted, forlorn, disconsolate, inconsolable
ANT. cheerful, hopeful

hearty *adj.* **1** warm, cheery, cordial, jovial, sincere, earnest, true, deep, profound, heartfelt, unfeigned, active, lively, zealous, vigorous, energetic, animated **2** large, nourishing, rich, nutritious
ANT. **1** cold, indifferent

heat *n.* **1** warmth, high temperature, hotness, fever **2** excitement, ardour, ardor (*N. Am.*), earnestness, fervour, fervor (*N. Am.*), zeal, flush, vehemence, impetuosity, passion, intensity, violence **3** contest, race, competition, trial
ANT. **1** cold **2** coolness, indifference

heathen *adj.* pagan, ungodly, godless, unbelieving
ANT. godly

heave *v.* **1** pull, drag, draw, haul **2** lift, hoist, raise, boost, elevate
ANT. **1** push **2** lower

heaven *n.* **1** firmament, sky, paradise, Elysium **2** bliss, ecstasy, happiness, rapture
ANT. **1** hell **2** misery, agony, torment

heavenly *adj.* **1** celestial, divine, angelic, godlike, saintly, sainted, blessed, holy, beatific, beatified, glorified, blest **2** wonderful, delightful, lovely, exquisite, glorious, great, super, fantastic
ANT. **1** hellish **2** awful

heavy *adj.* **1** weighty, ponderous, large, bulky, massive **2** intense, extreme, severe, great, concentrated **3** oppressive, grievous, burdensome, cumbersome, depressing, overwhelming **4** dull, sluggish, inert, inactive, stupid, torpid, indolent, slow, lifeless, inanimate **5** sad, gloomy, dejected, depressed, sorrowful, despondent, melancholy, disconsolate, crushed, downcast, crestfallen **6** difficult, onerous, laborious, hard, tedious, weary, tiresome, wearisome **7** dark, gloomy, cloudy, lowering, overcast, dull **8** miry, muddy, clayey, cloggy, soggy **9** impenetrable, solid, stolid, thick
ANT. **1** light **2** light, slight, minima **3** light **4** active **5** happy, cheerful, light **6** simple, easy **7** fine, bright, fresh **8** light

hectic *adj.* busy, rushed, frantic, excited, riotous, wild
ANT. calm

hector *v.* bully, menace, browbeat, threaten, vex, tease, annoy, worry, provoke, harass,
swagger, bluster, boast, vaunt

heed *v.* listen to, obey, observe, regard, notice, mind, attend
ANT. ignore, disregard, neglect

heed *n.* attention, mind, care, notice, regard, watchfulness, carefulness

heedful *adj.* mindful, attentive, regardful, watchful, careful, cautious, wary, observing, provident, circumspect
ANT. careless, thoughtless, inattentive, negligent, regardless, unmindful, neglectful, remiss, inconsiderate

height *n.* 1 altitude, elevation, tallness, loftiness, summit, top, apex, acme, climax, maximum, culmination 2 hill, mountain
ANT. 1 depth 2 depression

heighten *v.* 1 increase, enhance, augment, intensify, exaggerate, amplify, aggravate 2 elevate, raise, lift, magnify, exalt, ennoble
ANT. 1 moderate 2 lower

heinous *adj.* evil, wicked, hateful, detestable, odious, abominable, execrable, flagrant, infamous, villainous, nefarious, atrocious, enormous, monstrous
ANT. excellent, laudable, distinguished, praiseworthy, justifiable, meritorious, excusable

heir *n.* child, descendant, offspring, inheritor

hell *n.* perdition, underworld, torment, misery, anguish
ANT. heaven

help *v.* 1 aid, assist, encourage, foster, succour, succor (*N. Am.*), sustain, support, abet, cooperate, second, stand by, promote 2 improve, relieve, alleviate, remedy, restore 3 avoid, prevent, withstand, refrain from
ANT. 1 hinder, obstruct 2 aggravate

help *n.* aid, assistance, support, backing, cooperation, encouragement, succour, succor (*N. Am.*), relief

helper *n.* assistant, aide, supporter, backer, ally, partner, colleague
ANT. opponent, enemy

helpful *adj.* beneficial, advantageous, profitable, useful, valuable
ANT. useless

helpless *adj.* impotent, weak, feeble, powerless, defenceless, defenseless (*N. Am.*), unprotected
ANT. strong

hem *n.* edge, border, trimming

herald *n.* messenger, announcer, forerunner, harbinger

herb *n.* spice, plant, flavouring, flavoring (*N. Am.*)

herd *n.* drove, pack, flock, crowd, group

herd *v.* gather, congregate, collect, assemble
ANT. disperse, scatter

hereditary *adj.* ancestral, lineal, inherited, transmitted
ANT. acquired

heresy *n.* heterodoxy, error, schism, unorthodoxy
ANT. orthodoxy, soundness

heritage *n.* inheritance, legacy, bequest, tradition, portion, estate

hermetical *adj.* air-tight, close
ANT. loose, open

hermit *n.* recluse, anchorite, eremite

hero *n.* champion, conqueror, warrior, star, idol

heroic *adj.* brave, courageous, bold, daring, intrepid, valiant, fearless, dauntless, noble, magnanimous, gallant, chivalrous
ANT. cowardly, fearful, timorous

heroism *n.* bravery, courage, boldness, daring, fearlessness, gallantry
ANT. cowardice, fearfulness

hesitate *v.* 1 pause, delay, wait, waver, vacillate 2 falter, stammer, stutter
ANT. 1 proceed

heterogeneous *adj.* unlike, variant, various, conglomerate, mingled, mixed, discordant, miscellaneous, dissimilar, strange, different, opposed, contrary, contrasted., alien
ANT. homogeneous, identical, like, same, uniform, similar, like, congruous

hew *v.* 1 cut, chop, hack 2 engrave, carve, sculpture, smooth, fashion, form, mould, mold (*N. Am.*), model

hidden *adj.* concealed, unseen, masked, veiled, obscure
ANT. open

hide *v.* conceal, secrete, mask, veil, cloak, protect, store, disguise, screen, cover, suppress, shelter, withhold, bury, inter, entomb
ANT. expose, disclose, reveal, unveil, unmask, uncover

hide *n.* skin, leather, pelt, fur

hideous *adj.* ugly, monstrous, frightful, dreadful, appalling, horrible, ghastly, terrible, horrid, grim, shocking, grisly
ANT. beautiful, attractive, lovely

hierarchy *n.* system, authority, bureaucracy, officialdom

high *adj.* 1 tall, towering, lofty, uplifted, elevated, eminent, steep, noble, exalted 2 prominent, superior, distinguished, pre-eminent, eminent, important, powerful, dignified, great 3 shrill, raised, sharp, high-pitched 4 proud, haughty, arrogant, supercilious, lordly, despotic, domineering, overbearing, tyrannical, extreme, intense, great, strong, sharp 5 expensive, dear, costly
ANT. 1 low 2 inferior, unimportant 3 deep 4 humble 5 cheap, inexpensive

highlight *v.* stress, emphasize, underline, accentuate, spotlight
ANT. play down

highly *adv.* extremely, very, exceptionally

hike *n.* walk, trek, ramble

hill *n.* mound, rise, incline, slope

hinder *v.* interrupt, obstruct, oppose, prevent, stay, stop, delay, retard, hamper, impede, check, bar, clog, counteract, frustrate, foil, resist, thwart, block
ANT. quicken, hasten, speed, accelerate, expedite, enable, facilitate, promote

hindrance *n.* impediment, obstacle, obstruction, opposition, resistance, frustration, block, bar
ANT. assistance, hastening

hinge *v.* depend, rely, be dependent, pivot, turn, move, work, rotate

hint *n.* suggestion, intimation, clue, tip

hint *v.* suggest, intimate, imply, mention, tip off

hire *v.* 1 engage, commission, rent, employ 2 lease, let, rent

hire *n.* lease, let, rent, rental, charter

hiss *v.* boo, shout down, jeer

historic *adj.* momentous, significant, important, famous, remarkable
ANT. unimportant

history *n.* chronicle, annals, record, register, story, tale, memoir, narrative, account, archives, narration, muniment, memorial, autobiography, biography

hit *v.* 1 strike, beat, smack, batter, slap, thump, clash, collide 2 reach, achieve, attain, win, secure, gain

hit upon discover, find, come upon, think of

hit *n.* stroke, blow, beat, smack, slap, thump, clash, collision

hitch *v.* tie, attach, fasten, unite, connect
ANT. untie

hoard *v.* accumulate, amass, store, deposit, save, husband, treasure
ANT. waste, squander

hoarse *adj.* rough, harsh, low, husky, raucous, grating, guttural, gruff
ANT. clear

hoary *adj.* white, grey, gray (*N. Am.*), silvery, frosty
ANT. dark, black

hoax *n.* trick, practical joke, deception, prank, fraud, cheat

hobble *v.* limp, falter, stumble, totter, dodder

hobby *n.* pastime, recreation, diversion, leisure activity, amusement

hoist *v.* raise, lift, elevate, winch, erect
ANT. lower

hold *v.* 1 clasp, grasp, clutch, clinch, grip, seize 2 possess, have, keep, retain 3 convene, run, call, assemble, carry on, conduct, observe 4 think, consider, maintain, believe, notice, judge, esteem, count, reckon, deem 5 detain, imprison, restrain, confine, stop, stay, arrest 6 stick, cohere, adhere, cling, persist, last, endure, remain, stay 7 stand, be true, be valid, exist
ANT. 1 drop 2 lose 3 cancel 5 release 6 fall apart

hold *n.* 1 grip, clasp, grasp 2 influence, sway, power, control

hole *n.* 1 opening, gap, break, aperture, breach, rift, tear, rip 2 hollow, cavity, depression, pit, cave, cavern, burrow, den, lair

holiday *n.* vacation, rest, break, time off

hollow *adj.* **1** empty, void, unfilled, vacant, vacuous, cavernous **2** insincere, false, empty, meaningless, pointless, faithless, hypocritical, treacherous, deceitful
ANT. **1** solid, full **2** firm, sincere

holy *adj.* blessed, hallowed, sacred, consecrated, devoted, set apart, righteous, saintly, spiritual, devout, saintlike, sanctified, divine, godly, religious, heavenly-minded, pious, pure
ANT. wicked, profane, evil, unsanctified, unconsecrated, unhallowed

homage *n.* reverence, obeisance, respect, deference, duty, service, honour, honor (*N. Am.*), allegiance, devotion, loyalty, fidelity, fealty, submission, veneration
ANT. disrespect, rebellion

home *n.* house, residence, dwelling, domicile, abode, habitation, hearth, fireside

homely *adj.* **1** domestic, homelike, family, household **2** plain, everyday, simple, crude, coarse, unattractive, inelegant, homespun
ANT. **2** attractive, elegant

honest *adj.* **1** upright, virtuous, conscientious, just, true, faithful, trusty, reliable, trustworthy, truthful, honourable, honorable (*N. Am.*), fair, open, straightforward, equitable, moral, decent, reputable, respectable **2** open, candid, truthful, ingenuous, sincere, unreserved
ANT. **1** lying, unscrupulous, deceitful, dishonest, false, hypocritical, fraudulent **2** insincere, vicious

honesty *n.* **1** integrity, uprightness, probity, justice, fairness, equity, honour, honor (*N. Am.*), truth, truthfulness, veracity, fidelity, faithfulness **2** sincerity, candour, candor (*N. Am.*), frankness, openness, unreserve, ingenuousness, straightforwardness
ANT. **1** dishonesty, guile, fraud, deception, unfairness **2** insincerity, chicanery

honour, honor (*N. Am.*) *n.* **1** reverence, respect, homage, deference, civility, reputation, repute, fame, esteem, credit, glory, consideration, dignity, elevation, distinction **2** integrity, probity, rectitude, pride, nobility, eminence,

high-mindedness, spirit, self-respect, grandeur, renown
ANT. **1** contempt, irreverence, disrespect **2** dishonesty, deception

honour, honor (*N. Am.*) *v.* **1** respect, value, esteem **2** admire, revere, worship, venerate **3** accept, acknowledge, pay, clear, discharge
ANT. **1** shame **2** despise

honourable, honorable (*N. Am.*) *adj.* **1** honest, upright, high-minded, great, just, fair, trustworthy, conscientious, virtuous, estimable, reputable, right, proper, creditable, equitable **2** famous, illustrious, noble, distinguished, eminent
ANT. **1** shameful **2** notorious

honorary *adj.* unofficial, nominal, gratuitous, titular
ANT. professional, official

hood *n.* covering, bonnet, veil, shawl, mantle

hook *n.* clasp, fastener, catch

hoot *v.* screech, shriek, howl, bellow, cry, yell

hoot *n.* screech, shriek, howl, bellow, cry, yell

hop *v.* skip, jump, leap

hope *n.* **1** anticipation, expectancy, expectation, possibility, prospect, longing, vision, desire **2** trust, confidence, faith, reliance
ANT. **1** distrust **2** despair, despondency

hope *v.* expect, believe, desire, wish, long, yearn

hopeful *adj.* **1** optimistic, confident, assured **2** encouraging, favourable, favorable (*N. Am.*), promising
ANT. **1** despairing, pessimistic **2** discouraging, unfavourable, unfavorable (*N. Am.*)

hopeless *adj.* **1** despairing, dejected, desperate, despondent, downcast, pessimistic **2** useless, worthless, pointless, vain, futile **3** inadequate, poor, weak, incompetent
ANT. **1** hopeful, optimistic **2** worthwhile, useful **3** good, proficient

horizontal *adj.* plain, level, straight, even, plane
ANT. vertical, upright, inclined, uneven, slanting, sloping

horrible *adj.* horrid, frightful, terrible, awful, harrowing, dreadful, hideous, alarming, dire, portentous, appalling, horrific, horrifying, dreadful, hideous, abominable, ghastly, detestable, hateful
ANT. lovely, wonderful, enjoyable, attractive

horrid *adj.* horrible, frightful, terrible, awful, dreadful, hideous

horror *n.* **1** alarm, dread, fear, fright, consternation, terror, dismay, panic **2** abomination, abhorrence, detestation, disgust, hatred, aversion, loathing, shuddering, antipathy

horse *n.* steed, charger, stallion, gelding, mare, colt, pony, foal, nag, filly

hospitable *adj.* generous, liberal, bountiful, open, kind, warm, unconstrained, unreserved, receptive, sociable, neighbourly, neighborly (*N. Am.*), charitable
ANT. unsociable, exclusive

hospital *n.* clinic, infirmary, medical centre, medical center (*N. Am.*)

hospitality *n.* generosity, liberality, openness, kindness, warmth

host¹ *n.* **1** entertainer, compere, presenter, MC, emcee, leader of ceremonies, moderator **2** innkeeper, landlord, landlady
ANT. **2** guest, traveller, traveler (*N. Am.*), boarder, lodger

host² *n.* multitude, crowd, horde, throng, number, army, legion

hostage *n.* captive, prisoner, security, bail, surety

hostel *n.* inn, guest house, boarding house, lodging house

hostile *adj.* unfriendly, antagonistic, adverse, opposite, contrary, repugnant, opposing, opposed, inimical, warlike
ANT. friendly, kind

hostility *n.* enmity, animosity, hatred, unfriendliness, ill will, opposition, repugnance
ANT. friendship, sympathy

hot *adj.* **1** burning, fiery, blazing, scorching, scalding, heated, very warm **2** passionate, excitable, impetuous, irascible, furious, violent, ardent, fervent, vehement, eager, glowing, animated, fervid **3** pungent, sharp, acrid, spicy, peppery, stinging, biting, piquant, highly flavoured, highly flavored (*N. Am.*)
ANT. **1** cold, frigid, cool, arctic, chilled, chilly, wintry, frosty, icy **2** unresponsive, unfeeling, stoical, passionless, uninspiring, dull, dead, indifferent, apathetic, unconcerned

hotel *n.* guest house, motel, lodge, boarding house, inn

hot-headed *adj.* hasty, rash, reckless, impetuous
ANT. calm, composed

hound *v.* chase, dog, pursue, hunt, persecute, pester, harry

house *n.* home, building, dwelling, residence, domicile

house *v.* accommodate, lodge, shelter, contain, hold

hover *v.* float, fly, drift, hang

howl *v.* yowl, cry, shriek, roar

hubbub *n.* noise, uproar, tumult, turmoil, racket, commotion, fuss

huddle *v.* crowd, bunch, throng, nestle, snuggle

hue *n.* shade, colour, color (*N. Am.*), tone, tint, tinge, complexion

hug *v.* embrace, clasp, cuddle, grasp, press

hug *n.* embrace, clasp, cuddle, grasp, press

huge *adj.* immense, enormous, big, large, great, colossal, gigantic, monstrous
ANT. small, minute

human *n.* human being, person, individual, mortal, man, woman, child, young person

humane *adj.* kind, tender, compassionate, charitable, benevolent, sympathetic, gentle, kind-hearted, tender-hearted
ANT. unkind, cruel

humanity *n.* **1** human race, people, human beings, humans, humankind, mankind **2** kindness, tenderness, sympathy, charity, humaneness, good nature, benevolence, philanthropy
ANT. **2** unkindness, cruelty

humanize *v.* civilize, cultivate, refine, polish, improve, enlighten, educate, soften, mellow
ANT. barbarize, degrade, debase, brutalize

humble *adj.* meek, modest, unassuming, unobtrusive, lowly, unpretending, submissive, poor, low
ANT. proud, assuming, pretentious, boastful, arrogant

humid *adj.* damp, wet, moist, muggy, close, sultry, clammy, sticky
ANT. dry, arid, moistureless, parched

humiliate *v.* shame, disgrace, abase, humble, mortify, embarrass

humour, humor (*N. Am.*) *n.* **1** fun, comedy, amusement, joking, jocularity, wit, facetiousness **2** disposition, temper, mood, frame of mind, fancy, caprice, whim, vagary, bent, bias
ANT. **1** seriousness

humorous *adj.* funny, comical, comic, ludicrous, farcical, pleasant, witty, amusing, entertaining, facetious, jocular, jocose
ANT. serious, sober, solemn

hump *n.* bulge, protuberance, swelling, knob

hunch *n.* guess, feeling, intuition, suspicion

hunch *v.* stoop, crouch, bend, arch

hungry *adj.* famished, starving, ravenous
ANT. full

hunt *v.* **1** chase, pursue, trail, track, stalk **2** search, seek, look for
ANT. **2** find

hunt *n.* chase, pursuit, tracking, stalking, search, quest

hurdle *n.* **1** fence, barrier, barricade **2** impediment, hindrance, difficulty, obstacle, problem

hurl *v.* throw, fling, pitch, cast, sling

hurry *v.* **1** rush, race, run, speed **2** urge, rush, expedite, dispatch, accelerate
ANT. **1** loiter, dawdle, saunter, move slowly **2** delay, retard, slow down

hurry *n.* haste, rush, flurry, precipitation, confusion, bustle, agitation, perturbation, celerity, expedition, quickness, promptness
ANT. slowness

hurt *v.* injure, harm, damage, impair, mar, wound, distress, grieve, pain, afflict, bruise
ANT. heal, soothe

hurt *n.* damage, harm, injury, wound, pain, mischief, disadvantage, detriment
ANT. benefit, pleasure

hurtful *adj.* harmful, injurious, mischievous, detrimental, disadvantageous, pernicious, noxious, prejudicial
ANT. helpful, beneficial, good, advantageous, wholesome

hush *v.* silence, still, quiet, quieten

hustle *v.* hurry, push, jostle, elbow, rush

hut *n.* shed, cabin, hovel, shanty, lodge, shelter

hybrid *adj.* mixed, impure, mongrel, cross, crossbreed, half-breed
ANT. pure, unmixed, thoroughbred

hygienic *adj.* clean, disinfected, pure, healthy

hypnotize *v.* mesmerize, fascinate, entrance

hypocrisy *n.* pretence, pretense (*N. Am.*), sham, affectation, hollowness, deceit, deception, dissimulation, false profession, imposture, formalism, Pharisaism, cant, pietism, sanctimoniousness, assumed piety
ANT. sincerity, transparency, truth, honesty, genuineness, ingenuousness

hypocrite *n.* deceiver, impostor, pretender, cheat, fraud, dissembler, formalist

hypocritical *adj.* false, hollow, faithless, deceitful, insincere, dissembling, pharisaical, sanctimonious
ANT. sincere, transparent, genuine, candid, truthful

hypothesis *n.* supposition, conjecture, guess, surmise, theory, speculation

hysterical *adj.* crazed, crazy, mad, frenzied, wild, uncontrollable, delirious

I

icy *adj.* frozen, freezing, ice-cold, cold, chilly
ANT. hot

idea *n.* **1** thought, concept, conception, impression, judgment, plan, opinion, design, theory, belief, notion, supposition **2** aim, purpose, meaning, intention, design
ANT. **1** fact, reality

ideal *n.* example, original, model, standard, prototype, archetype

ideal *adj.* perfect, supreme, model, exemplary

identical *adj.* same, alike, indistinguishable, particular
ANT. different, separate, contrary

identify *v.* recognize, name, classify

identity *n.* personality, individuality, uniqueness, self

idiocy *n.* stupidity, folly, senselessness, imbecility, foolishness, irrationality, insanity
ANT. wisdom, common sense, soundness

idiom *n.* phrase, expression, turn of phrase

idiosyncrasy *n.* peculiarity, mannerism, quirk, characteristic, individuality, singularity, eccentricity

idiot *n.* fool, imbecile, moron, nincompoop, blockhead

idiotic *adj.* foolish, silly, stupid, daft, senseless, inane, moronic
ANT. wise

idle *adj.* **1** lazy, indolent, inert, slothful, unoccupied, vacant, inactive, sluggish, unemployed **2** useless, unavailing, vain, abortive, futile, ineffectual, fruitless **3** trivial, unimportant, empty
ANT. **1** active, busy, diligent, industrious, employed, working, occupied **2** useful, profitable

idol *n.* image, statue, god, graven image

idolize *v.* deify, adore, worship, revere, venerate
ANT. loathe, abominate, abhor

ignite *v.* fire, light, set fire to, kindle

ignition *n.* firing, timing

ignoble *adj.* worthless, insignificant, contemptible, low, base, mean, disgraceful, inferior, unworthy, humble, plebeian, vulgar
ANT. eminent, exalted, noble

ignominious *adj.* dishonourable, dishonorable (*N. Am.*), infamous, disgraceful, contemptible, shameful, scandalous, disreputable, despicable, base
ANT. honourable, honorable (*N. Am.*), creditable, reputable, worthy

ignominy *n.* dishonour, dishonor (*N. Am.*), disgrace, discredit, shame, infamy, disrepute, contempt, scandal, reprobation, reproach
ANT. credit, honour, honor (*N. Am.*), reputation, glory, distinction, renown

ignorance *n.* illiteracy, stupidity, unintelligence, blindness, darkness
ANT. knowledge, wisdom, sense, learning, erudition

ignorant *adj.* **1** uneducated, untrained, illiterate, unlearned, unlettered, unskilled, untaught, untutored, ill-informed, uninstructed, uninformed **2** unaware, unconscious, unmindful, in the dark
ANT. **1** educated, learned, instructed, wise, skilled, cultured, trained, well-informed **2** aware, conscious, mindful

ignore *v.* disregard, neglect, overlook, omit, reject, disown, repudiate
ANT. notice, recognize

ill *adj.* sick, ailing, diseased, poorly, unwell, unhealthy, indisposed
ANT. healthy, well, strong, good, robust, hearty, hale

ill-bred *adj.* impolite, uncivil, uncourteous, uncourtly, uncouth, unpolished, rude, ill-behaved, ill-mannered
ANT. polite, well-behaved, civil, refined, courteous

illegal *adj.* unlawful, forbidden, prohibited, illicit
ANT. legal, allowed

illegible *adj.* unreadable, indecipherable, unintelligible
ANT. legible, readable

illness *n.* sickness, ailment, disease, infirmity, malady

illuminate *v.* 1 light, illumine, light up 2 enlighten, make wise, instruct, inspire
ANT. 1 darken, obscure 2 dim, mislead, delude

illusion *n.* delusion, hallucination, mirage, dream, vision, myth, deception, error, fallacy, mockery, fantasy, chimera
ANT. reality

illusive *adj.* delusive, deceptive, deceitful, fallacious, unreal, erroneous, false, imaginary, illusory, disappointing
ANT. substantial, real, true

illustrate *v.* 1 explain, exemplify, make clear, elucidate, interpret, demonstrate, represent, image 2 decorate, adorn, embellish
ANT. 1 obscure, misinterpret, confuse, mystify, darken, misrepresent

illustration *n.* 1 picture, photograph, figure, drawing 2 explanation, interpretation, example, instance, demonstration

illustrator *n.* painter, artist

illustrious *adj.* famous, famed, noted, renowned, distinguished, celebrated, eminent, remarkable, glorious, splendid
ANT. ignominious, disgraceful, infamous

ill will *n.* malevolence, unkindness, malice, enmity, hatred, hate, dislike, antipathy, aversion, grudge, uncharitableness, bitterness
ANT. good will, benevolence, beneficence

image *n.* 1 likeness, representation, picture, resemblance, effigy, figure, similitude 2 idea, copy, picture, notion, conception, fiction, shadow, vision 3 statue, idol, object of worship
ANT. 1 original 2 reality, original

imaginary *adj.* unreal, fanciful, fictitious, legendary, mythical, pretend
ANT. real, actual

imagination *n.* creative power, originality, inventiveness, ingenuity, conception, fantasy

imaginative *adj.* inventive, creative, ingenious, romantic, ideal, original, poetical, poetic
ANT. unimaginative, literal, uninventive

imagine *v.* 1 conceive, think, image, fancy, picture, envisage, devise, contrive, frame, project, invent, create 2 suppose, think, believe, assume, surmise, understand, presume, deem, apprehend

imbecile *n.* fool, idiot, moron, simpleton
ANT. sage

imbibe *v.* absorb, assimilate, take in, suck in, swallow, receive, gather, gain, learn, acquire, get, pick up
ANT. reject

imitate *v.* copy, follow, mimic, ape, duplicate, impersonate, take off, represent, resemble, portray, depict, repeat, counterfeit
ANT. misrepresent, distort

imitative *adj.* imitating, copying, mimicking, apish, unoriginal
ANT. original, creative, inventive

immaculate *adj.* spotless, unspotted, clean, pure, stainless, unsullied, unsoiled, untainted, unblemished, untarnished, undefiled, innocent, guiltless, sinless, faultless, holy, saintly
ANT. impure, corrupt, sinful, contaminated, defiled, polluted, tainted, spotted

immaterial *adj.* 1 unimportant, insignificant, trivial, trifling 2 spiritual, incorporeal, unbodied, unfleshly
ANT. 1 important, essential 2 material, corporeal, physical

immature *adj.* inexperienced, youthful, childish, puerile
ANT. mature

immeasurable *adj.* illimitable, unbounded, boundless, limitless, measureless, immense, infinite, vast, unfathomable
ANT. finite, limited, restricted

immediate *adj.* **1** instantaneous, instant, present **2** close, near, next, proximate **3** direct, unmediated
ANT. **1** future **2** distant, remote

immediately *adv.* straight away, directly, at once, now, right off, instantly, without delay, forthwith
ANT. after a while

immense *adj.* vast, huge, big, enormous, gigantic, great, colossal
ANT. small, tiny

immerse *v.* dip, plunge, submerge, sink, douse, duck, soak, steep, drown, inundate, overwhelm, bury

immigration *n.* migration, colonization, settlement
ANT. emigration

imminent *adj.* impending, approaching, coming, forthcoming, threatening

immobile *adj.* stationary, motionless, unmoving, still
ANT. mobile

immoderate *adj.* excessive, extreme, unreasonable, inordinate
ANT. moderate, reasonable

immoral *adj.* corrupt, depraved, obscene, impure, wicked
ANT. moral, virtuous

immortal *adj.* eternal, everlasting, endless, undying
ANT. mortal

immunity *n.* freedom, exemption, release
ANT. liability, susceptibility

imp *n.* sprite, hobgoblin, demon, devil

impact *n.* **1** shock, collision, crash, knock, striking, contact **2** effect, impression, influence, consequence

impair *v.* injure, harm, damage, spoil, destroy, lessen, diminish, decrease, weaken
ANT. improve, better

impartial *adj.* unbiased, neutral, fair, objective, dispassionate
ANT. biased, prejudiced

impassioned *adj.* passionate, fervent, ardent, zealous, vehement, spirited, animated, exciting, glowing, intense
ANT. impassive, apathetic, indifferent

impatience *n.* restlessness, uneasiness, eagerness, haste, irritability

ANT. patience, calmness, endurance, composure

impatient *adj.* restless, anxious, uneasy, nervy, irritable, eager, rash, hasty
ANT. patient, calm

impediment *n.* hindrance, obstacle, obstruction, difficulty, encumbrance, stumbling

impend *v.* approach, come, loom, threaten, menace

imperative *adj.* urgent, essential, vital, irresistible
ANT. optional

imperious *adj.* dictatorial, despotic, domineering, tyrannical, overbearing, lordly, haughty, arrogant, authoritative
ANT. submissive, gentle, mild

impersonate *v.* mimic, imitate, copy, ape

impertinent *adj.* rude, cheeky, impudent, insolent, disrespectful
ANT. polite, courteous, respectful

impetuous *adj.* rash, hasty, precipitate, impulsive, overzealous, reckless, excitable, fierce, vehement, violent, furious, passionate
ANT. careful, slow, deliberate, thoughtful, cautious

implement *n.* tool, utensil, appliance, device, instrument

implement *v.* put into operation, carry out, realize, achieve, fulfil

implicate *v.* involve, connect, associate, charge, incriminate, entangle
ANT. disconnect, extricate, dissociate

implication *n.* involvement, connection, association, entanglement

implicit *adj.* **1** understood, implied, inferred, tacit, indirect **2** unreserved, unquestioning, unhesitating, firm, certain, absolute, steadfast, undoubting
ANT. **1** expressed, explicit **2** reserved

implore *v.* ask, beg, beseech, entreat, supplicate

imply *v.* hint, suggest, intimate, mention, signify, mean, indicate
ANT. express, declare

impolite *adj.* rude, discourteous, disrespectful, bad-mannered, unpleasant
ANT. polite, civil, courteous

import *v.* bring in, introduce
ANT. export

import *n.* meaning, sense, importance, drift, significance, gist, spirit, bearing, tenor, intention, purport
ANT. statement, proceeding

importance *n.* significance, momentousness, consequence, moment, weight, import, concern
ANT. insignificance, unimportance

important *adj.* 1 significant, weighty, momentous, consequential, serious, material, leading, main, relevant, essential 2 influential, prominent, famous, distinguished
ANT. 1 insignificant, trivial, inconsiderable, irrelevant, secondary 2 uninfluential, minor, unimportant

importunate *adj.* urgent, persistent, pressing, busy

importune *v.* urge, entreat, press, solicit, trouble, harass, pester, badger

impose *v.* put, set, lay, place, levy, demand, exact, require, inflict, subject
ANT. remove, lift, free

imposing *adj.* impressive, striking, stately, majestic, grand, noble, commanding
ANT. unimposing, insignificant

imposition *n.* imposing, putting, placing, laying, burden, levy, tax, constraint

impossible *adj.* 1 impracticable, unworkable, unfeasible 2 hopeless, unthinkable, inconceivable, unimaginable 3 outrageous, unreasonable
ANT. possible, likely

impostor *n.* deceiver, pretender, cheat, hypocrite, charlatan, mountebank, trickster, dissembler

impotence *n.* weakness, disability, incapacity, incompetence, powerlessness, infirmity, frailty, inability, incapability, helplessness, disqualification
ANT. vigour, vigor (*N. Am.*)

impoverish *v.* make poor, exhaust, deplete, ruin, rob
ANT. enrich

impractical *adj.* unrealistic, unworkable, idealistic
ANT. realistic, practical, sensible

impregnable *adj.* invincible, unassailable, invulnerable, immovable, secure
ANT. weak, exposed, vulnerable

impregnate *v.* saturate, soak, permeate, pervade, imbue, infuse, fertilize

impress *v.* 1 influence, affect, stir, move 2 imprint, mark, stamp, engrave, emboss

impression *n.* 1 effect, influence, mark, impact, awareness, sensation, notion, idea, opinion, fancy 2 printing, stamping, imprinting, stamp, brand, mark

impressive *adj.* striking, touching, moving, stirring, powerful, overpowering, grand, imposing, important
ANT. unimpressive, insignificant

imprison *v.* jail, incarcerate, put in prison, confine, detain, lock up
ANT. release, free

improbable *adj.* unlikely, doubtful, questionable, uncertain
ANT. probable, likely

improper *adj.* 1 unseemly, impolite, indecent, naughty 2 unsuitable, inappropriate, unfit
ANT. 1 proper 2 appropriate, suitable

improve *v.* make better, become better, better, progress, amend, correct, reform, ameliorate, rectify
ANT. deteriorate

improvement *n.* betterment, advancement, amendment, increase, correction, progress, development, change, growth, modernization, amelioration, efficiency, proficiency, use
ANT. degeneration, deterioration

improvise *v.* ad-lib, play by ear, extemporize

impudence *n.* impertinence, pertness, rudeness, effrontery, forwardness, insolence, presumption
ANT. humility, diffidence, meekness, lowliness, modesty, submissiveness, coyness

impudent *adj.* impertinent, pert, rude, cheeky, insolent, presumptuous, saucy (*informal*), sassy (*N. Am.* informal)
ANT. humble, meek, modest, submissive

impugn *v.* question, challenge, dispute, contradict, oppose, resist

impulse *n.* 1 thrust, push, impetus, surge, force, boost, motive, influence, incitement, instigation, incentive 2 urge, fancy, desire, passion, inclination, appetite

impulsive *adj.* rash, impetuous, hasty, passionate, hot, quick
ANT. cautious, careful, hesitating, reluctant, wary

impure *adj.* unclean, dirty, contaminated, polluted, sullied, tainted, adulterated
ANT. clean, pure, unadulterated

impute *v.* ascribe, attribute, credit, reckon

inability *n.* incapacity, disability
ANT. ability, skill

inaccurate *adj.* incorrect, wrong, mistaken
ANT. correct, accurate

inactive *adj.* idle, unoccupied, inoperative
ANT. active, working

inadequate *adj.* insufficient, deficient, defective, imperfect, unsatisfactory, faulty
ANT. adequate, sufficient

inane *adj.* silly, stupid, idiotic, worthless, trifling, vacuous, weak, empty, vain, pointless, feeble, vapid, puerile, frivolous
ANT. sensible

inappropriate *adj.* unsuitable, irrelevant, inapplicable, out of place
ANT. appropriate, suitable

inaugural *adj.* first, initial, opening, introductory

inaugurate *v.* 1 invest, install, induct 2 commence, begin, initiate, originate, open
ANT. divert, deprive, conclude, terminate

incandescence *n.* heat, glow

incantation *n.* charm, enchantment, spell, magic, witchcraft, sorcery, witchery, necromancy

incapable *adj.* unable, helpless, incompetent, unfit
ANT. able, capable

incarnation *n.* embodiment, impersonation, exemplification, personification
ANT. disembodiment, spiritualization

incense[1] *v.* enrage, infuriate, anger, exasperate, irritate, provoke, inflame, nettle, gall
ANT. soothe, pacify, appease, conciliate, mollify

incense[2] *n.* perfume, aroma, fragrance, scent

incentive *n.* inducement, incitement, stimulus, spur, impulse, motive, cause, encouragement, rousing, excitation
ANT. deterrent, warning, discouragement, disincentive

inception *n.* beginning, start, commencement, inauguration
ANT. ending, finish, conclusion, termination

incessant *adj.* ceaseless, continual, unceasing, unremitting, perpetual, constant, everlasting, eternal, uninterrupted
ANT. periodic, occasional, intermittent

incident *n.* event, occurrence, circumstance, chance, accident, fact

incidental *adj.* minor, unimportant, secondary, subsidiary, appertaining, natural, relating, impinging, casual, occasional

incipient *adj.* beginning, commencing, embryonic
ANT. final, terminal

incite *v.* rouse, stimulate, provoke, urge, goad, spur, excite

inclement *adj.* stormy, cold, rough
ANT. clement, mild

inclination *n.* 1 tendency, leaning, disposition, bent, bias, proneness, aptitude, propensity, desire, wish, fondness, liking, partiality, attachment, affection 2 slope, leaning, slant
ANT. 1 dislike

incline *v.* 1 slant, lean, slope, verge, tend 2 be disposed, tend, verge, lean, sway, dispose, predispose, turn, bias

ANT. 1 ascend, rise 2 deter, indispose, disincline

include *v.* contain, comprise, embody, comprehend, embrace, take in, encompass, hold
ANT. exclude, leave out

inclusive *adj.* including, comprehending, embracing, comprehensive
ANT. exclusive

incoherent *adj.* unconnected, disordered, disjointed, rambling, illogical, muddled, inarticulate, unclear
ANT. coherent, logical, clear

income *n.* salary, wages, earnings, pay, revenue, profits, gains, proceeds, allowance
ANT. expenditure, outlay, expense

incompatible *adj.* conflicting, contradictory, inconsistent, incongruous, out of place
ANT. compatible, consistent

incompetent *adj.* incapable, unskilful, unskillful (*N. Am.*), unfit, unqualified, inexpert, bungling
ANT. competent, skilled

incomplete *adj.* imperfect, unfinished, partial
ANT. complete, finished

incongruous *adj.* inconsistent, unsuitable, absurd, conflicting, discordant, incompatible, inapposite, contrary, contradictory, inappropriate
ANT. consistent, harmonious, suitable, compatible

inconsistent *adj.* conflicting, contradictory, incompatible, incongruous, out of keeping
ANT. consistent, in keeping

inconvenient *adj.* awkward, difficult, troublesome, unsuitable, untimely
ANT. convenient

incorrect *adj.* wrong, mistaken, erroneous, inaccurate, inexact
ANT. right, correct

increase *v.* grow, enlarge, expand, swell, raise, advance, heighten, enhance, magnify, spread, augment, extend, prolong, intensify, multiply, be fruitful
ANT. decrease, lessen, diminish, decline, abate, lower, reduce, curtail

increase *n.* growth, extension, addition, enlargement, expansion, increment, product, produce, gain, profit
ANT. decrease, deduction, contraction, curtailment, reduction, impoverishment

incredible *adj.* 1 fantastic, wonderful, marvellous, amazing 2 unbelievable, unlikely, unthinkable, impossible, beyond belief
ANT. 1 awful 2 believable

incriminate *v.* involve, implicate, accuse, charge

inculcate *v.* impress, instil, implant, urge, teach, infuse

incumbent *adj.* 1 obligatory, binding, necessary 2 lying, leaning, reclining, resting, prone
ANT. 1 optional, discretionary, voluntary

incur *v.* bring on, sustain, draw, contract, become liable to
ANT. avoid

incursion *n.* inroad, raid, invasion, foray, sally, encroachment

indebted *adj.* owing, obliged, grateful, thankful, under obligation

indecent *adj.* vulgar, obscene, immoral, dirty, shocking
ANT. decent

indecision *n.* hesitation, uncertainty, doubt, wavering, vacillation, irresolution

indeed *adv.* truly, really, positively, absolutely, in fact, certainly, truthfully

indefatigable *adj.* unwearied, untiring, unflagging, persevering, persistent, assiduous, unremitting, never-tiring, indomitable
ANT. idle, indolent

indefinite *adj.* uncertain, unsure, inexact, unclear, vague, general, indeterminate
ANT. definite, sure, clear

indelible *adj.* ineffaceable, indestructible, irreversible, persistent
ANT. erasable, effaceable

indemnify *v.* compensate, remunerate, reimburse

indemnity *n.* security, guarantee, protection, compensation, reimbursement

independence *n.* sovereignty, autonomy, self-rule, self-government, freedom

independent *adj.* separate, self-governing, autonomous, self-ruling, self-determining, free

index *n.* catalogue, catalog (*N. Am.*), list, classification, direction, file

indicate *v.* show, denote, mark, signify, point out, designate, specify, evidence, evince, betray, manifest, declare
ANT. conceal, hide, falsify

indication *n.* sign, mark, note, index, symptom, token, hint, suggestion, manifestation, evidence, demonstration, proof

indictment *n.* accusation, charge, impeachment, arraignment

indifference *n.* neutrality, impartiality, disinterestedness, unconcern, apathy, coolness, negligence, carelessness, inattention, heedlessness
ANT. concern

indifferent *adj.* **1** neutral, unbiased, impartial, disinterested, unconcerned, unmoved, cold, cool, inattentive, apathetic, dead, regardless, heedless, unmindful **2** passable, tolerable, ordinary, middling, mediocre, rather poor, lukewarm, careless
ANT. **1** concerned **2** excellent

indigent *adj.* poor, needy, destitute, necessitous, reduced, penniless, moneyless, distressed, insolvent, in want, impecunious, straitened
ANT. wealthy, rich, affluent, opulent

indignant *adj.* angry, exasperated, irate, incensed, furious
ANT. calm

indignation *n.* resentment, anger, wrath, fury, rage, exasperation

indignity *n.* insult, outrage, affront, slight, snub, dishonour, dishonor (*N. Am.*), abuse, disrespect, reproach, rudeness, contempt, ignominy, disgrace
ANT. deference, respect

indirect *adj.* circuitous, roundabout, devious, deviating, incidental, secondary
ANT. direct, immediate

indiscriminate *adj.* random, haphazard, careless, unsystematic
ANT. selective

indispensable *adj.* necessary, essential, vital, crucial, required
ANT. unnecessary

indisposed *adj.* unwell, ill, sick, ailing
ANT. healthy

individual *n.* person, human being, being, character

individual *adj.* particular, special, separate, single, unique, one, distinct, specific
ANT. general, common, universal

individuality *n.* personality, character, originality, uniqueness

indolence *n.* laziness, inertness, idleness, sluggishness, slothfulness
ANT. activity, energy

indomitable *adj.* unyielding, unconquerable, invincible, irrepressible
ANT. weak, effortless, feeble

induce *v.* persuade, influence, impel, move, cause, produce, effect, bring on, prompt, instigate, actuate, urge, incite, spur, prevail upon
ANT. prevent, dissuade, deter, hinder, restrain

inducement *n.* lure, incentive, stimulus, encouragement
ANT. disincentive, discouragement

induction *n.* introduction, installation, inauguration

indulge *v.* gratify, yield, satisfy, humour, humor (*N. Am.*), pamper, spoil, allow, permit, foster
ANT. thwart, deny, disappoint, counteract, mortify, discipline

indulgence *n.* gratification, satisfying, humouring, humoring (*N. Am.*), pampering
ANT. abstinence, self-sacrifice, repression, restraint

indulgent *adj.* pampering, spoiling, lenient, tolerant, gentle, kind, tender, forbearing
ANT. harsh, severe, rough

industrial *adj.* commercial, business, trade, manufacturing

industrious *adj.* hard-working, diligent, active, busy, assiduous, engaged, employed, occupied, laborious
ANT. lazy, idle

industry *n.* business, commerce, trade, production, manufacturing

ineffable *adj.* unspeakable, indescribable, inexpressible, unutterable, inconceivable, unsurpassable, exquisite, perfect
ANT. common, commonplace

inefficient *adj.* wasteful, careless, extravagant
ANT. efficient

inert *adj.* 1 inactive, lifeless, dead, passive, motionless 2 dull, boring, uninteresting, heavy, dormant
ANT. 1 active, alert, brisk, energetic, quick, vigorous 2 interesting, exciting

inevitable *adj.* necessary, unavoidable, inescapable, certain, fixed, irresistible
ANT. uncertain, avoidable, indeterminate

inexperienced *adj.* untrained, unskilled, unversed, green, raw
ANT. experienced, trained

infamous *adj.* notorious, scandalous, shocking, shameful

infamy *n.* notoriety, dishonour, dishonor (*N. Am.*), shame, disgrace, discredit, ignominy, scandal, disgracefulness, wickedness, atrocity, shamefulness

infantile *adj.* young, childish, babyish, weak, puerile, immature
ANT. adult, mature, robust

infatuation *n.* obsession, fascination, charm

infect *v.* contaminate, taint, pollute, corrupt

infection *n.* contagion, contamination, taint, corruption, defilement, pollution
ANT. purification, disinfection, antidote

infectious *adj.* contagious, catching, contaminating, corrupting, defiling, polluting
ANT. beneficial, antiseptic

infer *v.* deduce, conclude, gather, derive, argue

inference *n.* conclusion, deduction, corollary, consequence, generalization, induction

inferior *adj.* subordinate, minor, mediocre, second-rate
ANT. superior, excellent

infernal *adj.* hellish, diabolical, devilish, fiendish, satanic, atrocious, accursed, abominable
ANT. angelic, cherubic

infest *v.* throng, overrun, beset, swarm, plague, harass, trouble, torment, worry, pester

infidelity *n.* 1 unfaithfulness, disloyalty, faithlessness 2 unbelief, disbelief, scepticism, skepticism (*N. Am.*)
ANT. 1 faithfulness, loyalty 2 fidelity, belief, faith, religiousness

infinite *adj.* limitless, boundless, unbounded, immeasurable, eternal, unlimited, unmeasured, measureless, unfathomable, numberless, innumerable, countless
ANT. limited, finite, restricted

infinitesimal *adj.* minute, tiny, microscopic
ANT. enormous, vast, infinite, immeasurable

infinity *n.* limitlessness, measurelessness, boundlessness, vastness, immensity, infiniteness, eternity

infirm *adj.* weak, feeble, ill, frail, weakened, enfeebled, debilitated
ANT. healthy

infirmity *n.* weakness, feebleness, frailness, frailty, debility
ANT. strength, health

inflame *v.* excite, stimulate, incite, enkindle, rouse, arouse, animate, inspire, work up, irritate, exasperate, anger, provoke, enrage, incense, infuriate
ANT. allay, cool, pacify, quiet

inflammation *n.* swelling, soreness, tenderness, redness, rash

inflate *v.* expand, swell, bloat, blow up, puff up, increase, enlarge, distend
ANT. collapse, deflate

inflexible *adj.* rigid, firm, unbending, unyielding, stubborn, steadfast
ANT. flexible, pliant, yielding

inflict *v.* impose, lay on, put on, levy, apply, afflict
ANT. remove

influence *n.* effect, power, authority, control, weight, sway, predominance

influence *v.* control, affect, persuade, move, stir, induce, incite, incline, actuate, sway, compel, urge, instigate, prompt, lead, impel, excite, drive, draw, direct, bias
ANT. prevent, restrain, retard, deter, discourage, impede, inhibit, hinder, dissuade

influential *adj.* powerful, controlling, authoritative, persuasive, forcible, guiding
ANT. weak, ineffective

inform *v.* mention to, notify, advise, tell, educate, enlighten, instruct, impart, communicate, acquaint, apprise
ANT. deceive, misinform

informal *adj.* relaxed, friendly, easygoing, casual, natural
ANT. formal, serious, official

information *n.* knowledge, facts, data, news, advice, notice, intelligence

informative *adj.* instructive, enlightening, educational

informer *n.* betrayer, traitor, rat (*informal*)

infrequent *adj.* occasional, unusual, rare
ANT. frequent, common

infringe *v.* break, disobey, transgress, violate
ANT. keep

infuriate *v.* anger, exasperate, enrage, incense, annoy

infuse *v.* instil, inspire, introduce, inculcate, implant, steep, soak, water, infiltrate, insinuate, breathe into

ingenious *adj.* skilful, skillful (*N. Am.*), clever, gifted, inventive, able, bright, ready, adept
ANT. unskilful, unskillful (*N. Am.*), uninventive

ingenuity *n.* inventiveness, ingeniousness, skill, ability, aptitude, cunning, gift, genius
ANT. inability, ineptitude, clumsiness

ingenuous *adj.* artless, open, candid, frank, sincere, straightforward, honest, transparent, guileless, truthful, childlike, naive, generous
ANT. insincere, disingenuous

ingratiate *v.* insinuate, flatter, fawn, crawl, suck up to (*informal*)
ANT. alienate, estrange

ingredient *n.* element, component, constituent

inhabit *v.* live, occupy, settle, dwell

inhabitant *n.* native, resident, citizen, occupant, dweller

inherent *adj.* essential, necessary, natural, innate, intrinsic, indispensable
ANT. unconnected, incidental

inherit *v.* receive, come into, be left, succeed to, get
ANT. bequeath, leave

inheritance *n.* legacy, heritage, patrimony, bequest, possession

inheritor *n.* heir, successor, legatee, devisee
ANT. testator, devisor

inimical *adj.* antagonistic, hostile, unfriendly, adverse, opposite, contrary, repugnant, noxious, pernicious, hurtful, harmful
ANT. friendly, agreeable

iniquity *n.* injustice, wickedness, sin, crime, offence, offense (*N. Am.*), misdeed, grievance, evil
ANT. justice, integrity, virtue, holiness, honesty, uprightness, righteousness

initial *adj.* first, opening, primary, beginning, introductory, inaugural
ANT. final, last

initiate *v.* begin, start, commence, introduce, open
ANT. finish, stop

initiation *n.* beginning, start, introduction, opening, inauguration, commencement
ANT. finish, completion, termination

initiative *n.* **1** enterprise, ambition, drive, resourcefulness **2** start, lead, leadership, example

inject *v.* vaccinate, inoculate, insert

injunction *n.* order, command, mandate, precept, exhortation

injure *v.* harm, damage, spoil, mar, disfigure, wound, cripple, maltreat, wrong, abuse
ANT. benefit, profit

injurious *adj.* wrong, unjust, hurtful, detrimental, fatal, destructive, damaging, ruinous, disadvantageous, iniquitous
ANT. helpful, advantageous, beneficial

injury *n.* hurt, damage, harm, disadvantage, detriment, loss, wrong, evil, prejudice, injustice, mischief, outrage
ANT. benefit, service, help, blessing, improvement

injustice *n.* wrong, unrighteousness, iniquity, grievance, unfairness, injury
ANT. equity, fairness, justice, right, integrity, honesty, impartiality, uprightness, lawfulness, righteousness, fair play

inlet *n.* opening, entrance, commencement
ANT. outlet

inmate *n.* patient, convict, prisoner, occupant, dweller, tenant, resident

inn *n.* hotel, public house, tavern

innate *adj.* inherent, inborn, natural, inbred, native, congenital
ANT. unnatural

inner *adj.* inmost, within, interior, inside, inward, internal, secret, close
ANT. outer, outermost, exterior, outside, outward

innocence *n.* harmlessness, inoffensiveness, innocuousness, sinlessness, purity, simplicity, guilelessness, guiltlessness, blamelessness
ANT. guilt, sinfulness, impurity, guile, corruption

innocent *adj.* blameless, guiltless, harmless, inoffensive, righteous, pure, sinless, virtuous, upright, stainless, right, faultless, guileless, clear, clean, spotless, immaculate, innocuous
ANT. criminal, culpable, immoral, guilty, blameworthy

innocuous *adj.* harmless, inoffensive, wholesome
ANT. hurtful, obnoxious

innovation *n.* change, alteration, novelty

innumerable *adj.* countless, numberless, incalculable, numerous
ANT. few

inoculate *v.* vaccinate, impregnate, insert, imbue

inquire, enquire *v.* investigate, inspect, examine, study, explore, ask, question

inquiry, enquiry *n.* query, interrogation, question, study, investigation, research, exploration, examination, scrutiny, asking, search

inquisitive *adj.* curious, meddlesome, intrusive, searching, prying, inquiring, meddling, peeping, scrutinizing, nosy (*informal*)
ANT. uninterested, unconcerned

inroad *n.* incursion, foray, raid, encroachment, trespass, infringement

insane *adj.* crazy, lunatic, mad, deranged, demented, crazed
ANT. sane, sound, sensible

insanity *n.* madness, derangement, craziness, delirium, dementia, lunacy, mania, aberration, alienation, hallucination
ANT. sanity, rationality, lucidity

inscribe *v.* **1** write, engrave, impress, imprint **2** label, letter, mark, delineate **3** address, dedicate

inscrutable *adj.* incomprehensible, unsearchable, impenetrable, unintelligible, hidden, mysterious, untraceable, insolvable, profound
ANT. obvious, intelligible, explainable, self-evident

insert *v.* introduce, put in, set in

insidious *adj.* artful, crafty, secret, deceptive, scheming, cunning, intriguing, tricky
ANT. straightforward, sincere

insignificant *adj.* unimportant, irrelevant, meaningless, trivial, trifling
ANT. significant, important

insinuate *v.* introduce, infiltrate, hint, intimate, suggest, ingratiate

insipid *adj.* tasteless, flavourless, flavorless (*N. Am.*), stale, spiritless, heavy, stupid, uninteresting, prosaic, tame, dull, unentertaining, characterless
ANT. interesting, engaging, piquant, spirited, lively

insist *v.* demand, maintain, urge, require, command, contend, persist, press, persevere

insolence *n*. rudeness, contempt, disrespect, impertinence, pertness, impudence, forwardness, disobedience, insubordination, arrogance, assumption
ANT. deference, modesty, respect, politeness

insolvent *adj*. bankrupt, penniless, beggared, ruined
ANT. solvent, rich, wealthy, flourishing, thriving

inspect *v*. examine, study, scrutinize, investigate, oversee, superintend, supervise

inspection *n*. examination, study, investigation, inquiry, analysis

inspector *n*. examiner, tester, critic, superintendent, censor, supervisor

inspiration *n*. encouragement, stimulus, motivation, spur

inspire *v*. stimulate, encourage, invigorate, arouse, excite, hearten, cheer

instability *n*. unsteadiness, imbalance, insecurity
ANT. stability, steadiness, firmness

install *v*. put in, place, establish, set up

instance *n*. illustration, example, case, exemplification, specification, point, occurrence

instant *n*. moment, twinkling, second, minute, flash, trice, jiffy (*informal*)

instant *adj*. immediate, instantaneous, quick, pressing, earnest, urgent

instantly *adv*. immediately, directly, at once, presently, straightaway, forthwith
ANT. after a time

instigate *v*. incite, impel, move, urge, prompt, provoke, stimulate, rouse, influence, encourage, persuade, prevail upon
ANT. restrain, discourage

instil *v*. introduce, infuse, implant, impress, inculcate, imbue
ANT. extract, remove

instinct *n*. intuition, feeling, impulse, tendency, inclination, prompting
ANT. reason

instinctive *adj*. natural, spontaneous, impulsive, voluntary, intuitive
ANT. rational, logical, reasonable, reasoning

institute *v*. 1 found, establish, organize, launch, set up, begin, commence 2 ordain, enact, pass

institute *n*. institution, establishment, university, college, school, academy, seminary

institution *n*. 1 establishment, university, college, school, academy, seminary 2 custom, practice, tradition, convention, usage

instruct *v*. 1 teach, inform, train, educate, school, enlighten, indoctrinate 2 direct, command, tell, order
ANT. 1 misinform, misguide, mislead, deceive

instruction *n*. 1 teaching, education, training, schooling, information, discipline, tuition, advice, counsel 2 direction, order, command, mandate, precept

instrument *n*. 1 tool, utensil, implement, device 2 agency, agent, medium, means, vehicle

instrumentality *n*. medium, means, agency, vehicle, mediation, intervention, use, employment

insufficient *adj*. inadequate, lacking, deficient, scarce, in short supply

insulate *v*. wrap, line, protect, shield, isolate

insult *n*. offence, offense (*N. Am.*), affront, outrage, abuse, rudeness, dishonour, dishonor (*N. Am.*), slight, disrespect
ANT. respect, compliment

insult *v*. outrage, offend, dishonour, dishonor (*N. Am.*), abuse, provoke, mock, ridicule
ANT. respect, salute, honour, honor (*N. Am.*), compliment

insurgent *n*. rebel, mutineer, traitor, rioter

insurgent *adj*. rebellious, disobedient, mutinous, unruly, insubordinate, seditious
ANT. obedient, loyal, patriotic

insurrection *n*. rebellion, revolt, uprising, mutiny, sedition, riot, tumult, anarchy
ANT. law, order, peace, obedience, submission

intact *adj.* whole, entire, unbroken, safe, inviolate, sacred, undefiled, uncorrupted, uncontaminated, untouched, unhurt, unharmed, uninjured, unscathed
ANT. defiled, hurt, injured, affected, contaminated

integrate *v.* unite, combine, consolidate, solidify, incorporate, complete

integrity *n.* **1** honesty, virtue, goodness, principle, uprightness, honour, honor (*N. Am.*), probity, rectitude, truthfulness, conscientiousness **2** completeness, entirety, wholeness
ANT. **1** unfairness, underhandedness

intellect *n.* reason, mind, sense, brains (*informal*), understanding, judgment, intelligence

intellectual *adj.* mental, academic, scholarly, erudite, highbrow, learned, cultured

intellectual *n.* academic, scholar, thinker, brains (*informal*), egghead (*informal*)

intelligence *n.* **1** knowledge, information, understanding, apprehension, discernment, acumen, penetration, quickness, brightness, comprehension **2** news, announcement, report, statement, notice, notification, publication, advice
ANT. **1** ignorance, stupidity

intelligent *adj.* clever, bright, knowledgeable, quick, sharp, brainy (*informal*)
ANT. stupid, ignorant

intelligible *adj.* clear, plain, obvious, understandable, distinct, comprehensible, explainable, familiar, self-evident
ANT. hidden, impenetrable, unfathomable, inscrutable

intend *v.* design, mean, expect, plan, propose, purpose, contemplate, determine, meditate

intense *adj.* **1** extreme, great, immoderate, powerful, strong, concentrated **2** serious, earnest, deep
ANT. **1** moderate, mild **2** easygoing, relaxed

intensify *v.* heighten, magnify, enhance, strengthen, reinforce
ANT. moderate

intensity *n.* power, strength, concentration, activity, forcefulness

intent *n.* purpose, aim, object, design, end, meaning, intention, scope, drift, view, purport

intent *adj.* set, eager, fixed, earnest, close, bent

intention *n.* plan, design, purpose, intent, meaning, purport

intentional *adj.* deliberate, purposeful, designed, intended, studied, purposed, premeditated
ANT. casual, accidental, undesigned, fortuitous

inter *v.* bury, entomb
ANT. exhume, disinter

intercede *v.* mediate, arbitrate, interpose, plead, make intercession, advocate

intercept *v.* stop, seize, catch, obstruct, interrupt, ambush
ANT. send, dispatch, delegate, forward, commission, interchange

interdict *v.* prohibit, forbid, proscribe, inhibit, restrain, stop, debar, disallow
ANT. grant, allow

interest *n.* **1** attention, notice, curiosity, care, concern **2** activity, hobby, pastime, diversion **3** advantage, benefit, profit, gain **4** share, stake, part, right, claim
ANT. **1** indifference, apathy

interest *v.* absorb, fascinate, intrigue, attract, engage
ANT. weary, bore

interested *adj.* absorbed, fascinated, intrigued, curious, inquisitive
ANT. uninterested, bored

interesting *adj.* exciting, appealing, absorbing, fascinating, intriguing, engaging
ANT. boring

interfere *v.* meddle, intervene, butt in

interference *n.* meddling, intervention, butting in

interior *adj.* inside, internal, inner, inward, inland
ANT. outside, exterior

interior *n.* inside, contents
ANT. exterior, outside, surface

interloper *n*. intruder, meddler

intermediate *adj*. intervening, middle, mean, halfway, in-between, moderate
ANT. extreme

interminable *adj*. endless, ceaseless, unending, never-ending, long, boring

intermission *n*. interval, pause, interlude, rest, stop, suspension, interruption, stoppage, suspense, respite, remission, cessation, discontinuance, interregnum
ANT. continuity, continuance, uninterruptedness

intermittent *adj*. occasional, irregular, spasmodic, sporadic
ANT. continuous, uninterrupted

internal *adj*. 1 inner, interior, inside 2 domestic, home, native
ANT. 1 outer, exterior, outside 2 foreign

international *adj*. foreign, worldwide, global, multinational, universal
ANT. national, domestic

internecine *adj*. destructive, deadly, irreconcilable

interpolate *v*. introduce, insert, interweave, intersperse

interpose *v*. interrupt, mediate, meddle, arbitrate

interpret *v*. explain, define, expound, elucidate, make sense of, understand, unfold, translate, render, construe, declare, represent, solve, decipher
ANT. misconceive, misunderstand, falsify, misinterpret, distort, misrepresent

interpretation *n*. explanation, definition, exposition, elucidation, version, account, construction, rendering, translation, sense, meaning, signification, solution
ANT. misinterpretation

interrogate *v*. question, ask, examine, inquire of, cross-examine, grill (*informal*)

interrupt *v*. 1 disturb, interfere with, break in, cut in on 2 separate, disconnect, stop, hinder, delay, divide, cut, dissolve, suspend, discontinue, break off
ANT. 1, 2 continue

interval *n*. pause, rest, intermission, stop, respite, suspension
ANT. continuity, uninterruptedness

intervene *v*. come between, interrupt, intrude, step in, mediate

intervention *n*. intrusion, mediation, agency, interruption, interference
ANT. continuance, non-interference

interview *n*. meeting, conference, consultation, dialogue, discussion, talk

interview *v*. question, interrogate

intimate[1] *adj*. 1 close, personal, dear, friendly, private, secret, confidential 2 thorough, profound, exhaustive, complete
ANT. 1 distant 2 superficial

intimate[1] *n*. confidant(e), associate, crony, companion, friend

intimate[2] *v*. suggest, hint, imply, indicate, insinuate, allude to, remind of

intimidate *v*. frighten, alarm, scare, daunt, dismay, threaten, appal, terrify, deter, dishearten
ANT. encourage, inspire

intolerable *adj*. unbearable, unendurable, painful, insupportable, insufferable
ANT. comfortable, tolerable

intolerant *adj*. biased, prejudiced, bigoted, extreme
ANT. tolerant

intoxication *n*. inebriety, inebriation, drunkenness
ANT. sobriety, abstinence

intrepid *adj*. bold, brave, fearless, undaunted, courageous, daring, unterrified, dauntless, heroic, undismayed, valiant, doughty
ANT. cautious, timid, fearful, cowardly, dismayed, terrified

intricacy *n*. complexity, complication, entanglement, perplexity, difficulty, intricateness, obscurity, confusion

intricate *adj*. complex, involved, perplexed, complicated, puzzling, entangled
ANT. simple, easy, direct, obvious, plain, uninvolved

intrigue *v*. attract, charm, interest, fascinate

intrigue *n*. plot, scheme, conspiracy, machination, artifice, cunning, duplicity, trickery, chicanery, ruse

intrinsic *adj.* inward, internal, essential, real, genuine, true, inherent, native, innate, natural, inbred, inborn
ANT. extrinsic, acquired

introduce *v.* 1 present, make acquainted, familiarize 2 propose, submit, present, offer, put forward

introduction *n.* 1 introducing, presentation, acquaintance 2 preface, foreword, prelude, preamble

introductory *adj.* preliminary, preparatory, prefatory, initiatory, precursory
ANT. final, conclusive, terminal

intrude *v.* infringe, trespass, interfere, meddle, obtrude, encroach

intruder *n.* prowler, snooper, trespasser, burglar, thief

intrusion *n.* encroachment, interference, intruding, infringement

intuition *n.* apprehension, perception, instinct, insight, recognition, cognition

inundate *v.* flood, deluge, overflow, submerge, cover, overwhelm
ANT. drain, dry, reclaim

invade *v.* attack, march into, enter in, assault, assail, occupy, infringe, violate, encroach on
ANT. abandon

invalid[1] *n.* patient, convalescent

invalid[1] *adj.* ill, weak, feeble, infirm, sick, frail
ANT. strong, well, healthy, vigorous

invalid[2] *adj.* null, void, unsound, baseless, untrue, unfounded, fallacious
ANT. sound, legal, legitimate, authorized, genuine, true, correct, exact

invalidate *v.* nullify, cancel, annul, overthrow, make void
ANT. conserve, maintain, establish, confirm, enact, institute

invasion *n.* attack, assault, occupation, infringement, violation, trespass, incursion, encroachment, inroad
ANT. abandonment, relinquishment

invective *n.* abuse, censure, denunciation, diatribe, railing, obloquy, vituperation, reproach, castigation
ANT. praise, commendation

invent *v.* conceive, contrive, fabricate, originate, design, concoct, discover, find out, devise, contrive, produce

invention *n.* contrivance, construction, device, gadget

inventive *adj.* ingenious, skilful, skillful (*N. Am.*), clever, adept, resourceful
ANT. unskilful, unskillful (*N. Am.*), uninventive

inventor *n.* contriver, originator, author, creator

inventory *n.* list, catalogue, catalog (*N. Am.*), register, record, enrolment, enumeration

inversion *n.* reversal, transposition, alteration, change, permutation
ANT. fixity, order, sequence

invert *v.* upset, overthrow, reverse, subvert
ANT. restore, set up, make upright

invest *v.* spend, lay out, advance, fund, supply, put in, lend, loan

investigate *v.* inquire, examine, test, scrutinize, prove, search, explore, inspect, discuss, study

investigation *n.* search, examination, inquiry, research, exploration, scrutiny, study, analysis

investiture *n.* installation, induction, investment

inveterate *adj.* long-established, confirmed, chronic, ingrained, incarnate, habitual, deep-rooted, hardened, accustomed, besetting

invidious *adj.* unpopular, undesirable, unfair, partial, inconsiderate
ANT. fair, just

invigorate *v.* strengthen, brace, harden, nerve, refresh, stimulate, animate, exhilarate
ANT. weaken, enfeeble, debilitate, deteriorate, relax, enervate

invisible *adj.* hidden, concealed, unseen, inconspicuous, imperceptible, indiscernible
ANT. visible, apparent

invitation *n.* call, request, offer, summons, invite (*informal*)
ANT. rebuff, snub

invite *v.* ask, summon, bid, request, solicit, call, attract, entice, persuade, allure, tempt, incite, challenge
ANT. repel, forbid

inviting *adj.* alluring, attractive, tempting, appealing
ANT. repulsive, abhorrent

invoke *v.* supplicate, implore, solicit, summon, call, beseech, invite, challenge, appeal to, imprecate

involuntary *adj.* automatic, uncontrolled, reflex, spontaneous, unintentional
ANT. voluntary, intentional

involve *v.* 1 include, entail, concern, contain, comprise, embrace 2 implicate, entangle, complicate, embroil, embarrass, include, overwhelm, imply
ANT. 1 exclude 2 extricate

inward *adj.* internal, interior, inner
ANT. outward, external, exterior

iota *n.* jot, particle, atom, tittle
ANT. whole, mass

irate *adj.* angry, enraged, incensed, choleric, irritable
ANT. good-tempered, calm, forbearing, gentle, mild

ire *n.* anger, wrath, rage, fury, indignation, resentment, displeasure, vexation
ANT. goodwill, patience, forbearance, mildness, forgiveness, reconciliation, peaceableness

ironic *adj.* incongruous, paradoxical, mocking, sarcastic, derisive

irony *n.* sarcasm, satire, ridicule, mockery

irrational *adj.* unreasonable, absurd, illogical, incoherent
ANT. rational, reasonable, logical

irregular *adj.* 1 uneven, rough 2 variable, erratic, random, haphazard 3 unusual, exceptional, abnormal, eccentric, odd, unorthodox

ANT. 1 level, even, smooth 2 regular 3 normal

irrelevant *adj.* inappropriate, unconnected, inapplicable, unimportant
ANT. relevant

irresistible *adj.* overwhelming, compelling, invincible, inescapable

irreverent *adj.* disrespectful, rude, impolite, sacrilegious
ANT. deferential

irritable *adj.* crotchety, touchy, sensitive, short-tempered, snappish
ANT. easygoing, even-tempered

irritate *v.* 1 annoy, bother, aggravate, vex, provoke, nettle, rattle 2 chafe, rub, inflame

isolate *v.* separate, detach, disconnect, segregate, dissociate, insulate
ANT. associate, unite

isolation *n.* separation, segregation, detachment, disconnection, loneliness, solitariness, solitude, insulation
ANT. community

issue *n.* 1 copy, number, edition, impression 2 event, outcome, result, end, conclusion, consummation, effect, termination 3 children, offspring, posterity, progeny

issue *v.* 1 put out, release, send out, publish, announce, distribute, give out 2 emit, discharge, emerge, flow, emanate

item *n.* article, thing, object, point, note, entry

itinerant *adj.* travelling, traveling (*N. Am.*), wandering, roving, roaming, journeying, unsettled, nomadic, peripatetic
ANT. settled, fixed, local

itinerary *n.* schedule, route, programme, program (*N. Am.*), guide

jade *v.* tire, weary, fatigue, exhaust
ANT. refresh, invigorate, inspire

jagged *adj.* notched, indented, uneven, rough, ragged
ANT. smooth

jail *n.* prison, gaol, inside (*informal*), nick (*informal*)

jail *v.* gaol, imprison, confine, detain, incarcerate
ANT. release

jailer *n.* warden, guard, gaoler

jam¹ *v.* pack, cram, squeeze, wedge, press

jam² *n.* preserve, conserve

jangle *v.* clang, clank, rattle, jar

jar¹ *n.* pot, bottle, container, jug, pitcher

jar² *v.* **1** jolt, jerk, rattle, shake, agitate **2** clash, interfere, quarrel, contend, bicker, spar, squabble
ANT. **2** agree, harmonize, accord, concur

jargon *n.* **1** language, idiom, gobbledegook, cant, slang, lingo, patois **2** nonsense, twaddle, trash, stuff, gibberish, drivel

jaundiced *adj.* biased, prejudiced, pessimistic
ANT. unprejudiced, unbiased

jaunty *adj.* lively, brisk, breezy, sprightly

jealous *adj.* **1** envious, covetous, grudging, resentful **2** anxious, apprehensive, solicitous, zealous, suspicious, possessive, watchful
ANT. **2** content

jealousy *n.* envy, covetousness

jeer *v.* scoff, taunt, laugh, gibe, sneer, flout, mock, jest, deride, banter
ANT. flatter, compliment, praise

jejune *adj.* **1** unsophisticated, naive, simple, inexperienced **2** dull, boring, uninteresting

jeopardy *n.* danger, hazard, peril, risk, venture
ANT. security, safety

jerk *v.* jolt, bump, jar, shake, quiver

jerk *n.* jolt, bump, shake, twitch, spasm

jest *n.* joke, witticism, quip, play, fun, crack (*informal*)

jest *v.* joke, sport, banter, quip, tease, ridicule, mock

jet *n.* **1** stream, gush, spring, squirt **2** aeroplane, airplane (*N. Am.*), jumbo jet

jewel *n.* gem, precious stone, gemstone, diamond, pearl, emerald, ruby

job *n.* **1** occupation, profession, work, business, employment, trade, position, career, calling, vocation **2** task, duty, chore, responsibility

jog *v.* **1** jolt, nudge, jar, prod, shake **2** remind, prompt, stir **3** run, trot

join *v.* connect, couple, link, unite, associate, cement, add, attach, annex
ANT. separate, split, disconnect

joint *n.* connection, link, juncture, union, coupling
ANT. disconnection, separation

joke *n.* quip, witticism, trick, prank, caper, crack (*informal*), play, sport, fun, game

joke *v.* quip, jest, tease, kid (*informal*)

jolly *adj.* happy, joyful, glad, cheery, cheerful, merry, jovial, mirthful, sprightly
ANT. sad, cheerless, joyless, gloomy, morose

jolt *v.* jerk, jostle, push, bump, shake

jolt *n.* jerk, jostle, push, bump, shake

jostle *v.* push, shake, jog, jolt, hustle, collide, strike against

jot *n.* little, iota, particle, atom, grain, bit, mite, whit, scrap, scintilla, trifle, morsel, fraction

journal *n.* 1 diary, log, logbook, record 2 magazine, periodical, newspaper

journalist *n.* writer, reporter, correspondent, columnist, editor

journey *n.* trip, expedition, excursion, tour, voyage, pilgrimage

journey *v.* go, travel, tour, voyage, roam, rove

jovial *adj.* jolly, convivial, merry, joyful, hearty, festive
ANT. gloomy, melancholy

joy *n.* happiness, gladness, delight, pleasure, felicity, exultation, ecstasy, bliss, rapture, glee, ravishment
ANT. sorrow, sadness, grief, melancholy, depression, despondency, misery, trouble, despair

joyful happy, delighted, glad, joyous, merry, jubilant, jolly, jovial, elated, buoyant
ANT. sad, solemn, mournful, melancholy

jubilant *adj.* rejoicing, exultant, triumphant, joyous, festive, exulting, congratulatory
ANT. doleful, sorrowful, remorseful

jubilee *n.* festival, feast, holiday, festivity, revel, carnival, merriment, season of rejoicing
ANT. fast, mourning

judge *n.* 1 justice, magistrate, referee, arbiter, arbitrator, umpire 2 critic, reviewer, connoisseur, authority, expert

judge *v.* 1 referee, arbitrate, find, try, rule, convict, sentence, condemn 2 decide, consider, believe, think, reckon, assess, estimate

judgment *n.* 1 decision, opinion, notion, conclusion 2 understanding, discernment, intelligence, wisdom, sense, prudence, estimate, criticism, discrimination, sagacity 3 verdict, ruling, sentence, reward, condemnation

judicious *adj.* discreet, wise, prudent, sensible, reasonable, rational, sound, politic, enlightened, well-considered, sagacious
ANT. foolish, imprudent, indiscreet, ill-judged, inexpedient, rash, impolitic

jug *n.* pitcher, jar, bottle, carafe, ewer, urn, flask

jumble *n.* confusion, muddle, mess, chaos, disorder, hotchpotch, hodgepodge
ANT. order, system, neatness

jump *v.* leap, bound, hop, spring, vault, skip, caper

jump *n.* leap, hop, spring, vault

jumpy *adj.* nervous, apprehensive, agitated, jittery, sensitive, touchy, on edge
ANT. calm, unruffled

junction *n.* joining, joint, juncture, union, intersection, combination, coalition, connection, linking, coupling
ANT. division, separation, disconnection

jungle *n.* thicket, forest, bush, undergrowth, entanglement
ANT. open, clearing

junior *adj.* younger, minor, inferior, subordinate, less advanced
ANT. senior, elder, older, more advanced, superior

junk *n.* rubbish, waste, scrap, refuse, garbage, trash

jurisdiction *n.* right, authority, power, control, sway, sphere, judicature, government, administration

just *adj.* 1 upright, equitable, fair, impartial, right, rightful, lawful, righteous, honest, true, exact, reasonable, due 2 deserved, fit, merited, appropriate, suitable, rightful, proper, harmonious
ANT. 1 unjust, dishonest, unfair, unreasonable, partial, unlawful 2 undeserved, unmerited, unfit

justice *n.* legality, equity, rectitude, fairness, law, lawfulness, right, truth, uprightness, virtue, fair play, faithfulness, impartiality, integrity, righteousness, reasonableness, propriety
ANT. injustice, dishonesty, partiality, wrong, unlawfulness, unfairness, unreasonableness

justification *n.* vindication, defence, defense (*N. Am.*), apology, advocacy, plea, exoneration, exculpation
ANT. censure, condemnation, conviction

justify *v.* vindicate, maintain, defend, absolve, clear, exonerate, pardon, excuse, exculpate
ANT. condemn, convict, censure

juvenile *adj.* young, youthful, boyish, girlish, adolescent, teenage, immature, puerile, childish
ANT. mature, adult

juvenile *n.* child, minor, boy, girl, young person, young adult, youth, young man, young woman, adolescent, teenager

juxtaposition *n.* contiguity, adjacency, proximity, contact, closeness, nearness
ANT. distance, remoteness, separateness

K

keen *adj.* **1** enthusiastic, eager, earnest, zealous **2** sharp, acute, bitter, severe, piercing, stinging, cutting, biting, sarcastic, penetrating, poignant, acrimonious, caustic **3** discerning, quick, astute, shrewd, clever
ANT. 1 apathetic **2** blunt, obtuse **3** undiscerning, slow, simple

keep *v.* **1** retain, hold, reserve, detain, preserve, restrain, withhold, maintain, support, sustain, guard, protect **2** observe, comply with, adhere to, obey, fulfil **3** store, save, amass, accumulate **4** maintain, support, provide for, look after, take care of **5** continue, carry on, persist, keep on **6** celebrate, honour, honor (*N. Am.*), remember, mark, commemorate
ANT. 1 release, discard, neglect **2** disregard, disobey **4** neglect **5** cease

keeper *n.* warden, warder, custodian, jailer

keeping *n.* **1** charge, guardianship, custody, care, preservation **2** maintenance, support, feed, provision **3** harmony, consistency, congruity, conformity, agreement
ANT. 1, 2 neglect, abuse, disregard **3** disagreement, incongruity

keepsake *n.* souvenir, token, remembrance

kernel *n.* seed, grain, nucleus, core, essence
ANT. shell, husk

key *n.* clue, guide, solution, answer, explanation

kick *v.* **1** strike, boot, hit, tap **2** recoil, resist, rebel, oppose, spurn

kidnap *v.* abduct, make off with, seize, capture, hijack, hold to ransom
ANT. free, liberate, release

kill *v.* murder, put to death, massacre, assassinate, butcher, execute, slay, slaughter, bump off (*informal*)

kin *n.* family, birth, blood, descent, race, relationship, kind, kindred, affinity, alliance

kind¹ *n.* **1** character, sort, variety, nature, fashion, description, designation **2** species, breed, class, genus, race, family

kind² *adj.* good, friendly, tender, tender-hearted, sympathetic, affectionate, generous, indulgent, humane, compassionate, gentle, forbearing, lenient, bounteous, mild, obliging, amicable, philanthropic, charitable
ANT. harsh, severe, hard, cruel, unkind, rough, stern, forbidding

kindle *v.* **1** light, ignite, inflame, fire, set on fire **2** excite, arouse, awaken, stir up, stimulate, incite, animate, foment, inflame, exasperate, provoke, enrage
ANT. 1 extinguish **2** quell, suppress

kindness *n.* friendliness, tenderness, benevolence, humanity, charity, sympathy, compassion, good nature, mildness, gentleness, softness
ANT. harshness, cruelty, severity, roughness

kindred *n.* **1** relationship, family, birth, blood, descent, race **2** relations, kin, kith and kin, relatives, kinsfolk

kindred *adj.* related, cognate, akin, allied

kingdom *n.* empire, monarchy, realm, sovereignty, domain, dominion

kiosk *n.* booth, stall, stand

kiss *v.* **1** embrace, peck (*informal*), neck (*informal*) **2** touch, graze, brush

kit *n.* set, equipment, outfit, gear, tackle

knack *n.* skill, dexterity, adroitness, facility, gift, aptitude, expertness, quickness
ANT. inability, clumsiness, awkwardness

knave *n.* rascal, rogue, scoundrel, cheat, swindler, villain

knife *n.* cutter, blade, spear

knob *n.* 1 handle 2 bump, protuberance, swelling, projection

knock *v.* strike, hit, rap, tap, hammer, pound

knock *n.* hit, blow, rap, tap

knot *n.* tie, bond, connection, bow, loop, joint, splice
ANT. loosening, unfastening

knotty *adj.* difficult, tough, hard, complicated, intricate, perplexing
ANT. plain, simple, easy

know *v.* 1 understand, comprehend, see, realize, perceive, apprehend
2 recognize, be familiar with, distinguish, discern, discriminate, identify, tell
ANT. 1 misunderstand

knowing *adj.* 1 intelligent, skilful, skillful (*N. Am.*), competent, well-informed, proficient, qualified, experienced, accomplished, shrewd, astute, discerning 2 expressive, significant, meaningful
ANT. 1 stupid

knowledge *n.* learning, wisdom, scholarship, comprehension, erudition, intelligence, perception, recognition, acquaintance, intuition, experience, information, data, facts, apprehension, notice, understanding, cognizance, familiarity, instruction, enlightenment
ANT. ignorance, illiteracy, unfamiliarity, misunderstanding

L

label *n.* tag, marker, sticker, brand

label *v.* tag, mark, stamp, brand, name, call

laborious *adj.* hard, burdensome, toilsome, difficult, tiresome, onerous, wearisome, fatiguing, arduous, tedious, irksome
ANT. easy, light, simple

labour, labor (*N. Am.*) *n.* **1** work, effort, task, toil, exertion, travail, drudgery, industry, burden, duties **2** workers, working class, employees
ANT. **1** ease, laziness, idleness, rest **2** management

labour, labor (*N. Am.*) *v.* work, toil, struggle, strive

laboured, labored (*N. Am.*) *adj.* stiff, heavy, slow, studied, overwrought
ANT. easy, natural, simple, effortless

labourer, laborer (*N. Am.*) *n.* worker, operative, hand, employee
ANT. employer

labyrinth *n.* maze, confusion, intricacy, perplexity, difficulty, complexity, bewilderment

lack *n.* want, need, deficiency, destitution, failure, scantiness, dearth, scarcity, deficit, shortness, insufficiency
ANT. plenty, abundance, supply, sufficiency

lack *v.* need, want, require, be short of
ANT. have, possess

laconic *adj.* short, terse, succinct, epigrammatic, brief, concise, pithy
ANT. wordy, diffuse, prosy, loquacious, garrulous, prolix

lad *n.* boy, youth, youngster, chap, fellow

lag *v.* fall behind, hang back, linger, dawdle

laggard *n.* dawdler, idler, loiterer, lingerer, sluggard, saunterer

lame *adj.* **1** hobbling, crippled, limping, disabled, deformed, faltering **2** weak, feeble, poor, unsatisfactory, insufficient, imperfect
ANT. **1** strong **2** effective, strong, convincing, telling

lament *v.* mourn, weep, bemoan, bewail, deplore, sorrow over, regret, grieve
ANT. rejoice

lamentable *adj.* deplorable, regrettable, shocking, unfortunate, miserable

lamp *n.* light, candle

land *n.* **1** ground, earth, soil **2** property, estate, real estate, realty, grounds

land *v.* come down, touch down, settle, arrive

lane *n.* alley, passage, passageway

language *n.* **1** speech, tongue **2** idiom, dialect, patois, vernacular, vocabulary, mother tongue, phraseology, discourse, conversation, talk **3** diction, expression, articulation, accent, style, utterance, voice

languid *adj.* drooping, feeble, weak, faint, sickly, pining, weary, listless, heavy, dull, exhausted, heartless, enervated, flagging, spiritless
ANT. strong, vigorous, robust, active, braced, healthy, energetic, animated, alert

languish *v.* pine, droop, sink, faint, decline
ANT. thrive, prosper, flourish, bloom

languor *n.* feebleness, weakness, faintness, weariness, lassitude, listlessness, heaviness
ANT. strength, vigour, vigor (*N. Am.*), energy, freshness

lap *n.* circuit, circle, round

lapse *v.* sink, decline, fall, drop, stop, end

lapse *n.* **1** error, fault, mistake, slip **2** interval, period, time

large *adj.* big, great, huge, immense, gigantic, colossal, ample, broad, bulky, extensive, vast, massive, spacious, wide, enormous, capacious, considerable, abundant
ANT. small, little, microscopic, minute, tiny

largely *adv.* mainly, chiefly, mostly, principally

lash *v.* strike, whip, scourge, flog, beat

lash *n.* whip, scourge, thong, cane, rod

lassitude *n.* languor, weariness, weakness, debility, inertia
ANT. energy, strength, robustness, freshness

last *v.* continue, endure, remain, hold, persist
ANT. end, stop, cease

last *adj.* final, latest, concluding, ultimate, extreme
ANT. first, initial, opening, introductory

lasting *adj.* durable, permanent, unending, enduring, abiding, perpetual
ANT. temporary, momentary, occasional, transient, ephemeral

late *adj.* slow, tardy, delayed, overdue, behind time
ANT. early

lately *adv.* recently, of late, not far past, just

latent *adj.* hidden, secret, invisible, dormant, concealed, potential, implicit, undeveloped, inherent
ANT. visible, explicit, apparent, developed, active

latitude *n.* scope, range, extent, room, space, freedom, liberty
ANT. restriction

latter *adj.* later, last, final
ANT. former, previous

laudable *adj.* praiseworthy, commendable, worthy, admirable
ANT. blameworthy

laugh *v.* chuckle, giggle, snigger, chortle, guffaw

laugh *n.* chuckle, giggle, snigger, chortle, guffaw

laughable *adj.* funny, amusing, humorous, ludicrous, ridiculous, absurd, farcical

laughter *n.* laughing, chuckling, giggling, mirth, merriment, glee
ANT. weeping, tears, sorrow

launch *v.* **1** hurl, throw, let fly, propel, move, drive **2** start, begin, commence, found, set up, originate, initiate

lavish *adj.* generous, liberal, profuse, superabundant, excessive, extravagant, bountiful, wasteful
ANT. sparing, economical, niggardly

law *n.* rule, ruling, regulation, code, canon, edict, decree, order, mandate, legislation, ordinance, enactment, command, commandment, formula, principle, statute

lawful *adj.* legitimate, competent, constituted, authorized, legal, permissible, right, allowable, fair, constitutional, rightful
ANT. illegal, unlawful, wrong

lawless *adj.* illegal, unrestrained, unregulated, uncontrolled, wild, rebellious, savage, disorderly
ANT. peaceful, law-abiding, civilized

lawyer *n.* barrister, attorney, counsel, advocate

lax *adj.* slack, loose, remiss, negligent
ANT. strict, rigid

lay[1] *v.* put, place, set down, establish, deposit, arrange, spread, dispose
ANT. lift up

lay[2] *adj.* laic, laical, unordained, non-professional
ANT. ordained, professional

layer *n.* coating, coat, seam, stratum, bed

lazy *adj.* idle, inactive, slothful, slow, sluggish, shirking
ANT. industrious, energetic, active, assiduous

lead *v.* **1** guide, conduct, steer, direct, counsel **2** rule, govern, direct, command, persuade, influence
ANT. **1** follow

lead *n.* guidance, direction, initiative, control, precedence, priority

leader *n.* director, chief, head, commander, ruler, guide, conductor
ANT. follower, disciple

league *n.* alliance, union, coalition, confederacy, confederation, bond, combination

leak *v.* seep, ooze, drip, trickle, flow

lean¹ *v.* **1** incline, slope, slant, bend, rest **2** depend, rely, trust, rest, confide

lean² *adj.* slender, spare, thin, lanky, gaunt, skinny, bony, scraggy
ANT. fat, plump, heavy, obese, stout

leaning *n.* tendency, inclination, bias, liking, partiality, proclivity, propensity

leap *v.* jump, vault, spring, bound, hop

learn *v.* acquire, master, memorize, discover, attain, collect, know, gather, understand, study, imbibe
ANT. forget

learned *adj.* educated, erudite, versed, scholarly, skilled, literary, conversant, well-informed, well-read
ANT. ignorant, unlearned, illiterate, unscholarly

learner *n.* pupil, scholar, student, disciple, novice
ANT. teacher, professor, authority, master, doctor

learning *n.* knowledge, education, culture, tuition, attainments, scholarship, erudition, skill, literature, science, lore, letters
ANT. ignorance, stupidity

least *adj.* smallest, shortest, lowest, most unimportant, slightest
ANT. most, greatest, longest, highest, most important, first, main, leading

leave *v.* **1** depart, go from, quit, abandon, give up, cease, stop, desist, forego, resign, surrender, forbear **2** bequeath, will, consign, entrust
ANT. **1** arrive

leave *n.* **1** permission, consent, freedom, liberty **2** holiday, vacation

lecture *n.* speech, talk, address, discourse, sermon

ledge *n.* shelf, sill, strip

legal *adj.* lawful, authorized, legitimate, constitutional, allowable
ANT. illegal, unlawful, unconstitutional

legend *n.* myth, fable, story, tale
ANT. fact, history, truth

legendary *adj.* **1** famous, renowned, celebrated, illustrious **2** fabled, fictitious, mythical

legible *adj.* decipherable, well-written, distinct, plain, apparent, discernible, clear
ANT. illegible, indecipherable

legitimate *adj.* lawful, valid, legal, authorized, real, genuine, allowable
ANT. illegitimate, unallowable, unfair, unauthorized, illicit, false

leisure *n.* spare time, recreation, relaxation, ease
ANT. employment, work

leisurely *adj.* deliberate, convenient, easy, unhurried, relaxed, casual
ANT. hurried, hasty, difficult, forced

lend *v.* loan, advance, grant, entrust
ANT. refuse, withhold

length *n.* measure, extent, reach, span, stretch

lengthen *v.* elongate, stretch, extend, prolong
ANT. shorten, contract

lengthy *adj.* long, interminable, long-winded, long-drawn-out, tedious, verbose, diffuse, prolix
ANT. concise, short, brief, condensed, succinct, compact

lenient *adj.* merciful, mild, tolerant, soft, compassionate
ANT. harsh, cruel, hard, severe, stern

lessen *v.* diminish, reduce, decrease, abate, lower, shrink, dwindle
ANT. increase, enlarge, extend, develop, heighten, multiply, strengthen, spread, enhance

lesson *n.* **1** class, period, teaching, instruction, lecture, seminar, tutorial **2** exercise, task, assignment, practice, homework **3** example, model, reproof, warning

let *v.* **1** permit, allow, grant, authorize **2** rent, lease, charter, hire, hire out

lethal *adj.* fatal, deadly, mortal, poisonous, venomous
ANT. safe

lethargy *n.* drowsiness, torpor, sluggishness, trance, stupor, oblivion
ANT. alertness, liveliness

letter *n.* **1** note, communication, message, missive, epistle **2** mark, character, symbol

level *adj.* even, plane, smooth, uniform, flat, horizontal
ANT. rough, uneven

level *v.* **1** smooth, flatten, even, equalize **2** demolish, raze, devastate, knock down, bulldoze **3** aim, direct, focus, point

level *n.* position, status, rank, standard, degree, surface, floor

lever *n.* bar, crowbar, handle

levity *n.* frivolity, fickleness, flippancy, flightiness, volatility
ANT. gravity, earnestness, seriousness

levy *n.* tax, charge, fee, toll, tariff, duty, imposition

levy *v.* impose, charge, raise, collect, exact

liable *adj.* accountable, responsible, answerable, subject, amenable

liar *n.* fibber, cheat, deceiver, perjurer

libel *n.* defamation, detraction, slander, aspersion

liberal *adj.* **1** generous, unselfish, kind, charitable, lavish, munificent, beneficent **2** tolerant, progressive, permissive, indulgent, open-minded
ANT. **1** mean, greedy, niggardly **2** narrow-minded, bigoted, prejudiced

liberate *v.* set free, free, loose, release, deliver
ANT. confine, imprison

liberty *n.* choice, emancipation, freedom, licence, license (*N. Am.*), independence, leave, permission, exemption, privilege, franchise, immunity
ANT. slavery, captivity, servitude

licence, license (*N. Am.*) *n.* **1** permit, authorization, certificate, permission, leave, privilege, right, warrant **2** laxity, disorder, indulgence, anarchy, lawlessness

license *v.* permit, authorize, let, allow, warrant
ANT. prohibit, forbid

licentious *adj.* unrestrained, dissolute, profligate, loose, impure, unchaste, lascivious, unruly, lawless, immoral, lewd, riotous, wanton, lax
ANT. temperate, strict, moderate, controlled, self-controlled

lick *v.* touch, stroke, rub, taste

lid *n.* cover, top, cap

lie[1] *n.* untruth, fiction, fable, deception, falsehood, falsification, delusion, illusion, prevarication
ANT. truth, reality, fact

lie[2] *v.* fib, fabricate, prevaricate, misrepresent

lie[2] *v.* **1** rest, recline, lodge, sleep **2** be situated, exist, be, belong, consist, remain, continue, abide

life *n.* **1** being, existence, vitality, soul, spirit **2** liveliness, vivacity, energy, vigour, vigor (*N. Am.*), spirit, animation **3** biography, autobiography, life story, memoirs
ANT. **1** death **2** lethargy

lifeless *adj.* **1** dead, deceased, defunct **2** lethargic, inactive, sluggish, slow
ANT. **1** living **2** lively, active

lift *v.* raise, elevate, pull up, hoist, jack (up)
ANT. lower, sink, depress

light[1] *n.* **1** illumination, radiance, gleam, shine, glitter, flame, blaze, incandescence, glow, flash, flare, sparkle, twinkle, flicker, glare, glimmer, glistening, sheen, lustre, luster (*N. Am.*), shimmer, shining, scintillation **2** lamp, lantern, candle, bulb, chandelier, torch, flashlight **3** enlightenment, comprehension, understanding, knowledge, information, prosperity, joy, happiness, felicity
ANT. **1** dark, darkness, dimness, blackness **2** confusion, mystification, ignorance, misunderstanding

light[1] *v.* **1** illuminate, light up, brighten **2** ignite, burn, kindle, fire
ANT. **1** darken **2** extinguish

light¹ *adj.* bright, clear, illuminated, whitish
ANT. dark

light² *adj.* **1** insubstantial, buoyant, airy, flimsy, delicate, portable **2** trivial, small, trifling, inconsiderable, moderate, insignificant, superficial, porous, spongy **3** frivolous, entertaining, amusing, humorous, funny
ANT. **1** weighty, ponderous **2** weighty **3** serious, heavy

light-hearted *adj.* cheerful, happy, carefree, glad
ANT. sad, unhappy, serious

like *v.* be pleased with, approve, enjoy, love, admire, care for, cherish, relish, esteem, fancy
ANT. dislike, hate, loathe, detest, abhor, abominate

like *adj.* resembling, similar, alike, correspondent, equivalent
ANT. different, dissimilar

likelihood *n.* probability, possibility
ANT. improbability, impossibility, unlikelihood

likely *adj.* probable, presumable, reasonable, possible, liable, conceivable
ANT. improbable, unlikely, doubtful

likeness *n.* **1** resemblance, similarity, correspondence, sameness **2** picture, portrait, copy, imitation, image, representation, effigy
ANT. **1** unlikeness, dissimilarity

likewise *adv.* also, moreover, besides, too

liking *n.* inclination, preference, approval, affection, pleasure, desire, fondness, taste, partiality
ANT. dislike, abhorrence, hatred, loathing, repugnance, aversion

limit *n.* **1** boundary, termination, restriction, confine, bound, enclosure, border **2** restraint, restriction, check, limitation

limit *v.* restrict, restrain, confine, check

limitless *adj.* immeasurable, vast, immense, infinite, boundless, interminable, unrestricted, unhindered, unobstructed
ANT. limited, restricted

limp¹ *v.* hobble, stagger, falter, shuffle

limp² *adj.* flabby, soft, slack, supple, flexible
ANT. stiff

limpid *adj.* clear, transparent, lucid, pellucid, pure, translucent, bright, crystal
ANT. opaque, turbid, foul, muddy, dark, black

line *n.* **1** row, series, file, column, queue, rank **2** mark, band, strip, stripe, bar **3** thread, string, rope, cable, wire, cord **4** wrinkle, crease, seam, furrow **5** boundary, edge, limit, border, frontier **6** way, route, direction, track, course, path, channel **7** business, occupation, trade, profession **8** lineage, house, family, descent, extraction

lineage *n.* ancestry, family, descendants, house, breed, race, descent, progeny

linear *adj.* direct, straight, lineal, rectilinear
ANT. crooked, zigzag, wandering

linger *v.* loiter, remain, stay, tarry, delay, halt, stop, hesitate, wait, pause, lag, saunter

link *n.* bond, tie, connection, joint

link *v.* connect, tie, join, unite, couple, associate

lip *n.* edge, rim, brim

liquid *n.* fluid, solution, gas, vapour, vapor (*N. Am.*)
ANT. solid

liquid *adj.* fluid, flowing, running, liquefied
ANT. solid

list *n.* series, roll, catalogue, catalog (*N. Am.*), schedule, inventory, record, register, index

list *v.* record, register, file, catalogue, catalog (*N. Am.*)

listen *v.* hear, attend, pay attention, hark, heed
ANT. ignore, neglect

listless *adj.* lethargic, spiritless, weary, heedless, indifferent, careless, languid, uninterested
ANT. energetic, lively

literal *adj.* word for word, specific, accurate, correct, exact, grammatical, positive, verbal, close, plain, actual
ANT. free, liberal

literate *adj.* learned, bookish, lettered, erudite, scholarly, well-read, studious, instructed, educated
ANT. illiterate, unlettered, unscholarly

literature *n.* books, literary works, publications, writings, plays, novels, essays, poetry, belles-lettres

lithe *adj.* agile, pliant, flexible, limber, supple, elastic
ANT. stiff, inflexible, unresponsive

litter *n.* rubbish, waste, refuse, clutter, disorder, untidiness
ANT. order, cleanliness, tidiness

litter *v.* scatter, disorder, strew, clutter, mess up

little *adj.* 1 small, diminutive, tiny, minute, petite 2 insignificant, unimportant, inconsiderable, trivial, petty, paltry 3 short, brief, fleeting, passing
ANT. 1 big, large, huge, colossal, enormous 2 important, momentous 3 long

live *v.* 1 have life, be, exist, breathe, survive, remain, last, grow, continue, behave, act 2 abide, dwell, reside
ANT. 1 die, wither, fade, vanish, fail

live *adj.* 1 alive, living, active, vigorous, earnest, energetic, animate 2 important, current, topical, controversial, burning
ANT. 1 inanimate, dead, moribund, deceased, departed, gone

livelihood *n.* employment, work, job, occupation, support, maintenance, sustenance, subsistence

lively *adj.* quick, energetic, active, alert, nimble, sprightly, brisk, animated, prompt, vivacious, keen, eager, spirited, vigorous
ANT. lifeless, dull, languid, indifferent

livery *n.* uniform, clothing, uniform, dress, costume, attire

livid *adj.* angry, furious, wild, enraged, fuming
ANT. calm

living *n.* livelihood, support, subsistence, existence

load *n.* burden, onus, cargo, freight, charge, weight, pack, lading, encumbrance, oppression, pressure

load *v.* burden, weight, weigh down, encumber, oppress, lade

loaf *v.* idle, lounge, laze, loll

loan *v.* lend, advance
ANT. borrow

loan *n.* advance, credit

loath *adj.* averse, unwilling, reluctant, indisposed, disinclined
ANT. eager, ardent, zealous, enthusiastic

loathe *v.* hate, detest, dislike, abhor, abominate, execrate
ANT. desire, like, long for, love

lobby *n.* foyer, vestibule, hall, hallway

lobby *v.* persuade, influence, urge

local *adj.* nearby, neighbourhood, neighborhood (*N. Am.*), provincial, regional, suburban

locality *n.* area, neighbourhood, neighborhood (*N. Am.*), district, region, province, town, village, city

locate *v.* 1 place, set, situate 2 discover, find, unearth, track down

location *n.* situation, place, position, spot, site

lock[1] *v.* secure, fasten, bolt, latch, padlock

lock[1] *n.* clasp, catch, bar, bolt, fastening, hasp, hook, latch

lock[2] *n.* curl, tress, plait, braid

lodge *n.* hut, cabin, cottage, chalet

lodge *v.* 1 rest, remain, shelter, stay, live, abide, stop 2 fix, stick, embed
ANT. 1 move on 2 remove

lofty *adj.* 1 sublime, exalted, noble, dignified, stately, majestic, elevated, towering, tall, high 2 arrogant, condescending, proud, haughty

logical *adj.* reasonable, sensible, rational, coherent, consistent, sound
ANT. illogical, unsound, inconsistent, unreasonable, fallacious

lonely *adj.* 1 friendless, isolated, by oneself, solitary, forsaken, bereft 2 forlorn, forsaken, remote, isolated, desolate, secluded

long[1] *adj.* 1 extensive, lengthy, drawn out, extended, stretched, protracted
ANT. short, brief

long² *v.* desire, yearn, crave, wish, pine, hunger, thirst

long-suffering *adj.* patient, forbearing, tolerant, uncomplaining, philosophical, resigned
ANT. impatient, complaining

look *v.* 1 see, glance, watch, stare, scan, contemplate, view, discern, gaze, regard, inspect, survey 2 seem, appear

look after take care of, mind, tend, attend to **look for** search, try to find, seek, hunt, rummage **look into** investigate, study, examine, explore, probe

look *n.* 1 glance, view, stare, gaze, sight 2 appearance, aspect, expression, manner, air

loom *v.* be imminent, appear, menace, threaten

loop *n.* circle, ring, coil, hoop

loose *adj.* 1 untied, free, unattached, unfastened, unbound, unconstrained, wobbly 2 lax, slack, baggy, hanging, drooping 3 vague, indefinite, imprecise, unconnected, rambling 4 immoral, promiscuous, unchaste, dissolute, debauched
ANT. 1 secure, fastened, firm 2 tight, close, close-fitting 3 precise, accurate 4 chaste

loosen *v.* unfasten, untie, undo, loose, ease, slacken, relax
ANT. fasten, tighten

loot *n.* bounty, plunder, spoils

loot *v.* plunder, ravage, sack, pillage, ransack, rob, steal

loquacious *adj.* garrulous, talkative, voluble
ANT. taciturn, silent

lord *n.* peer, noble, nobleman, aristocrat, duke, earl, baron

lordly *adj.* arrogant, overbearing, proud, haughty, lofty, imperious, noble
ANT. humble, lowly

lore *n.* knowledge, wisdom, learning, erudition, advice, counsel, instruction
ANT. ignorance, illiteracy, inexperience

lose *v.* 1 mislay, misplace, miss, forget, part with, deprive of 2 fail, be defeated, be unsuccessful, go wrong
ANT. 1 find 2 win, succeed

loss *n.* 1 deprivation, defeat, failure, destruction, injury, hurt, harm, damage, disadvantage, forfeiture, waste, detriment, ruin 2 death, bereavement
ANT. 1 restoration, gain

lost *adj.* 1 missing, misplaced, mislaid, gone, vanished, disappeared 2 wasted, squandered, ruined, misspent, forfeited
ANT. found

lot *n.* 1 plenty, abundance, large number, large amount, great extent, great degree 2 set, group, collection, batch 3 chance, accident, fate, fortune, hazard, destiny, doom 4 portion, allotment, share, apportionment, division, part

lotion *n.* cream, salve, ointment, balm

loud *adj.* noisy, deafening, thundering, ear-splitting, booming, blaring, clamorous
ANT. quiet, soft, silent, inaudible

lounge *n.* sitting room, living room, parlour, parlor (*N. Am.*)

love *n.* affection, devotion, fondness, adoration, friendship, liking, tenderness, regard, attachment, attraction
ANT. hate, hatred

love *v.* enjoy, like, be fond of, adore, be attached to, be devoted to, hold dear
ANT. hate, dislike

lovely *adj.* attractive, beautiful, charming, delightful, pretty, enchanting, pleasing, winning, sweet, admirable
ANT. hideous, ugly, unattractive, plain

low *adj.* 1 short, small, sunken, depressed, squat 2 inadequate, insufficient, poor, meagre, meager (*N. Am.*), inferior 3 rude, vulgar, base, mean, contemptible, despicable 4 cheap, inexpensive, reasonable
ANT. 1 high 2 high, good 3 honourable, honorable (*N. Am.*) 4 expensive

lower *v.* 1 decrease, lessen, depress, sink, reduce, diminish, humble 2 let down, drop, fall, descend, sink 3 degrade, disgrace, debase, abase, humble
ANT. 1 increase 2 raise

lower *adj.* inferior, subordinate, minor, lesser
ANT. higher, superior

lowly *adj.* low, humble, unimportant, meek, modest, unpretentious
ANT. proud, arrogant, haughty

loyal *adj.* faithful, true, constant, devoted, staunch, dependable, trustworthy, obedient, submissive
ANT. disloyal, unfaithful, inconstant, untrue, traitorous, mutinous, rebellious, disobedient

loyalty *n.* allegiance, fidelity, devotion, faithfulness, constancy
ANT. treason, treachery, unfaithfulness, disloyalty, rebellion

lucid *adj.* 1 clear, intelligible, plain 2 transparent, clear, bright, shining, resplendent, limpid
ANT. 1 unintelligible, unclear, confused 2 dark, opaque

luck *n.* chance, fate, fortune, hazard, accident, fluke

lucky *adj.* fortunate, successful, prosperous, happy, favoured (*N. Am.*), favourable, favorable (*N. Am.*), blessed, auspicious
ANT. unlucky, unfortunate

lucrative *adj.* profitable, gainful, paying, remunerative
ANT. unremunerative, unprofitable

ludicrous *adj.* absurd, farcical, preposterous, funny, laughable, ridiculous, comical, odd, comic, burlesque, droll, sportive
ANT. grave, serious

luggage *n.* baggage, suitcases, trunks, bags, belongings, things (*informal*)

lugubrious *adj.* melancholy, morose, mournful, woeful, pitiable, doleful, sad, sorrowful, complaining
ANT. cheerful, happy, lively

lull *n.* calm, peace, quiet, still, stillness, tranquillity

lull *v.* compose, calm, quiet, soothe, hush, still
ANT. disturb

luminous *adj.* light, glowing, shining, brilliant, bright, illuminated
ANT. dark, black

lump *n.* 1 piece, block, mass, chunk 2 bump, protuberance, swelling, growth, tumour, tumor (*N. Am.*)

lunacy *n.* madness, insanity, derangement, mania, craziness, aberration
ANT. sanity, reason

lunatic *adj.* insane, mad, crazy, deranged, demented
ANT. sane, rational, reasonable, sound

lunatic *n.* maniac, madman, madwoman, psychopath, obsessive

lure *n.* enticement, decoy, bait, temptation, attraction

lure *v.* allure, entice, draw, tempt, attract, seduce

lurid *adj.* 1 shocking, explicit, sensational 2 brightly-coloured, brightly-colored (*N. Am.*), vivid, dazzling, intense

lurk *v.* lie hidden, lie in wait, hide, skulk

luscious *adj.* sweet, delicious, mouthwatering, succulent, appetizing, delightful, delectable

lustre, luster (*N. Am.*) *n.* 1 brilliance, brightness, splendour, splendor (*N. Am.*), glitter, gleam, radiance, resplendence 2 fame, renown, distinction, glory, honour, honor (*N. Am.*), eminence, repute, celebrity
ANT. 1 darkness, blackness, gloom 2 detraction, infamy, disrepute, dishonour, dishonor (*N. Am.*), notoriety

luxuriant *adj.* profuse, lush, exuberant, excessive, rank, abundant, plentiful, plenteous
ANT. scanty, scarce, feeble

luxuriate *v.* indulge, bask, wallow, revel, delight

luxurious *adj.* sumptuous, splendid, lavish, plush, rich, opulent, affluent, expensive, self-indulgent
ANT. austere, Spartan

luxury *n.* splendour, splendor (*N. Am.*), lavishness, richness, sumptuousness, affluence, opulence, self-indulgence

lying *adj.* false, deceitful, dishonest, untruthful, untrue
ANT. truthful, true, honest

lyric *n.* words, libretto, text

M

macabre *adj.* gruesome, chilling, horrible, horrifying, frightening, grim, grisly

macerate *v.* soak, steep, soften

machination *n.* plot, conspiracy, intrigue, stratagem, design, scheme, trick, artifice, contrivance

machine *n.* 1 engine, motor, mechanism, device, instrument, tool 2 organization, system, agency

mad *adj.* 1 crazy, insane, lunatic 2 furious, angry, deranged, demented, enraged, exasperated, infuriated, raging, fuming, provoked, incensed, wrathful
ANT. 1 sane, sound 2 pleased

madden *v.* make mad, enrage, anger, incense, irritate, provoke, inflame, infuriate
ANT. calm, pacify

madness *n.* insanity, craziness, derangement, mania, delirium, frenzy, fury, rage
ANT. sanity, rationality

magazine *n.* periodical, journal, review

magic *n.* sorcery, witchcraft, wizardry, enchantment, incantation, necromancy

magical *adj.* mystical, mysterious, supernatural, enchanting

magician *n.* conjuror, wizard, juggler, sorcerer, witch, warlock

magistrate *n.* judge, police officer, chief official

magnanimous *adj.* generous, unselfish, benevolent, kind, chivalrous, high-minded, honourable, honorable (*N. Am.*)
ANT. mean, selfish

magnificent *adj.* splendid, glorious, grand, majestic, imposing, stately, showy, admirable, superb
ANT. ordinary, unimposing

magnify *v.* enlarge, increase, amplify, intensify, exaggerate, augment
ANT. diminish

magnitude *n.* 1 extent, size, volume, dimension, mass 2 importance, greatness, significance, weight, consequence
ANT. 2 insignificance, unimportance

maid *n.* servant, chambermaid, maidservant, domestic

maim *v.* disable, cripple, injure, mutilate, disfigure, lame

main *adj.* principal, chief, leading, most important, first, foremost, necessary, vital, essential, indispensable, requisite, cardinal, capital
ANT. subordinate, non-essential, minor

mainly *adv.* chiefly, principally, mostly, generally, greatly, primarily
ANT. partially, somewhat, slightly

maintain *v.* 1 claim, uphold, assert, affirm, vindicate, allege, support, sustain 2 preserve, defend, continue, keep, supply, provide, look after
ANT. 1 retract, deny, withdraw 2 neglect, abandon

maintenance *n.* sustenance, support, upkeep, preservation, provisions, subsistence, livelihood

majestic *adj.* grand, impressive, imposing, splendid, magnificent, regal, royal, pompous, stately, dignified
ANT. lowly, ordinary

majesty *n.* grandeur, dignity, power, authority, loftiness, stateliness, augustness, elevation

major *adj.* greater, main, chief, leading, important, significant, older, senior, elder
ANT. minor

majority *n.* greater part, bulk, preponderance, mass
ANT. minority

make v. **1** produce, create, fabricate, manufacture, build, construct, fashion, shape **2** cause, bring about, occasion, accomplish, perform, achieve, render, execute **3** force, compel, cause, constrain, require, urge, drive **4** appoint, elect, select **5** earn, obtain, gain, get, net, gross, bring in **6** reach, attain, arrive at, make for, head for, head towards, aim for, make out discern, perceive, recognize, detect, make up invent, create, fabricate, formulate

maker n. creator, producer, manufacturer, builder, constructor

malefactor n. wrongdoer, evildoer, criminal, convict, culprit, felon

malice n. spite, ill will, resentment, grudge, pique, bitterness, animosity, malevolence
ANT. goodwill, benevolence, kindness

maltreat v. mistreat, ill-treat, abuse, harm, injure

mammoth adj. enormous, colossal, immense, huge
ANT. tiny, minute

man n. **1** human beings, humanity, human race, humankind, people **2** person, individual, human being, adult **3** male, fellow, gentleman, chap, bloke (informal)

manage v. **1** direct, govern, control, order, contrive, conduct, transact, administer, regulate, supervise, superintend, handle, rule **2** succeed, bring about, arrange, make work
ANT. **2** fail

manageable adj. controllable, tractable, governable, docile, obedient
ANT. unmanageable, uncontrollable

management n. **1** control, supervision, regulation, administration, government, guidance, direction, care, charge **2** directors, board, managers, executive
ANT. **1** maladministration, mismanagement

manager n. director, superintendent, executive, supervisor, governor, overseer, boss

mandate n. authority, command, commission, order, charge, precept, injunction, requirement, edict

mangle v. mutilate, destroy, mar, spoil, cut, bruise, lacerate, maim, tear
ANT. restore, heal

manhood n. virility, maturity, masculinity

mania n. insanity, derangement, madness, lunacy, craze, obsession, aberration, delirium, frenzy
ANT. soundness

maniac n. lunatic, madman, madwoman, psychopath

manifest adj. patent, obvious, unmistakable, distinct, plain, clear, evident, apparent, visible, conspicuous, indubitable
ANT. hidden, indistinct, inconspicuous

manifest v. show, display, disclose, reveal, declare, evince, make known, discover, exhibit, expose
ANT. hide, cover, conceal

manifold adj. various, numerous, many, diverse
ANT. few, rare

mankind n. humanity, human race, human beings, humankind, people, society

manner n. **1** way, method, form, style, means, fashion, practice, mode, custom, habit **2** behaviour, behavior (N. Am.), conduct, bearing, carriage, demeanour, demeanor (N. Am.), air, look, mien, aspect, appearance

mannerism n. idiosyncrasy, characteristic, peculiarity, uniformity, affectation
ANT. unaffectedness, simplicity, naturalness

manoeuvre, maneuver (N. Am.) v. **1** move, steer, drive, push **2** manipulate, contrive, scheme, plot, intrigue

manoeuvre, maneuver (N. Am.) n. movement, action, motion, exercise, operation

manual n. guide, guidebook, handbook, instruction book

manual adj. physical, human, hand-operated
ANT. automatic

manufacture v. make, produce, assemble, fabricate

manufacture *n.* making, production, fabrication, construction

many *adj.* several, numerous, various, abundant
ANT. few

map *n.* plan, chart, diagram, graph

map *v.* plot, plan, chart

mar *v.* harm, injure, mark, spoil, ruin, blemish, damage, disfigure, deface, hurt, impair, maim, deform
ANT. restore, improve, reinstate

marauder *n.* plunderer, robber, ravager, pillager, outlaw, bandit, brigand, freebooter, invader

march *n.* **1** procession, parade, demonstration **2** walk, step, pace, stride

march *v.* walk, proceed, parade, step, pace

margin *n.* border, edge, brim, lip, rim, brink, verge, limit, boundary, extremity
ANT. centre, center (*N. Am.*)

marine *adj.* naval, nautical, maritime, oceanic

marital *adj.* wedded, matrimonial, conjugal, connubial, nuptial

maritime *adj.* marine, oceanic, nautical

mark *n.* **1** spot, stain, blemish, scratch **2** impression, imprint, track, evidence, proof, characteristic, indication, stamp, vestige **3** sign, badge, symbol, emblem **4** goal, target, objective

mark *v.* **1** stamp, imprint, impress, brand, identify **2** stain, bruise, blemish, scratch **3** grade, assess, correct **4** remark, notice, note, regard, heed, show **5** denote, characterize, label, designate, observe, stigmatize, signalize, specify, specialize

marked *adj.* noticeable, obvious, evident, conspicuous, noted, notable, prominent, remarkable, eminent, distinguished
ANT. ordinary, undistinguished

market *n.* mart, stall, bazaar, fair

market *v.* sell, deal, retail, trade, merchandise

marriage *n.* **1** wedding, matrimony, wedlock, espousal, nuptials, union **2** union, alliance, merger, association
ANT. **1** divorce, celibacy **2** separation, division

marrow *n.* pith, essence, substance, kernel, quintessence

marry *v.* wed, join, unite, betroth, get hitched (*informal*), get spliced (*informal*)

marsh *n.* fen, swamp, bog, quagmire, morass

marshal *v.* order, arrange, direct, organize, rank, array, dispose, draw up
ANT. disarrange, disorder

martial *adj.* warlike, military, soldierly

martyr *n.* sufferer, sacrifice, victim

marvel *n.* wonder, miracle, phenomenon, surprise, astonishment, amazement, admiration

marvel *v.* wonder, be amazed, be surprised, be astounded, be in awe

marvellous, marvelous (*N. Am.*) *adj.* wonderful, astonishing, surprising, astounding, incredible, stupendous, extraordinary, wondrous
ANT. everyday, ordinary, commonplace

masculine *adj.* male, manly, manlike
ANT. feminine, womanly, female

mask *n.* cover, disguise, camouflage, screen, blind, veil, protection

mask *v.* disguise, cover, hide, conceal, veil, shroud, screen, protect
ANT. expose, unmask, discover, detect

mass *n.* **1** pile, heap, stack, collection, quantity **2** bulk, magnitude, body, size, main part, majority, aggregate, whole, totality

mass *v.* gather, collect, assemble, accumulate, amass

massacre *v.* murder, butcher, kill, slaughter, slay

massacre *n.* mass murder, genocide, slaughter, butchery

massage *v.* rub, manipulate, knead

massive *adj.* huge, immense, vast, solid, colossal, weighty, heavy, massy, ponderous, bulky
ANT. small, slight

mast *n.* pole, spar, post

master *n.* **1** ruler, director, manager, head, chief, leader, employer, owner, governor, superintendent, commander, captain **2** expert, genius, maestro, dab hand (*informal*)

master v. **1** acquire, learn, grasp, understand **2** conquer, overcome, overpower, subdue, vanquish

masterly adj. skilful, skillful (N. Am.), clever, expert, dexterous, adroit, excellent, artistic, consummate
ANT. clumsy, bungling

mastermind v. play, arrange, organize, manage, direct, supervise

mastermind n. genius, expert, brains (informal)

masterpiece n. magnum opus, model, chef-d'oeuvre

mastery n. **1** command, control, authority, dominion, supremacy, victory, triumph, pre-eminence, ascendancy, superiority **2** knowledge, grasp, command, understanding, skill, dexterity, cleverness, ability
ANT. **1** subservience **2** ignorance

mat n. rug, carpet, covering

match n. **1** competition, trial, contest, game **2** equal, mate, equivalent, fellow, mate

match v. **1** harmonize, fit, adapt, blend, suit **2** equal, resemble, compare **3** join, unite, marry, couple, combine
ANT. **1** clash **3** separate

matchless adj. unequalled, unequaled (N. Am.), peerless, unparalleled, incomparable, inimitable, consummate, exquisite, excellent, surpassing, unrivalled, unrivaled (N. Am.)
ANT. common, ordinary, mediocre, everyday, commonplace, general

mate n. companion, associate, assistant, subordinate, fellow, intimate, match, equal

mate v. breed, couple, pair

material n. substance, fabric, stuff, matter

material adj. physical, real, concrete, substantial, tangible
ANT. spiritual, immaterial

maternal adj. motherly, kind, caring, protective

matter n. **1** substance, material, body, constituency **2** interest, concern, affair, business, subject, topic, question **3** trouble, difficulty **4** importance, significance, consequence
ANT. **1** immateriality, spirituality

matter v. be important, count, signify

mature adj. **1** ripe, perfect, ready, perfected, completed, full-grown **2** adult, grown-up, experienced, wise
ANT. **1** immature, undeveloped, unripe **2** immature, puerile, childish

maudlin adj. tearful, sentimental, weak, emotional, mawkish, soppy (informal)

maxim n. principle, axiom, saying, dictum, precept, rule, proverb, aphorism, apothegm, adage

maximize v. increase, enlarge, extend
ANT. minimize, reduce

maximum n. greatest, climax, culmination, completion, utmost, ultimate, zenith, apex, acme
ANT. minimum

maybe adv. perhaps, possibly

maze n. labyrinth, network, intricacy

meadow n. field, pasture, pastureland, grassland

meagre, meager (N. Am.) adj. scanty, sparse, inadequate, deficient, insufficient
ANT. abundant, copious

meal n. snack, breakfast, lunch, tea, dinner, supper, refreshment

mean¹ v. **1** intend, design, plan, expect, propose, purpose **2** signify, indicate, denote, express, suggest, import

mean² adj. **1** miserly, niggardly, stingy, selfish **2** unkind, cruel, nasty, unpleasant, contemptible, base, abject, shameful, wretched
ANT. **1** generous, unselfish, liberal **2** kind, noble

mean³ n. middle, medium, average, intermediate point, centre
ANT. extreme

meaning n. **1** sense, explanation, significance, interpretation, definition, purport **2** purpose, aim, intention, design, object

meanness n. stinginess, illiberality, niggardliness, abjectness, baseness
ANT. nobleness, generosity, unselfishness, liberality, large-heartedness

means *n. pl.* **1** resources, money, funds, wealth **2** agency, medium, instrument, vehicle, channel, method, way

measure *n.* **1** dimension, capacity, quantity, amount, extent, weight, size, bulk, volume, proportion **2** rule, standard, test

measure *v.* weigh, quantify, assess, compute, work out, be long, be high, be wide, be deep

measureless *adj.* unlimited, infinite, immeasurable, immense, boundless, limitless, vast, unbounded
ANT. finite, limited, bounded, restricted

measurement *n.* dimension, length, height, width, depth, weight, assessment

mechanic *n.* operative, worker, hand

mechanical *adj.* automatic, involuntary, blind, instinctive, habitual, unreflective, spontaneous, effortless

mechanism *n.* machine, engine, motor, device, tool, instrument

mechanize *v.* automate, industrialize

medal *n.* decoration, award, reward, badge, gong (*informal*)

meddle *v.* interfere, intrude, interpose, intervene, pry, snoop, butt in

meddlesome *adj.* meddling, intrusive, interfering, obtrusive
ANT. unobtrusive

mediate *v.* intervene, interpose, intercede, arbitrate, reconcile

mediation *n.* arbitration, adjustment, reconciliation, interposition, intercession, intervention

mediator *n.* intermediary, peacemaker, reconciler, intercessor, interceder, advocate, umpire

medicine *n.* drug, remedy, potion, cure, antidote, corrective, prescription

mediocre *adj.* moderate, indifferent, ordinary, mean, medium, average, middling, commonplace
ANT. superior, extraordinary, distinguished, distinctive

meditate *v.* consider, think, reflect, ponder, revolve, study, weigh, contemplate, muse, cogitate

medium *n.* **1** middle, mean, average **2** means, agency, instrument, instrumentality, factor

medium *adj.* middle, mean, middling, intermediate, average
ANT. outer, extreme

medley *n.* mixture, jumble, miscellany, variety, pot-pourri

meek *adj.* mild, patient, humble, lowly, modest, submissive, yielding, unassuming, gentle
ANT. bold, arrogant, proud, self-assertive

meet *v.* **1** come across, encounter, run into, bump into (*informal*) **2** collect, gather, assemble, congregate **3** fulfil, satisfy, match, carry out, discharge **4** join, converge, cross, intersect, come together
ANT. **1** miss, escape **2** disperse **4** diverge, separate

meeting *n.* conference, interview, encounter, gathering, assembly, company, convention, congregation, junction, union, confluence

melancholy *n.* sadness, depression, dejection, gloominess
ANT. happiness, gladness

melancholy *adj.* sad, dejected, depressed, gloomy, sorrowful, moody, despondent, dispirited, low-spirited, down-hearted, unhappy, heavy, doleful
ANT. happy, cheerful, glad

mellow *adj.* **1** ripe, soft, tender, mature **2** smooth, sweet, rich
ANT. **1** unripe **2** harsh, discordant

mellow *v.* ripen, develop, season, soften

melodious *adj.* tuneful, rhythmical, musical, agreeable, harmonious, dulcet, sweet
ANT. discordant, harsh, dissonant, jarring

melody *n.* tune, music, harmony, rhythm, air, song
ANT. discord, jarring, dissonance, harshness, discordance

melt *v.* liquefy, fuse, thaw, dissolve, soften, be dissipated, run, blend, flow
ANT. harden, consolidate, unite, crystallize

member *n.* partner, sharer, subscriber, associate, participator

memoir *n*. memorial, biography, record, narrative, chronicle, register

memorable *adj*. important, historic, remarkable, extraordinary, unforgettable, distinguished, famous, celebrated, great, conspicuous, prominent
ANT. ordinary, trivial, commonplace, insignificant, mediocre

memorial *n*. monument, commemoration, remembrance, record

memorize *v*. remember, learn, learn by heart, commit to memory
ANT. forget

memory *n*. remembrance, recollection, recall, reminiscence, thought
ANT. forgetfulness

menace *n*. threat, intimidation, warning, denunciation

menace *v*. threaten, intimidate, warn, scare, frighten, terrorize

mend *v*. repair, patch, fix, improve, reform, better, restore, recover, heal
ANT. damage, harm, deteriorate

menial *adj*. common, lowly, humble, servile, mean

mental *adj*. intellectual, cerebral, thinking

mention *v*. refer to, allude to, speak of, touch on, notice, announce, observe, remark, hint, declare, tell, state, report, disclose, name

mention *n*. reference, allusion, comment, remark, notice, remembrance, hint, communication, observation, declaration

merchandise *n*. wares, commodities, goods, stock, trade, traffic, commerce

merchant *n*. trader, shopkeeper, dealer, retailer, storekeeper, trafficker

merciful *adj*. kind, mild, forgiving, compassionate, pitiful, tender, humane, gracious, tender-hearted, lenient
ANT. cruel, hard, severe, pitiless, unrelenting

merciless *adj*. ruthless, pitiless, cruel, hard, brutal, unfeeling, harsh, unkind, callous, severe, unrelenting, unforgiving
ANT. kind, merciful, compassionate, pitying

mercy *n*. compassion, grace, favour, favor (*N. Am.*), clemency, forbearance, tenderness, forgiveness, gentleness, pardon, blessing, pity, kindness, mildness, lenity, benevolence
ANT. hardness, cruelty, implacability, ruthlessness, inhumanity, harshness, severity, justice, vengeance, revenge, punishment

mere *adj*. simple, bare, sheer, pure, absolute, unqualified, unadulterated

merely *adv*. barely, simply, purely, only

merge *v*. join, combine, unite, fuse, blend, amalgamate
ANT. separate

merger *n*. amalgamation, union, fusion, coalition, combination
ANT. separation

meridian *n*. zenith, height, culmination, summit, peak, apex, pinnacle

merit *v*. deserve, earn, be worthy of, be entitled to

merit *n*. worth, value, excellence, reward, quality, worthiness, credit
ANT. worthlessness, unworthiness

merry *adj*. cheerful, happy, joyful, jovial, lively, gleeful
ANT. sad, gloomy

mesh *n*. net, netting, network, web

mess *n*. 1 confusion, disorder, disarray, clutter, muddle, jumble, dirtiness
2 difficult, trouble, predicament, quandary, fix (*informal*), hole (*informal*)
ANT. 1 order

mess *v*. confuse, muddle, bungle, disorder, disarrange, dirty
ANT. clear

message *n*. communication, letter, note, notice, word, intimation

messenger *n*. courier, bearer, agent, runner, carrier, harbinger, forerunner, herald, precursor

messy *adj*. untidy, cluttered, muddled, confused, sloppy, dirty

metaphysical *adj*. abstract, theoretical, philosophical, abstruse, conceptual
ANT. physical, material

mete *v*. mete out dispense, administer, allot, allocate, assign

method *n.* way, manner, means, technique, order, system, rule, course, arrangement, process

methodical *adj.* ordered, orderly, systematic, organized, efficient, structured
ANT. disorganized

meticulous *adj.* exact, precise, scrupulous, accurate, painstaking
ANT. careless, sloppy

middle *n.* midpoint, centre, center (*N. Am.*), mean
ANT. edge

middle *adj.* central, intermediate, halfway, mean
ANT. extreme

midst *n.* middle, centre, center (*N. Am.*), heart

mien *n.* manner, bearing, look, aspect, carriage, deportment, appearance

might *n.* power, force, strength, energy, means, resources
ANT. weakness, feebleness

mighty *adj.* powerful, strong, forceful, muscular, vigorous
ANT. weak, feeble, frail

migrate *v.* move, relocate, resettle, journey, travel, emigrate, immigrate
ANT. remain, stay

mild *adj.* 1 gentle, pleasant, kind, compassionate, placid, tender, soft 2 moderate, temperate, pleasant
ANT. 1 harsh 2 stormy

militant *adj.* aggressive, belligerent, fighting
ANT. peaceful

military *adj.* armed, martial

mimic *v.* imitate, copy, impersonate, ape, mirror

mimic *n.* imitator, impersonator, impressionist, copycat (*informal*)

mind *n.* 1 understanding, intellect, intelligence, brain, reason, sense, consciousness, thought 2 opinion, judgment, belief, thought, view 3 choice, inclination, liking, intention, will, disposition 4 remembrance, memory, recollection

mind *v.* 1 care about, object to, dislike, take offence, take offense (*N. Am.*)

2 look after, care for, take care of, watch, tend 3 pay attention, heed, regard, watch, observe
ANT. 1 like 2 neglect 3 ignore

mindful *adj.* careful, thoughtful, attentive, heedful, observant
ANT. inattentive, careless

mine *n.* 1 excavation, pit, shaft, colliery 2 source, supply, reserve, fund, treasury

mine *v.* dig, excavate, bore, drill, quarry, tunnel

mingle *v.* combine, join, blend, amalgamate, compound, mix, unite, associate
ANT. separate

minister *n.* clergyman, clergywoman, priest, preacher, vicar, curate, chaplain, pastor, parson

minor *adj.* inferior, unimportant, smaller, less, junior, secondary, younger
ANT. major

mint *v.* coin, stamp, punch, strike

minute[1] *n.* moment, second, instant, jiffy (*informal*)

minute[2] *adj.* tiny, diminutive, slight, little, wee, microscopic, minuscule
ANT. enormous, huge

miracle *n.* wonder, marvel, phenomenon

miraculous *adj.* marvellous, wonderful, extraordinary, phenomenal, incredible, supernatural
ANT. ordinary

mirror *n.* looking-glass, reflector, glass

mirror *v.* reflect, copy, imitate

miscellaneous *adj.* assorted, varied, mixed, various, different, diverse

miscellany *n.* assortment, mixture, collection, medley, jumble, variety, diversity

mischief *n.* 1 naughtiness, misbehaviour, misbehavior (*N. Am.*), misconduct, roguishness 2 harm, hurt, damage, injury

mischievous *adj.* naughty, playful, roguish, impish, teasing

miser *n.* niggard, skinflint, Scrooge, cheapskate (*informal*), curmudgeon, churl
ANT. spendthrift

miserable *adj.* **1** unhappy, sad, despondent, downcast, depressed, dejected, heartbroken, melancholy, disconsolate **2** contemptible, despicable, mean, low, wretched **3** poor, impoverished, penniless, needy, destitute
ANT. **1** happy, cheerful **2** noble **3** rich, wealthy

miserly *adj.* mean, niggardly, stingy, covetous, cheeseparing
ANT. generous, liberal

misery *n.* unhappiness, wretchedness, woe, agony, distress, grief, sorrow
ANT. happiness

misfortune *n.* calamity, trouble, adversity, failure, ill luck, hardship, harm, ill, affliction, blow, disaster, disappointment, trial, tribulation, sorrow, ruin, distress, stroke, misery, reverse, misadventure
ANT. triumph, success, comfort, good fortune

misgiving *n.* doubt, hesitation, qualm, uncertainty

mishap *n.* accident, misfortune, bad luck, calamity, disaster

misjudge *v.* misunderstand, misinterpret, miscalculate

mislay *v.* misplace, lose
ANT. find

mislead *v.* misinform, deceive, trick, fool, delude

misprint *n.* error, mistake, literal

miss *v.* **1** fail, lose, overlook, skip **2** desire, need, want, yearn for
ANT. **1** hit, seize

missile *n.* projectile, weapon

mission *n.* duty, task, undertaking, message, errand, commission

missionary *n.* evangelist, preacher, minister

mist *n.* fog, vapour, vapor (*N. Am.*), cloud, steam, haze

mistake *n.* error, slip, fault, oversight, misunderstanding

mistake *v.* misjudge, misunderstand, get wrong, misinterpret

mistaken *adj.* wrong, in error, incorrect, inaccurate, inexact, erroneous
ANT. correct

misunderstand *v.* misinterpret, confuse, misjudge, misconceive
ANT. understand, comprehend

mitigate *v.* alleviate, moderate, lessen, relieve, reduce, diminish
ANT. aggravate

mix *v.* combine, blend, amalgamate

mix up confuse, humble, muddle (up)

mixture *n.* combination, blend, amalgamation, assortment, medley, jumble

moan *v.* complain, grumble, grieve, cry, groan, wail

moan *n.* complaint, grumble, lament, groan

mob *n.* crowd, rabble, swarm, throng, masses, populace

mobile *adj.* movable, portable, changeable
ANT. immovable, firm, set, steady, unchangeable

mock *v.* ridicule, laugh at, scorn, tease, jeer
ANT. respect, praise

mock *adj.* counterfeit, imitation, fake, spurious, simulated
ANT. authentic, real, genuine

mockery *n.* **1** ridicule, laughter, derision, scorn, taunt, contempt, jeering, teasing **2** travesty, imitation, pretence, pretense (*N. Am.*), parody, sham

mode *n.* way, method, manner, style, technique

model *n.* copy, design, example, image, imitation, standard, type, representation, pattern, prototype, facsimile, original, mould, mold (*N. Am.*), archetype

model *v.* form, shape, mould, mold (*N. Am.*), make, design, style, fashion, carve, sculpt, cast

moderate *adj.* **1** limited, restrained, reasonable, controlled, cautious **2** temperate, calm, mild, equable
ANT. **1** immoderate, extreme

moderate *v.* control, regulate, attenuate, reduce, lessen
ANT. aggravate

modern *adj.* new, up-to-date, contemporary, recent, fresh, novel, modish, fashionable, present, present-day
ANT. old, ancient, antiquated, antique, obsolete, former

modernize *v.* bring up to date, improve, renovate, renew

modest *adj.* humble, lowly, meek, reserved, unassuming, unobtrusive, self-effacing, shy, timid, coy
ANT. immodest, arrogant

modesty *n.* humility, lowliness, humbleness, meekness, shyness, reserve, bashfulness, backwardness, constraint, timidity, unobtrusiveness, coyness
ANT. impudence, self-conceit, arrogance

modify *v.* change, alter, vary, transform, convert, revise

moist *adj.* damp, wet, humid, clammy, muggy
ANT. dry

moisture *n.* damp, dampness, wet, wetness, vapour, vapor (*N. Am.*), condensation, dew
ANT. dryness

molest *v.* abuse, attack, assault, pester, accost

moment *n.* **1** second, trice, instant, twinkling, jiffy (*informal*) **2** importance, significance, consequence, weight, consideration, force, value
ANT. **2** insignificance, unimportance, triviality

momentary *adj.* brief, short, short-lived, temporary, transient, fleeting, ephemeral

momentous *adj.* important, significant, historic, critical, vital
ANT. unimportant, trivial

monarch *n.* ruler, sovereign, king, emperor, empress

money *n.* coin, cash, currency, notes, bills, capital, gold, silver, bullion, funds, property

monitor *v.* check, supervise, watch, observe, control

monopolize *v.* take over, control, dominate

monopoly *n.* control, domination, exclusiveness, possession

monotonous *adj.* dull, tedious, boring, unvarying, uniform, wearisome, same, humdrum, undiversified
ANT. varied, interesting

monster *n.* beast, brute, ogre, demon, fiend, dragon

monstrous *adj.* shocking, revolting, repulsive, dreadful, atrocious, horrible, hateful, terrible, hideous
ANT. lovely

monument *n.* statue, commemoration, obelisk, stone, pillar, column, cenotaph

mood *n.* temper, disposition, spirit, humour, humor (*N. Am.*), frame of mind

moody *adj.* temperamental, irritable, sullen, touchy (*informal*)
ANT. even-tempered

mop *v.* wipe, wash, clean, sponge, soak

moral *adj.* right, ethical, good, virtuous, just, worthy, honourable, honorable (*N. Am.*)
ANT. immoral, wrong

morale *n.* confidence, assurance, spirit(s), mood

morbid *adj.* unhealthy, unwholesome, ghoulish, macabre, gruesome

more *adj.* extra, additional, added, further, fresh
ANT. fewer

moreover *adv.* besides, further, furthermore, in addition, also, likewise

morning *n.* dawn, daybreak, sunrise

morose *adj.* gruff, gloomy, depressed, crusty, crabbed, acrimonious, severe, snappish, sullen, surly, churlish, dogged, ill-natured, sulky
ANT. good-natured, pleasant, sympathetic, friendly

morsel *n.* scrap, piece, bit, bite

mortal *adj.* **1** human, perishable, ephemeral, transient, transitory **2** serious, deadly, destructive, poisonous
ANT. **1** immortal, undying, everlasting, eternal, divine

most *adj.* greatest, nearly all, almost all, the majority

mostly *adv.* mainly, generally, chiefly, principally, on the whole, as a rule

mother *n.* parent, mum (*informal*), mom (*N. Am.* informal), mummy

motherly *adj.* maternal, motherlike, parental, kind, loving, affectionate
ANT. fatherly

motion *n.* movement, change, action, act, passage, process, transition
ANT. rest, stillness, immobility

motion *v.* signal, gesticulate, gesture, wave, indicate

motivate *v.* inspire, stimulate, spur, impel, prompt, cause, make, drive

motive *n.* reason, spur, stimulus, cause, incentive, incitement, inducement, object, purpose, impulse, prompting

motor *n.* engine, machine

motto *n.* slogan, watchword, maxim

mould[1], **mold** (*N. Am.*) *n.* cast, form, frame, stamp, pattern

mould[1], **mold** (*N. Am.*) *v.* form, fashion, pattern, shape, model

mould[2], **mold** (*N. Am.*) *n.* mildew, fungus, decay

mound *n.* pile, heap, hill, earthwork

mount *v.* **1** put on, display, prepare, set up, stage, launch, present, organize **2** increase, intensify, grow, escalate, rise **3** climb, ascend, go up, rise
ANT. **2** decrease **3** descend

mount *n.* **1** horse, steed, charger, stallion **2** mountain, hill **3** backing, mounting, setting, frame

mountain *n.* mount, hill, peak

mourn *v.* lament, grieve, regret, rue, bewail, sorrow
ANT. exult, rejoice, be joyful

mournful *adj.* sad, sorrowful, grievous, calamitous, lugubrious, heavy
ANT. happy, cheerful, joyful, jubilant

mouth *n.* **1** lips, jaws, gob (*informal*) **2** opening, aperture, entrance

move *v.* **1** go, advance, progress, proceed, stir, budge **2** leave, relocate, migrate **3** prompt, stimulate, urge, incite, persuade, inspire, motivate **4** touch, affect, stir, excite, influence
ANT. **1** stop **2** stay, remain

movement *n.* **1** motion, activity, action, advance, progress **2** campaign, drive, action, crusade

much *adv.* a lot, a great deal, greatly, considerably, to a great extent, often, frequently

mud *n.* clay, mire, dirt, muck, marsh, bog, swamp

muddle *n.* mess, confusion, jumble, mix-up, disorder

muddle *v.* confuse, jumble, mix up, mess up, disorder

muddy *adj.* **1** boggy, marshy, dirty, grimy **2** dull, cloudy, murky
ANT. **1** clean **2** clear

muffle *v.* deaden, quieten, stifle, soften, suppress
ANT. louden

multiplication *n.* increase, reproduction, swarming, teeming, multiplicity, multitude, plurality, augmentation, multifariousness, multitudinousness
ANT. diminution, reduction

multiply *v.* increase, grow, augment, reproduce, breed, swarm, teem, double, triple, treble
ANT. decrease

multitude *n.* throng, crowd, assembly, mass, rabble, mob, swarm, populace

mumble *v.* mutter, murmur, speak indistinctly

munch *v.* chomp, chew

mundane *adj.* ordinary, banal, everyday, commonplace, routine, boring, tedious
ANT. exciting, unusual

murder *n.* killing, manslaughter, homicide, assassination, slaughter, massacre

murder *v.* kill, slay, assassinate, butcher, massacre, do in (*informal*), bump off (*informal*)

murderer *n.* killer, slayer, assassin, butcher

murky *adj.* dark, dull, dim, cloudy, gloomy, dirty
ANT. clear, bright

murmur *v.* speak softly, say quietly, whisper

music *n.* melody, tune, harmony, rhythm, composition

musical *adj.* tuneful, melodious, harmonious, rhythmical, mellifluous
ANT. discordant, harsh

musician *n.* player, performer, instrumentalist, singer, composer

muster *v.* assemble, collect, gather, summon
ANT. disperse

mute *adj.* silent, dumb, speechless, voiceless
ANT. loud, noisy

mutilate *v.* maim, disable, cripple, disfigure

mutiny *n.* rebellion, revolt, revolution, uprising, insurrection, sedition

mutiny *v.* rebel, revolt, rise up

mutter *v.* mumble, complain, grumble

mutual *adj.* common, reciprocal, joint, interchangeable, correlative

mysterious *adj.* hidden, secret, obscure, inexplicable, incomprehensible, recondite, inscrutable, abstruse, enigmatical, dark, mystical, transcendental, unknown, unfathomable
ANT. clear, plain, apparent, obvious

mystery *n.* secret, enigma, puzzle, riddle

mystical *adj.* spiritual, transcendental, unknowable, obscure, mysterious, allegorical, enigmatical

mystify *v.* baffle, bewilder, puzzle, perplex

myth *n.* **1** fable, tradition, legend, parable, fiction, allegory **2** falsehood, lie, fib, fabrication

N

nab *v.* seize, collar, grab, snatch

nag *v.* pester, badger, harass, scold, annoy, irritate, bother, vex

naive *adj.* unsophisticated, unrealistic, simple, innocent, ingenuous, guileless
ANT. sophisticated, shrewd

naked *adj.* 1 nude, bare, unclothed, denuded, undressed 2 simple, plain, stark, obvious, unadorned, undisguised
ANT. 1 clothed 2 concealed

name *n.* 1 title, style, surname, appellation, denomination, designation, epithet 2 reputation, honour, honor (*N. Am.*), character, esteem, renown

name *v.* call, indicate, designate, specify, mention, style, nominate

nap *n.* snooze, doze, sleep, rest, forty winks (*informal*)

nap *v.* doze, sleep, rest, snooze, have forty winks (*informal*)

narrate *v.* relate, tell, recount, describe, detail, report, recite

narrative *n.* story, tale, description, narration, recital, account, rehearsal, history

narrow *adj.* 1 thin, fine, slender, tapering, attenuated 2 tight, limited, cramped, constricted
ANT. 1 wide 2 broad

narrow-minded *adj.* bigoted, prejudiced, biased, parochial
ANT. liberal, tolerant

nascent *adj.* budding, embryo, rudimentary, incipient
ANT. grown, developed, mature

nasty *adj.* 1 horrible, unpleasant, disgusting, revolting, foul, loathsome, offensive, vile 2 unkind, cruel, disagreeable, unpleasant, wicked, evil
ANT. 1 nice, lovely, pleasant 2 kind, pleasant

nation *n.* country, state, community, people, realm

national *n.* state, civil, general, public, political

native *n.* inhabitant, citizen, national, resident, aborigine
ANT. foreigner, alien

native *adj.* 1 local, resident, indigenous, original 2 innate, natural, original, inborn, indigenous

natural *adj.* 1 normal, typical, ordinary, usual, regular 2 inbred, inborn, native, congenital, intrinsic, inherent, indigenous 3 simple, naive, artless, unsophisticated, unaffected 4 real, genuine, authentic
ANT. 1 abnormal, unusual 2 acquired 3 artful, affected 4 artificial

naturally *adv.* of course, obviously, usually, normally, typically

nature *n.* 1 world, earth, creation, universe 2 essence, constitution, kind, sort, character, quality, temper, disposition, mood

naughty *adj.* 1 mischievous, disobedient, unmanageable, unruly, perverse 2 rude, obscene, bawdy, improper, indecent
ANT. 1 good, well-behaved

nausea *n.* sickness, vomiting, queasiness, biliousness

nautical *adj.* marine, maritime, naval, oceanic

navigate *v.* steer, pilot, direct, guide, sail, fly

near *adj.* close, nearby, adjacent, adjoining, neighbouring, neighboring (*N. Am.*)
ANT. distant, remote, far

nearly *adv.* almost, practically, virtually, well-nigh, intimately, closely, approximately

neat *adj.* clean, orderly, tidy, trim, prim, precise, spruce, natty, dapper
ANT. sloppy, slovenly, dirty, disorderly, untidy

necessary *adj.* essential, needed, needful, important, indispensable, required, requisite, unavoidable
ANT. unnecessary, optional, dispensable

necessitate *v.* force, compel, coerce, make necessary, oblige, constrain, make, drive, impel

necessity *n.* **1** need, requirement, want, compulsion, requisite, essential, indispensableness, urgency, unavoidableness, sine qua non
2 poverty, need, destitution, indigence
ANT. **2** wealth

need *v.* require, want, miss, lack, call for

need *n.* **1** necessity, want, lack, requirement **2** poverty, destitution, indigence

needful *adj.* required, necessary, requisite, essential, indispensable
ANT. unnecessary, optional

needless *adj.* unnecessary, useless, superfluous, redundant, groundless, gratuitous
ANT. necessary, obligatory

needy *adj.* poor, impoverished, poverty-stricken, deprived, destitute
ANT. rich, wealthy, well-off

negation *n.* denial, disavowal, disclaimer, contradiction
ANT. declaration, affirmation

negative *adj.* denying, opposing, contrary, cynical
ANT. positive, constructive, affirmative, declarative

neglect *v.* ignore, disregard, overlook, miss, skip
ANT. pay attention to

neglect *n.* negligence, failure, omission, disregard, oversight, indifference
ANT. care, attention, notice

negligent *adj.* neglectful, careless, remiss, thoughtless, lax
ANT. attentive, thoughtful

negotiate *v.* arrange, bargain, trade, transact, transfer, sell

neighbourhood, neighborhood (*N. Am.*) *n.* area, vicinity, surroundings, locality

nerve *n.* **1** courage, strength, endurance, steadiness, firmness, fortitude, resolution, pluck, presence of mind
2 impudence, impertinence, insolence, boldness, effrontery, cheek (*informal*)
ANT. **1** weakness, frailty **2** timidity

nervous *adj.* excitable, agitated, restless, irritable, weak, fearful. shy, timid
ANT. self-possessed, self-controlled, calm, composed

nestle *v.* snuggle, cuddle, huddle, settle, shelter

net *n.* netting, mesh, web, network

network *n.* system, organization, structure

neutral *adj.* impartial, undecided, indifferent, uninterfering
ANT. prejudiced, biased, partial

neutralize *v.* incapacitate, invalidate, counteract, counterbalance, countervail

new *adj.* **1** recent, modern, latest, current, contemporary **2** original, novel, fresh, unusual
ANT. **1** old, ancient, old-fashioned **2** old, usual

newcomer *n.* beginner, novice, new person

news *n.* information, knowledge, data, intelligence, word, report, account, announcement

next *adj.* **1** following, subsequent, succeeding **2** nearest, adjoining, adjacent, touching
ANT. **1** preceding **2** distant

nibble *v.* peck, nip, bite, gnaw

nice *adj.* **1** pleasant, agreeable, charming, delightful **2** fine, minute, subtle, accurate, correct, precise, particular
ANT. **1** disgusting, nasty, awful

nicety *n.* accuracy, precision, subtlety, distinction, exactness, fastidiousness, scrupulousness, delicacy, daintiness
ANT. inaccuracy

niggardly *adj.* stingy, mean, miserly, sparing, parsimonious, avaricious, covetous
ANT. generous

night *n.* nightfall, darkness, dark, evening, sunset, sundown
ANT. day

nimble *adj.* agile, sprightly, active, alert, brisk, bustling, lively, prompt, quick, speedy, swift, spry
ANT. clumsy, slow

nobility *n.* greatness, dignity, superiority, nobleness, eminence, elevation, worthiness, family, rank, title, aristocracy, peerage
ANT. obscurity, meanness

noble *adj.* honourable, honorable (*N. Am.*), worthy, dignified, elevated, superior, sublime, great, eminent, stately, aristocratic, illustrious, grand, lordly
ANT. ignoble, low

nobody *n.* no person, no one, not anybody, nonentity
ANT. somebody

nocturnal *adj.* nightly, dark, gloomy
ANT. light

nod *v.* agree, approve, assent, acknowledge

noise *n.* cry, outcry, clamour, clamor (*N. Am.*), din, clatter, uproar
ANT. silence, hush, stillness

noiseless *adj.* silent, quiet, inaudible
ANT. noisy, uproarious, tumultuous, loud

noisome *adj.* noxious, unpleasant, unwholesome, destructive, hurtful, harmful
ANT. wholesome, beneficial

noisy *adj.* loud, clamorous, tumultuous, booming, boisterous, turbulent
ANT. quiet, noiseless, subdued, inaudible, whispering

nominal *adj.* literal, theoretical, formal, pretended, ostensible, titular
ANT. actual, real, true

nominate *v.* name, specify, appoint, designate, choose, select, propose
ANT. withdraw, reject

nonsense *n.* folly, silliness, absurdity, rubbish, trash, twaddle, balderdash, inanity, pretence, pretense (*N. Am.*)
ANT. sense

norm *n.* standard, rule, measure

normal *adj.* regular, ordinary, natural, standard, usual, typical, common
ANT. exceptional, abnormal, uncommon, unusual, irregular, peculiar, rare, remarkable, unprecedented

normally *adv.* usually, typically, commonly, regularly
ANT. exceptionally, unusually

notable *adj.* plain, evident, noted, noticeable, remarkable, noteworthy, distinguished, memorable, extraordinary, notorious
ANT. ordinary, common, everyday, usual, undistinguished

note *n.* 1 message, memorandum, comment, remark, record 2 heed, notice, observation 3 reputation, eminence, distinction, celebrity, fame, repute, renown

note *v.* notice, remark, observe, heed, regard, pay attention to

noted *adj.* famous, well-known, noteworthy, famed, renowned, illustrious
ANT. obscure, anonymous, unknown

notice *n.* 1 information, news, intelligence, intimation, announcement, instruction, warning 2 attention, consideration, observation, regard, heed 3 sign, poster, note, announcement, advertisement
ANT. 2 oversight, disregard, neglect

notice *v.* mark, observe, note, attend, mind, heed, regard, perceive, see, remark, mention, comment on
ANT. overlook, disregard, ignore, neglect

noticeable *adj.* obvious, conspicuous, apparent, clear, distinct, plain, evident
ANT. unclear, inconspicuous

notification *n.* information, notice, declaration, publication, announcement, advertisement

notify *v.* inform, advise, intimate, declare, publish, announce, acquaint, warn, apprise, communicate
ANT. conceal, suppress, misinform, misreport

notion *n.* idea, conception, apprehension, sentiment, judgment, opinion, belief, impression, estimation, conceit, conviction
ANT. misconception, misapprehension

notorious *adj.* infamous, disreputable, scandalous, ignominious, dishonourable, dishonorable (*N. Am.*)

notwithstanding *prep.* despite, in spite of

nourish *v.* feed, foster, cherish, nurse, tend, sustain, supply, support, maintain, train, educate
ANT. starve, destroy, kill

nourishment *n.* nutrition, sustenance, support, nutriment, food, aliment, provision

novel *adj.* new, recent, modern, fresh, original, uncommon, rare, unusual
ANT. ancient, old-fashioned

novel *n.* story, tale, narrative, book, fiction

novice *n.* beginner, newcomer, tyro, learner, neophyte

noxious *adj.* noisome, injurious, hurtful, pernicious, unwholesome, harmful
ANT. wholesome, beneficial

nucleus *n.* kernel, core, centre, center (*N. Am.*)

nude *adj.* naked, bare, undressed, unclothed
ANT. clothed, dressed

nudity *n.* nakedness, exposure, bareness
ANT. clothing, clothes, dress

nuisance *n.* annoyance, irritation, bother, trouble, affliction, bane
ANT. pleasure, delight, benefit, blessing

nullify *v.* revoke, annul, cancel, abolish, render void, abrogate, neutralize, repeal
ANT. enact, confirm, perpetuate, establish

numb *adj.* dead, deadened, enfeebled, insensible, paralysed, paralyzed (*N. Am.*)
ANT. alive, alert, sensitive

number *n.* **1** digit, numeral, figure, cipher, character **2** quantity, collection, multitude, aggregation

number *v.* count, total, calculate, compute, reckon, estimate, enumerate

numberless *adj.* innumerable, infinite, countless
ANT. few, scarce, rare, infrequent

numerous *adj.* many, abundant, diverse, manifold
ANT. few, scarce, rare, infrequent

nuptial *n.* wedding, marriage, bridal, espousal, connubial

nurse *v.* nourish, cherish, look after, take care of, care for, tend, foster, attend, feed, nurture

nurse *n.* attendant, orderly, staff nurse, sister, matron

nurture *v.* nourish, nurse, tend, cherish, support, feed
ANT. neglect

nutrition *n.* food, nutrition, nourishment, sustenance, nutriment, feeding

oath *n.* **1** pledge, vow, promise **2** curse, imprecation, profanity, swearing, swear word, adjuration, anathema, blasphemy, denunciation, execration, malediction
ANT. **2** blessing, benediction, benison

obdurate *adj.* obstinate, stubborn, firm, unbending, inflexible, unyielding, impenitent, callous, unfeeling, insensible
ANT. yielding, teachable, tender, flexible

obedience *n.* submission, duty, compliance, respect, dutifulness, subservience
ANT. disobedience, resistance, rebellion, insubordination

obedient *adj.* dutiful, respectful, compliant, submissive, humble, yielding, docile
ANT. disrespectful, undutiful, disobedient, insubordinate, unyielding, obstinate, stubborn

obesity *n.* fatness, corpulence, fleshiness, corpulency
ANT. leanness, thinness

obey *v.* submit, do, carry out, yield, comply
ANT. disobey, resist, refuse

object *n.* **1** thing, item, article, reality, fact, existence **2** aim, intention, end, purpose, view, goal, motive, design, sight

object *v.* protest, complain, disapprove of, oppose, take exception
ANT. agree

objection *n.* protest, disapproval, opposition
ANT. agreement, approval

objective *n.* aim, goal, intention, purpose, design, view

obligation *n.* responsibility, duty, necessity, debt, compulsion, engagement, contract, agreement, bond, covenant, stipulation

oblige *v.* necessitate, bind, constrain, compel, force, coerce
ANT. release

obliging *adj.* civil, courteous, kind, considerate, accommodating, agreeable, compliant
ANT. discourteous, inconsiderate, rude

oblique *adj.* indirect, slanting, inclined, sloping, diagonal, divergent, angular

obliterate *v.* destroy, wipe out, erase, eradicate, expunge
ANT. restore

oblivion *n.* forgetfulness, unconsciousness, blankness, obscurity
ANT. memory, awareness

oblivious *adj.* unaware, unconscious, unmindful, forgetful, blind, deaf
ANT. conscious, aware

obnoxious *adj.* unpleasant, disagreeable, objectionable, odious, detrimental, offensive
ANT. pleasant, agreeable

obscene *adj.* vulgar, coarse, indecent, immoral, improper, disgusting, offensive

obscure *adj.* **1** unknown, minor, insignificant **2** vague, indefinite, uncertain, mysterious, enigmatic, unfathomable **3** dim, faint, murky, blurred
ANT. **1** famous, well-known **2** definite, clear **3** clear, bright

obsequious *adj.* servile, cringing, fawning, sycophantic, compliant, submissive, deferential, flattering
ANT. impudent, self-assertive, independent, arrogant

observance *n.* observation, keeping, heeding, form, practice, custom, attention, celebration, ceremony, performance
ANT. inobservance, inattention, disuse, disregard

observant *adj.* observing, watchful, attentive, keen, vigilant, obedient, mindful, careful, heedful
ANT. unmindful

observation *n.* 1 watching, attention, notice, consideration 2 comment, remark, note, statement, thought, view, conclusion, judgment
ANT. 1 inattention, oversight, ignorance

observe *v.* 1 remark, note, watch, heed, see, discover, attend, comment 2 honour, honor (*N. Am.*), mark, celebrate, keep 3 keep, obey, follow
ANT. 2 ignore, disregard 3 break

obsolete *adj.* old, old-fashioned, rare, obsolescent, disused, ancient, neglected, antiquated, archaic, past
ANT. new, modern, current, customary

obstacle *n.* impediment, obstruction, difficulty, hindrance, block, barrier
ANT. support, aid, assistance

obstinacy *n.* stubbornness, inflexibility, perverseness
ANT. flexibility

obstinate *adj.* stubborn, inflexible, unyielding, intractable, perverse, obdurate, determined, unflinching, dogged, mulish, heady, headstrong, opinionated, persistent, refractory
ANT. pliant, docile, submissive, compliant, tractable, yielding, amenable

obstruct *v.* bar, barricade, block, hinder, oppose, impede, stay, stop, arrest, check, clog, choke, retard, interfere, interrupt
ANT. aid, facilitate, accelerate, forward, promote, clear, open, pave the way for, further, free, expedite

obstruction *n.* obstacle, barrier, bar, block, blockage, impediment, check, clog, interference, hindrance
ANT. aid, support

obtain *v.* 1 gain, attain, acquire, earn, win, procure 2 be valid, exist, prevail
ANT. 1 lose, forfeit, surrender

obtrude *v.* force, interfere, thrust, push, intrude

obtrusive *adj.* conspicuous, noticeable, obvious
ANT. unobtrusive

obtuse *adj.* dull, stupid, unintelligent, dense, thick, blunt, stolid

ANT. keen, quick, sharp, intelligent, acute, clever

obverse *n.* reverse, opposite

obvious *adj.* plain, evident, clear, apparent, discovered, perceived, open, transparent, explicit, manifest, patent
ANT. hidden, obscure

obviously *adv.* clearly, plainly, evidently, surely, certainly

occasion *n.* 1 time, incident, event, opportunity 2 function, celebration, ceremony, party

occasion *v.* cause, produce, bring about, create, induce, originate, generate

occasional *adj.* irregular, rare, periodic, intermittent

occasionally *adv.* sometimes, infrequently, irregularly, now and then, rarely
ANT. always, often, constantly

occult *adj.* mystical, supernatural, magical, mysterious, secret, concealed, hidden, unknown, invisible, latent

occupancy *n.* possession, occupation, tenancy

occupation *n.* 1 job, profession, trade, business, employment, vocation, calling, pursuit 2 invasion, defeat, conquest, seizure, capture

occupy *v.* 1 inhabit, live in 2 invade, defeat, conquest, capture, seize 3 hold, take up, use, fill 4 absorb, engage, engross

occur *v.* happen, appear, meet, take place, befall, betide

occurrence *n.* event, happening, incident, affair, adventure, circumstance, episode

ocean *n.* sea, deep, main

odd *adj.* unusual, strange, peculiar, queer, curious, quaint, unmatched, eccentric, fantastical, singular
ANT. common, usual, normal

odious *adj.* hateful, detestable, disgusting, abominable, repulsive, offensive, invidious, loathsome
ANT. pleasing, pleasant, acceptable, agreeable, charming

odium *n.* hatred, abhorrence, detestation, antipathy, dislike, offensiveness

odour, odor (*N. Am.*) *n.* scent, perfume, smell, fragrance, aroma, bouquet, redolence

odorous *adj.* fragrant, perfumed, balmy, aromatic
ANT. fetid

offend *v.* **1** upset, insult, displease, affront, harm, pain, annoy, irritate **2** sin, transgress, infringe, violate, err, trespass
ANT. please, gratify, conciliate

offender *n.* criminal, lawbreaker, culprit, wrongdoer, transgressor

offence, offense (*N. Am.*) *n.* **1** crime, wrongdoing, wrong, sin, trespass, transgression, infringement, violation **2** outrage, insult, affront **3** resentment, indignation, annoyance, anger, umbrage

offensive *adj.* objectionable, disagreeable, obnoxious, distasteful, unpleasant, nasty, disgusting, attacking, abusive, invading, assailant
ANT. pleasing, grateful

offensive *n.* attack, invasion, assault, aggression, onslaught
ANT. defence, defense (*N. Am.*)

offer *v.* present, tender, put forward, bid, propose, suggest, submit, extend, undertake, attempt, try, proffer
ANT. withhold, withdraw, retract

offer *n.* tender, bid, proposal, suggestion

offhand *adj.* casual, informal, instant, ready, extemporaneous, unpremeditated, unstudied, impromptu
ANT. premeditated, elaborate, studied, thought-out

office *n.* position, post, occupation, situation, appointment, commission, function, business, service, duty, custom, charge, authority

officer *n.* official, functionary, officeholder, civil servant, bureaucrat, director, dignitary, manager, administrator

official *adj.* administrative, authoritative, functional, formal, ceremonial, professional
ANT. private, unofficial, unprofessional

official *n.* officer, functionary, officeholder, civil servant, bureaucrat, director, dignitary, manager, administrator

officiate *v.* be in charge, act, serve, perform

officious *adj.* impertinent, meddlesome, interfering, forward, intrusive, rude, pushing
ANT. retiring, modest

offset *v.* compensate for, balance out, neutralize, counterbalance, cancel out

offshoot *n.* spin-off, by-product, derivative

offspring *n.* child, children, young, descendant(s)

often *adv.* frequently, repeatedly, commonly, many times, usually, regularly
ANT. infrequently, seldom, rarely

oil *n.* grease, lubricant, fat

OK *adj.* okay, all right, fine, satisfactory, acceptable, fair

old *adj.* **1** elderly, aged, hoary, senile, grey, gray (*N. Am.*) **2** old-fashioned, outmoded, antiquated, obsolete, passé, ancient, antique, archaic, original, primitive, worn-out, decrepit, dilapidated, time-honoured, time-honored (*N. Am.*), time-worn **3** former, previous, one-time
ANT. **1** young, youthful **2** new, recent, fresh, contemporary, fashionable, up-to-date **3** current, present

old-fashioned *adj.* old, outmoded, antiquated, obsolete, passé, ancient, antique, archaic, original, primitive, worn-out, decrepit, dilapidated, time-honoured, time-honored (*N. Am.*), time-worn
ANT. new, recent, fresh, contemporary, fashionable, up-to-date

omen *n.* sign, portent, foreboding, augury, presage

ominous *adj.* threatening, menacing, inauspicious, foreboding, premonitory, suggestive, significant, portentous

omit *v.* leave out, neglect, fail, miss, overlook, forbear
ANT. include, notice

one *adj.* single, individual, solitary, certain, particular, undivided, united, unitary
ANT. many, several

onerous *adj.* burdensome, oppressive, difficult, heavy, toilsome, troublesome, laborious
ANT. light, easy, trivial

only *adv.* merely, barely, just, solely, singly, exclusively

only *adj.* single, sole, lone, alone

onset *n.* beginning, start, commencement, opening
ANT. end, finish, conclusion

ooze *v.* seep, trickle, exude, leak, flow, filter, escape

opaque *adj.* hazy, dull, cloudy, darkened, impervious, obscure
ANT. transparent, clear

open *v.* 1 unfasten, unlock, undo, uncover, expose, disclose 2 expand, spread, extend, unfold, unfurl 3 start, begin, commence, launch, initiate
ANT. 1 close, shut, cover, fasten, lock 3 end, finish, conclude, terminate

open *adj.* 1 unclosed, unfastened, unlocked, clear, accessible, free, unobstructed 2 obvious, evident, plain, unconcealed, visible, apparent 3 frank, candid, honest, sincere, straightforward, artless, ingenuous 4 unsettled, undecided, debatable, moot 5 liable, susceptible, exposed, vulnerable, defenceless, defenseless (*N. Am.*)
ANT. 1 closed, shut, barred, inaccessible 2 hidden, concealed 3 secretive, devious 4 decided, settled 5 safe

opening *n.* 1 aperture, hole, space, gap, breach, gap, fissure 2 start, beginning, inauguration, commencement, initiation, opportunity
ANT. 1 obstruction 2 close, end, conclusion

open-minded *adj.* tolerant, liberal, broad-minded, unprejudiced, unbiased
ANT. narrow-minded, prejudiced, biased

operate *v.* function, go, work, use, run, manage, perform

operation *n.* action, performance, function, effect, exercise, production, influence, force, result, process, procedure, execution

opinion *n.* belief, idea, view, point of view, viewpoint, conviction, judgment, notion, impression, estimation, sentiment

opponent *n.* antagonist, foe, adversary, enemy, rival, competitor, contestant
ANT. helper, assistant, ally, colleague

opportune *adj.* timely, seasonable, convenient, ready, suitable, auspicious, appropriate
ANT. untimely, unseasonable, inopportune, infelicitous

opportunity *n.* occasion, chance, occurrence, opening

oppose *v.* resist, withstand, contradict, deny, obstruct, fight, battle
ANT. support, aid, abet

opposite *adj.* facing, contrary, reverse, adverse, counter, contradictory, opposed
ANT. agreeing, coincident

opposition *n.* resistance, antagonism, disapproval, defiance, hostility, obstacle, obstruction, animosity
ANT. agreement

oppress *v.* weigh down, burden, overwhelm, crush, afflict, overpower, subdue, persecute
ANT. encourage, support

oppression *n.* cruelty, tyranny, hardship, injustice, persecution, severity
ANT. kindness, mercy, justice

oppressive *adj.* heavy, oppressing, burdensome, overbearing, tyrannical, harsh, cruel
ANT. light, easy

opt *v.* opt for choose, select, prefer, go for, decide

optimistic *adj.* cheerful, confident, hopeful, positive, sanguine
ANT. pessimistic

option *n.* choice, preference, selection, alternative, discretion, wish, election

optional *adj.* voluntary, discretionary, elective, unforced
ANT. compulsory, obligatory, mandatory

opulence *n.* wealth, riches, fortune, affluence
ANT. poverty, indigence, want

oral *adj.* verbal, unwritten, vocal, spoken, said, uttered, traditional
ANT. written, printed

oration *n.* address, speech, discourse, lecture, sermon, declamation

orb *n.* sphere, globe, ball

orbit *n.* revolution, path, circuit, course, lap

ordain *v.* set, regulate, establish, appoint, decree, constitute, prescribe, dictate

ordeal *n.* test, trial, difficulty, trouble, misfortune, suffering, hardship, affliction, tribulation

order *v.* 1 command, direct, instruct, demand, ordain, decree 2 reserve, book, apply for, request 3 arrange, organize, tidy, neaten, classify, sort, group

order *n.* 1 command, instruction, direction, rule, demand, requirement, injunction 2 reservation, booking, application, request 3 arrangement, organization, structure, system, method, plan, sequence, grouping

orderly *adj.* 1 organized, well-organized, methodical, planned, structured, controlled, regulated, neat, tidy 2 disciplined, well-behaved, obedient
ANT. 1 chaotic 2 disobedient

ordinance *n.* regulation, institute, rule, statute, law, edict, decree

ordinary *adj.* 1 normal, usual, common, customary, settled, frequent, wonted, habitual 2 mediocre, average, medium, indifferent
ANT. 1 extraordinary, superior, unusual, uncommon 2 superior, excellent

organic *adj.* 1 natural, animate, living 2 inherent, fundamental, essential, basic, radical, vital
ANT. 1 inorganic

organization *n.* 1 arrangement, structure, form, construction, order, classification 2 association, club, society, group, company, business

organize *v.* arrange, plan, order, sort, constitute, shape, adjust, frame, establish, construct, systematize
ANT. disorganize

organized *adj.* planned, methodical, ordered, arranged, neat, tidy

orgy *n.* party, revelry, debauchery, carousal, binge (*informal*)

orientate *v.* incline, tend, position, direct, align, acclimatize

origin *n.* source, rise, spring, fountain, derivation, cause, root, foundation, commencement
ANT. end, termination, conclusion

original *adj.* primitive, new, beginning, primary, first, unique, pristine, genuine, inventive, ancient, former
ANT. later, derivative

originate *v.* begin, start, invent, create, spring, rise, cause, commence
ANT. finish, end, conclude

ornament *n.* decoration, adornment, embellishment

ornate *adj.* decorated, adorned, beautiful, embellished, elaborate rich, ornamented
ANT. plain

orthodox *adj.* sound, conventional, conforming, standard, conservative, approved, correct
ANT. heretical, unorthodox, unconventional, liberal, radical

oscillate *v.* sway, swing, fluctuate, vibrate, vary, waver, vacillate

ostensible *adj.* alleged, exhibited, avowed, professed, apparent, seeming, pretended, specious, plausible, outward
ANT. real, actual, genuine, concealed, hidden

ostentation *n.* display, boasting, show, boast, vaunting, flourish, pageant, pomp, parade, pageantry
ANT. modesty, reserve, quietness, unobtrusiveness

ostracism *n.* banishment, exclusion, expulsion, separation, excommunication
ANT. admittance, enlistment, enrolment

oust *v.* eject, throw out, expel

outbreak *n.* outburst, eruption, conflict, tumult, commotion, rebellion, riot
ANT. quiet, order, subsidence, quelling

outcast *n.* exile, vagabond, reprobate, castaway, pariah, vagrant

outcome *n.* result, effect, consequence, upshot, sequel
ANT. cause

outcry *n.* clamour, clamor (*N. Am.*), tumult, noise, yell, scream, alarm
ANT. quiet, silence

outdo v. beat, excel, surpass, top, eclipse, transcend, outrun, outstrip

outer adj. outside, outward, external, exterior, outermost
ANT. inward, inside, internal, interior

outfit n. 1 clothes, clothing, get-up, gear (*informal*) 2 equipment, kit, tackle, gear

outlaw n. bandit, robber, criminal, brigand, highwayman, marauder, freebooter

outlet n. opening, channel, escape, exit, vent
ANT. entrance

outline n. 1 sketch, draft, plan, contour, delineation 2 summary, précis, résumé, synopsis, plan, sketch

outline v. draft, sketch, plan, delineate, map out, rough out, summarize

outlook n. 1 attitude, perspective, viewpoint, frame of mind 2 prospect, future, opportunity, expectation

output n. production, manufacture, yield, work

outrage n. offence, offense (*N. Am.*), violence, abuse, affront, insult, indignity, atrocity, enormity

outrage v. offend, insult, affront, shock, horrify, abuse

outrageous adj. shocking, disgraceful, scandalous, offensive, shameful, abominable
ANT. reasonable

outset n. beginning, start, opening, commencement
ANT. end

outsider n. stranger, foreigner, alien, non-member

outskirts n. border, edge, precincts, environs, suburbs
ANT. interior, centre, center (*N. Am.*)

outspoken adj. forthright, frank, candid, blunt, direct, straightforward
ANT. reserved

outstanding adj. 1 excellent, remarkable, superb, exceptional, striking, impressive 2 unpaid, due, overdue, owing

outward adj. outer, external, exterior, visible, extraneous, superficial, apparent, extrinsic
ANT. inward, inner, internal, intrinsic

overall adj. general, comprehensive, complete, total, all-embracing, blanket

overcast adj. cloudy, obscured, murky, darkened, overspread, eclipsed
ANT. cloudless, clear

overcome v. conquer, beat, defeat, overthrow, vanquish, surmount, excel, subjugate, rule, domineer over
ANT. lose, surrender, fail, submit

overcrowded adj. congested, crowded, full

overdue adj. late, delayed, behind, in arrears, tardy

overflow v. run over, flood, overrun, spill over, swamp

overrule v. govern, control, dominate, direct, prevail

oversight n. 1 omission, error, fault, inadvertence, omission, slip, lapse, neglect, blunder 2 charge, superintendence, management, supervision, command, care, watchfulness, surveillance, control, inspection, direction, watch

overt adj. manifest, plain, clear, apparent, deliberate, open
ANT. secret, implied

overtake v. pass, leave behind, catch up, outrun, overhaul

overthrow v. defeat, overcome, overpower, ruin, demolish, destroy

overthrow n. defeat, fall, collapse, downfall, ruin

overture n. 1 opening, prelude, introduction, initiation 2 proposal, proposition, offer, invitation, advance

overweening adj. arrogant, egoistic, vain, haughty, conceited

overwhelm v. defeat, conquer, subdue, overpower, submerge, engulf, immerse, extinguish, bury, crush, sink, vanquish

owe v. be indebted to, be obliged to, borrow, attribute
ANT. repay

own adj. private, personal

own v. possess, keep, have, hold
ANT. lose, disown, abandon

pace *n.* **1** step, walk, stride **2** speed, velocity, rate, progress

pace *v.* step, walk, stride

pacific *adj.* calm, peaceful, mild, tranquil, gentle
ANT. rough, turbulent

pacify *v.* calm, quiet, quieten, appease, conciliate, compromise, reconcile
ANT. aggravate

pack *v.* store, load, cram, press, stuff

pack *n.* bundle, package, parcel, collection

package *n.* parcel, packet, pack

packet *n.* container, box, parcel, package

pact *n.* agreement, league, contract, covenant, bargain, stipulation, alliance, bond, compact

pad *n.* cushion, wad, bolster, buffer, padding, filling, stuffing

paddle *n.* oar, scull, pole

pagan *adj.* heathen, ungodly, godless, unbelieving
ANT. believing

pageant *n.* spectacle, exhibition, display, show, ceremony, procession, parade

pageantry *n.* pomp, parade, display, show, spectacle, splendour, splendor (*N. Am.*), magnificence

pain *n.* agony, ache, distress, suffering, torture, anguish, torment, misery, pang, throe, twinge, woe, grief
ANT. ease, comfort, enjoyment, relief, comfort, delight

pain *v.* hurt, grieve, afflict, disquiet, trouble, distress, agonize, torment, torture
ANT. please, delight, charm, refresh

painful *adj.* aching, sore, tender, agonizing, throbbing, excruciating
ANT. soothing

painstaking *adj.* careful, diligent, attentive, faithful, laborious, exacting, scrupulous
ANT. careless, negligent

paint *v.* colour, color (*N. Am.*), picture, sketch, draw, portray, depict, delineate
ANT. misrepresent

painting *n.* picture, sketch, composition, portrait, landscape, abstract

pair *n.* two, couple, brace, team

pale *adj.* pallid, white, wan, colourless, colorless (*N. Am.*), sallow, ashen, dim, faint
ANT. ruddy, brilliant

palliate *v.* mitigate, alleviate, soothe, ease, allay, cover, conceal, extenuate, hide, veil, screen, cloak, gloss over, apologize for
ANT. aggravate, heighten, increase, intensify

palpable *adj.* perceptible, obvious, plain, evident, distinct. patent, manifest
ANT. impalpable, indistinct, imperceptible

paltry *adj.* contemptible, worthless, mean, vile, pitiful, trifling
ANT. valuable, estimable, admirable, worthy, excellent, magnificent

pamper *v.* spoil, mollycoddle, cosset, overindulge

pan *n.* saucepan, container, bowl, vessel

pander *v.* pander to indulge, satisfy, please, gratify, humour

panel *n.* **1** board, sheet, section **2** committee, board, group, team

pang *n.* pain, throe, agony, anguish, distress, paroxysm

panic *n.* fear, alarm, terror, dread, scare

panic *v.* terrify, alarm, frighten

pant *v.* gasp, puff, blow, wheeze

paper *n.* **1** newspaper, journal
2 document, certificate, deed **3** essay,
article, report, dissertation, monograph

parable *n.* fable, allegory, story, tale,
similitude

parade *n.* march, display, show, pageant,
spectacle, procession

parade *v.* march, walk, process

paradise *n.* heaven, bliss, ecstasy
ANT. hell, torture, misery, torment

paradox *n.* puzzle, contradiction,
ambiguity, enigma, mystery

parallel *adj.* corresponding, similar, like,
analogous
ANT. different, divergent

parallel *n.* **1** counterpart, equivalent,
match, equal **2** resemblance, similarity,
likeness

parallel *v.* resemble, equal, match, be
like, correspond to

paralyse, paralyze (*N. Am.*) *v.* deaden,
numb, unnerve, destroy, impair,
enfeeble, debilitate
ANT. nerve, strengthen, invigorate

paramount *adj.* supreme, pre-eminent,
greatest, chief, superior, principal
ANT. minor, inferior, secondary,
subordinate

parcel *n.* package, packet, bundle, bunch

pardon *n.* mercy, forgiveness,
forbearance, remission, acquittal,
indulgence, absolution, amnesty
ANT. penalty, punishment, vengeance,
retribution, retaliation

pardon *v.* excuse, overlook, forgive,
absolve, remit, pass over, condone,
acquit
ANT. condemn, punish

pardonable *adj.* excusable, forgivable
ANT. inexcusable, unpardonable

pare *v.* cut, peel, prune, dock, reduce,
diminish

parentage *n.* descent, extraction, lineage,
birth, stock, pedigree

park *n.* garden, green, land

parody *n.* satire, mockery, caricature,
burlesque, lampoon, send-up (*informal*),
spoof (*informal*), skit (*informal*)

parsimonious *adj.* stingy, niggardly,
selfish, avaricious, frugal, sparing, close,
penurious, illiberal
ANT. generous, liberal, profuse,
unsparing, extravagant

part *n.* **1** fraction, fragment, section,
atom, segment, element, piece, portion,
instalment, installment (*N. Am.*),
constituent, component, ingredient,
member, particle **2** share, subdivision,
allotment **3** character, role, office, duty,
responsibility
ANT. **1** whole, mass, bulk

part *v.* **1** divide, separate, split,
disconnect, break up **2** leave, depart, go,
withdraw

partake *v.* share, participate
ANT. relinquish

partial *adj.* **1** unfinished, incomplete,
undone, fragmentary **2** biased, unfair,
unjust, inequitable
ANT. **1** unrestricted, universal, total
2 unbiased, impartial

participate *v.* join, share, take part,
partake, be involved

particle *n.* atom, bit, scrap, speck, iota,
grain, jot, mite, molecule, element,
whit, tittle, shred, scintilla
ANT. mass, quantity, sum

particular *adj.* **1** specific, exact, distinct,
single, individual **2** special, unusual,
remarkable, notable, important **3** fussy,
fastidious, finicky, careful, methodical
ANT. **1** general **2** ordinary **3** careless

particular *n.* detail, point, feature, item
ANT. whole

parting *n.* separation, leave-taking,
farewell, dividing, division, disruption,
detachment
ANT. union, attachment

partisan *adj.* prejudiced, biased, partial,
one-sided
ANT. impartial

partisan *n.* adherent, follower,
supporter, disciple
ANT. opponent, antagonist, adversary

partition *n.* **1** division, distribution,
separation, allotment, apportionment
2 screen, compartment, wall, barrier

partly *adv.* in part, somewhat, partially, not wholly
ANT. altogether, entirely, completely, to the full extent

partner *n.* associate, colleague, confederate, participator, partaker, friend, companion, comrade, spouse, mate
ANT. rival, competitor, opponent, adversary

partnership *n.* company, firm, union, alliance, connection, society, interest, house, association, cooperation, participation
ANT. independence, disconnection, dissociation

party *n.* **1** social, get-together, celebration **2** group, crowd, gang, body **3** faction, side, set, clique, circle

pass *v.* **1** go, move, proceed, run, depart, take place, occur, elapse, advance **2** spread, circulate, transmit, send, deliver **3** get through, succeed in **4** transcend, exceed, surpass **5** accept, adopt, enact, establish

passable *adj.* **1** acceptable, tolerable, admissible, moderate, mediocre **2** navigable, free, unobstructed, unblocked
ANT. **1** excellent **2** impassable, impenetrable

passage *n.* **1** corridor, hall, hallway, aisle, alley **2** route, way, course, path, avenue, opening, channel **3** section, paragraph, piece, excerpt, extract **4** journey, trip, voyage **5** passing, transition, movement, flow

passenger *n.* traveller, commuter, rider, tourist

passion *n.* feeling, emotion, susceptibility, sentiment, ardour, ardor (*N. Am.*), excitement, desire, anger, warmth, vehemence
ANT. indifference, apathy, coldness, coolness, frigidity

passionate *adj.* fervent, excited, emotional, enthusiastic, earnest, sincere, zealous

passive *adj.* inert, inactive, quiescent, unopposing, enduring, submissive, patient, unresisting, relaxed, negative
ANT. active, alert, resistant, positive, impatient, vehement

past *adj.* gone by, elapsed, ended, spent, departed, late, preceding
ANT. present, future

paste *n.* adhesive, glue

paste *v.* stick, flue, join

pastime *n.* hobby, entertainment, recreation, sport, play, amusement, diversion
ANT. business, work, task, labour, labor (*N. Am.*), occupation, study

pastor *n.* minister, clergyman, clergywoman, vicar, cleric

pastry *n.* tart, pie, cake

pasture *n.* field, meadow, grass

pat *v.* tap, stroke, caress, hit, slap

patch *n.* piece, scrap

patent *n.* right, licence, license (*N. Am.*), copyright

patent *adj.* clear, obvious, evident, apparent, manifest, public
ANT. ambiguous, questionable, dubious

paternal *adj.* fatherly, kind, caring, protective

path *n.* walk, way, footway, track, pathway, route, course, road, trail, course, method

pathetic *adj.* **1** affecting, emotional, moving, pitiful, tender, touching, melting **2** mediocre, worthless, paltry, inadequate, bad, awful

patience *n.* composure, calmness, long-suffering, leniency, passiveness, submission, endurance, forbearance, resignation
ANT. anger, impatience, fury, rage, temper

patient *adj.* forbearing, long-suffering, resigned, passive, enduring, submissive, calm, quiet
ANT. impatient, resistant

patient *n.* client, case, invalid

patrimony *n.* heritage, inheritance, estate

patrol *v.* guard, defend, protest, watch

patrol *n.* guard, watch, sentry, protector

patron *n.* **1** sponsor, backer, promoter, guardian **2** customer, client, buyer, purchaser

patronize *v.* **1** condescend, talk down to, look down on **2** support, buy from, deal with

patter *n.* tapping, rattle

pattern *n.* **1** plan, system, arrangement, order **2** design, motif, decoration, ornamentation **3** model, standard, original, mould, mold (*N. Am.*), exemplar

paucity *n.* lack, want, scantiness, deficiency, fewness, rarity
ANT. abundance, quantity

pause *n.* stop, hesitation, interruption, suspension, suspense, cessation
ANT. continuance, continuity, progress, progression

pause *v.* stop, hesitate, rest, interrupt, cease, wait, stay, demur
ANT. continue, proceed, persist, persevere, advance

pave *v.* cover, tile, floor, prepare, smooth

pay *n.* earnings, payment, salary, wages, allowance, retainer, remuneration, compensation, hire, fee, requital, honorarium, stipend

pay *v.* recompense, reward, remunerate, requite, satisfy, compensate, discharge, settle, fulfil, expend, disburse
ANT. deprive, defraud, retain, exact, hoard, invest

payment *n.* pay, compensation, income, fee, salary, reward, wages, recompense, requital, return

peace *n.* quiet, calm, repose, tranquillity, stillness, silence, serenity, harmony, amity, concord, reconciliation, order, pacification
ANT. noise, disturbance, disorder, war, strife, discord, tumult, agitation, hostility

peaceable *adj.* peaceful, undisturbed, tranquil, quiet, mild, serene, still
ANT. warlike, quarrelsome, hostile, savage, fierce, violent, restless

peaceful *adj.* quiet, still, calm, tranquil, serene, restful

peak *n.* summit, top, height, pinnacle, apex, acme
ANT. base

peal *v.* ring, chime, sound, resound

peasant *n.* country dweller, rustic, villager, bumpkin

peculiar *adj.* **1** odd, strange, unusual, uncommon, weird, bizarre **2** special, distinct, particular, distinctive, characteristic
ANT. **1** ordinary, usual **2** general

peculiarity *n.* individuality, characteristic, particularity, singularity, idiosyncrasy, distinctiveness

pedantic *adj.* fussy, particular, precise, punctilious

peddle *v.* sell, hawk, push (*informal*)
ANT. buy

pedestrian *n.* walker

pedestrian *adj.* dull, boring, commonplace
ANT. exciting, interesting, extraordinary

pedigree *n.* lineage, descent, family, ancestry, genealogy, birth, parentage

pedlar, peddler (*N. Am.*) *n.* hawker, seller, vendor, canvasser

peel *v.* skin, pare, flake, strip

peel *n.* rind, skin

peep *v.* peek, glimpse, glance, look quickly

peep *n.* peek, glimpse, glance, quick look

peer[1] *n.* **1** equal, match, mate, like, fellow, comrade, associate **2** nobleman, noblewoman, lord, lady, aristocrat

peer[2] *v.* squint, examine, scrutinize

peerless *adj.* unmatched, matchless, unequalled, unequaled (*N. Am.*), unique, superlative, paramount
ANT. ordinary, mediocre, commonplace

peevish *adj.* irritable, irascible, querulous, cross, testy, ill-tempered, captious, discontented, petulant, ill-natured
ANT. good-natured, genial, mild

peg *n.* hook, knob, holder

pen *n.* **1** ballpoint pen, felt-tip pen, fountain pen **2** enclosure, coop, cage, fold

penal *adj.* punitive, retributive, corrective
ANT. preventive

penalize *v.* condemn, punish, discipline, sentence

penalty *n.* punishment, fine, forfeiture, retribution
ANT. reward, prize

penetrate *v.* **1** enter, pierce, bore, hole, perforate, permeate **2** grasp, fathom, comprehend, discern, understand
ANT. **2** misunderstand, mistake

penetrating *adj.* piercing, sharp, acute, shrill

penitence *n.* repentance, contrition, remorse, sorrow, regret, compunction
ANT. self-approval

penitent *adj.* repentant, contrite, remorseful, regretful
ANT. impenitent, obdurate, hardhearted

pensive *adj.* thoughtful, sad, wistful, meditative, dreamy, serious, mournful, melancholy, solemn, reflective
ANT. thoughtless, unreflecting

penury *n.* poverty, need, want, privation, indigence, destitution, beggary
ANT. wealth, affluence

people *n.* **1** human beings, humans, persons, humankind, mankind, men, women, children **2** nation, race, population, state, community, tribe, clan

perceive *v.* see, notice, discern, sense, observe, understand, comprehend, apprehend, conceive
ANT. ignore, lose, miss, misconceive, misapprehend

perception *n.* understanding, comprehension, discernment, apprehension, recognition, feeling, sensation, sense
ANT. misunderstanding

perceptive *adj.* discerning, observant, alert, sharp, intuitive, aware
ANT. unobservant

percolate *v.* filter, strain, exude, drain, ooze
ANT. rush, stream, run

perennial *adj.* perpetual, unceasing, never failing, enduring, continual, constant, permanent, uninterrupted
ANT. occasional, intermittent, periodic, ephemeral, transient, fleeting

perfect *adj.* finished, complete, whole, faultless, consummate, accurate, ideal, absolute, correct, immaculate, sinless, blameless, holy, undefiled, stainless, spotless, unblemished
ANT. imperfect, bad, deficient, blemished, faulty, corrupt, poor, inferior, incomplete

perfect *v.* complete, finish, achieve, accomplish, consummate

perfection *n.* excellence, completeness, faultlessness, maturity, wholeness, consummation
ANT. defect, imperfection, incompleteness, blemish

perfectly *adv.* thoroughly, completely, faultlessly, entirely, fully, wholly, exactly, accurately
ANT. imperfectly, partially, inaccurately

perforate *v.* pierce, puncture, drill, bore

perforation *n.* hole, notch

perform *v.* **1** complete, accomplish, execute, do, discharge, fulfil, carry out **2** represent, act, play, produce

performance *n.* **1** show, entertainment, play, presentation, production, rendition, work **2** completion, consummation, execution, accomplishment, achievement, action, deed, exploit, feat

performer *n.* actor, actress, player, entertainer, artiste

perfume *n.* fragrance, smell, aroma, scent, redolence, balminess
ANT. stink

perhaps *adv.* by chance, maybe, possibly, peradventure, perchance
ANT. certainly, inevitably

peril *n.* danger, hazard, risk, jeopardy, venture, insecurity, liability
ANT. safety

perimeter *n.* edge, border, circumference, boundary

period *n.* time, cycle, age, epoch, phase, interval, era, duration, date, term

periodical *n.* magazine, journal, review, weekly, monthly

periodical *adj.* recurring, regular, recurrent, serial
ANT. irregular

perish *v.* die, expire, breathe one's last

perk *v.* perk up cheer up, liven up, revive, buck up (*informal*)

permanent *adj.* enduring, lasting, persistent, perpetual, abiding, changeless, constant, durable, steadfast, unchangeable, immutable, invariable, fixed, unchanging, stable
ANT. transient, brief, fleeting, passing, impermanent, transitory, momentary, temporary, ephemeral, evanescent

permeate *v.* pervade, infiltrate, impregnate, penetrate

permission *n.* permit, authorization, authority, allowance, consent, liberty, leave, licence, license (*N. Am.*)
ANT. prohibition, refusal

permit *v.* allow, let, authorize, approve
ANT. prohibit, forbid, refuse

permit *n.* authorization, authority, consent, licence, license (*N. Am.*)

pernicious *adj.* harmful, hurtful, destructive, noisome, deleterious, noxious, pestilential, detrimental, deadly, injurious, ruinous
ANT. helpful, advantageous, good

perpendicular *adj.* vertical, upright
ANT. horizontal

perpetual *adj.* continual, endless, unceasing, unfailing, incessant, constant, eternal, everlasting, perennial, permanent, enduring
ANT. periodic, transient, temporary, occasional, casual, momentary

perplex *v.* confuse, bewilder, puzzle, embarrass, distract, annoy, confound, trouble, worry, disturb, pester, bother, mystify
ANT. enlighten, clear, explain, make intelligible

perplexity *n.* confusion, bewilderment, disturbance, distraction, doubt, embarrassment, astonishment, amazement

persecute *v.* oppress, torment, torture, abuse, harass, martyr, ill-treat

perseverance *n.* persistency, tenacity, steadfastness, steadiness, constancy, indefatigableness, resolution
ANT. fitfulness, caprice, instability

persevere *v.* endure, persist, carry on, continue, stand firm

persist *v.* last, continue, persevere, endure

person *n.* individual, human, human being, man, woman, child

personal *adj.* **1** private, secret, confidential, intimate **2** individual, particular, special, exclusive
ANT. **1** public

personify *v.* embody, exemplify, represent

personnel *n.* staff, workers, human resources

perspective *n.* outlook, view, angle, aspect

perspicacity *n.* astuteness, discernment, acuteness, keenness, penetration, insight, sagacity, distinctness, explicitness

perspire *v.* sweat, exude, secrete

persuade *v.* influence, win over, convince, lead, induce, incite, dispose, allure, entice, urge, move, prevail upon, coax, bring over, incline, impel
ANT. deter, discourage, restrain, hinder, repel, dissuade, hold back

pert *adj.* impertinent, bold, forward, saucy, flippant, impudent
ANT. diffident, humble, modest, shy, bashful, demure

pertinent *adj.* relevant, suitable, appropriate, proper, fit, apposite
ANT. unrelated, unsuitable, incongruous, unconnected

pervade *v.* spread, fill, diffuse, saturate, impregnate

perverse *adj.* wilful, willful (*N. Am.*), wayward, stubborn, obstinate, contrary, fractious, intractable, petulant, ungovernable
ANT. compliant, accommodating, obliging, complaisant, amenable

pessimistic *adj.* gloomy, despondent, unhappy, negative, cynical
ANT. optimistic, cheerful

pest *n.* nuisance, bother, annoyance, irritation

pester *v.* nag, bother, trouble, harass, badger, annoy, irritate

pet *n.* favourite, favorite (*N. Am.*), darling

pet *v.* pamper, spoil, pat, stroke, fondle

petition *n.* appeal, supplication, entreaty, solicitation, application, suit, address, prayer

petition *v.* appeal, ask, entreat, request

petrified *adj.* terrified, staggered, appalled, horrified

petty *adj.* 1 trivial, unimportant, insignificant, minor, paltry, slight, trifling 2 mean, miserly, stingy
ANT. 1 important, significant 2 generous

phantom *n.* ghost, spectre, specter (*N. Am.*), apparition, spirit

phantom *adj.* unreal, imaginary, illusory
ANT. real, actual

phase *n.* period, stage, step, level

phenomenal *adj.* incredible, unbelievable, extraordinary
ANT. ordinary

phenomenon *n.* event, occurrence, incident, happening, fact, wonder, marvel

philanthropy *n.* goodwill, charity, benevolence, humanity, public-spiritedness
ANT. misanthropy, ill will, selfishness

phobia *n.* dread, feat, terror, horror

phone See **telephone**

photograph *n.* picture, photo, snapshot, snap, print, slide, transparency

physical *adj.* material, natural, corporal, visible, tangible, bodily, corporeal
ANT. mental, spiritual, immaterial, unsubstantial, intangible

pick *v.* 1 choose, select, decide for, opt for 2 harvest, gather, glean, pluck

pick out 1 recognize, spot, identify, distinguish 2 choose, select

picture *n.* 1 illustration, painting, drawing, sketch, photograph, representation, image 2 description, account, report

picture *v.* imagine, visualize, envisage, conceive

picturesque *adj.* beautiful, scenic, attractive, graphic, vivid, artistic
ANT. ugly, hideous

piece *n.* bit, part, section, portion, division, fragment

pierce *v.* perforate, stab, puncture, penetrate, prick

piety *n.* sanctity, godliness, holiness, religion, reverence, devotion, grace
ANT. impiety, sacrilege, ungodliness, hypocrisy, formalism

pigment *n.* colour, color (*N. Am.*), dye, paint, stain, tint

pile *n.* heap, mass, mound, collection, accumulation

pile *v.* heap, amass, stack, store, accumulate

pilgrim *n.* traveller, traveler (*N. Am.*), wanderer, worshipper, worshiper (*N. Am.*)

pill *n.* tablet, capsule, pellet

pillar *n.* column, post, prop, shaft, support

pillow *n.* cushion, bolster

pilot *n.* aviator, navigator, flyer, flight engineer, steerer, guide, director, leader

pilot *v.* steer, guide, direct, lead

pin *n.* fastener, peg, clip, nail, bolt, brooch

pin *v.* fix, attach, fasten

pinch *v.* squeeze, press, grip, nip

pinch *n.* squeeze, nip

pioneer *n.* settler, explorer, trailblazer, leader, innovator, initiator

pioneer *v.* explore, invent, discover, lead

pious *adj.* godly, holy, religious, devoted
ANT. impious, irreligious

pipe *n.* tube, line, passage, channel, duct

piquant *adj.* tart, sharp, pungent, stimulating, biting, racy

pique *n.* resentment, umbrage, irritation, displeasure, grudge, offence, offense (*N. Am.*)
ANT. delight, gratification pleasure, satisfaction

pirate *n.* buccaneer, plunderer, freebooter, robber, marauder

pirate *v.* copy, plagiarize, steal

pistol *n.* gun,. handgun, revolver

pit *n.* hole, mine, excavation, trench, ditch, well, shaft

pitch *n.* field, ground, area, land

pitch *v.* throw, hurl, fling, toss

pitcher *n.* jug, jar, bottle, container, carafe, ewer, urn, flask

piteous *adj.* sad, pitiable, pitiful, sorrowful, mournful, doleful, lamentable, woeful, rueful
ANT. joyous, happy, cheerful

pitfall *n.* difficulty, disadvantage, trap, snare, catch, drawback

pitiful *adj.* sad, lamentable, mournful, piteous, pathetic, pitiable, touching, sorrowful, woeful, wretched, despicable, moving, paltry
ANT. happy, cheerful, exalted

pity *n.* sympathy, mercy, tenderness, condolence, compassion, commiseration, charity
ANT. cruelty, severity, mercilessness, sternness, hardness, harshness

pity *v.* sympathize with, feel for, feel sorry for, commiserate with

pivot *n.* fulcrum, focal point, hinge, axis

placard *n.* poster, bill, sign, notice, advertisement, card

place *n.* 1 point, spot, position, situation, area, location, district, region, village, town, city 2 establishment, office, building, house, home, institution

place *v.* 1 put, lay, arrange, set, position, locate 2 identify, recognize

placid *adj.* quiet, gentle, collected, calm, composted, pleased, contented, unruffled, undisturbed, peaceful, serene, tranquil, passionless
ANT. distressed, anxious, distracted

plague *n.* disease, epidemic, pestilence

plague *v.* torment, pester, trouble, annoy, vex

plain *adj.* 1 simple, basic, unadorned, unembellished 2 obvious, evident, clear, distinct, apparent, unmistakable 3 forthright, blunt, candid, outspoken, honest 4 unattractive, ugly, unappealing
ANT. 1 decorated, fancy, elaborate 2 unclear, hidden, obscure 3 affected, insincere, devious 4 attractive, beautiful, pretty

plan *n.* 1 scheme, strategy, method, proposal, idea 2 diagram, drawing, map, chart, blueprint

plan *v.* arrange, decide, work out, prepare, organize, design

plane *n.* 1 aeroplane, airplane 2 level, degree, position, status

plank *n.* board, timber

plant *n.* 1 flower, shrub, tree, bush 2 machinery, equipment, factory, works

plant *v.* sow, seed, set, set out
ANT. eradicate, uproot, weed out, root up

plaster *n.* 1 cement, mortar 2 bandage, dressing

plate *n.* dish, bowl

platform *n.* 1 stage, rostrum, podium 2 programme, program (*N. Am.*), policies, principles

plausible *adj.* reasonable, feasible, likely, specious, seeming, pretending, fair-spoken, passable, ostensible, apparent
ANT. implausible

play *v.* 1 have fun, have a good time, enjoy oneself, caper, frolic, romp 2 compete, take part, participate, contend 3 perform, act, present, represent

play down minimize, underplay, make light of, underestimate, belittle **play up** 1 emphasize, stress, highlight, underline, stress, accentuate 2 misbehave, be naughty, annoy, irritate, bother, trouble

play *n.* 1 performance, show, drama 2 sport, recreation, diversion, entertainment, amusement

player *n.* contestant, competitor, participant, team member, sportsman, sportswoman, sportsperson

playful *adj.* friendly, cheerful, high-spirited, lively, frisky

plea *n.* 1 appeal, request, entreaty, petition 2 reason, excuse, pretext, justification, apology

plead *v.* ask, beg, urge, argue, solicit, entreat, implore, advocate

pleasant *adj.* delightful, pleasurable, agreeable, attractive, pleasing, kind, good-natured, kindly, obliging
ANT. unpleasant, disagreeable, repulsive, offensive

please *v.* 1 satisfy, gratify, delight, humour, humor (*N. Am.*) 2 like, want, wish, desire, choose

pleased *adj.* contented, happy, glad, delighted, satisfied

pleasing *adj.* agreeable, pleasant, delightful, attractive, charming, nice, lovely
ANT. unpleasant, disagreeable

pleasure *n.* **1** delight, enjoyment, happiness, gladness, satisfaction, comfort, solace, joy, gratification, self-indulgence **2** choice, preference, luxury
ANT. **1** sadness, distress, misery, suffering, pain

pledge *n.* promise, vow, agreement, oath, undertaking, commitment

pledge *v.* promise, swear, vow, agree, undertake

plenitude *n.* fullness, abundance, completeness, plenty, luxury, affluence, exuberance, wealth, richness, profusion
ANT. scarcity, scantiness, dearth, insufficiency, want, need

plentiful *adj.* large, abundant, adequate, enough, full, profuse, rich, sufficient, complete, exuberant, bountiful, generous, plenteous, replete, teeming, ample, lavish, liberal, overflowing, abounding
ANT. deficient, drained, impoverished, scanty, insufficient, small, sparing, stingy

plenty *n.* fullness, abundance, profusion, wealth, riches

plight *n.* predicament, quandary, difficulty, trouble, dilemma, fix (*informal*), jam (*informal*)

plod *v.* walk, trudge, tramp, toil, drudge, labour, labor (*N. Am.*)

plot *n.* **1** scheme, strategy, project, intrigue, conspiracy, cabal, machination, contrivance **2** story, theme, outline, thread

plot *v.* scheme, conspire, contrive, machinate

plough, plow (*N. Am.*) *v.* turn over, cultivate, till, furrow

pluck *v.* pull, take, snatch, draw, pick, gather

pluck *n.* courage, bravery, determination, boldness, spirit, guts (*informal*)

plug *n.* stopper, bung, cork

plug *v.* block, stop (up), clog, obstruct

plump *adj.* rounded, chubby, fat, stout
ANT. slim, thin

plunder *v.* rob, raid, loot, sack, savage

plunge *v.* fall, drop, dive, dip, immerse, submerge, thrust

plunge *n.* fall, drop, dive, leap, jump

pocket *n.* bag, pouch

pocket *v.* steal, take, pilfer, filch

poem *n.* verse, ode, rhyme, sonnet, ballad

poet *n.* bard, singer, rhymester, versifier

poetical *adj.* metrical, rhythmical, lyric, versified

poetry *n.* verse, poem, song, metre, meter (*N. Am.*), rhyme, metrical composition

poignant *adj.* distressing, touching, moving, piercing, sharp, pungent

point *n.* **1** item, detail, part, aspect, feature **2** aim, purpose, intention, object, goal **3** essence, core, heart, gist, meaning, drift **4** place, spot, location, locality, position, juncture **5** tip, end, prong

point *v.* show, direct, indicate, designate

poison *n.* toxin, venom, virus, bane

poison *v.* contaminate, infect, pollute

poisonous *adj.* toxic, venomous, baneful, corrupting, noxious, malignant, virulent
ANT. wholesome, healthful, beneficial

poke *v.* jab, push, prod, dig

pole *n.* stick, staff, shaft, rod, post

policy *n.* plan, strategy, programme, program (*N. Am.*), procedure, approach

polish *n.* **1** wax, varnish **2** sheen, lustre, luster (*N. Am.*), brilliance **3** sophistication, refinement, grace, style

polish *v.* clean, rub, shine, buff, wax, burnish

polite *adj.* courteous, well-behaved, well-mannered, well-bred, cultivated, cultured, genteel, urbane, civil, courtly, obliging, gracious, polished, accomplished, complaisant
ANT. impolite, insolent, coarse, rude, discourteous

politeness *n.* courtesy, civility, gentility, refinement, courtliness, urbanity, good breeding, decorum, complaisance, affability
ANT. rudeness, arrogance, incivility, insolence

poll *n.* survey, election, vote

pollute *v.* contaminate, corrupt, taint, soil, dirty, foul
ANT. purify, clean

pomp *n.* ceremony, splendour, splendor (*N. Am.*), magnificence, display

ponder *v.* consider, deliberate, think, contemplate, study, reflect

poor *adj.* **1** impoverished, needy, hard-up, destitute, broke (*informal*) **2** inferior, substandard, weak, unsatisfactory, mediocre, worthless **3** miserable, unfortunate, sorry, wretched, unlucky
ANT. **1** rich, wealthy **2** excellent **3** fortunate, happy, lucky

popular *adj.* **1** favourite, favorite (*N. Am.*), liked, well-liked, approved, accepted **2** current, prevalent, general, prevailing
ANT. **1** unpopular, rejected, undesirable, disliked

port *n.* harbour, harbor (*N. Am.*), haven, refuge

portable *adj.* handy, light, movable, transportable

portion *n.* **1** part, share, allocation, section, division **2** serving, helping

portrait *n.* picture, drawing, painting, likeness

portray *v.* depict, represent, describe, picture

pose *v.* **1** present, put, ask, assert **2** sit, model **3** pretend, impersonate, feign

position *n.* **1** situation, place, location, locality, site **2** role, state, condition, circumstances, status **3** job, employment, post, office, role, duty **4** stance, attitude, opinion, belief, view

position *v.* place, put, lay, arrange, set, locate

positive *adj.* **1** constructive, optimistic, practical, useful, hopeful **2** clear, direct, definite, categorical, unmistakable, incontrovertible **3** sure, certain, confident, definite

ANT. **1** adverse, negative **2** vague, indefinite **3** uncertain, unsure

possess *v.* own, have, acquire, hold, enjoy

possession *n.* **1** control, ownership, retention, management, occupation, tenure **2** belongings, assets, property, estate, wealth, dominion

possibility *n.* likelihood, probability
ANT. impossibility, unlikelihood, improbability

possible *adj.* imaginable, conceivable, probably, likely, feasible, potential
ANT. impossible, unlikely, inconceivable

possibly *adv.* perhaps, maybe, by chance
ANT. certainly, definitely

post *n.* **1** pole, stake, shaft, prop, support **2** job, position, employment, duty, office

post *v.* mail, send, dispatch

poster *n.* advertisement, placard, bill, notice

postpone *v.* put off, delay, defer, shelve, procrastinate

postulate *v.* suppose, assume, think, presuppose

posture *n.* bearing, carriage, deportment, stance

pot *n.* saucepan, pan, vessel, container, bowl, jar

potent *adj.* strong, powerful, mighty, able, forcible, cogent, influential, effective, active, energetic, efficacious
ANT. impotent, powerless, weak, feeble, infirm

potential *adj.* **1** possible, likely **2** hidden, latent, dormant, implicit, undeveloped, virtual, immanent, inherent, intrinsic
ANT. **1** definite **2** explicit, real, developed

pottery *n.* ceramics, earthenware, crockery

pouch *n.* bag, container, sack

pound *v.* strike, hit, beat, hammer, pummel

pour *v.* flow, run, rush, gush, stream, spout, discharge, emit

poverty *n.* want, need, distress, beggary, indigence, destitution, penury, privation
ANT. wealth, riches, affluence, luxury, comfort

powder *n.* dust, particles, grains

power *n.* **1** ability, capability, skill, capacity, faculty, aptitude, dexterity, cleverness, expertness, efficacy, efficiency **2** energy, strength, might, force, cogency **3** authority, influence, rule, command, control
ANT. **1** incompetence, inability **2** feebleness, weakness

powerful *adj.* **1** strong, mighty, energetic, forceful **2** effective, influential, authoritative, commanding
ANT. **1** weak, feeble **2** ineffective, weak, feeble

practical *adj.* useful, sensible, achievable, workable, actual, pragmatic, realistic, down-to-earth
ANT. theoretical, impractical, unworkable

practice *n.* **1** usage, habit, custom, tradition **2** exercise, drill, study, training, repetition **3** performance, application, operation, effort, system

practise, practice (*N. Am.*) *v.* **1** do, perform, exercise, carry out, function, execute **2** teach, exercise, drill, train, repeat **3** apply, use, follow, observe, pursue

pragmatic *adj.* realistic, practical, functional, workable
ANT. impractical, theoretical

praise *v.* celebrate, magnify, glorify, laud, eulogize, honour, honor (*N. Am.*), commend,
applaud, extol, compliment
ANT. condemn, blame, censure, reprove, disparage, discredit

praise *n.* approval, cheering, compliment, acclaim, adulation, flattery, acclamation, cheers, applause, plaudit, eulogy, laudation, panegyric
ANT. abuse, blame, censure, disapproval, contempt, reproach, scorn

pray *v.* ask, call upon, beg, beseech, entreat, implore, invoke, petition, supplicate, appeal, request, importune, bid, plead

prayer *n.* supplication, request, appeal, plea, entreaty, devotion, adoration, praise, worship, thanksgiving

preach *v.* teach, declare, proclaim, urge, exhort, advocate

precarious *adj.* dangerous, hazardous, perilous, risky, insecure, uncertain, unsettled, unsteady, unstable
ANT. firm, settled, stable, sure, certain, undoubted, immutable, steady

precaution *n.* measure, step, safeguard, foresight, prudence, forethought, providence, wariness, care
ANT. thoughtlessness, improvidence, carelessness, imprudence

precede *v.* go before, introduce, lead, herald
ANT. go after

precedence *n.* priority, preference, antecedence

precedent *n.* example, case, instance, model, pattern, authority, antecedent, warrant

precept *n.* rule, direction, principle, maxim, commandment, law, injunction, mandate

precious *adj.* **1** valuable, expensive, dear, costly **2** cherished, dear, treasured, prized, beloved
ANT. **1** cheap

precipitate *v.* hasten, quicken, accelerate, further, expedite
ANT. retard, slow down, obstruct

precipitous *adj.* steep, sheer, abrupt
ANT. gradual

précis *n.* summary, abridgment, abstract, synopsis, compendium

precise *adj.* accurate, exact, correct, definite, well-defined, scrupulous, punctilious, meticulous, particular, nice, formal
ANT. inaccurate, inexact, incorrect, careless, vague

precisely *adv.* exactly, accurately

precision *n.* exactness, accuracy, correctness, strictness, punctiliousness, meticulousness

precocious *adj.* forward, developed, advanced, premature

preconception *n.* assumption, presumption, presupposition, bias, prejudice

predatory *adj.* plundering, pillaging, ravaging, marauding, rapacious
ANT. protecting, guarding, keeping

predestination *n.* fate, necessity, foreknowledge, foreordination
ANT. choice, freedom, free will, independence

predicament *n.* dilemma, quandary, difficulty, trouble, fix (*informal*), tight spot (*informal*)

predict *v.* forecast, foretell, prophesy, prognosticate

prediction *n.* prophecy, prognostication, foretelling, forecast, augury, soothsaying, presage

predominant *adj.* main, chief, major, dominant, prevailing, prevalent, controlling
ANT. minor, secondary

predominate *v.* prevail, dominate, rule

pre-eminent *adj.* outstanding, supreme, distinguished, incomparable, matchless, peerless
ANT. inferior, secondary

preface *n.* introduction, foreword, prelude, prologue, proem, preamble, exordium
ANT. conclusion, postscript, appendix, epilogue

preface *v.* begin, introduce, open

prefer *v.* 1 choose, elect, select, desire, wish, pick out, fancy, single out, fix upon 2 advance, promote, elevate
ANT. 1 reject, discard, decline, refuse 2 degrade, demote

preference *n.* choice, selection, option, desire, wish, decision, election

pregnant *adj.* 1 with child, expecting, in the family way (*informal*), in the club (*informal*) 2 meaningful, expressive, significant

prejudice *n.* bias, partiality, unfairness, favouritism, favoritism (*N. Am.*), preconception, presumption
ANT. impartiality

prejudice *v.* influence, bias, sway, dispose

preliminary *adj.* prior, introductory, preparatory, prefatory, previous, precedent, antecedent
ANT. subsequent, following, consequent, succeeding

premature *adj.* early, untimely, forward, advanced, unexpected
ANT. late

premium *n.* reward, remuneration, recompense, prize, bonus, bounty, enhancement

preoccupied *adj.* busy, engaged, distracted, engrossed, absorbed, immersed

preparation *n.* arrangement, plan, measure, foundation, groundwork, readiness

preparatory *adj.* preliminary, opening, introductory, basic
ANT. final, advanced

prepare *v.* get ready, make ready, arrange, make arrangements, plan, make plans, supply, provide, equip

preposterous *adj.* absurd, ridiculous, exorbitant, foolish, irrational
ANT. reasonable, moderate

prerogative *n.* right, privilege, authority

prescribe *v.* order, command, direct, recommend
ANT. forbid, prohibit

presence *n.* 1 attendance, existence, being 2 appearance, mien, carriage, bearing 3 nearness, immediacy, vicinity, neighbourhood, neighborhood. (*N. Am.*)
ANT. 1 absence, distance, remoteness, separation

present[1] *adj.* 1 existing, current, present-day 2 here, attending
ANT. 1 past, future 2 absent

present[2] *n.* gift, donation, offering, tip, benefaction

present[2] *v.* 1 give, donate, award, bestow, grant 2 stage, mount, produce, offer, show, display, exhibit

presentation *n.* 1 show, display, appearance, representation, exhibition, introduction, launch, demonstration 2 award, gift, donation

presently *adv.* at present, now, currently, shortly, soon

preservation *n.* security, safety, maintenance, conservation, integrity, protection, care, guardianship
ANT. exposure, abandonment, peril, damage, injury

preserve *v.* **1** keep, maintain, conserve, save, protect **2** store, bottle, can, treat, salt, pickle, cure
ANT. **1** destroy, waste

president *n.* leader, director, chief, head

press *v.* **1** push, compress, crush, squeeze **2** smooth, iron **3** embrace, hug, clasp, squeeze **4** urge, plead, beg, demand

press *n.* newspapers, reporters, journalists

pressure *n.* force, stress, influence, compulsion, constraint

prestige *n.* reputation, influence, renown, fame, eminence, distinction

presume *v.* assume, support, think, believe, presuppose, take for granted

presumption *n.* **1** assumption, presupposition, hypothesis, guess, conjecture, belief, opinion, judgment, understanding **2** arrogance, effrontery, audacity, assurance
ANT. **2** modesty, diffidence, bashfulness, hesitation

pretence, pretense (*N. Am.*) *n.* simulation, affectation, disguise, excuse, mask, show, pretension, semblance, wile, trick, subterfuge, ruse, assumption, pretext, dissimulation
ANT. honesty, truth, sincerity, frankness, guilelessness

pretend *v.* claim, imagine, make believe, represent, allege, simulate, deceive, fake, feign, profess

pretentious *adj.* affected, mannered, showy, ostentatious, flamboyant
ANT. natural, simple

pretext *n.* excuse, reason, allegation, claim, cover, mask, cloak

pretty *adj.* attractive, beautiful, good-looking, lovely, charming, fair
ANT. ugly, hideous

prevail *v.* predominate, hold sway, reign, rule, succeed, win
ANT. lose

prevalence *n.* success, superiority, predominance, preponderance, influence, force, power, strength

prevalent *adj.* current, predominating, influential, widespread

prevent *v.* hinder, obstruct, stop, slow, interrupt, bar, block, thwart
ANT. help, encourage

previous *adj.* before, earlier, precedent, preliminary, introductory, prior, preceding, front, forward, former, foregoing, antecedent
ANT. later, concluding, following, consequent

prey *n.* game, victim, quarry, target

prey *v.* hunt, seize, victimize, feed

price *n.* value, cost, charge, expense, outlay, worth, expenditure

price *v.* value, rate, cost, assess

priceless *adj.* invaluable, precious, dear, treasured
ANT. cheap, inexpensive

prick *v.* pierce, puncture, perforate, stab

pride *n.* **1** conceit, vanity, haughtiness, arrogance, insolence, presumption, superciliousness, ostentation, disdain **2** self-respect, self-esteem, dignity
ANT. **1** humility, modesty

primarily *adv.* chiefly, essentially, mainly, firstly

primary *adj.* **1** chief, principal, main, leading **2** first, fundamental, primitive, original, preparatory
ANT. **1** secondary, unimportant, subordinate, auxiliary, inferior **2** subsequent, later, following

prime *adj.* **1** chief, main, primary **2** best, superior, top, classic, supreme

prime *v.* prepare, train, break in

prime *n.* perfection, culmination, opening, beginning, cream, flower
ANT. decadence, decay

primeval *adj.* original, old, primitive, ancient, immemorial, primordial
ANT. modern, new, fresh, recent

primitive *adj.* **1** uncivilized, simple, unsophisticated **2** primeval, original, old, ancient, primordial
ANT. **1** civilized **2** modern

principal *adj.* most important, chief, main, highest, leading, foremost, pre-eminent, primary, first, prime
ANT. minor, subordinate, inferior, secondary, auxiliary, supplementary, dependent, ancillary

principle *n.* **1** rule, law, standard, criteria, formula, postulate, truth, maxim, axiom, proposition **2** honesty, integrity, uprightness, probity, virtue, worth, honour, honor (*N. Am.*), morals, rectitude

print *v.* publish, issue, reproduce, copy, develop, enlarge

print *n.* **1** copy, photograph, picture, duplicate, reproduction **2** impression, imprint **3** lettering, type, printing

prior *adj.* earlier, preceding, previous, former, foregoing, antecedent
ANT. later

priority *n.* precedence, superiority, supremacy

prise, prize (*N. Am.*) *v.* lever, open, press, force open

prison *n.* jail, gaol, inside (*informal*), nick (*informal*)

private *adj.* **1** secret, confidential, hidden, concealed, hush-hush (*informal*) **2** personal, individual, particular, intimate
ANT. **1** public **2** general, public, communal

privilege *n.* right, advantage, due, entitlement, liberty, freedom, exemption, immunity

prize *n.* trophy, honour, honor (*N. Am.*), reward, premium, palm, laurels
ANT. loss, failure, fine

prize *v.* value, appreciate, treasure, hold dear, cherish
ANT. underrate

probable *adj.* likely, believable, reasonable, plausible, feasible

probably *adv.* in all probability, doubtless, no doubt, most likely, as likely as not

probation *n.* examination, trial, test, proof, experiment, ordeal, assay

probe *v.* investigate, search, look into, examine, scrutinize

probe *n.* inquiry, scrutiny, investigation, examination, exam

problem *n.* **1** difficulty, predicament, trouble, dilemma **2** question, puzzle, enigma

procedure *n.* process, system, method, course, approach, policy, course of action

proceed *v.* **1** move ahead, go on, progress, advance **2** arise, result, originate, derive, spring, issue
ANT. **1** retreat, withdraw **2** cause

proceedings *n. pl.* records, annals, minutes, affairs, action

proceeds *n. pl.* income, money, receipts, return, profit

process *n.* procedure, operation, system, method, course, approach, policy

process *v.* treat, prepare, handle

procession *n.* march, parade, cavalcade

proclaim *v.* announce, declare, report, make known, herald, advertise, enunciate, utter, blaze abroad, promulgate
ANT. silence, repress, suppress, conceal

proclamation *n.* announcement, declaration, pronouncement, report, statement

prod *v.* poke, jab, push, dig

prodigal *adj.* wasteful, squandering, extravagant, profuse, lavish
ANT. economical, thrifty, saving, frugal

prodigious *adj.* very large, enormous, immense, vast, huge
ANT. tiny, minuscule

prodigy *n.* genius, marvel, wonder, whizz kid (*informal*)

produce *v.* **1** make, create, form, occasion, bring about, originate, generate **2** bear, beget, bring forth, give, supply, yield **3** show, present, demonstrate

produce *n.* product, fruit, crop, harvest, yield

product *n.* **1** article, work, produce, goods, commodity, merchandise, stock **2** result, consequence, effect, fruit, yield, crop, harvest

production *n.* **1** making, manufacture, construction, assembly, creation, fabrication, generation **2** output, work, yield **3** show, performance, play

productive *adj.* fruitful, worthwhile, profitable, creative
ANT. fruitless

profess *v.* declare, state, avow, claim, allege, pretend

profession *n.* **1** claim, declaration, avowal, assertion, acknowledgment **2** occupation, vocation, calling, employment, job
ANT. **1** denial, suppression **2** leisure, hobby

professional *adj.* specialist, expert, qualified, trained, experienced, skilled
ANT. amateur

professional *n.* specialist, expert, authority
ANT. amateur

proficient *adj.* expert, skilful, skillful (*N. Am.*), skilled, competent, conversant, qualified, accomplished, trained, adept
ANT. unskilled, inexpert, ignorant, untrained

profit *n.* **1** gain, benefit, emolument, proceeds, returns, value, receipts **2** advantage, usefulness, gain, avail, expediency, good, service
ANT. **1** loss **2** disadvantage

profit *v.* gain, help, benefit, better, improve

profitable *adj.* lucrative, beneficial, useful, advantageous, productive, desirable, gainful, remunerative
ANT. useless, vain, fruitless, unprofitable, disadvantageous, detrimental

profound *adj.* **1** deep, bottomless, fathomless, abysmal **2** intense, very great, extreme, thorough **3** wise, learned, intelligent, mysterious, abstruse, occult, obscure, recondite
ANT. **1** shallow **2** stupid **3** shallow, superficial

programme, program (*N. Am.*) *n.* **1** show, production, broadcast, performance **2** plan, scheme, schedule, calendar, record

progress *n.* advance, increase, improvement, proficiency, progression, growth, development, attainment
ANT. delay, check, regression, falling back

progress *v.* advance, move on, make headway, improve, grow, develop

prohibit *v.* forbid, prevent, hinder, inhibit, ban, bar, proscribe, preclude, disallow
ANT. allow, permit, let, authorize

prohibition *n.* ban, bar, restriction, prevention, hindrance
ANT. permission, authorization

project *n.* plan, scheme, proposal, design, study, task, work, activity

project *v.* plan, expect, propose, calculate, predict, extrapolate

proliferate *v.* multiply, increase, breed, reproduce, grow, mushroom

prolific *adj.* fertile, fruitful, active, productive, generating, teeming
ANT. barren, sterile, unproductive, unfruitful

prolong *v.* extend, lengthen, draw out, stretch
ANT. curtail, shorten

prominent *adj.* **1** eminent, distinguished, famous, well-known, celebrated, important, main, principal, leading, characteristic **2** conspicuous, obvious, noticeable, projecting, protuberant
ANT. **1** insignificant, secondary, unimportant, minor **2** inconspicuous

promiscuous *adj.* immoral, loose, dissolute

promise *v.* give one's word, pledge, assure, vow, swear

promise *n.* pledge, vow, assurance, word

promote *v.* encourage, forward, foster, push, advance, aid, assist, excite, further, help, raise, urge forward, urge on, elevate, exalt
ANT. hinder, prevent, foil, frustrate

prompt *adj.* **1** punctual, timely, on time **2** immediate, direct, quick, brisk
ANT. **1** late **2** slow, lingering

prompt *v.* **1** urge, encourage, move, stimulate, arouse **2** remind, suggest, propose, mention, hint

pronounce *v.* **1** deliver, speak, utter, articulate, enunciate, express **2** declare, affirm, announce, state
ANT. **1** mispronounce, gabble, mumble **2** deny, retract

pronounced *adj.* distinct, noticeable, obvious, clear, definite, marked, conspicuous
ANT. unclear

proof *n.* demonstration, evidence, confirmation, verification, substantiation, corroboration, testimony

prop *n.* support, stay, brace, shore

prop *v.* support, hold up, brace, shore up

propaganda *n.* information, indoctrination, publicity, advertising

propagate *v.* increase, spread, extend, generate, circulate, promote, promulgate, diffuse, disseminate
ANT. stifle, extinguish, suppress, repress

proper *adj.* 1 real, actual, true, genuine 2 correct, right, fit, fitting, suitable, appropriate, decent, respectable, polite, well-mannered, seemly 3 own, individual, personal, particular
ANT. 2 wrong, inappropriate, unsuitable, indecent, improper, unbecoming, unbefitting

property *n.* 1 belongings, possessions, effects, goods, assets, wealth, fortune 2 building, house, land, real estate

prophecy *n.* prediction, forecast, prognostication, augury

prophesy *v.* predict, forecast, foretell, foresee, prognosticate

prophet *n.* forecaster, augur, oracle, soothsayer, diviner, clairvoyant, seer, fortune-teller

propitiation *n.* atonement, reconciliation, appeasement, satisfaction, expiation
ANT. reprobation, retribution, vengeance, wrath, estrangement, penalty, punishment, condemnation

propitious *adj.* auspicious, kind, gracious, friendly, benign, clement, favourable, favorable (*N. Am.*), merciful
ANT. adverse, antagonistic, hostile, unfriendly, unpropitious, unfavourable, unfavorable (*N. Am.*), ill-disposed, forbidding, inauspicious

proportion *n.* 1 ratio, symmetry, relation, comparison, balance, harmony, equality, similarity, share, lot, adjustment, distribution 2 share, part, portion, allocation, section, piece
ANT. 1 disproportion, disparity

proposal *n.* offer, suggestion, recommendation, plan, overture, proposition, bid

propose *v.* 1 suggest, put forward, present, recommend, offer, tender 2 intend, plan, mean, contemplate, expect

proposition *n.* 1 proposal, suggestion, statement, offer, declaration, overture 2 position, thesis, dictum, assertion, affirmation, doctrine

prosecute *v.* try, charge, accuse, sue, take to court, indict, impeach, arraign

prospect *n.* 1 possibility, chance, hope, likelihood, probability 2 view, outlook, vista, landscape, panorama

prospect *v.* search, explore, seek

prosperity *n.* happiness, well-being, success, good fortune, welfare, thrift
ANT. misfortune, bad luck, failure, adversity, calamity, affliction, distress, disaster

prosperous *adj.* wealthy, rich, affluent, successful, flourishing, thriving
ANT. failing

protect *v.* defend, guard, look after, take care of, cover, shield
ANT. attack

protection *n.* defence, defense (*N. Am.*), guard, shield, shelter, security, safety, precaution, safeguard

protest *v.* complain, object, disagree, oppose, denounce, remonstrate, repudiate, deprecate
ANT. support, agree, endorse, subscribe

protest *n.* complaint, objection, opposition, disagreement, denunciation, remonstration
ANT. agreement, support

protocol *n.* etiquette, convention, custom, rule

prototype *n.* model, original, pattern, example, type, exemplar

protract *v.* prolong, draw out, defer, continue, delay, postpone, extend, lengthen, elongate, procrastinate
ANT. shorten, contract, abridge, curtail

protrude *v.* stick out, project, extend, jut out

proud *adj.* 1 arrogant, haughty, vain, self-important, presumptuous, lordly, lofty, supercilious, imperious, boastful 2 self-respecting, worthy, admirable, grand, splendid, magnificent
ANT. 1 humble, unassuming, unobtrusive, meek, lowly

prove *v.* show, demonstrate, confirm, verify, substantiate, corroborate, testify

proverb *n.* saying, adage, axiom, byword, dictum, aphorism, maxim, motto, precept, truism, saw, apothegm

provide *v.* prepare, supply, furnish, give, afford, bestow, contribute
ANT. neglect, withhold, refuse

province *n.* district, county, area, region, division, territory

provisional *adj.* temporary, interim, contingent, conditional

provisions *n. pl.* stores, supplies, rations, food

provocation *n.* annoyance, irritation, vexation, incitement, stimulus, affront, insult, offence, offense (*N. Am.*), indignity
ANT. pacification

provoke *v.* 1 annoy, irritate, anger, enrage, bother, goad, vex, wind up (*informal*) 2 cause, bring about, occasion, prompt, produce

prowess *n.* heroism, valour, valor (*N. Am.*), gallantry, bravery, courage, intrepidity
ANT. fear, timidity, cowardice

prowl *v.* sneak, lurk, steal, slink, skulk

prudence *n.* care, caution, foresight, wisdom, consideration, carefulness, discretion, forethought, judgment, judiciousness, providence, circumspection
ANT. imprudence, thoughtlessness, rashness, folly, heedlessness, recklessness, indiscretion, improvidence

prudent *adj.* cautious, considerate, judicious, provident, circumspect, sagacious, wise, discreet, frugal, economical, thrifty
ANT. imprudent, foolish, rash, reckless, indiscreet, unwise, wasteful, extravagant

pry *v.* meddle, interfere, nose, snoop, peep, peer

public *n.* people, society, community, population

public *adj.* common, general, national, civil, community, popular, social, open
ANT. private, individual, secret, domestic

publicity *n.* advertising, advertisement, promotion, plug (*informal*), puff (*informal*), hype (*informal*)

publish *v.* 1 distribute, circulate, issue, bring out, edit 2 announce, declare, proclaim

pull *v.* draw, drag, tug, yank, haul, tow

pull off succeed, achieve **pull out** quit, leave, depart **pull through** survive, recover

pull *n.* 1 haul, tow, drag, tug, yank 2 influence, attraction, weight

pulse *n.* throb, beat, rhythm

pump *v.* force, push, drive

punch *v.* hit, knock, strike, wallop, thump, box

punch *n.* blow, knock, wallop, thump

punctilious *adj.* exact, particular, precise, careful, nice, scrupulous, conscientious
ANT. careless

punctual *adj.* on time, prompt
ANT. late

punish *v.* correct, discipline, chastise, reprove, castigate, scold, beat, flog

puny *adj.* small, feeble, weak, undeveloped, stunted
ANT. large, great, developed, vigorous

pupil *n.* learner, student, disciple, novice, ward, tyro
ANT. teacher

purchase *v.* buy, get, obtain, secure, acquire, bargain for, barter for, procure
ANT. sell, dispose of

pure *adj.* 1 unmixed, undiluted, unadulterated, natural 2 clean, spotless, immaculate, untainted, unpolluted, uncontaminated 3 utter, sheer, absolute, downright 4 chaste, undefiled, virtuous, innocent
ANT. 1 mixed 2 dirty 4 defiled

purify *v.* cleanse, clean, purge, sanitize

purpose *n.* intention, aim, meaning, object, plan, design, end, effect

pursue *v.* 1 follow, chaste, go after, harass, dog, hound 2 engage in, undertake, do, carry out

pursuit *n.* 1 chase, hunt 2 activity, interest, occupation, recreation, hobby, pastime

push *v.* thrust,. shove, move, drive, press, propel

put *v.* **1** deposit, place, set, lay **2** express, say, utter, state **3** attach, attribute, assign, establish

put across communicate, explain, make clear **put away 1** save, set aside, put by **2** lock up, confine **put down** quash, crush, quell, suppress **put off** delay, postpone **put on** stage, present, produce, mount **put out** extinguish, quench, douse **put up** build, construct, erect **put up with** tolerate, stand, endure

putrid *adj.* rotten, stinking, decayed, decomposed, putrefied, foul ANT. fresh

puzzle *n.* riddle, problem, question, conundrum, enigma

puzzle *v.* perplex, confuse, baffle, mystify

Q

quaint *adj*. **1** odd, strange, curious, unusual, extraordinary, fanciful, affected, whimsical **2** old-fashioned, archaic, antique, antiquated
ANT. **1** usual, ordinary, common **2** fashionable, modern, contemporary

quake *v*. tremble, shake, shudder, vibrate, quiver

qualification *n*. **1** skill, experience, ability, capacity, achievement, accomplishment, attainment **2** restriction, limitation, condition, requirement

qualify *v*. **1** fit, suit, prepare **2** restrict, limit, moderate, restrain
ANT. **1** disqualify

quality *n*. **1** characteristic, property, character, attribute, condition, tendency **2** excellence, worth, high standard, value

quantity *n*. greatness, measure, number, amount, bulk, extent, size

quarrel *n*. argument, disagreement, dispute, squabble, difference, fight

quarrel *v*. argue, disagree, squabble, dispute, wrangle, fight

quash *v*. crush, put down, quell, suppress, subdue

queer *adj*. odd, peculiar, strange, uncommon, curious, bizarre, unusual, anomalous, erratic, extraordinary
ANT. normal, ordinary, usual, regular, common, customary

quell *v*. put an end to, put down, quash, crush, suppress

quench *v*. satisfy, slake

querulous *adj*. murmuring, discontented, dissatisfied, lamenting, complaining, whining, bewailing, mourning
ANT. contented, uncomplaining, satisfied

query *n*. question, inquiry, interrogation, point, topic, subject, investigation, examination, dispute, discussion, debate, experimentation, scrutiny
ANT. answer, reply, response

query *v*. question, inquire, ask, challenge, doubt, suspect

question *n*. **1** query, inquiry, interrogation, point, experimentation **2** uncertainty, doubt, problem, issue

question *v*. ask, interrogate, examine, inquire, investigate, query, call in question, doubt, dispute
ANT. answer, reply, respond

questionable *adj*. dubious, uncertain, doubtful, suspicious

queue *n*. line, file, chain, series

queue *v*. line, line up, stand in line, file

quick *adj*. **1** fast, speedy, expeditious, hasty, swift, rapid, active, nimble, alert, agile, brisk, ready, lively, sprightly **2** impatient, quick-tempered, irritable **3** sensitive, perceptive, intelligent, discerning, quick-witted
ANT. **1** slow, tardy, inactive, inert, sluggish **2** even-tempered **3** insensitive, unresponsive

quicken *v*. hasten, hurry, accelerate, further, speed, urge, promote, advance, make haste, press forward, dispatch, drive, expedite, facilitate
ANT. hinder, impede, delay, check, obstruct, retard

quiet *adj*. still, silent, noiseless, hushed, tranquil, calm, patient, unruffled, peaceful, undisturbed, contented, gentle, mild, undemonstrative, meek
ANT. noisy, loud

quiet *n*. calm, peace, stillness, still, rest, repose, tranquillity, silence
ANT. noise, commotion, unrest

quieten *v.* still, silence, hush, rest, calm, tranquillize
ANT. disturb

quirk *n.* peculiarity, idiosyncrasy, eccentricity, mannerism

quit *v.* stop, give up, abandon, resign, go, leave, depart

quite *adv.* 1 fairly, rather, moderately, somewhat 2 definitely, totally, completely, absolutely
ANT. 1 very 2 partly

quiver *v.* tremble, shudder, shake, quake, vibrate

quiz *n.* test, examination, investigation

quiz *v.* question, interrogate, test, examine, cross-examine, grill (*informal*)

quotation *n.* 1 extract, excerpt, passage, citation, saying 2 estimate, cost, price

quote *v.* cite, mention, refer to, adduce, excerpt, extract, paraphrase, plagiarize

rabble *n.* mob, crowd, people, herd, the masses, multitudes, populace

race¹ *n.* competition, contest

race¹ *v.* run, rush, hurry, compete, contend, dash, fly, tear

race² *n.* people, tribe, clan, family, nation

racial *adj.* tribal, ethnic, national

rack *n.* frame, framework

rack *v.* torment, torture, agonize, afflict

racket *n.* noise, uproar, disturbance, din, tumult
ANT. quiet

racy *adj.* lively, spirited, forcible, rich, piquant, pungent, spicy
ANT. dull, flat, cold, insipid

radiant *adj.* bright, brilliant, shining, splendid, gorgeous, glittering, glaring, radiating, beaming, resplendent, sparkling, luminous, glorious, lustrous, effulgent
ANT. dull, dark

radiate *v.* spread, emanate, scatter, diffuse

radical *adj.* 1 fundamental, basic, essential, natural, original, organic 2 entire, complete, extreme, thorough, positive, perfect, thorough-going, total, revolutionary
ANT. 1 superficial, tentative, trial 2 incomplete, moderate, partial, slight, conservative

rag *n.* cloth, scrap

rage *n.* 1 anger, fury, wrath, ire, passion 2 fashion, fad, craze, mania

ragged *adj.* torn, tattered, worn, untidy, uneven, rough

raid *n.* attack, invasion, assault, seizure

raid *v.* attack, invade, seize, capture, pillage, plunder

rail *n.* bar, railing, fence

rain *n.* rainfall, precipitation, drizzle, shower, storm, downpour, cloudburst, deluge

rain *v.* pour down, drizzle, teem, bucket down (*informal*)

raise *v.* 1 lift, elevate, heave, hoist 2 increase, aggravate, intensify, heighten, improve, advance, enhance 3 collect, gather, assemble 4 breed, rear, bring up, propagate, grow, cultivate 5 awaken, arouse, incite, start, originate, put forward, present, produce, effect, cause
ANT. 1 depress, lower, drop, sink, let down 2 lessen, diminish, decrease, reduce

rally *n.* meeting, assembly, gathering

rally *v.* assemble, meet, gather, collect
ANT. disperse

ramble *v.* rove, roam, wander, range, stroll, saunter, amble, stray

rampant *adj.* uncontrolled, unrestrained, unchecked, wild, violent

random *adj.* chance, haphazard, fortuitous, casual, aimless, purposeless, accidental, unpremeditated
ANT. deliberate, intentional, regular, systematic, planned, specific

range *n.* variety, assortment, span, extent, expanse, area, compass, sweep

range *v.* vary, change, fluctuate, waver

rank *n.* position, grade, standing, level, class, order

rank *v.* order, arrange, classify, grade, sort

ransack *v.* search, loot, plunder, pillage

ransom *n.* redemption, liberation, rescue, deliverance, release, compensation, indemnification

ransom *v.* redeem, liberate, rescue, deliver, release, emancipate, compensate, indemnify
ANT. kidnap, hold as hostage

rap *n.* tap, knock, blow, stroke

rap *v.* tap, knock, hit, strike

rape *v.* assault, violate, abuse, molest

rapid *adj.* quick, fast, swift, speedy, hurried, hasty, brisk, expeditious
ANT. slow, deliberate, lingering, tardy

rapidity *n.* quickness, haste, speed, velocity, agility, swiftness, fleetness
ANT. slowness, dilatoriness, tardiness, delay

rare *adj.* strange, uncommon, unusual, unprecedented, unique, unparalleled, infrequent, curious, extraordinary, incomparable, odd, peculiar, remarkable, precious, scarce, singular
ANT. usual, normal, ordinary

rash *adj.* hasty, thoughtless, precipitate, headlong, indiscreet, foolhardy, heedless, incautious, careless, inconsiderate, unwary
ANT. cautious, wary, discreet, thoughtful, prudent, timid, hesitating, reluctant

rate *n.* 1 speed, velocity, pace 2 charge, price, cost, fee 3 proportion, ratio

rate *v.* consider, esteem, regard, evaluate, assess, appraise

rather *adv.* quite, fairly, somewhat, moderately
ANT. very, extremely

ratio *n.* proportion, relation, relationship

ration *n.* allowance, quota, share, portion

ration *v.* distribute, divide, allocate, share (out), apportion

rational *adj.* sane, sound, intelligent, reasonable, logical, sensible, wise, discreet, judicious, reasoning, intellectual
ANT. irrational, insane, foolish, crazy

rationalize *v.* justify, explain, explain away

rattle *v.* shake, clatter, knock, hit, bang

rattle *n.* shaking, clatter, knock, hit, bang

raucous *adj.* harsh, rough, grating

ravage *v.* damage, wreck, ruin, destroy

rave *v.* rant, roar, storm

raw *adj.* 1 fresh, uncooked, natural, unprocessed, untreated, unrefined 2 immature, untrained, inexperienced 3 green, tender, sore, painful
ANT. 1 cooked, processed 2 experienced

ray *n.* beam, shaft, glimmer, glint, flicker

reach *v.* 1 extend, stretch 2 arrive at, get to, come to

reach *n.* extent, range, distance, stretch

react *v.* respond, answer, reply, behave, act

reaction *n.* response, answer, reply, feedback

read *v.* study, peruse, understand, comprehend, take in

readable *adj.* 1 enjoyable, interesting, entertaining, pleasant, absorbing 2 legible, decipherable, clear
ANT. 1 dull, boring 2 illegible

readily *adv.* willingly, easily, promptly, cheerfully, gladly
ANT. reluctantly

ready *adj.* 1 prepared, organized, arranged, set 2 keen, eager, willing, cheerful 3 prompt, quick, clever, skilful, skillful (*N. Am.*)
ANT. 1 unready, unprepared 2 hesitant, reluctant, unwilling 3 slow

real *adj.* actual, true, genuine, demonstrable, substantial, authentic, certain, veritable
ANT. illusory, imaginary, unreal, untrue, fictitious, hypothetical

realistic *adj.* practical, sensible, pragmatic, down-to-earth
ANT. unrealistic

reality *n.* truth, fact, actuality, existence

realize *v.* 1 understand, grasp, comprehend, take in, perceive, recognize 2 carry out, put into effect, achieve, accomplish 3 sell for, make, get, bring in

really *adv.* actually, in fact, indeed, certainly

realm *n.* 1 kingdom, domain, empire, principality, province 2 activity, area, domain, sphere, department

reap *v.* harvest, gather, crop, glean
ANT. sow, plant

rear[1] *n.* back, end, rail, buttocks, rump, posterior
ANT. front

rear[1] *adj*. back, tail, hind
ANT. front

rear[2] *v*. **1** bring up, raise, nurture **2** raise, lift, elevate **3** build, erect, construct, put up
ANT. **2** lower **3** demolish

reason *n*. **1** cause, ground, aim, motive, explanation, account, argument, design, end, object, purpose, principle **2** mind, intellect, intelligence, judgment, understanding

reason *v*. **1** decide, think, believe, suppose, infer **2** debate, argue, contend, discuss, prove, establish, question, demonstrate, controvert, wrangle, dispute

reasonable *adj*. **1** sensible, logical, rational **2** moderate, fair, tolerable, just, equitable
ANT. **1** irrational, crazy, mad **2** extreme, unreasonable

reassure *v*. comfort, encourage, inspire, hearten

rebel *n*. mutineer, insurgent, revolutionary, dissenter, non-conformist
ANT. conformist

rebel *v*. mutiny, revolt, defy, rise up

rebellious *adj*. disobedient, insubordinate, defiant, mutinous, ungovernable, uncontrollable, intractable, refractory, seditious, unmanageable
ANT. obedient

rebuff *v*. reject, spurn, repel, refuse, turn down, snub, slight

rebuff *n*. rejection, spurn, snub, refusal

rebuke *v*. scold, reproach, chide, reprimand, criticize, admonish, tell off (*informal*)
ANT. praise

rebuke *n*. scolding, reprimand, criticism, telling-off (*informal*)
ANT. praise, commendation

recall *v*. **1** remember, recollect, think back, look back **2** call back, take back, summon, withdraw

recall *n*. memory, recollection, remembrance

receive *v*. **1** accept, take, acquire, obtain, get **2** welcome, greet, entertain

recent *adj*. new, fresh, modern, contemporary, up-to-date
ANT. old, old-fashioned, out-of-date

reception *n*. function, party, gathering

recess *n*. **1** niche, alcove, corner, bay **2** holiday, vacation, rest, pause, break, interval

recipe *n*. formula, directions, instructions, prescription, method, technique

reciprocal *adj*. mutual, interchangeable

recite *v*. go over, repeat, tell, recount, narrate

reckless *adj*. careless, mindless, negligent, thoughtless, regardless, unconcerned, inattentive, remiss, improvident, rash, inconsiderate
ANT. careful, wary, thoughtful, mindful, attentive, considerate, prudent

reckon *v*. **1** think, believe, suppose, imagine, expect **2** calculate, work out, total, compute

recognize *v*. **1** know, identify, distinguish **2** acknowledge, accept, concede, confess **3** honour, honor (*N. Am.*), mark, observe, celebrate

recoil *v*. draw back, flinch, shrink, withdraw

recommend *v*. **1** advise, suggest, counsel, urge **2** praise, commend, approve

recompense *n*. compensation, reparation, amends, indemnification

reconcile *v*. bring together, unite, resolve, settle

record *n*. **1** note, account, report, diary, journal, list, inventory **2** disc, disk (*N. Am.*), CD, cassette, album, recording **3** best result, fastest time, furthest distance, highest, best, top

record *v*. note (down), enter, write (down), register, log

recover *v*. **1** get better, get well, improve, convalesce, mend **2** retrieve, regain, recapture, reclaim, get back

recreation *n*. relaxation, sport, fun, games, entertainment, amusement, diversion, hobby, pastime

recruit *n*. novice, beginner, trainee, tyro, rookie (*informal*)

rectify *v.* correct, amend, put right, right, remedy

redress *v.* correct, compensate for, balance, offset

redress *n.* compensation, recompense, amends, damages

reduce *v.* lessen, decrease, lower, diminish, attenuate, abridge, contract
ANT. increase, expand, amplify, promote

redundant *adj.* surplus, superfluous, unnecessary, excessive
ANT. necessary, indispensable, essential

refer *v.* 1 mention, talk about, touch on 2 mean, signify, indicate, denote 3 direct, point, guide, send

referee *n.* umpire, judge, adjudicator, arbitrator

reference *n.* 1 mention, allusion, citation 2 regard, concern, relation, respect

refine *v.* 1 purify, cleanse, polish 2 improve, amend, polish, tweak (*informal*)
ANT. pollute

refined *adj.* polite, well-mannered, respectful, civil, sophisticated, cultured, genteel
ANT. rude, coarse, impolite

reflect *v.* 1 mirror, reproduce, copy, imitate, echo 2 think, ponder, meditate, consider, contemplate, deliberate

reflection *n.* 1 mirror image, likeness 2 thought, consideration, contemplation, study, deliberation

reflex *adj.* spontaneous, automatic, involuntary, mechanical
ANT. voluntary, premeditated

reform *n.* improvement, correction, change, progress, reformation, modernization

reform *v.* improve, change, modernize, remodel

refresh *v.* invigorate, revitalize, restore, renew, stimulate, exhilarate
ANT. weary, tire, exhaust

refreshment *n.* food, drink, snack

refuge *n.* shelter, asylum, retreat, protection, sanctuary, stronghold, defence, defense (*N. Am.*), hiding-place

refugee *n.* fugitive, exile, evacuee

refund *n.* reimbursement, repayment

refund *v.* reimburse, repay, pay back

refuse[1] *v.* reject, turn down, decline

refuse[2] *n.* waste, rubbish, garbage, trash

regard *v.* 1 consider, contemplate, observe, look at, remark, attend, notice, heed, mind 2 revere, honour, honor (*N. Am.*), value, respect, esteem, estimate
ANT. 1 overlook, disregard, dismiss, neglect, omit 2 dislike, hate, loathe

regard *n.* attention, consideration, note, care, respect

regardless *adv.* anyway, in any case, notwithstanding

regime *n.* government, system, rule, management

region *n.* area, district, province, zone, territory

regional *adj.* provincial, district, local

register *n.* record, list, catalogue, catalog (*N. Am.*), roll

register *v.* enrol, enter, sign in, sign up

regret *v.* feel sorry about, morn, deplore, bemoan

regret *n.* grief, concern, sorrow, lamentation, repentance, penitence, self-condemnation, compunction, remorse, contrition
ANT. joy, exultation, happiness, delight

regular *adj.* 1 usual, normal, customary, ordinary, typical, common, everyday 2 steady, even, uniform, unchanging, constant, methodical, systematic
ANT. 1 unusual, exceptional, rare, irregular, abnormal 2 variable, uncertain, erratic

regulate *v.* control, direct, manage, govern, organize, arrange, adjust

regulation *n.* law, rule, direction, statute, ordinance, decree, edict

rehabilitate *v.* reform, improve, restore, renew

rehearse *v.* practise, practice (*N. Am.*), exercise, train, drill

reign *v.* rule, govern

reign *n.* rule, government, control, power, dominion

reimburse *v.* refund, repay, pay back

reinforce v. strengthen, support, consolidate, back, buttress, brace

reject v. refuse, turn down, discard, exclude, deny
ANT. accept, agree with

rejoice v. delight, joy, exult, triumph, please, cheer, exhilarate, gladden, charm, enliven, gratify, make happy
ANT. mourn, grieve, weep, lament, distress, sadden, trouble

relapse v. slip back, revert, decline
ANT. improve

relate v. 1 concern, refer, apply, connect, link, associate 2 tell, report, describe, narrate

relation n. 1 connection, relationship, link, association, reference, relevance 2 relative, member of one's family

relative n. relation, family, kin, kinsman, kinswoman

relative adj. corresponding, comparative, proportionate, connected, associated

relax v. 1 unwind, rest, become less tense, take it easy 2 slacken, loosen, weaken
ANT. 2 tighten

relaxation n. rest, leisure, recreation, entertainment, diversion, sport, hobby, pastime

release v. 1 free, set free, let go, liberate, turn loose, acquit 2 publish, announce, make known, issue
ANT. 1 hold 2 suppress

release n. liberation, freedom, acquittal
ANT. imprisonment

relegate v. demote, degrade, transfer

relentless adj. remorseless, unrelenting, merciless, pitiless, implacable
ANT. merciful, compassionate

relevant adj. applicable, pertinent, appropriate, suitable, germane
ANT. irrelevant, out of place, inapplicable

reliable adj. dependable, trustworthy, faithful, loyal, stable
ANT. unreliable, untrustworthy, unstable

relief n. comfort, ease, respite, refreshment, alleviation, mitigation, aid, help, support, assistance

relieve v. comfort, ease, refresh, aid, help, support, assist, alleviate, soothe

religion n. faith, creed, belief

religious adj. godly, holy, pious, devout, reverent
ANT. irreligious, impious

relinquish v. resign, leave, quit, forsake, abandon, renounce, desert, give up, forgo, surrender, discontinue
ANT. retain, hold, keep, detain

relish v. enjoy, delight in, like, appreciate, savour, savor (N. Am.)
ANT. dislike, hate

reluctant adj. unwilling, hesitant, disinclined, loath, averse
ANT. eager, willing, inclined, disposed

rely v. depend, trust, count, bank, have confidence

remain v. stay, continue, endure, wait, rest, linger, last
ANT. leave, abandon, depart, remove, go, disappear

remainder n. remains, rest, remnant, surplus, leftovers

remark v. comment, mention, note, notice, observe

remark n. comment, note, statement, observation, utterance

remarkable adj. unusual, exceptional, extraordinary, strange, peculiar, uncommon, notable, noteworthy, surprising
ANT. ordinary, usual, commonplace, mediocre, everyday, common, general

remedy n. cure, medicine, therapy, treatment

remedy v. cure, treat, restore, correct, improve

remember v. recall, recollect, reminisce, call to mind
ANT. forget

remembrance n. memory, recollection, reminiscence, recall

remind v. bring back, prompt, jog the memory of

reminiscence n. memory, recollection, remembrance, remnant, relic, trace
ANT. oblivion, forgetfulness, announcement, warning, suggestion, prognostic

remiss adj. negligent, careless, thoughtless, forgetful
ANT. attentive, diligent

remit v. send, mail, post, forward, pass

remnant n. remainder, remains, residue, rest, trace, vestige

remorse n. regret, grief, sorrow, contrition, compunction

remote adj. 1 distant, far, removed, out-of-the-way 2 aloof, cold, unfriendly, standoffish, detached 3 slight, unlikely, slim, inconsiderable
ANT. 1 near, close 2 warm, friendly 3 considerable

remove v. take away, take off, move, get rid of, transfer

render v. 1 make, cause to become 2 give, provide, supply, furnish, deliver, present

rendition n. performance, interpretation, version, production, presentation

renew v. start again, begin again, repeat, restore, resume, revive

renounce v. give up, abandon, deny, disavow, disown, disclaim, retract, repudiate, revoke, recall, refuse, reject, discard, recant

renovate v. restore, renew, repair, recondition, refurbish, do up (*informal*)

renown n. fame, distinction, repute, name, reputation, celebrity, honour, honor (*N. Am.*), glory, eminence
ANT. disgrace, shame, dishonour, dishonor (*N. Am.*), disrepute, discredit

rent v. hire, let, lease, charter

repair v. mend, fix, restore, renovate, patch up, make good
ANT. destroy

repay v. pay back, refund, reimburse, recompense

repeal v. cancel, abrogate, annul, rescind, revoke
ANT. enact

repeat v. say again, restate, reiterate, recapitulate

repel v. 1 drive back, check, reject 2 disgust, revolt, offend, nauseate, sicken
ANT. 1 welcome 2 attract

repentance n. penitence, regret, remorse, sorrow, compunction, contrition
ANT. impenitence, obstinacy

replace v. 1 supersede, substitute, take the place of, take over (from) 2 put back, give back, return

replica n. copy, facsimile, reproduction, duplicate

reply n. answer, response, riposte, reaction

reply v. answer, respond, retort, react, rejoin

report n. account, description, narration, narrative, record, tale, rumour, rumor (*N. Am.*), statement, story

report v. account, describe, tell, narrate, record

represent v. 1 symbolize, stand for, show, express, illustrate, describe, depict, typify 2 act for, speak for, impersonate

representation n. spokesperson, agent, mouthpiece, speaker, stand-in

repress v. control, check, restrain, hold back, suppress
ANT. release

reprimand v. rebuke, admonish, scold, reproach, criticize, chide, tell off
ANT. praise

reprimand n. rebuke, admonition, scolding, criticism
ANT. praise, commendation

reproach v. blame, censure, criticize, reprimand, chide

repudiate v. reject, denounce, disown, deny, disclaim
ANT. acknowledge, accept

repulsive adj. disgusting, horrible, revolting, repugnant
ANT. attractive, pleasing

reputable adj. honourable, honorable (*N. Am.*), respectable, estimable, creditable
ANT. disreputable, disgraceful, dishonourable, dishonorable (*N. Am.*), discreditable, despicable

reputation n. repute, name, renown, fame, distinction

request v. ask, appeal, entreat, petition

request n. appeal, entreaty, petition, supplication

require v. 1 want, need, demand, call for 2 command, oblige, instruct, order, direct

rescue v. save, free, release, liberate

rescue n. release, freedom, liberation, deliverance, recovery, salvation

research n. inquiry, examination, experimentation, exploration, discovery, investigation, study, observation

research v. inquire, examine, investigate, study, observe, explore

resemblance n. likeness, similarity

resemble v. be like, be similar to, look like, take after

resentment n. bitterness, ill will, indignation, grudge
ANT. satisfaction, goodwill

reserve v. 1 set aside, keep back, hold, withhold 2 book, arrange
ANT. 1 waste, squander

reserve n. 1 supply, store, stock, fund 2 backwardness, shyness, coyness, modesty, taciturnity

reside v. live, dwell, stay, remain, exist, be

residence n. 1 home, house, dwelling, accommodation 2 stay, sojourn, occupancy

resident n. citizen, inhabitant, dweller, householder, tenant, lodger, inmate

residue n. remainder, rest, remains, surplus, excess, leftovers, dregs

resign v. give up, leave, stand down, step down, abandon, abdicate, relinquish, quit

resignation n. relinquishment, forsaking, abandonment, abdication, renunciation

resist v. stand firm, withstand, oppose, face, hold out
ANT. give in, surrender, yield

resolute adj. determined, firm, bold, unshaken, steady, decided, fixed, steadfast, constant, persevering, undaunted, unflinching
ANT. irresolute, timid, hesitating, doubtful, wavering, vacillating

resolution n. 1 decision, conclusion, judgment, statement 2 determination, firmness, resolve, steadfastness, tenacity, perseverance
ANT. 2 hesitation, doubt, vacillation

resolve v. 1 decide, determine, settle, conclude 2 solve, sort out, unravel, explain

resolve n. resolution, determination, firmness, steadfastness, tenacity, perseverance

resort v. turn, go, use, apply, have recourse

resort n. holiday centre, retreat, haunt

resources n. pl. supplies, funds, means, money, wealth

respect v. honour, honor (N. Am.), admire, look up to, think highly of, appreciate, esteem
ANT. despise, scorn, dislike

respect n. 1 honour, honor (N. Am.), admiration, appreciation, esteem 2 detail, point, particular, feature, regard, relation
ANT. 1 dishonour, dishonor (N. Am.), scorn

respectable adj. 1 estimable, honourable, honorable (N. Am.), worthy, reputable, honest 2 passable, adequate, acceptable, fair
ANT. 1 unworthy, dishonourable, dishonorable (N. Am.) 2 unacceptable, inadequate

respectful adj. courteous, polite, well-mannered, considerate, thoughtful
ANT. disrespectful, rude, impolite

respite n. rest, interval, pause, lull, break, intermission, reprieve

respond v. answer, reply, rejoin, retort, react

response n. answer, reply, rejoinder, retort, reaction, feedback

responsibility n. 1 duty, obligation, burden, charge, onus 2 accountability, liability, blame

responsible adj. accountable, liable, to blame, culpable, answerable

rest[1] n. pause, peace, quiet, stillness, tranquillity, ease, calm, peacefulness, calmness, stop, repose, quietness, recreation, sleep
ANT. agitation, commotion, disturbance, excitement, restlessness, stir, tumult, work, unrest, toil, disquiet, motion, movement, rush

rest[2] n. remainder, residue, balance, excess

restless adj. agitated, excited, unsettled, active, nervous, fidgety
ANT. rested, peaceful, still

restore v. **1** replace, give back, put back, return **2** renovate, renew, repair, fix, mend, recondition, modernize

restrain v. control, constrain, hold in, keep back, keep down, keep in, keep under, check, repress, confine, curb, hinder, hold, hold back, restrict, suppress, withhold, bridle
ANT. let loose, set free, release, arouse, animate, incite, excite

restraint n. control, constraint, check, confinement, curb, restriction, suppression, repression
ANT. liberation, freedom, release

restrict v. confine, limit, bound, confine

result n. conclusion, effect, consequence, issue, end, event, termination, product, outcome, inference, deduction, resolution, determination
ANT. cause, beginning, commencement, rise, origin

result v. happen, arise, spring, be caused, follow, ensue

resume v. recommend, restart, continue, proceed

retain v. hold, keep, preserve, maintain, support
ANT. relinquish, discard, get rid of

retaliate v. take revenge, avenge, repay, return
ANT. forget, forgive

retire v. leave, resign, go away, depart, withdraw, retreat

retort v. answer, reply, respond, rejoin

retort n. answer, reply, response, rejoinder, riposte

retract v. withdraw, take back, deny, cancel, go back on
ANT. confirm, verify

retreat v. move away, withdraw, leave, depart, retire

retreat n. **1** withdrawal, departure, retirement **2** refuge, shelter, sanctuary, asylum

return v. **1** go back, turn back, come back **2** replace, put back, give back, restore

reveal v. disclose, expose, uncover, divulge, communicate, tell, inform, betray
ANT. hide, conceal

revelation n. disclosure, divulgence, communication
ANT. hiding, concealment, shrouding, veiling

revenge n. vengeance, retaliation, retribution, vengeance, avenging, requital
ANT. mercy, pardon, pity, compassion, excuse, grace, forgiveness

revenue n. income, receipts, proceeds, return, taxes, excise, customs, duties
ANT. outgoings, expenditure, expense, deductions

reverberate v. echo, resonate, ring, resound

reverence n. respect, honour, honor (N. Am.), awe, worship, adoration
ANT. irreverence, contempt, blasphemy, sacrilege

reverse v. **1** change, cancel, revoke, annul, repeal, overthrow **2** invert, turn round, transpose **3** drive backwards, go back
ANT. **1** enact **2** right **3** drive forwards

reverse adj. opposite, inverse, converse, contrary

reverse n. **1** opposite, inverse, converse, contrary **2** setback, defeat, misfortune, adversity
ANT. **2** success

review n. **1** evaluation, assessment, study, inspection, examination, analysis, appraisal **2** critique, commentary, criticism, opinion

review v. evaluate, assess, inspect, examine, analyse, analyze (N. Am.), appraise, criticize

revise v. change, amend, correct, alter, revise, update

revive v. renew, refresh, restore, recover, revitalize
ANT. destroy, decline

revoke v. rescind, annul, cancel, abrogate, nullify, withdraw, take back
ANT. enact, confirm, ratify

revolt n. mutiny, rebellion, uprising, insurrection

revolt v. rebel, rise up, mutiny
ANT. conform

revolution n. 1 lawlessness, insurrection, revolt, riot, sedition, anarchy, insubordination, rebellion, mutiny, confusion, disorder, tumult 2 cycle, rotation, turn, spin, circle

revolve v. roll, rotate, turn, spin, circle

revulsion n. disgust, loathing, repugnance, aversion

reward n. award, prize, recompense, compensation, remuneration

reward v. pay, recompense, compensate

rhyme n. verse, poem, poetry, jingle

rhythm n. beat, tempo, metre, meter (*N. Am.*), accent

rich adj. 1 wealthy, well-off, affluent, well-to-do, opulent, loaded (*informal*) 2 abundant, copious, bountiful, fertile, productive 3 juicy, succulent, luscious 4 bright, vivid, deep, intense
ANT. 1 poor, indigent, needy, impoverished, destitute, impecunious, penniless

rid adj. **get rid of** discard, throw away, dispose of, clear

riddle n. puzzle, problem, mystery, enigma, conundrum

ride v. travel, drive, journey, move, go, sit on

ridicule v. mock, deride, insult, sneer, taunt
ANT. respect, honour, honor (*N. Am.*)

ridicule n. derision, mocking, sarcasm, gibe, jeer, sneer, teasing
ANT. respect, deference, honour, honor (*N. Am.*)

ridiculous adj. absurd, ludicrous, nonsensical, foolish, preposterous, farcical
ANT. sensible, reasonable

right adj. 1 correct, exact, precise, accurate, true 2 appropriate, suitable, proper, fit, fitting, apt 3 just, fair, good, lawful, upright, honest, virtuous
ANT. 1 incorrect, wrong 2 unsuitable, inappropriate 3 dishonest

right n. 1 claim, privilege, authority, power, prerogative, title 2 uprightness, integrity, justice, fairness, honesty, virtue

right adv. 1 correctly, accurately, exactly 2 fairly, well, lawfully, honestly

right v. rectify, correct, put right, remedy

righteous adj. holy, uncorrupt, honest, equitable, rightful, upright, virtuous, just, good
ANT. unholy, corrupt, dishonest, unjust, wicked, evil, unscrupulous

rigid adj. 1 stiff, unbending, unyielding, inflexible 2 harsh, severe, tough, fixed, firm, inflexible

rigorous adj. thorough, meticulous, scrupulous, exact, painstaking
ANT. careless

rim n. edge, brink, verge

rind n. peel, skin, shell, husk

ring¹ v. 1 resound, sound, reverberate, peal, tinkle 2 telephone, phone, call

ring² n. circle, band, hoop

ring² v. encircle, circle, surround, enclose

rinse v. wash, clean, dip, bathe
ANT. dry

riot n. tumult, uproar, commotion, disturbance, disorder

riot v. fight, brawl, rebel, revolt

rip v. tear, split, cut, slash

rip n. tear, split, cut, slash

ripe adj. grown, mature, mellow, seasoned
ANT. raw, unripe

ripen v. mature, grow, develop, mellow

ripple n. wave, undulation

ripple v. wave, roll, swell, lap, splash, flutter

rise v. 1 climb, mount, ascend, go up, grow, increase 2 stand up, arise, get up 3 improve, advance, succeed, progress, prosper, flourish
ANT. 1 fall, descend 3 decline

risk n. danger, peril, hazard, jeopardy

risk v. endanger, hazard, chance, put in jeopardy

risky adj. dangerous, hazardous, unsafe, precarious
ANT. safe, secure

ritual *n.* ceremony, rite, custom, formality, service, observance

rival *n.* competitor, contestant, challenger, adversary, opponent

rival *v.* compete, contest, vie, oppose

river *n.* tributary, stream, brook, rivulet, beck, burn

road *n.* street, way, highway, motorway, carriageway, thoroughfare, lane, avenue, drive, way, course

roam *v.* wander, drift, rove, ramble, range

roar *v.* bellow, shout, cry, yell

roar *n.* bellow, shout, cry, yell

rob *v.* burgle, steal, pilfer, burglarize, ransack, plunger, pillage, sack

robber *n.* burglar, thief, pilferer, swindler, bandit, highwayman, brigand, marauder

robbery *n.* burglary, theft, hold-up, larceny, embezzlement, piracy

robust *adj.* strong, sturdy, healthy, vigorous, forceful
ANT. weak, delicate

rock¹ *n.* stone, boulder

rock² *v.* sway, roll, swing, pitch

rod *n.* stick, pole, baton, cane, wand, staff

rogue *n.* rascal, scoundrel, cheat, swindler

role *n.* 1 position, function, task, job, purpose 2 part, character

roll *v.* 1 turn, rotate, revolve, spin, whirl 2 flow, move, go, run 3 wrap, enfold, tie, wind, twist 4 smooth, flatten, level

roll *n.* 1 bun, cake, pastry, bread 2 list, register, roster, inventory, schedule 3 cylinder, spool

romance *n.* 1 love affair, affair, liaison, relationship 2 excitement, pleasure, passion 3 story, novel, fiction, tale

romantic *adj.* 1 sentimental, loving, passionate, amorous 2 fanciful, fantastic, unrealistic, idealistic, impractical, extravagant
ANT. 1 unromantic, cold 2 realistic

romp *v.* play, frolic, caper

roof *n.* shelter, top, cover

room *n.* 1 chamber, apartment 2 space, extent, margin

root *n.* origin, foundation, base, source, stem, beginning, commencement, radical, radix, radicle, parent, bottom

rope *n.* string, cable, cord, line

rosy *adj.* 1 pink, red, ruddy, blooming 2 optimistic, cheerful, hopeful, bright, promising
ANT. 1 pale 2 pessimistic, hopeless

rot *v.* decompose, decay, go bad, corrupt, putrefy, mould, mold (*N. Am.*)

rot *n.* decay, decomposition, corruption, putrefaction, mould, mold (*N. Am.*)

rotate *v.* 1 revolve, turn, spin, gyrate 2 alternate, take turns, take it in turns

rotten *adj.* 1 decayed, decomposed, bad, putrid, mouldy, moldy (*N. Am.*) 2 nasty, unpleasant, despicable, immoral, low, mean, base
ANT. 1 fresh 2 good

rough *adj.* 1 uneven, irregular, bumpy, coarse 2 harsh, severe, extreme, cruel, brutal 3 incomplete, unfinished, draft, preliminary 4 stormy, tempestuous, turbulent, violent, wild
ANT. 1 smooth 2 gentle, mild 3 finished, complete 4 calm

round *adj.* 1 circular, curved, rotund, spherical, cylindrical 2 approximate, rough
ANT. 1 straight 2 exact

round *n.* cycle, series, turn, course, route, circuit, lap

roundabout *adj.* indirect, evasive, periphrastic
ANT. direct

rouse *v.* wake, wake up, stir, animate, excite, stimulate

rout *v.* defeat, beat, conquer, overcome

rout *n.* defeat, beating, overthrow

route *n.* way, track, course, path

routine *n.* habit, system, pattern, method

routine *adj.* usual, regular, customary, everyday, habitual

row¹ *n.* series, sequence, line, file, queue

row² *n.* 1 disagreement, quarrel, fight, tiff 2 noise, din, disturbance, commotion, tumult

royal *adj.* regal, majestic, sovereign, noble, imperial, kingly, queenly

rub *v.* scrape, scour, wipe, stroke, polish, smooth, clean

rub out erase, obliterate, delete

rubbish *n.* **1** waste, litter, refuse, garbage **2** nonsense, drivel, twaddle, rot, balderdash

rude *adj.* impolite, discourteous, uncivil, brusque, abrupt, insulting, impertinent, insolent, cheeky, coarse, vulgar
ANT. polite, courteous, civil

rudimentary *adj.* basic, fundamental, primary, initial
ANT. advanced

ruffle *v.* rumple, disturb, disorder
ANT. tidy, arrange, smooth

rug *n.* carpet, mat

rugged *adj.* rough, uneven, cragged, harsh, hard, jagged, wrinkled
ANT. smooth, even

ruin *v.* destroy, harm, damage, spoil, wreck, devastate, demolish

ruin *n.* wreck, destruction, damage, decay, devastation

rule *n.* **1** regulation, ruling, order, law, statute, ordinance, principle, guide, criterion, formula **2** government, reign, control, direction, authority, dominion, mastery
ANT. **1** exception

rule *v.* **1** govern, reign, direct, control, manage, lead **2** declare, pronounce, decree, judge

ruler *n.* leader, commander, governor, controller, director, sovereign, monarch, king, queen

ruling *n.* decision, judgment, decree, verdict

rumble *v.* roll, thunder, roar, growl

rummage *v.* search, hunt, forage

rumour, rumor (*N. Am.*) *n.* gossip, story, talk, hearsay

run *v.* **1** dash, sprint, race, rush, hurry, speed, hasten **2** operate, function, go work **3** manage, organize, administer, lead, direct, control, govern, conduct, carry on **4** compete, stand, contend **5** extend, stretch, reach **6** flow, pour, stream, gush

run away run off, abscond, escape, flee, elope **run down 1** hit, knock down **2** criticize, belittle, disparage, knock (*informal*) **run out** exhaust, use up, consume

run *n.* **1** dash, sprint, race, rush **2** sequence, series, chain, period

rupture *n.* break, burst, split, crack, fracture

rupture *v.* break, burst, split, crack, fracture

rural *adj.* country, countrified, rustic, pastoral, agricultural
ANT. urban

rush *v.* hurry, dash, run, speed, hasten
ANT. dawdle, linger

rush *n.* hurry, haste

rustle *v.* swish, whisper, crackle

rut *n.* **1** furrow, groove **2** routine, habit, system

ruthless *adj.* cruel, pitiless, merciless, harsh, hard, severe, heartless, hard-hearted, relentless, unrelenting, unsparing
ANT. gentle, pitiful, compassionate

S

sabotage *v.* destroy, damage, wreck

sack *n.* **1** bag, pouch **2** dismissal, discharge, removal, notice

sacred *adj.* holy, divine, hallowed, consecrated, dedicated, devoted, religious, venerable, reverend
ANT. secular, profane

sacrifice *n.* offering, atonement, propitiation, expiation, oblation

sacrifice *v.* surrender, devote, give up, offer, let go

sad *adj.* **1** unhappy, sorrowful, mournful, dejected, gloomy, depressed, downhearted **2** distressing, upsetting, unfortunate, wretched, cheerless, tragic
ANT. **1** happy, cheerful **2** cheerful, joyful

sadden *v.* distress, upset, depress, deject, dishearten

safe *adj.* **1** secure, protected, guarded, impregnable, invulnerable **2** harmless, innocuous **3** certain, reliable, dependable, sure, trustworthy
ANT. **1** exposed **2** dangerous, harmful **3** unreliable

safeguard *v.* protect, shield, guard, defend

safeguard *n.* protection, defence, defense (*N. Am.*), shield, guard, security, precaution

safety *n.* security, protection, impregnability, invulnerability, sanctuary
ANT. insecurity

sag *v.* hang loosely, droop, drop, fall

sail *n.* cloth, sheet, material, fabric

sail *v.* set sail, travel, journey, voyage, navigate, cruise, drift

sailor *n.* mariner, seaman, seafarer, marine, crew member, deck hand

sake *n.* **1** purpose, reason, motive **2** advantage, benefit, behalf, account, interest

salary *n.* pay, wage(s), payment, earnings, remuneration

sale *n.* selling, trade, commerce, business, demand, market, auction, clearance, reduction, bargain
ANT. purchase

salient *adj.* prominent, conspicuous, noticeable, significant, striking
ANT. unimportant, inconspicuous, unnoticeable, minor, inconsiderable, subordinate, insignificant

salute *v.* greet, welcome, receive, acknowledge, praise

salute *n.* greeting, welcome, acknowledgment

salvation *n.* rescue, saving, preservation, deliverance, redemption, forgiveness
ANT. loss, destruction, condemnation, damnation, perdition

same *adj.* identical, duplicate, twin, similar, like, equivalent, corresponding
ANT. different, unlike

sample *n.* specimen, example, illustration, case, instance, token, exemplification

sample *v.* test, try, taste

sanction *v.* authorize, approve, let, allow, permit, support, confirm, ratify

sanction *n.* authorization, authority, approval, support, allowance, ratification, confirmation, approbation
ANT. disapproval, cancellation, nullification

sane *adj.* rational, sound, normal, lucid, sensible, intelligent
ANT. insane, irrational, crazy, deranged

sanguine *adj.* hopeful, cheerful, optimistic, confident, enthusiastic, buoyant, lively, animated
ANT. pessimistic, despondent, despairing

sanity *n.* saneness, soundness, rationality, lucidity
ANT. insanity, irrationality, madness, lunacy, dementia, folly

sap *v.* drain, exhaust, diminish, deplete

sarcasm *n.* mockery, irony, satire, scorn, contempt, sneer, ridicule

satire *n.* humour, humor (*N. Am.*), irony, ridicule, sarcasm, mocking, caricature, burlesque, parody, send-up (*informal*)

satisfaction *n.* 1 pleasure, enjoyment, contentment, indulgence, gratification 2 amends, compensation, reparation, recompense, payment
ANT. 1 dissatisfaction

satisfactory *adj.* adequate, passable, acceptable, tolerable, all right, fair
ANT. unsatisfactory, inadequate

satisfy *v.* 1 please, indulge, gratify, content 2 meet, fulfil, discharge
ANT. 1 dissatisfy

saturate *v.* drench, soak, flood, steep, waterlog

sauce *n.* 1 dressing, relish, seasoning, gravy 2 impudence, impertinence, cheek (*informal*), brass (*informal*)

saunter *v.* wander, stroll, amble

savage *adj.* wild, brutal, barbarous, cruel, inhuman, fierce, pitiless, merciless, violent, ferocious, uncivilized
ANT. tame, gentle, merciful

save *v.* 1 rescue, deliver, free, set free, liberate 2 reserve, keep, lay up, set aside, put by, store, hoard
ANT. 1 lose, destroy 2 waste, spend

savour, savor (*N. Am.*) *v.* enjoy, relish, appreciate, taste

say *v.* speak, express, utter, tell, state, declare, mention, suggest, propose, confirm, assert, affirm, comment, remark, answer, reply, respond

scale *n.* series, sequence, range, scope, extent, graduation

scale *v.* climb, ascend, go up, mount

scan *v.* 1 glance through, look over, skim through, browse 2 study, examine, scrutinize

scandal *n.* disgrace, dishonour, dishonor (*N. Am.*), outrage
ANT. honour, honor (*N. Am.*)

scant *adj.* little, small, inadequate, insufficient, meagre, meager (*N. Am.*)

scarce *adj.* rare, infrequent, uncommon, scant, sparing, meagre, meager (*N. Am.*), insufficient, inadequate
ANT. abundant, frequent, plentiful, common

scarcely *adv.* hardly, barely, only just, narrowly

scare *v.* make afraid, frighten, alarm, terrify

scatter *v.* spread, disperse, sprinkle, strew
ANT. gather, collect

scene *n.* place, site, spot, location, locale

scent *n.* 1 fragrance, smell, odour, odor (*N. Am.*), aroma, perfume 2 track, trail

sceptical, skeptical (*N. Am.*) *adj.* doubtful, suspicious, distrustful, unbelieving, cynical

schedule *n.* programme, program (*N. Am.*), plan, agenda, timetable

schedule *v.* plan, programme, program (*N. Am.*), arrange

scheme *n.* 1 plan, project, design, purpose, system, outline 2 plot, machination, intrigue, conspiracy, stratagem, cabal

scholar *n.* learner, pupil, schoolboy, schoolgirl, student, academic

school *n.* kindergarten, nursery, college, academy, institute, department, faculty, seminary

scoff *v.* mock, ridicule, make fun of, jeer

scold *v.* reprimand, rebuke, criticize, reprove, upbraid, berate, chide, blame, tell off
ANT. praise

scope *n.* opportunity, range, extent, reach

scorch *v.* burn, singe, char, scald

score *v.* gain, win, achieve, earn, make

score *n.* 1 record, reckoning, sum, total, tally, mark 2 wrong, injury, obligation, debt

scorn *n.* contempt, disrespect, disdain, ridicule, mockery, derision, slight
ANT. praise, commendation, respect, regard, esteem

scorn *v.* spurn, despise, look down on, mock
ANT. praise, commend, respect, think highly of

scour v. scrub, clean, wash, clear

scourge n. 1 bane, affliction, curse, misfortune 2 whip, lash, switch

scowl v. frown, glower, glare

scowl n. frown, glower, glare

scramble v. 1 clamber, climb, hurry, rush, hasten 2 mix, blend, jumble, confuse

scrap n. 1 fragment, bit, piece, part 2 waste, leftovers

scrap v. throw away, get rid of, discard, drop

scrape v. scratch, scour, rub, grate

scratch v. rub, scrape, mark, graze

scrawl v. write, scribble

scream v. yell, cry, shriek, screech

scream n. yell, cry, shriek, screech

screen n. divider, partition, protection, cover, curtain, shade, blind

screen v. protect, guard, shelter, hide, conceal
ANT. expose

script n. text, words, writing, handwriting, manuscript

scrub v. rub, scour, clean, wash

scruple n. hesitation, doubt, qualm, reluctance, misgiving, unwillingness

scrupulous adj. conscientious, meticulous, precise, exact, thorough
ANT. careless, sloppy

scrutinize v. examine, inspect, investigate, study

scrutiny n. examination, inspection, observation, search, exploration, inquiry

sea n. ocean, deep, waves, water

search v. look carefully for, explore, inspect, seek, examine, investigate, scrutinize, comb

search n. exploration, investigation, probe, inquiry, quest, pursuit

season n. time, period, term, interval, spell, occasion, opportunity

seat n. 1 chair, stool, bench, sofa 2 location, site, place, situation

secondary adj. subsidiary, minor, unimportant, subordinate
ANT. primary

secret adj. 1 confidential, private, personal, intimate 2 hidden, concealed, unseen
ANT. 1 public 2 open, exposed

secret n. confidence, mystery, enigma

sect n. group, faction, party, denomination

section n. part, division, piece, fragment, segment

secure adj. 1 safe, defended, guarded, protected, certain, sheltered 2 firm, stable, tight 3 self-assured, confident, self-confident
ANT. 1 unsafe, vulnerable 2 free, loose 3 insecure

secure v. 1 tighten, fix, fasten, guard, protect, defend 2 gain, obtain, acquire
ANT. 1 loosen, release 2 lose

security n. 1 safety, protection, refuge, shelter 2 self-assurance, confidence, self-confidence, assurance 3 guarantee, pledge, surety, warranty
ANT. 1 danger, vulnerability 2 insecurity

sedate adj. settled, composed, calm, quiet, tranquil, still, serene, unruffled, undisturbed, contemplative, sober, serious
ANT. disturbed, uneasy, restless, discomposed

sediment n. grounds, residue, deposit, dregs, lees

seduce v. lure, allure, tempt, entice, lead astray

see v. 1 perceive, glance, look at, view, watch, notice, observe, discern, make out, examine, inspect 2 imagine, visualize, envisage, expect 3 understand, comprehend, grasp, realize, recognize, appreciate 4 discover, find out, learn, ascertain 5 experience, go through, meet, encounter 6 think, ponder, reflect, consider 7 escort, attend, accompany, lead, usher
ANT. 1 overlook, neglect, ignore 3 misunderstand

seed n. germ, grain, origin, start, beginning, source

seek v. look for, search, try for, inquire for, strive after, hunt, follow, trace, attempt, endeavor, investigate

seem v. appear, look

seep *v.* leak, ooze, drip, trickle, flow

segment *n.* portion, section, part, fragment, piece
ANT. whole

seize *v.* **1** grasp, take hold of, catch, snatch **2** capture, take, gain
ANT. drop, release

seldom *adv.* rarely, infrequently, occasionally, hardly ever
ANT. often, frequently

select *v.* choose, pick, prefer, go for, opt for, elect

select *adj.* choice, exclusive, fine, precious

selection *n.* choice, pick, preference, election, option

self-conscious *adj.* embarrassed, shy, awkward, sheepish

self-control *n.* self-restraint, discipline

selfish *adj.* self-centred, self-seeking, self-indulgent, mean, narrow, illiberal, mercenary, greedy
ANT. unselfish, generous, liberal, altruistic, philanthropic

sell *v.* trade, deal in, retail, market, exchange, barter
ANT. buy

send *v.* mail, post, dispatch, forward, transmit, remit
ANT. receive

senior *adj.* older, elder, superior, more advanced
ANT. junior, younger, minor, inferior

sensation *n.* **1** feeling, emotion, sense, impression, awareness, perception, sensibility **2** excitement, thrill, frisson

sensational *adj.* exciting, thrilling, spectacular, dramatic, breathtaking
ANT. boring, dull

sense *n.* **1** feeling, sensation, awareness, perception, recognition, apprehension **2** understanding, mind, intelligence, judgment, reason, wisdom, common sense **3** meaning, significance, import, substance, definition
ANT. **2** nonsense, misunderstanding

sense *v.* feel, be aware of, realize, perceive, discern

sensibility *n.* feeling, sensitiveness, susceptibility
ANT. insensibility, insensitivity, coldness, unconsciousness

sensible *adj.* reasonable, logical, wise, judicious, responsible, rational, intelligent, thoughtful
ANT. foolish, stupid, silly

sensitive *adj.* **1** aware, conscious, receptive, responsive **2** touchy, tense, nervous, irritable, on edge **3** delicate, difficult, thorny, awkward
ANT. **1** insensitive, unaware, hardened

sentiment *n.* **1** attitude, idea, opinion, view, thought **2** feeling, emotion, tenderness, sentimentality

separate *v.* **1** divide, sever, disconnect, part, break up, move apart, come between, divorce, disengage, detach **2** remove, segregate, isolate, dissociate
ANT. **1** unite, consolidate, integrate, connect, join, attach, link **2** gather, collect

separate *adj.* different, distinct, discreet, unconnected, independent, divided, isolated
ANT. united, joined, connected

sequence *n.* series, order, succession, arrangement

series *n.* sequence, order, chain, string

serious *adj.* **1** sober, earnest, grave, thoughtful, solemn **2** important, momentous, significant, weighty
ANT. **1** thoughtless, frivolous, laughing, joking, careless **2** trivial, unimportant, light, insignificant

sermon *n.* talk, address, lecture, message

servant *n.* domestic, attendant, maid, butler, valet

serve *v.* **1** wait on, attend, minister to, give, distribute, help, aid, assist, benefit **2** perform, function, act

service *n.* **1** work, function, duty, business **2** help, aid, assistance, benefit **3** maintenance, overhaul, check-up, repair **4** ceremony, ordinance, observance, worship

session *n.* meeting, gathering, assembly, period

set *v.* **1** put, place, deposit, situate, locate, position, fix **2** determine, decide, fix, designate, assign, settle, establish, confirm **3** adjust, control, regulate, adapt **4** sink, go down, drop **5** harden, thicken, solidify, congeal, stiffen
ANT. **1** move, remove, transfer **4** rise **5** melt

set about tackle, begin, start, embark on
set aside reserve, save, keep back, put by
set off 1 start out, begin, go, leave, depart **2** detonate, explode, let off
set out set off, start out, begin, go, leave, depart **set up** establish, found, build, construct, raise

set *n.* **1** collection, group, assortment, batch **2** group, gang, band, company, circle

set *adj.* fixed, firm, unchangeable, appointed, decided, settled, established

setback *n.* reversal, disappointment, hindrance, difficulty

settle *v.* **1** agree, decide, resolve, determine, arrange **2** pay, discharge **3** inhabit, live, reside, people, dwell **4** subside, sink, drop, depress, lower
ANT. **1** disagree **3** move **4** rise

settlement *n.* agreement, decision, arrangement, resolution

sever *v.* cut, divide, separate, split
ANT. join, connect

several *adj.* some, a few, different

severe *adj.* **1** stern, strict, harsh, hard, relentless, unrelenting, inexorable, inflexible, rigid, uncompromising, unmitigated, unyielding **2** austere, plain, Spartan
ANT. **1** mild, gentle, flexible **2** decorated

sew *v.* embroider, stitch

shabby *adj.* scruffy, dirty, worn, ragged, tattered, threadbare

shack *n.* hut, cabin, hovel

shade *n.* **1** shadow, darkness, obscurity **2** screen, shutter, blind, veil, shelter, protection **3** colour, color (*N. Am.*), tint, hue
ANT. **1** light, illumination, sunshine

shade *v.* **1** obscure, darken, eclipse **2** hide, conceal, cover, screen

shadow *n.* shade, darkness, gloom, dusk

shaft *n.* **1** rod, stick, bar, pole **2** ray, beam

shake *v.* tremble, waver, wave, sway, swing, vibrate, agitate, fluctuate, flutter, oscillate, quake, quiver, quaver, rock, shiver, shudder, totter, jar

shallow *adj.* slight, superficial, petty, silly, foolish, trifling
ANT. deep, profound

sham *n.* fake, counterfeit, pretence, pretense (*N. Am.*)

shame *n.* **1** humiliation, embarrassment, mortification, abashment **2** disgrace, reproach, dishonour, dishonor (*N. Am.*), ignominy, degradation, contempt, infamy

shame *v.* humiliate, embarrass, mortify, disgrace, dishonour, dishonor (*N. Am.*)

shameful *adj.* humiliating, disgraceful, scandalous, ignominious
ANT. honourable, honorable (*N. Am.*)

shameless *adj.* bold, brazen, barefaced, impudent, insolent, indecent, immodest, unembarrassed
ANT. ashamed, humiliated

shape *n.* **1** appearance, outline, form, aspect, likeness, guise **2** character, fashion, mould, mold (*N. Am.*), pattern, cast, model, frame

share *n.* portion, part, division, allocation

share *v.* **1** join, participate, take part **2** apportion, allocate, divide, distribute

sharp *adj.* **1** cutting, keen, pointed, fine **2** quick, clever, witty, discerning, shrewd, intelligent **3** sour, acid, tart, acrid, biting, poignant, acrimonious, caustic, cutting, sarcastic, bitter **4** strong, intense, severe, extreme, sudden, violent, abrupt, harsh
ANT. **1** dull, blunt **2** stupid **3** sweet, mild **4** gentle, gradual

shatter *v.* **1** smash, break, split, burst **2** shock, upset, disturb, devastate

shave *v.* cut, trim, clip, scrape

sheer *adj.* **1** absolute, complete, utter, unqualified **2** steep, abrupt, vertical, perpendicular
ANT. **2** gentle

sheet *n.* covering, layer, coating, blanket, cloth

shell *n.* case, casing, pod, husk

shelter *n.* protection, sanctuary, retreat, refuge, haven

shelter *v.* protect, guard, defend, shield, cover

shield *n.* protection, guard, defence, defense (*N. Am.*), screen, shelter

shield *v.* protect, guard, defend
ANT. expose

shift *v.* move, remove, transfer, change, vary, alter

shift *n.* move, transfer, change, alteration

shimmer *v.* shine, flicker, twinkle, glisten, glimmer

shine *v.* **1** beam, glow, flash, radiate **2** rub, polish, burnish, buff

shine *n.* lustre, luster (*N. Am.*), polish, gloss, sheen

ship *n.* boat, vessel, tanker, ferry

shirk *v.* avoid, evade, dodge, get out of

shiver *v.* tremble, quiver, quake, shudder, shake

shock *n.* **1** disturbance, upset, trauma **2** collision, blow, impact

shock *v.* disturb, upset, stun, horrify, appal, offend
ANT. delight

shocking *adj.* appalling, horrifying, scandalous, outrageous, shameful, disgraceful, dreadful, terrible, repulsive, offensive, revolting
ANT. delightful, attractive, charming

shoe *n.* boot, sandal, footwear, trainer

shoot *v.* fire, discharge, explode, burst, launch, fling

shop *n.* store, supermarket

shore *n.* beach, coast, seaside, strand

short *adj.* **1** small, little, petite **2** brief, contracted, concise, condensed, succinct, terse, pithy, curt, laconic
ANT. **1** tall **2** long, protracted

shorten *v.* curtail, cut, reduce, abridge, abbreviate
ANT. lengthen

shortly *adv.* soon, presently, before long
ANT. later

shout *v.* yell, cry, roar, scream, bellow

shout *n.* yell, cry, roar, scream, bellow

shove *v.* push, move, elbow, jostle

show *v.* **1** exhibit, present, display, demonstrate **2** clear, prove, manifest, explain, point out, inform, teach, tell, reveal, elucidate **3** direct, guide, lead, conduct

show off boast, brag, flaunt **show up** arrive, appear, turn up

show *n.* **1** exhibition, exhibit, presentation, display, demonstration, pageant, parade, exposition **2** pretence, pretense (*N. Am.*), illusion, affectation

shred *v.* tear, cut, strip

shred *n.* strip, piece, bit, scrap, fragment

shrewd *adj.* astute, discerning, penetrating, clever, sharp, intelligent, cunning, artful, crafty
ANT. stupid

shriek *v.* yell, screech, squeal

shrill *adj.* high-pitched, high, sharp, piercing

shrink *v.* **1** contract, wither, shrivel **2** draw back, flinch, wince, recoil, withdraw
ANT. **1** expand, swell

shudder *v.* quiver, shiver, quake, tremble

shuffle *v.* **1** hobble, falter, crawl **2** mix, jumble, muddle, disorder

shun *v.* avoid, steer clear of, evade, shirk

shut *v.* close, fasten, lock
ANT. open

shut up be quiet, hush, silence, still

shy *adj.* bashful, reserved, retiring, timid, coy
ANT. bold, forward

sick *adj.* unwell, poorly, ill, unhealthy, indisposed, infirm, weak
ANT. healthy, well, strong

side *n.* **1** edge, verge, margin, border, boundary, face, surface, aspect, plane **2** team, party, faction, interest, cause, policy, behalf

side *adj.* subsidiary, secondary, minor, unimportant
ANT. main

side *v.* join, associate, support, back

sift *v.* filter, strain, screen, separate, scrutinize, examine, analyse, analyze (*N. Am.*), evaluate

sigh *v.* exhale, breathe, groan, lament

sight *n.* **1** vision, seeing, eyesight **2** spectacle, scene, display, shoe, view

sign *n.* symbol, type, token, emblem, note, mark, manifestation, indication, presage, omen, signal, prognostic, symptom

signal *n.* sign, flag, gesture, indication

significant *adj.* important, weighty, momentous, consequential, critical, decisive, vital, crucial
ANT. insignificant, unimportant

signify *v.* indicate, mean, denote, show, represent, symbolize, express, communicate, convey

silence *n.* **1** stillness, hush, restfulness, quiet, noiselessness, calm, peace, tranquillity **2** muteness, dumbness, speechlessness
ANT. **1** noise, sound, tumult, din **2** talkativeness, loquacity, garrulity

silent *adj.* **1** still, quiet, hushed, noiseless, soundless, calm, peaceful, tranquil **2** mute, dumb, speechless
ANT. **1** noisy, tumultuous **2** talkative

silly *adj.* foolish, stupid, senseless, idiotic, daft, ridiculous, absurd, nonsensical, childish, puerile
ANT. sensible, wise

similar *adj.* like, alike, resembling, corresponding, uniform, homogeneous
ANT. dissimilar, unlike, different

similarity *n.* resemblance, likeness, correspondence

simmer *v.* boil, bubble, stew

simmer down calm down, cool off

simple *adj.* **1** easy, uncomplicated, effortless, straightforward, elementary, clear, plain, unadorned **2** naive, unsophisticated, guileless, artless, ingenuous, credulous, green
ANT. **1** difficult, complicated, complex, ornate **2** sophisticated, artful

simulate *v.* imitate, copy, reproduce, pretend, feign

simultaneous *adj.* concurrent, happening at the same time, synchronous, contemporaneous

sin *n.* transgression, trespass, wrong, wrong-doing, evil, crime, guilt, offence, offense (*N. Am.*), wickedness, fault, misdeed, iniquity, ungodliness, unrighteousness, immorality, depravity

sin *v.* transgress, trespass, commit wrong, be guilty

sincere *adj.* genuine, true, real, honest, truthful, heartfelt, direct, plain
ANT. insincere, unreal

sing *v.* chant, carol, chirp, hum, warble, chirrup, croon

single *adj.* **1** lone, sole, only, one, solitary **2** unmarried, unattached, on one's own, celibate
ANT. **1** many **2** married

sinister *adj.* ominous, bad, unfavourable, unfavorable (*N. Am.*), menacing, inauspicious
ANT. favourable, favorable (*N. Am.*), good

sink *v.* **1** subside, drop, fall, descend, droop, decay, lower, lessen, decline, dwindle, decrease, reduce, depress, diminish **2** submerge, immerse, engulf, drown
ANT. **1** rise, ascend, increase

sip *v.* taste, drink

sit *v.* rest, settle, seat, crouch, squat

site *n.* location, place, spot, ground, position

situation *n.* **1** location, position, place, site, locality, seat, ground, spot **2** condition, circumstance, state, predicament **3** employment, job, post, position

size *n.* dimensions, proportions, measurements, bigness, greatness, amount, extent, scope

skeleton *n.* framework, frame, bones

sketch *n.* drawing, plan, outline, draft

sketch *v.* draw, outline, draft, portray, depict

skilful, skillful (*N. Am.*) *adj.* skilled, trained, proficient, accomplished, practised, practiced (*N. Am.*), expert, dexterous, apt, handy, adroit, clever, deft
ANT. unskilled, clumsy, inexpert, unskilful, unskillful (*N. Am.*), awkward, incompetent

skill *n.* ability, capability, talent, gift, proficiency, aptitude, expertise, dexterity

skim *v.* **1** graze, touch, brush **2** browse, flick, scan, glance

skin *n.* peel, shell, rind, covering, surface, outside

skin *v.* peel, flay, pare

skinny *adj.* thin, lean, gaunt, lank, scrawny, emaciated
ANT. plump, fat

skip *v.* hop, jump, leap, bound, spring, gambol

sky *n.* atmosphere, air, firmament, heaven

slack *adj.* **1** loose, lax, limp **2** careless, negligent, lazy, slow, inactive, idle, sluggish
ANT. **1** tight **2** careful, active, busy

slam *v.* bang, crash, close, shut

slander *n.* defamation, disparagement, abuse, libel
ANT. praise

slant *v.* slope, incline, lean, tilt

slant *n.* slope, incline, angle, gradient, tilt

slap *v.* blow, hit, strike, smack

slash *v.* **1** cut, gash, slit **2** reduce, cut, lower

slaughter *v.* kill, butcher, slay, massacre, murder

slaughter *n.* killing, butchery, bloodshed, massacre, carnage, murder

sleep *v.* rest, slumber, doze, snooze, nap, drop off, nod off

sleep *n.* rest, slumber, snooze, nap, siesta, forty winks (*informal*)

slender *adj.* slight, thin, slim, svelte
ANT. fat, thick, stout, broad, bulky, considerable

slide *v.* glide, slip, skid, skate

slight *adj.* **1** small, insignificant, inconsiderable, minor **2** slim, delicate, little, frail, slender
ANT. **1** large, considerable. major **2** fat

slight *v.* snub, disregard, ignore, insult, scorn
ANT. praise, flatter

sling *v.* throw, fling, hurl, cast, toss

slip *v.* slide, glide, fall, drop

slip *n.* mistake, error, blunder, indiscretion

slippery *adj.* **1** icy, dangerous, insecure, perilous, unsafe **2** shifty, crafty, cunning, deceptive, dishonest, elusive
ANT. **1** firm, safe **2** dependable, honest

slit *v.* cut, slash, gash, tear, rip

slit *n.* cut, tear, opening, split

slogan *n.* catchphrase, watchword, motto, cry, saying

slope *v.* lean, slant, incline

slope *n.* incline, gradient, acclivity, declivity

slouch *v.* stoop, slump, lounge

slow *adj.* **1** unhurried, leisurely, deliberate, dawdling **2** stupid, unintelligent, dense, thick (*informal*) **3** tedious, boring, dull, uninteresting
ANT. **1** fast, quick, hurried **2** clever, intelligent, bright **3** interesting, exciting, lively

slow *v.* brake, delay, decelerate, hinder, obstruct
ANT. speed

slump *v.* fall, sink, drop, plunge

slump *n.* depression, recession, fall, collapse

slur *n.* insult, slight, smear, aspersion

sly *adj.* cunning, crafty, deceitful, devious, insidious, mischievous, artful, wily, foxy
ANT. guileless, artless

smack *v.* hit, strike, spank, slap

small *adj.* **1** little, tiny, minute, short, diminutive, inconsiderable **2** insignificant, unimportant, minor, inconsequential, trifling, trivial
ANT. **1** large, great, big, extensive, enormous, massive **2** important, significant

smart *adj.* **1** neat, tidy, fashionable, stylish, modish **2** clever, bright, intelligent, shrewd, sharp
ANT. **1** untidy, shabby, dowdy **2** stupid, slow

smash *v.* break, crash, crush, shatter, demolish, ruin, wreck

smash *n.* crash, collision, accident, pile-up, ruin, wreck

smear *v.* spread, rub, wipe, cover, coat

smell *n.* scent, odour, odor (*N. Am.*), aroma, fragrance, perfume, stink, stench

smell v. sniff, detect, scent

smile v. grin, beam, smirk
ANT. scowl

smooth adj. 1 level, even, flat, regular
2 still, calm, peaceful, glassy 3 easy,
effortless, uncomplicated 4 suave, glib,
slick
ANT. 1 uneven, rough 2 rough, stormy
3 troublesome, difficult

smooth v. level, plane, even, flatten,
iron, press

smother v. stifle, choke, strangle,
suffocate, asphyxiate

smug adj. complacent, self-satisfied,
conceited

snap v. break, crack, fracture, sever

snare n. trap, net, noose

snarl v. growl, roar

snatch v. seize, catch, grab, grasp, clutch

sneak v. crawl, steal, slink, skulk, sidle

sneer v. jeer, mock, gibe, taunt, fling,
scoff, scorn

sneer n. taunt, jeer, scorn

snip v. cut, crop, clip, trim

snub v. insult, slight, ignore, rebuff,
humiliate, cold-shoulder

snub n. insult, slight, rebuff, humiliation

snug adj. 1 comfortable, cosy, cozy (N.
Am.), warm, safe, secure, protected,
sheltered 2 close-fitting, tight-fitting,
tight

soak v. immerse, drench, wet, saturate,
steep

soar v. mount, rise, tower

sob v. weep, cry, blubber

sober adj. 1 abstemious, abstinent,
moderate, temperate 2 solemn, serious,
grave, staid, sombre, somber (N. Am.),
sedate
ANT. 1 drunk, intoxicated 2 frivolous

so-called adj. alleged, professed,
supposed

sociable adj. friendly, outgoing,
gregarious, genial, affable
ANT. unsociable

social adj. common, community, group

society n. 1 association, club,
organization, community, fellowship,
circle, group, league 2 people,
community, nation, humanity

soft adj. 1 flexible, yielding, impressible,
malleable 2 smooth, gentle, flowing
3 tender, kind, gentle, compassionate,
indulgent, permissive, mild 4 quiet,
faint, low, dim, peaceful, tranquil
ANT. 1 hard, unyielding, impervious,
tough, impermeable 2 rough, coarse
3 disagreeable, harsh, brusque, gruff,
unkind 4 loud, noisy

soften v. weaken, relax, abate, mellow,
moderate, cushion, temper
ANT. strengthen, harden, stiffen

soil n. earth, ground, dust

sole adj. only, one, exclusive, single,
lone

solemn adj. grave, serious, sober,
sombre, somber (N. Am.), staid
ANT. frivolous, light-hearted

solicit v. ask, seek, request, beg, beseech,
crave

solid adj. 1 hard, firm, dense, compact
2 reliable, dependable, trustworthy,
sensible
ANT. 1 hollow, yielding, soft, fluid,
liquid 2 unreliable

solitary adj. lone, single, sole, only

solitude n. loneliness, solitariness,
aloneness, recluseness, withdrawal,
remoteness, seclusion, retirement,
retreat, wilderness, desert, privacy,
isolation

solution n. 1 explanation, answer, key,
elucidation 2 liquid, compound,
mixture, blend, suspension

solve v. work out, explain, resolve,
answer, disentangle, unravel

sombre, somber (N. Am.) adj. serious,
solemn, sober, grave, sad, mournful,
gloomy, dismal
ANT. happy, bright, cheerful, frivolous

sometimes adv. occasionally, now and
then, now and again, at times
ANT. always

song n. ballad, hymn, anthem, psalm,
carol, melody, tune

soon adv. shortly, before long, in a
minute, in a little while

soothe *v.* assuage, calm, mollify, comfort, pacify, soften, allay, compose, mitigate, relieve, lull
ANT. rouse, excite, disturb, aggravate

sophisticated *adj.* 1 cultured, refined, educated, fashionable, worldly-wise 2 advanced, complex, complicated, intricate

sordid *adj.* immoral, dirty, filthy, seedy
ANT. moral, respectable

sore *adj.* 1 tender, painful, sensitive, raw, aching 2 annoyed, angry, irritated, upset, distressed

sorrow *n.* sadness, grief, unhappiness, distress, affliction, misery, anguish, woe
ANT. happiness, joy

sorry *adj.* 1 apologetic, regretful, penitent, remorseful 2 wretched, poor, miserable, pitiful, mean
ANT. 1 unrepentant, impenitent 2 splendid, magnificent

sort *n.* kind, type, variety, class, category, order, group, genus, species

sort *v.* arrange, classify, order, organize, catalogue, catalog (*N. Am.*), group, divide, separate

soul *n.* 1 spirit, life, mind, reason, intellect, emotions, ghost, spectre, specter (*N. Am.*) 2 passion, fervour, fervor, affection, feeling, emotion, energy, vitality, inspiration
ANT. 1 body

sound[1] *n.* noise, din, racket
ANT. silence

sound[1] *v.* make a noise, ring, echo, utter

sound[2] *adj.* 1 fit, healthy, well, robust, secure, whole, unbroken, unharmed, free, firm, strong, solid, safe, perfect 2 reliable, sensible, logical, rational, correct, true, orthodox
ANT. 1 unfit, insecure, imperfect 2 unreliable, unsound, incorrect

sour *adj.* 1 acid, bitter, sharp, tart 2 unpleasant, bad-tempered, bitter, nasty, acrimonious
ANT. 1 sweet 2 friendly, genial

source *n.* beginning, origin, derivation, spring

souvenir *n.* keepsake, token, memento

sovereign *n.* monarch, ruler, king, queen, emperor, empress

sovereign *adj.* supreme, primary, principal, superior, chief, independent, autonomous
ANT. secondary

sow *v.* plant, scatter, disseminate, propagate

space *n.* 1 room, area, place, expanse 2 interval, period, time, distance 3 outer space, cosmos, sky, galaxy

spacious *adj.* roomy, ample, big, large, extensive
ANT. small, narrow, cramped

span *n.* extent, distance, reach, stretch, spread

span *v.* extend, reach, stretch, spread

spare *adj.* extra, additional, surplus, superfluous

spare *v.* 1 save, reserve, set aside, make available 2 show mercy to, pardon, release, forgive
ANT. 2 condemn, punish

spark *n.* flash, gleam, flicker, sparkle

sparkle *v.* shine, glitter, gleam, glisten, flicker

sparse *adj.* scattered, sprinkled, infrequent, thin, scanty, meagre, meager (*N. Am.*) few
ANT. dense, thick, plentiful, many

spasm *n.* fit, seizure, attack, convulsion, paroxysm

speak *v.* say, talk, tell, utter, articulate, converse, express, chat, chatter, enunciate, pronounce, announce, declare, deliver, address

special *adj.* 1 different, unusual, exceptional, extraordinary 2 particular, certain, individual, definite, specific, distinct
ANT. 1 ordinary, average 2 general

specialist *n.* authority, expert, professional, master

specific *adj.* definite, particular, precise, exact, express, special, distinct
ANT. general, vague

specification *n.* detail, requirement, description, designation

specify *v.* name, state, mention, define, describe, designate

specimen *n.* sample, example, illustration, instance, exemplification

speck *n.* spot, mark, dot, stain, blemish

spectacle *n.* show, exhibit, display, sight, scene, performance, extravaganza

spectator *n.* viewer, onlooker, observe, watcher
ANT. participant, player

spectre, specter (*N. Am.*) *n.* ghost, apparition, phantom, spook (*informal*)

speculate *v.* guess, think, consider, contemplate, estimate, suppose, surmise

speculation *n.* theory, view, notion, conjecture, consideration, meditation, contemplation, thought, weighing, hypothesis, scheme, venture

speech *n.* **1** speaking, language, talking, utterance, diction, articulation, pronunciation **2** talk, address, discourse, oration, utterance, sermon, harangue, dissertation, oratory, disquisition

speed *n.* velocity, rapidity, haste, hurry, rate, tempo, pace
ANT. slowness

spell *n.* **1** period, time, stretch, term **2** incantation, charm, formula, enchantment

spend *v.* **1** pay out, expend, use up, consume, exhaust, waste, squander **2** use, employ, devote, pass
ANT. **1** save, set aside, hoard

sphere *n.* **1** ball, globe, orb **2** field, area, province, domain

spice *n.* condiment, flavouring, flavoring (*N. Am.*), seasoning

spike *n.* point, prong, nail, point

spill *v.* drop, scatter, pour out, shed

spin *v.* turn, rotate, revolve, twirl

spine *n.* vertebrae, backbone, spinal column

spirit *n.* **1** life, soul **2** ghost, spectre, specter (*N. Am.*), apparition, angel, devil, demon **3** liveliness, energy, vivacity, ardour, ardor (*N. Am.*), courage, enthusiasm **4** essence, meaning, substance, sense, intention, drift **5** mood, temper, attitude, outlook, disposition

spiritual *adj.* **1** immaterial, incorporeal, mental, intellectual **2** holy, sacred, religious, pious, divine, heavenly-minded
ANT. **1** temporal, physical

spite *n.* malice, malevolence, ill will, resentment, contempt, scorn
ANT. goodwill, benevolence

in spite of despite, notwithstanding, regardless of

splash *v.* spray, shower, wash, sprinkle

splendid *adj.* **1** very good, excellent, fine, wonderful, superb, marvellous **2** magnificent, grand, glorious, imposing, impressive, fine, rich, luxurious, resplendent, pompous, sumptuous, gorgeous
ANT. **1** poor, awful **2** plain, ugly

splinter *n.* sliver, fragment, piece, chip

split *v.* break, part, divide, separate, cut, crack, sever

split *n.* break, division, crack, opening, fracture

spoil *v.* **1** mar, harm, hurt, damage, destroy, ruin, wreck **2** pamper, indulge, cosset **3** go bad, go off, rot, decay, putrefy

spokesperson *n.* spokesman, spokeswoman, representative, speaker, source, voice, agent, mouthpiece

sponge *v.* mop, wipe, clean, rub, swab

sponsor *n.* backer, patron, supporter, promoter, friend

spontaneous *adj.* natural, free, unintentional, voluntary, unconscious, impulsive, automatic, instinctive
ANT. forced, compelled, coerced, unwilling, reluctant

sport *n.* **1** game, play, exercise, recreation, fun **2** joke, jest, fun, mockery

spot *n.* **1** dot, mark, speck, blemish, blot **2** place, location, site, scene

spot *v.* notice, make out, discern, recognize, identify

spout *v.* spurt, gush, jet, spray, squirt

sprawl *v.* sit, lie, lounge, relax

spray *n.* mist, drizzle, spatter

spray *v.* sprinkle, shower, scatter, spatter

spread *v.* **1** stretch, extend, reach, expand, open, unfurl **2** disperse, distribute, scatter, circulate, divulge, propagate, publish, diffuse, disseminate, dispense, extend, stretch, expand, amplify

spread *n.* **1** extent, reach, span, expanse, stretch **2** distribution, circulation, dissemination **3** jam, marmalade, preserve, jelly

spring *n.* **1** jump, leap, bound, hop, vault **2** well, source, origin, fount

spring *v.* **1** jump, leap, bound, hop, vault **2** start, begin, arise, rise, originate, derive, flow, emerge
ANT. **2** end, finish, terminate

sprinkle *v.* scatter, shower, spray

sprint *v.* run, race, dash, rush

sprout *v.* germinate, bud, grow, develop

spur *v.* urge, prompt, motivate, encourage, stimulate, induce, provoke

spur *n.* stimulus, motive, motivation, encouragement, incentive, inducement

spurious *adj.* unreal, false, fake, counterfeit
ANT. real, genuine

spy *n.* agent, informer, scout

spy *v.* watch, see, observe, pry

squalid *adj.* dirty, filthy, foul, unclean, seedy
ANT. clean

squander *v.* waste, fritter away, throw away, dissipate

square *n.* quadrangle, plaza, piazza, market place

squat *v.* crouch, sit

squat *adj.* dumpy, short, stubby, thickset

squeak *v.* cry, squeal, whine

squeeze *v.* pinch, squash, press, crush, wring, clasp, grip

stab *v.* stick, pierce, cut, jab

stable *adj.* fixed, established, constant, resolute, unwavering, steady, abiding, firm, strong, durable, secure, permanent, solid, lasting, perpetual, immobile, rigid, unmovable
ANT. unstable, vacillating, wavering, unsteady, toppling, weak, tottering, insecure, precarious

stack *n.* pile, heap, mound, mass

stack *v.* pile, heap, mound, amass

staff *n.* personnel, workers, employees, workforce, crew

stage *n.* **1** phase, period, step, point, level **2** platform, podium, rostrum, theatre

stage *v.* produce, mount, put on, perform, present

stagger *v.* totter, reel, sway, wobble, lurch

staggering *adj.* amazing, astounding, astonishing, surprising, extraordinary
ANT. familiar, usual

stagnant *adj.* standing, still, static, inert, sluggish, foul, brackish
ANT. flowing, moving, active

stain *n.* **1** blot, spot, mark, blemish, tint, colour, color (*N. Am.*) **2** shame, blemish, slur, taint, stigma

stain *v.* blot, spot, sully, tarnish, tinge, tint, colour, color (*N. Am.*), discolour, discolor (*N. Am.*), disgrace, soil

stake *n.* **1** risk, chance, venture, bet, wager **2** share, concern, interest, investment **3** post, stick, pole

stake *v.* risk, chance, venture, bet, wager, gamble

stale *adj.* **1** old, musty, dry, fusty, tasteless **2** dull, uninteresting, trite, hackneyed
ANT. **1** fresh **2** interesting, exciting, original

stalk[1] *n.* stem, shaft

stalk[2] *v.* chase, track, follow, pursue, shadow

stall *v.* stop, halt, delay

stall *n.* stand, booth, cubicle

stalwart *adj.* loyal, staunch, steadfast, hard-working, enthusiastic

stamina *n.* strength, endurance, energy, resilience

stammer *v.* stutter, falter, hesitate, stumble

stamp *v.* **1** step, tread, trample, beat, crush **2** brand, mark, impress, print
stamp out put an end to, eradicate, eliminate

stand *v.* **1** rise, arise, get up, stand up **2** cease, stop, pause, halt, endure, last **3** endure, sustain, bear, tolerate, abide, withstand, suffer

stand by defend, support, back, endorse
stand down resign, step down, leave, quit **stand for** represent, symbolize, illustrate **stand out** be prominent, be conspicuous, stick out **stand up for** champion, defend, support, stick up for

stand *n.* 1 platform, place, post, station 2 stance, attitude, position, viewpoint, standpoint

standard *n.* 1 measure, scale, gauge, example, model, type, norm, criterion, test, pattern 2 flag, colours, colors (*N. Am.*), banner, ensign, pennant

standard *adj.* normal, regular, typical, usual, official
ANT. irregular, unusual, special

staple *adj.* basic, primary, important, main, chief, principal, essential, necessary

stare *v.* gaze, gawk, gawp, watch

stark *adj.* 1 harsh, severe, plain, bare, barren, austere 2 absolute, utter, sheet

start *v.* 1 begin, commence, originate, arise, launch, open, initiate, set up, bring into being, come into being 2 jump, twitch, jerk, flinch, wince
ANT. 1 finish, end

start *n.* 1 beginning, commencement, onset, outset, launch, initiation, inception 2 jump, twitch, jerk, surprise, shock

startle *v.* surprise, shock, amaze, astound, take aback

starve *v.* die, perish, be famished

state *n.* 1 country, nation, kingdom, government 2 condition, situation, form, circumstance, case

state *v.* declare, say, tell, maintain, announce, assert, affirm, allege, testify, assure, swear, set forth, protest, pronounce, specify, propound, inform, express, claim, avow, aver, certify, asseverate
ANT. deny, dispute, oppose, retract

stately *adj.* grand, magnificent, splendid, imposing, majestic, dignified, lofty
ANT. lowly

statement *n.* declaration, assertion, announcement, affirmation, expression, claim, assurance

statesman *n.* stateswoman, politician, diplomat, leader

station *n.* 1 depot, stopping place, terminus 2 place, spot, position, stand 3 state, rank, condition, occupation, business, office, sphere

stationary *adj.* still, motionless, immobile, immovable
ANT. moving, mobile

statistics *n. pl.* data, figures, numbers, information, facts

status *n.* standing, position, rank, condition

statute *n.* law, ruling, decree

staunch *adj.* loyal, steadfast, constant, faithful, true, firm
ANT. disloyal, wavering

stay *v.* 1 remain, continue, keep, endure, last 2 wait, settle, remain, stop, halt, reside, rest, visit, linger 3 delay, prevent, hinder, put off, check, hold back, restrain
ANT. 1 leave, go

stay *n.* 1 visit, rest, stop, wait, halt, delay 2 support, prop, brace

steady *adj.* 1 even, regular, constant, uniform, unvarying 2 stable, firm, fixed, solid
ANT. 1 changeable, irregular 2 unstable

steal *v.* 1 take, rob, pilfer, filch, embezzle, nick (*informal*) 2 sneak, creep, slink, prowl

steam *n.* mist, vapour, vapor (*N. Am.*), fog, condensation

steep *adj.* sharp, abrupt, perpendicular, sheer, precipitous
ANT. gradual, level

steer *v.* control, guide, direct, pilot

stem *n.* stalk, trunk

stem *v.* 1 originate, arise, come, issue 2 stop, restrain, check, curb

step *n.* 1 pace, stride, footprint 2 measure, action, act, move, stage 3 stair, rung, level

step *v.* walk, go, move, pace

step up increase, boost, accelerate

sterile *adj.* 1 sterilized, germ-free, clean 2 barren, unfruitful, fruitless, unproductive, empty, impotent
ANT. 1 unsterilized, dirty 2 fruitful

stern *adj.* strict, hard, severe, harsh, unyielding, uncompromising, inflexible
ANT. lenient, gentle

stew *n.* goulash, ragout

stew *v.* simmer, seethe, boil

stick *n.* rod, twig, birch, cane, pole, staff

stick *v.* **1** pierce, stab, puncture **2** join, fix, attach, fasten **3** stay, remain, continue, be loyal

stick out protrude, project, jut out

stick up for support, champion, defend, stand up for

sticky *adj.* **1** adhesive, gluey, gummy **2** difficult, tricky, awkward, delicate **3** hot, close, muggy, oppressive
ANT. **2** easy **3** cool

stiff *adj.* **1** rigid, inflexible, strong, hard, solid, firm, unbending, unpliant **2** formal, strict, pompous, strait-laced **3** difficult, hard, harsh, tough, severe, arduous
ANT. **1** flexible, pliant, amenable, yielding **2** informal, unceremonious **3** easy

stiffen *v.* harden, tense (up)

stifle *v.* choke, smother, suffocate, repress

stigma *n.* mark, blot, stain, brand, blemish

still *adj.* motionless, stationary, inert, restful, quiet, serene, silent, calm, soundless, low, hushed, mute, placid, gentle, soft, mild, pacific, peaceful, noiseless
ANT. moving, agitated, restless, noisy, resonant

still *v.* quieten, quiet, hush, silence, soothe, calm, pacify
ANT. agitate, disturb

still *n.* quiet, rest, silence, calm
ANT. noise

stimulate *v.* arouse, excite, urge, prompt, incite, instigate

sting *v.* prick, injure, hurt, bite, wound, tingle, smart

stink *v.* smell, reek, pong (*informal*)

stink *n.* smell, stench, reek, pong (*informal*)

stint *n.* period, time, spell, term, task, work

stir *v.* **1** mix, blend, whip, beat, shake, agitate **2** move, budge, shift **3** rouse, stimulate, thrill, inspire, move, touch, excite

stock *n.* supply, store, reserve, fund, accumulation

stock *v.* supply, store, keep, carry

stone *n.* rock, pebble, cobble, boulder

stoop *v.* hunch, lean, bow, bend

stop *v.* **1** end, finish, conclude, complete, halt, cease **2** obstruct, hinder, delay, prevent, thwart, block, interrupt **3** remain, rest, settle, visit

stop *n.* halt, finish, end, conclusion

store *n.* **1** shop, supermarket, market **2** stock, supply, reserve, fund, accumulation

store *v.* keep, save, preserve, reserve, put aside

storm *n.* gale, hurricane, squall, tempest

storm *v.* attack, raid, charge, assault

story *n.* tale, narrative, legend, anecdote, account, record, recital, incident, myth, narration, novel

stout *adj.* fat, plump, heavy, large, big, overweight, obese, portly, corpulent
ANT. thin, slender

straight *adj.* **1** direct, undeviating, uncurving, unswerving **2** neat, tidy, orderly **3** honest, upright, respectable, trustworthy
ANT. **1** crooked, twisted

strain *v.* **1** stretch, tighten, extend **2** sprain, wrench, injure, hurt, harm

strait *n.* narrows, passage, channel

strand *v.* maroon, abandon, leave, desert, ground

strange *adj.* **1** odd, unusual, peculiar, uncommon, curious, bizarre, queer, exceptional **2** foreign, exotic, new, novel, unusual, unfamiliar, unknown, unaccustomed, inexperienced, distant
ANT. **1** common, usual, normal **2** familiar

stranger *n.* outsider, visitor, newcomer, foreigner, alien

strangle *v.* choke, throttle, suffocate, smother, asphyxiate

strap *n.* belt, strip, bond

strategy *n.* approach, technique, plan, method, policy, tactics

stray *v.* wander, roam, rove, ramble

stream *n.* **1** river, brook, rivulet, creek **2** flow, course, rush

stream *v.* flow, rush, issue, pour, gush

street *n.* road, thoroughfare, avenue, way, highway

strength *n.* power, might, toughness, force, brawn, energy, vigour, vigor (*N. Am.*), influence, intensity
ANT. weakness, feebleness, frailty

strengthen *n.* fortify, reinforce, energize, harden, toughen
ANT. weaken

strenuous *adj.* energetic, powerful, tough, vigorous, forceful, active, strong, determined, resolute, vehement
ANT. weak, irresolute

stress *v.* emphasize, accentuate, underline, highlight

stress *n.* 1 emphasis, accent, importance, weight 2 tension, strain, pressure, anxiety

stretch *v.* extend, spread, lengthen, draw out, elongate
ANT. contract

strict *adj.* 1 firm, harsh, stern, severe, stringent, inflexible 2 precise, exact, accurate
ANT. 1 lenient, flexible 2 loose, inexact, rough

stride *v.* walk, pace, step

strife *n.* conflict, disagreement, quarrel, dissension, friction
ANT. peace

strike *v.* 1 hit, collide, crash, beat, tap, pound 2 protest, walk out, down tools 3 impress, occur to, affect, move

strike out delete, cross out, erase

strike *n.* protest, walkout, sit-in

stringent *adj.* rigorous, tough, strict, demanding, exacting
ANT. lax

strip *n.* band, belt, piece, ribbon, stripe

strip *v.* undress, disrobe, remove, uncover, peel, skin

strive *v.* struggle, try, attempt, toil, labour, labor (*N. Am.*), endeavour, endeavor (*N. Am.*)

stroke *v.* caress, touch, rub, pat, fondle

stroke *n.* 1 blow, tap, hit, knock, rap, tap 2 attack, seizure, collapse, fit, shock

stroll *v.* wander, walk, saunter, amble, ramble

strong *adj.* 1 powerful, tough, sturdy, robust, muscular, brawny, sinewy, strapping, rugged, hardy 2 unbreakable, firm, tough, sturdy, solid, robust, substantial 3 spicy, sharp, hot, piquant, pungent 4 forceful, cogent, convincing, persuasive, robust, vehement
ANT. 1 weak, feeble 2 breakable, fragile, delicate 3 tasteless 4 feeble, unconvincing

structure *n.* 1 arrangement, organization, construction, make-up 2 building, edifice, fabric

struggle *v.* try, strive, endeavour, endeavor (*N. Am.*), labour, labor (*N. Am.*), fight

struggle *n.* 1 attempt, endeavour, endeavor (*N. Am.*), effort, exertion 2 fight, battle, clash, combat, conflict, engagement, encounter

stubborn *adj.* obstinate, inflexible, un-yielding, persistent, headstrong, harsh, intractable, firm, obdurate, refractory
ANT. yielding, pliant, tractable, flexible, pliable

student *n.* pupil, learner, scholar, trainee

study *v.* work, learn, read, swot up (*informal*), concentrate, examine, investigate, consider, research, ponder, contemplate, weigh

study *n.* learning, work, read, examination, investigation, research, thought, application, concentration

stuff *n.* 1 belongings, things, clothes, equipment 2 substance, material, fabric, textile

stuff *v.* cram, pack, press, push, squeeze, shove

stuffy *adj.* 1 airless, oppressive, close, sticky, sultry, musty 2 staid, dull, old-fashioned, strait-laced, stodgy
ANT. 1 ventilated 2 exciting

stumble *v.* trip, fall, lurch, falter

stun *v.* daze, stupefy, knock out, shock, surprise, amaze, astonish, astound, dumbfound

stupid *adj.* 1 foolish, unintelligent, daft, simple, dull, slow, half-witted 2 silly, idiotic, daft, absurd, ridiculous, ludicrous
ANT. 1 wise, sensible, intelligent, clever 2 clever, sensible

sturdy *adj*. strong, firm, robust, steady, well-built
ANT. flimsy

stutter *v*. stammer, falter, stumble, hesitate

style *n*. 1 way, method, manner, shape, form, kind, sort, type 2 fashion, vogue, trend, elegance, smartness, refinement

subconscious *adj*. inner, deep, hidden

subdue *v*. defeat, overcome, beat, crush, conquer, overpower

subdued *adj*. quiet, soft, low, toned down
ANT. loud, noisy

subject *n*. topic, theme, issue, point, area

subject *adj*. subordinate, dependent, depending, liable, susceptible

subject *v*. expose, submit, lay open

sublime *adj*. exalted, lofty, high, eminent, glorious, noble, majestic, grand, stately, magnificent, dignified, elevated, august, pompous
ANT. low, ignoble, debased, degraded

submerge *adj*. immerse, sink, plunge, dip, subside

submit *v*. 1 surrender, yield, obey, resign oneself 2 offer, present, tender, propose, put forward
ANT. 1 resist

subordinate *adj*. junior, inferior, lower, lesser, minor

subordinate *n*. junior, inferior, assistant

subscribe *v*. 1 sold, approve, support, agree, endorse 2 pay, contribute, donate, promise

subsequent *adj*. following, succeeding, later, future, ensuing
ANT. prior, previous

subside *v*. 1 abate, moderate, lower, diminish 2 sink, lower, decline
ANT. 1 intensify, increase 2 rise

subsidy *n*. allowance, grant, support, assistance, aid

substance *n*. stuff, matter, material, essence, gist

substantial *adj*. 1 large, significant, big, considerable 2 real, true, actual, material
ANT. 1 small 2 imaginary, unreal, insubstantial

substantiate *v*. prove, verify, confirm, corroborate, establish

substitute *v*. replace, change, exchange, interchange

substitute *n*. replacement, relief, understudy, stand-in

subtle *adj*. slight, indirect, faint, suggestive
ANT. obvious

subtract *v*. take away, deduct, lessen, reduce, remove, withdraw
ANT. add

subvert *v*. undermine, upset, destroy, ruin, overthrow, overturn
ANT. conserve, preserve, uphold, sustain, keep, perpetuate

succeed *v*. 1 flourish, prosper, thrive 2 follow, ensue, result, be subsequent
ANT. 1 fail 2 precede, antecede

success *n*. prosperity, triumph, achievement, accomplishment, fortune, luck
ANT. failure

successful *adj*. thriving, prosperous, flourishing, fortunate, lucky, triumphant, rewarding, favourable, favorable (*N. Am.*)
ANT. unsuccessful, failing

succession *n*. series, sequence, order, course, chain, lineage, descent, following, continuity, regularity

successive *adj*. consecutive, serial, following

successor *n*. follower, heir, inheritor

succinct *adj*. brief, concise, short, condensed, compact
ANT. long, wordy, rambling

succumb *v*. give way, yield, surrender, give in
ANT. resist

suck *v*. draw in, take in, absorb

sudden *adj*. unexpected, abrupt, hasty, rapid, unanticipated, unforeseen, unprovided for
ANT. anticipated, foreseen, expected, slow, gradual

sue *v*. prosecute, accuse, take to court

suffer *v*. endure, undergo, be affected by, experience, go through, bear, submit to

sufficient *adj.* adequate, enough, ample, plenty, satisfactory
ANT. insufficient, inadequate, lacking, deficient

suffocate *v.* stifle, choke, strangle, asphyxiate

suggest *v.* 1 put forward, submit, propose, advise 2 imply, intimate, evoke

suggestion *n.* 1 idea, plan, proposal, submission 2 hint, innuendo, intimation, insinuation, implication

suit *n.* outfit, costume

suit *v.* match, fit, correspond, harmonize, befit

suitable *adj.* appropriate, relevant, convenient, fitting, apt, becoming, seemly
ANT. unsuitable, inappropriate

sulk *v.* brood, mope, glower

sullen *adj.* morose, moody, surly, bad-tempered, bitter, resentful
ANT. cheerful, happy

sultry *adj.* hot, humid, oppressive, muggy, sticky, clammy

sum *n.* amount, total, whole, quantity, aggregate

sum up summarize, review, recapitulate, epitomize

summary *n.* outline, précis, résumé, synopsis, digest, abstract

summit *n.* top, peak, pinnacle, cap, crown
ANT. base

summon *v.* call, assemble, send for
ANT. dismiss

sumptuous *adj.* magnificent, lavish, splendid, extravagant, expensive, rich, opulent
ANT. poor

sundry *adj.* various, several, different, diverse, miscellaneous

super *adj.* great, wonderful, excellent, fine, marvellous
ANT. awful

superb *adj.* excellent, fine, wonderful, marvellous, great, magnificent
ANT. poor

superficial *adj.* shallow, slight, trivial
ANT. deep

superfluous *adj.* redundant, unnecessary, extra, surplus, needless

superintendent *n.* overseer, supervisor, manager, inspector, director, administrator

superior *adj.* higher, better, surpassing, greater, pre-eminent, excellent
ANT. inferior, lower, worse

superior *n.* boss (*informal*), manager, employer, director, senior
ANT. subordinate

supernatural *adj.* abnormal, paranormal, unnatural, preternatural, invisible, mysterious, spiritual
ANT. natural, ordinary, commonplace, everyday, usual

supersede *v.* replace, displace, supplant, succeed, oust

supervise *v.* oversee, superintend, administer, manage, direct

supple *adj.* pliant, flexible, bending, soft, yielding, compliant, submissive
ANT. firm, stiff, unyielding, inflexible, hard

supplement *v.* add, extend, top up

supplement *n.* addition, extension, enlargement

supply *v.* provide, give, grant, furnish, equip

supply *n.* stock, store, reserve, fund

support *v.* 1 back, encourage, advocate, promote, defend, champion, stand up for, help, aid, assist, sponsor 2 hold, hold up, bear, sustain, uphold, prop up, brace 3 maintain, look after, provide for 4 confirm, verify, corroborate, endorse

support *n.* 1 backing, encouragement, help, aid, assistance, sponsorship, patronage 2 prop, brace, buttress

supporter *n.* fan, enthusiast, follower, admirer, fanatic

suppose *v.* think, believe, judge, guess, imagine, assume, presume, surmise, say, allege

suppress *v.* repress, subdue, stop, restrain, restrict, overthrow, quell, overwhelm, conceal, stifle, smother, overpower, destroy, extinguish

supreme *adj.* best, highest, greatest, utmost, leading, top

sure *adj.* **1** certain, definite, decided, convinced, confident, positive **2** reliable, trustworthy, steady, firm, unfailing, infallible **3** bound, inevitable, destined
ANT. **1** doubtful, hesitating **2** unreliable, fallible

surface *n.* outside, covering, cover, exterior, façade

surge *v.* flow, rise, increase, gush, rush, swell
ANT. diminish

surmount *v.* overcome, conquer, triumph over, climb, scale

surpass *v.* exceed, excel, outdo, pass, transcend

surplus *n.* excess, surfeit, remainder, rest, balance

surplus *adj.* excess, spare, extra, remaining

surprise *v.* amaze, astound, astonish, startle, stupefy, shock, stun, stagger, dumbfound, flabbergast, bewilder
ANT. bore, tire

surprise *n.* amazement, astonishment, shock, bewilderment, marvel, wonder

surrender *v.* abandon, give up, give over, relinquish, resign, waive, yield, capitulate, cede, let go, sacrifice
ANT. resist, withstand, oppose

surround *v.* encircle, circle, encompass, ring, gird, enclose

surroundings *n. pl.* environment, setting, background, milieu, habitat, ambience

survey *n.* study, review, inquiry, examination, investigation, inspection, appraisal, assessment, evaluation

survey *v.* study, review, consider, examine, inquire into, investigate, inspect, appraise, assess, evaluate

survive *v.* last, live, continue, remain, persist
ANT. die

susceptible *adj.* liable, subject, vulnerable, disposed, open

suspect *v.* **1** think, guess, believe, suppose, assume, imagine, conjecture **2** doubt, mistrust, distrust
ANT. **2** trust, believe

suspect *adj.* suspicious, doubtful

suspend *v.* hang, dangle, swing, droop, sway

suspense *n.* uncertainty, expectation, apprehension, anxiety, doubt, indecision

suspicion *n.* doubt, mistrust, distrust, misgivings, qualm, scepticism, skepticism (*N. Am.*)

suspicious *adj.* doubtful, dubious, unbelieving, questioning, wary, distrustful, sceptical, skeptical (*N. Am.*)

sustain *v.* **1** continue, keep, maintain, hold onto **2** support, carry, hold up, uphold, bear **3** suffer, undergo, endure, experience

sustenance *n.* subsistence, food, livelihood, living, nutrition, provision, maintenance, support, supplies, aliment, nutriment, nourishment

swallow *v.* eat, drink, gulp, consume, down (*informal*)

swamp *n.* marsh, bog, quagmire, fen

swamp *v.* flood, deluge, inundate, overwhelm, engulf

swap *v.* exchange, barter, trade, switch

swarm *n.* crowd, throng, multitude, mob

swarm *v.* crowd, throng, mass, teem

sway *v.* **1** swing, wave, lean, bend, reel **2** influence, affect, stir, move, urge, compel, win over

swear *v.* **1** promise, declare, affirm, avow, asseverate **2** blaspheme, curse

sweat *n.* perspiration, secretion

sweat *v.* perspire, secrete

sweep *v.* brush, clear, clear

sweeping *adj.* general, comprehensive, broad, wide, all-inclusive, all-embracing, blanket

sweet *adj.* **1** sugary, saccharine, luscious **2** agreeable, attractive, charming, pleasant **3** fragrant, perfumed, pure, clean **4** melodious, dulcet, tuneful, musical, mellow, harmonious
ANT. **1** sour, bitter **2** nasty, unpleasant **3** foul **4** harsh, discordant

swell *v.* grow, spread, expand, extend, increase, enlarge
ANT. decrease

swerve v. turn, veer, swing, diverge, deviate

swift adj. quick, fast, rapid, prompt, speedy, fleet, nimble, expeditious
ANT. slow, lingering, loitering, inactive, sluggish

swim v. bathe, dive, float, paddle, drift, wade

swindle v. cheat, deceive, defraud, trick, con (informal), do (informal)

swindle n. deception, fraud, trickery, con (informal)

swing v. wave, rock, sway, turn, pivot, rotate

switch v. change, exchange, swap, interchange, transpose

swoop v. descend, dive, pounce

symbol n. sign, token, representation, badge, emblem, logo, figure, character

symmetry n. proportion, agreement, conformity, uniformity, similarity, regularity, shapeliness, harmony
ANT. disproportion, disharmony, irregularity

sympathetic adj. compassionate, caring, warm, tender, kind, considerate, concerned, supportive

ANT. harsh, unkind, pitiless, merciless, cruel

sympathize v. feel for, care for, listen to, show concern for, understand, comfort, commiserate with, console, pity

sympathy n. compassion, tenderness, care, warmth, kindness, consideration, concern, support, commiseration
ANT. harshness, unkindness, mercilessness, pitilessness, cruelty

symptom n. sign, warning, indication, mark

synonymous adj. similar, correspondent, like, identical, interchangeable, alike, same, corresponding, equivalent, associated

synthetic adj. artificial, man-made, handmade, manufactured, imitation
ANT. natural, genuine

system n. plan, scheme, order, method, technique, approach, way, practice, arrangement, procedure
ANT. confusion, chaos, disorder, irregularity

systematic adj. ordered, organized, orderly, planned, methodical
ANT. chaotic, disordered, irregular

table *n.* board, counter, stand

tacit *adj.* implicit, implied, granted, unexpressed, understood
ANT. expressed, explicit, declared

tackle *v.* **1** deal with, undertake, try, take on, set about **2** seize, obstruct, intercept, bring down

tackle *n.* equipment, gear, tools, apparatus, outfit, rig, rigging

tact *n.* diplomacy, prudence, sense, judgment, sensitivity
ANT. tactlessness

tactful *adj.* diplomatic, prudent, wise, astute, discreet, sensitive
ANT. tactless, blundering

tag *n.* label, tab, ticket, sticker

taint *v.* contaminate, pollute, defile, stain, tarnish

take *v.* **1** obtain, acquire, get, accept, receive, hold, lay hold of, catch, seize, grasp, win, capture **2** choose, select, pick, prefer **3** convey, transport, bring, accompany, guide, lead, conduct **4** remove, steal, take away, pinch (*informal*), nick (*informal*), filch **5** need, call for, demand, require **6** attract, charm, fascinate, captivate, engage
ANT. **1** lose, leave **3** drop **4** give **6** repel

take after be like, resemble **take back** withdraw, retract, deny **take in 1** welcome, receive, accommodate, let in **2** deceive, fool, trick, cheat **3** understand, comprehend, grasp **4** include, embrace, encompass, comprise **take on 1** employ, hire, engage **2** accept, undertake, assume, face, tackle **take up 1** begin, start, commence **2** occupy, fill, use up, consume

tale *n.* story, narrative, account, anecdote

talent *n.* ability, gift, endowment, genius, faculty, capacity, cleverness, aptitude, forte
ANT. inability, incompetence, imbecility, stupidity

talk *v.* speak, express, utter, communicate, discuss, chat, consult

talk *n.* **1** chat, conversation, discussion, consultation, interview **2** speech, lecture, address, oration

tall *adj.* high, towering, lofty, elevated
ANT. low

tame *adj.* **1** domesticated, trained, house-trained, docile, broken, meek, obedient **2** dull, boring, uninteresting, flat, tedious
ANT. **1** wild **2** exciting

tame *v.* domesticate, train, house-train, break, discipline

tamper *v.* interfere, meddle, mess about, fiddle

tangible *adj.* perceptible, apprehensible, evident, manifest, clear, material, substantial, sensible, obvious, tactile, palpable
ANT. imperceptible, intangible, immaterial

tangle *n.* mass, knot, jumble, confusion, muddle

tangle *v.* twist, knot, entangle, twist, snarl, involve, confuse, muddle

tank *n.* cistern, basin, container, receptacle

tap *v.* rap, knock, hit, strike

tap *n.* rap, knock, hit, strike

tape *n.* strip, ribbon, belt, band

tape *v.* tie, stick, fasten, bind

taper *v.* narrow, thin, lessen, decrease, diminish

target *n.* aim, objection, object, goal

tariff *n.* rate, charge, price list, tax

tarnish *v.* spoil, blemish, stain, deface, disfigure, disgrace

tart *adj.* sharp, sour, acid, bitter, biting
ANT. sweet, gentle, mild

task *n*. job, duty, exercise, assignment, undertaking

taste *v*. sample, try, savour, savor (*N. Am.*), relish

taste *n*. **1** flavour, flavor (*N. Am.*), savour, savor (*N. Am.*), relish, tang, zest, aroma **2** sample, sip, morsel **3** discernment, refinement, appreciation, judgment, style, elegance

tasteful *adj*. elegant, dainty, attractive, exquisite, fine, delicate, artistic

taunt *v*. ridicule, mock, jeer, deride, insult, scoff, scorn

tax *n*. duty, levy, excise

tax *v*. **1** charge, exact, demand **2** burden, load, overload, strain, tire, test

teach *v*. instruct, tutor, school, train, educate, enlighten, drill, inculcate, inform, initiate, instil, instill (*N. Am.*), nurture, indoctrinate, discipline

teacher *n*. instructor, tutor, trainer, coach, educator, lecturer, professor

team *n*. group, gang, crew, club

tear *v*. divide, split, rip, rend

tear *n*. split, rip, rent

tease *v*. make fun of, upset, annoy, irritate, bother, pester

technique *n*. procedure, system, method, way, style, approach

tedious *adj*. boring, dull, monotonous, tiresome
ANT. interesting, exciting, amusing, charming, delightful, stirring

tedium *n*. boredom, dullness, monotony
ANT. interest, excitement

teem *v*. swarm, be full, overflow, abound, bristle, crawl

teeter *v*. rock, totter, sway, stagger

telephone *n*. phone, receiver, blower (*informal*)

telephone *v*. phone, ring, call, dial, buzz (*informal*)

tell *v*. **1** inform, notify, let know, communicate, make known, explain, declare, reveal, disclose, divulge **2** report, narrate, relate **3** order, command, instruct, direct **4** find out, discover, determine, distinguish, differentiate

tell off reprimand, rebuke, scold, chide, tick off (*informal*)

temper *n*. **1** mood, temperament, disposition, character **2** tantrum, anger, fury, rage

temper *v*. **1** soothe, moderate, soften, mitigate **2** harden, toughen, anneal

temperament *n*. nature, character, disposition, frame of mind, personality

temperate *adj*. mild, calm, moderate, controlled, restrained
ANT. extreme

temporary *adj*. short-lived, fleeting, passing, momentary, ephemeral
ANT. permanent, lasting

tempt *v*. lure, allure, attract, draw, persuade, invite, entice, seduce

tend *v*. **1** lean, incline, be disposed, point **2** look after, take care of, mind, protect, guard, defend

tendency *n*. trend, inclination, leaning, bent, bias, liability, proneness, disposition

tender *adj*. **1** kind, gentle, caring, sensitive **2** delicate, weak, fragile **3** sore, sensitive, painful, inflamed
ANT. **1** hard, pitiless, callous **2** tough, strong

tender *v*. offer, present, suggest, propose, put forward

tense *adj*. **1** strained, stretched, tight, stiff **2** nervous, strained, stressed, worked up, uptight (*informal*), wound up (*informal*)
ANT. **1** lax, loose **2** relaxed, calm, composed

tension *n*. tightness, strain, tautness, anxiety, nervousness, pressure, stress

tentative *adj*. provisional, trial, experimental
ANT. firm, fixed

term *n*. **1** expression, phrase, word, name **2** time, period, spell, stint

terminate *v*. end, finish, stop, complete, conclude, cease, discontinue
ANT. begin, start, commence

terrible *adj*. horrible, shocking, awful, dreadful, frightful, terrifying

territory *n*. region, area, province, district, country, land, zone

terror *n.* horror, shock, fear, dread, fright, alarm

terse *adj.* brief, short, concise, succinct, abrupt, curt
ANT. long, lengthy, wordy

test *v.* examine, assess, inspect, review, evaluate, analyse, analyze (*N. Am.*), toy

test *n.* examination, quiz, assessment, inspection, review, evaluation, analysis, trial

testify *v.* declare, state, assert, attest, affirm, witness

testimony *n.* affirmation, proof, evidence, witness, certification, deposition

texture *n.* surface, fabric, feel, pattern

thank *v.* be grateful for, appreciate, show one's gratitude

thankful *adj.* grateful, appreciative, indebted, obliged
ANT. ungrateful

thaw *v.* melt, dissolve, liquefy

theft *n.* robbery, stealing, burglary, fraud, embezzlement

theme *n.* point, topic, subject, argument

theoretical *adj.* abstract, hypothetical, impractical
ANT. proved, practical, real

theory *n.* explanation, hypothesis, speculation, guess, conjecture, assumption, plan, scheme

therefore *adv.* so, then, thus, consequently, hence

thick *adj.* **1** broad, wide, solid, deep, dense, close, compact **2** full, packed, crowded, abundant **3** foggy, muddy, turbid, misty **4** husky, guttural, hoarse **5** stupid, dense, slow, dim
ANT. **1** thin **2** empty **3** clear **4** clear **5** clever, intelligent

thief *n.* robber, burglar, criminal, housebreaker, crook (*informal*)

thin *adj.* **1** narrow, slim, slender, fine, lean, skinny **2** delicate, fine, sheer, light, weak, watery **3** scattered, sparse, scanty, poor
ANT. **1** fat **2** thick **3** abundant

thing *n.* **1** article, object, device, something **2** idea, point, detail, feature, aspect, particular **3** event, occurrence, activity, situation

think *v.* **1** believe, imagine, feel, suppose, maintain, hold, judge, regard, assume **2** meditate, deliberate, contemplate, think over, reflect, ponder

thirst *n.* desire, longing, craving, appetite

thorn *n.* prickle, barb, bramble, point

thorough *adj.* meticulous, careful, painstaking, scrupulous
ANT. careless, sloppy

thought *n.* **1** idea, belief, view, opinion, concept, notion, judgment, fancy **2** meditation, deliberation, contemplation, reflection, cogitation

thoughtful *adj.* **1** pensive, quiet, serious, absorbed, contemplative, meditative, lost in thought **2** considerate, kind, careful, attentive, friendly
ANT. **2** thoughtless, inconsiderate

thrash *v.* whip, flog, beat, lash

threat *n.* intimidation, menace, warning, danger, hazard

threaten *v.* **1** intimidate, bully, menace **2** loom, be near, impend

threshold *n.* **1** doorstep, doorway, sill, entrance **2** verge, brink, beginning, start, commencement, outset

thrift *n.* saving, economy, care, prudence, frugality
ANT. extravagance

thrifty *adj.* economical, saving, careful, sparing, frugal, provident, foresighted
ANT. wasteful, prodigal, lavish, spendthrift, extravagant

thrill *n.* excitement, stimulation, tingle, kick (*informal*)

thrill *v.* excite, stimulate, stir, move, touch, arouse

thrive *v.* succeed, prosper, flourish, bloom

throng *n.* crowd, mass, multitude, swarm, horde

throng *v.* crowd, press, swarm

throttle *v.* strangle, choke, asphyxiate

throw *v.* fling, hurl, toss, pitch, sling, cast, chuck (*informal*)

thrust *v.* drive, push, force, press, shove

thrust *n.* drive, force, pressure, impetus

thump *v.* hit, beat, whack, smack, wallop

thump *n*. whack, smack, wallop

thwart *v*. prevent, hinder, stop, frustrate, foil, check, obstruct

tick *n*. mark, check

ticket *n*. certificate, token, voucher, coupon, card, pass, permit

tickle *v*. **1** stroke, touch, rub **2** delight, amuse, entertain, please, gratify

tide *n*. flow, ebb, current, stream

tidy *adj*. neat, orderly, clean, organized, methodical, systematic

tie *v*. fasten, join, bind, secure, lash, connect, link

tie *n*. **1** connection, link, bond, fastening, joint **2** necktie, bow tie, cravat

tight *adj*. **1** stretched, taut, tense, secure, fixed, fast **2** sealed, impervious, airtight, watertight **3** mean, miserly, stingy, niggardly **4** drunk, intoxicated, inebriated, tipsy
ANT. **1** loose **3** generous **4** sober

tilt *v*. lean, slope, incline, list

tilt *n*. slope, inclination, angle

time *n*. **1** period, epoch, era, date, age, interval, season, term, while, succession, sequence, duration **2** beat, rhythm, tempo, pace

time *v*. measure, count, set, regulate, control, adjust

timely *adj*. opportune, seasonable, convenient, suitable, appropriate, auspicious
ANT. untimely, inopportune

timetable *n*. schedule, programme, program (*N. Am.*), calendar, agenda, plan

timid *adj*. shy, retiring, fearful, timorous, cowardly, afraid, fainthearted, shrinking, diffident, bashful
ANT. bold, confident, assertive

tinge *adj*. tint, colour, color (*N. Am.*), shade, hue, dye, stain, hint

tingle *v*. prickle, sting, itch, shiver

tinkle *v*. ring, jingle, chime

tint *n*. colour, color (*N. Am.*), tinge, hue, shade, dye, stain

tint *v*. colour, color (*N. Am.*), tinge, dye, stain

tiny *adj*. minute, small, little, wee, miniature, minuscule
ANT. enormous, immense, huge, vast

tip¹ *n*. point, end, top, head, peak

tip² *v*. incline, tilt, overturn, upset

tip³ *n*. **1** gratuity, gift, reward, perk **2** hint, advice, clue, suggestion

tire *v*. exhaust, wear out, weary, fatigue, jade
ANT. refresh, recreate, rest, relax, restore, invigorate

tired *adj*. exhausted, worn out, weary, fatigued
ANT. fresh, rested

title *n*. **1** heading, name, designation, caption, inscription **2** right, claim, deed, ownership, possession

token *n*. voucher, certificate, sign, sample

tolerable *adj*. **1** bearable, endurable, supportable **2** reasonable, passable, ordinary, mediocre, indifferent
ANT. **1** intolerable, unendurable, insufferable, unbearable, insupportable

tolerant *adj*. patient, liberal, broad-minded, open-minded, easy-going
ANT. bigoted, prejudiced, narrow-minded

tolerate *v*. put up with, bear, endure, suffer, accept, allow, permit

tomb *n*. grave, vault, sepulchre, sepulcher (*N. Am.*), crypt

tone *n*. **1** sound, noise, note, modulation **2** quality, style, manner, mood, spirit, drift

tonic *n*. boost, stimulant, refresher, pick-me-up

tool *n*. instrument, implement, utensil, appliance, apparatus, device, mechanism, machine

top *n*. **1** peak, head, summit, pinnacle, crown, zenith **2** lid, cap, cover
ANT. **1** base, bottom

top *v*. exceed, excel, surpass, transcend

topic *n*. subject, theme, matter, point, question, issue

topical *adj*. current, present, contemporary, modern

torment *n*. anguish, pain, misery, agony, torture, distress
ANT. pleasure, comfort, ease, delight

torment v. distress, torture, agonize, annoy, irritate, vex

torrent n. flood, deluge, inundation

torture v. abuse, torment, agonize, distress

torture n. pain, misery, agony, anguish

toss v. throw, hurl, cast, fling, pitch, chuck (*informal*)

total n. sum, quantity, whole, entirety

total adj. whole, entire, full, absolute, complete, undivided
ANT. partial, imperfect, incomplete

total v. add up, sum up, amount to

totter v. falter, stumble, stagger

touch v. 1 feel, handle, stroke, pat, fondle, caress 2 affect, move, stir, influence 3 mention, refer, cover

touch n. 1 feel, feeling, contact, pat, stroke 2 trace, suggestion, hint, tinge, smack 3 skill, ability, talent, style

touching adj. moving, stirring, tender, pitiful

tough adj. 1 strong, firm, hard, durable, resilient, stiff, rigid, inflexible
2 stubborn, obstinate, unfeeling, callous
3 difficult, awkward, tricky, baffling
ANT. 1 weak 2 yielding 3 easy

tour n. journey, trip, excursion, voyage

tour v. travel, visit

tourist n. holiday-maker, visitor, sightseer

tournament n. match, contest, competition

tow v. pull, draw, drag, haul, lug

tower n. steeple, spire, belfry, minaret

tower v. soar, rise, mount, overlook, dominate

town n. city, borough, municipality, metropolis

toy n. game, plaything

toy v. play, sport, trifle, dally

trace n. mark, remains, sign, hint, vestige, track, token, trail, footmark, footprint, footstep, impression, suggestion

trace v. follow, trail, track, hunt, pursue

track n. 1 path, road, way, trail
2 footprint, footmark, footstep, impression, mark

track v. follow, pursue, trail, hunt, stalk

tract n. area, region, district, territory

trade n. 1 commerce, business, traffic, dealing, transaction 2 profession, occupation, office, calling, job, employment

tradition n. custom, convention, practice, habit

traditional adj. customary, conventional, usual, time-honoured, time-honored (*N. Am.*), established, habitual

traffic n. vehicles, transport, travel, movement, flow

tragedy n. catastrophe, calamity, adversity, disaster, affliction

tragic adj. disastrous, catastrophic, calamitous, awful, terrible, appalling, sad, miserable, dire

trail n. 1 path, road, way, track
2 footprint, footmark, footstep, impression, mark

trail v. 1 follow, pursue, track, hunt
2 drag, pull, bring, haul, tow

train v. teach, instruct, coach, school, guide, educate, drill

trait n. characteristic, feature, mark, attribute, quality, peculiarity

traitor n. betrayer, turncoat, renegade, deceiver, apostate, deserter, mutineer
ANT. patriot, defender, supporter

tramp n. down-and-out, hobo, vagrant

tramp v. plod, stamp, stomp, trudge

trample v. tread, crush, squash, infringe

tranquil adj. quiet, calm, undisturbed, peaceful, unruffled, composed, collected, cool
ANT. agitated, excited, restless

transaction n. deal, bargain, business, settlement, negotiation

transcend v. exceed, go beyond, surpass, excel

transfer v. move, remove, convey, shift, transport

transfer n. move, shift, change

transform v. change, alter, modify, convert

transient *adj.* transitory, temporary, short, brief, passing, fleeting
ANT. permanent, perpetual, lasting, enduring, abiding

translate *v.* put into, render, paraphrase, interpret

translation *n.* rendering, version, interpretation, paraphrase

transmit *v.* send, communicate, broadcast, relay
ANT. receive

transparent *adj.* 1 clear, lucid, translucent, pellucid, diaphanous, crystalline, limpid 2 obvious, clear, evident, patent
ANT. 1 opaque 2 obscure

transport *v.* move, carry, convey, transfer, shift

transport *n.* movement, carriage, conveyance, transfer, transportation

trap *n.* snare, net, ambush, trick, pitfall

trap *v.* catch, ensnare

trauma *n.* shock, injury, wound, ordeal

travel *v.* go, pass, journey, voyage, move, wander, roam, traverse, migrate
ANT. stay, remain, settle

travel *n.* tour, journey, voyage, trip

treacherous *adj.* 1 traitorous, disloyal, unfaithful, false, deceitful 2 dangerous, risky, hazardous, perilous
ANT. 1 loyal 2 safe

treachery *n.* disloyalty, treason, betrayal, unfaithfulness, deceit
ANT. loyalty

tread *v.* step, pace, walk, stride, trample

treason *n.* betrayal, disloyalty, treachery, mutiny
ANT. loyalty, allegiance

treasure *n.* wealth, riches, money, jewels, cash, valuables, hoard, abundance, plenty

treasure *v.* value, cherish, prize, hold dear

treat *v.* 1 deal with, use, manage, handle 2 heal, cure, nurse, minister to, care for, look after, attend 3 pay for, entertain, indulge

treat *n.* gift, present, surprise, delight, pleasure

treatment *n.* 1 handling, management, use, dealing 2 remedy, cure, medication, care, nursing, therapy

treaty *n.* agreement, alliance, convention, contract, negotiation, compact

tremble *v.* shake, shudder, quiver, vibrate

tremendous *adj.* 1 immense, vast, huge, great, large, enormous 2 fantastic, wonderful, terrific, marvellous, extraordinary
ANT. 1 small 2 awful

trench *n.* channel, ditch, gully, furrow

trend *n.* tendency, inclination, development, style, fashion, vogue

trial *n.* 1 lawsuit, case, hearing, inquiry 2 experience, examination, experiment, proof, test, analysis, criterion, ordeal, assay 3 trouble, affliction, distress, grief, suffering, ordeal, tribulation, temptation

tribe *n.* clan, race, family, people

tribute *n.* acknowledgment, honour, honor (*N. Am.*), praise, recognition, acclaim

trick *n.* 1 deceit, deception, hoax, fraud, swindle, wile, stratagem 2 joke, practical joke, prank, caper

trick *v.* deceive, defraud, swindle, cheat, con (*informal*)

trickle *v.* drip, seep, dribble

tricky *adj.* difficult, awkward, delicate, knotty, thorny

trim *adj.* neat, tidy, orderly, clean, spruce
ANT. untidy

trim *v.* 1 cut, clip, shorten, neaten 2 decorate, adorn, beautify, garnish, embellish

trip¹ *n.* journey, excursion, voyage, tour, cruise

trip² *v.* stumble, fall

triumph *n.* 1 victory, conquest, success 2 celebration, jubilation, exultation, achievement, attainment
ANT. 1 defeat, failure 2 disappointment

triumph *v.* win, conquer, be successful
ANT. fail

triumphant *adj.* exultant, jubilant, elated, joyful
ANT. sad, depressed

trivial *adj.* small, minor, unimportant, insignificant, trifling
ANT. important, significant

trophy *n.* prize, award, reward, cup, shield, medal, badge, laurels

trouble *n.* 1 worry, concern, misfortune, distress, suffering, adversity, inconvenience, difficulty, problem 2 disturbance, unrest, strife, disorder 3 effort, exertion, care, bother, pains, inconvenience
ANT. 1 relief 2 order

trouble *v.* worry, concern, upset, distress, disturb, bother, inconvenience

troublesome *adj.* difficult, awkward, bothersome, tricky
ANT. easy, simple

true *adj.* 1 correct, right, exact, precise, accurate, actual, real, genuine, valid, authentic, factual 2 loyal, faithful, reliable, trustworthy
ANT. 1 incorrect, wrong, mistaken, false, fictitious 2 disloyal, unfaithful, unreliable, vacillating, fickle

trust *n.* confidence, belief, expectation, faith, hope, reliance
ANT. doubt, misgiving, distrust

trust *v.* have confidence in, depend on, rely on, expect, hope

truth *n.* fact, reality, accuracy, precision, faithfulness, conformity, exactness
ANT. falsehood, falsity, lie, untruth, fiction, deceit, mistake

truthful *adj.* honest, open, sincere, straightforward, direct, frank, candid
ANT. untruthful, deceitful

try *v.* 1 attempt, have a go, seek, endeavour, endeavor (*N. Am.*), undertake, strive, essay 2 test, assess, evaluate, prove

trying *adj.* difficult, awkward, troublesome, annoying, exasperating
ANT. easy

tube *n.* pipe, conduit, passage, channel

tuck *v.* fold, put (in), push, insert

tug *v.* yank, pull

tumble *v.* fall, drop, slip, stumble, trip

tumult *n.* disturbance, confusion, turmoil, noise, turbulence, disorder, hubbub, brawl, riot

ANT. peace, order, orderliness

tune *n.* melody, music, harmony, rhythm, song, air

tunnel *n.* hole, excavation, burrow, trench, passage

turbulent *adj.* stormy, agitated, rough, wild, violent, restless
ANT. calm, peaceful

turn *v.* 1 rotate, revolve, roll, shift, transfer, spin, gyrate, twirl, whirl 2 change, alter, modify, convert, adjust, adapt, transform 3 become, go, grow, get 4 go bad, go off, go sour, spoil, curdle

turn down 1 reject, refuse, decline 2 lower, reduce **turn out** dismiss, expel, evict **turn up** 1 arrive, appear 2 increase, raise

turn *n.* 1 revolution, cycle, rotation 2 change, alteration, conversion, adjustment 3 opportunity, chance, go (*informal*), stint, period, spell

tussle *v.* struggle, fight, scuffle, grab

tutor *n.* teacher, instructor, trainer, mentor

twilight *n.* dusk, nightfall, evening, gloaming
ANT. dawn

twin *n.* match, double, counterpart, equivalent

twinkle *v.* sparkle, glisten, glitter

twirl *v.* spin, turn, twist, whirl

twist *v.* 1 curl, twirl, spin, twine, entwine 2 sprain, wrench 3 falsify, misrepresent, garble, pervert

twist *n.* roll, twirl, spin, coil, curl

twitch *v.* jerk, shake, quiver, shudder

type *n.* 1 kind, sort, variety, order, class 2 sample, specimen, example, pattern, model, standard

typical *adj.* representative, usual, normal, regular, conventional, characteristic
ANT. atypical, abnormal

tyranny *n.* despotism, oppression, dictatorship
ANT. democracy

tyrant *n.* despot, dictator, autocrat

ugly *adj.* **1** unsightly, repulsive, hideous, frightful **2** unpleasant, nasty, disagreeable, horrible
ANT. 1 attractive, beautiful, handsome **2** pleasant

ultimate *adj.* final, last, eventual, conclusive, decisive, extreme

ultimately *adv.* finally, eventually, in the end

umpire *n.* judge, referee, arbitrator, moderator

umpire *v.* judge, referee, arbitrate

unaware *adj.* ignorant, uninformed, oblivious, unmindful
ANT. aware, informed

unbelievable *adj.* incredible, amazing, wonderful, marvellous, unthinkable, impossible

uncertain *adj.* unsure, doubtful, vague, indefinite, undecided, questionable
ANT. sure, certain

uncomfortable *adj.* uneasy, awkward, embarrassed, anxious, apprehensive, troubled
ANT. relaxed

unconscious *adj.* **1** out, asleep, insensible, comatose **2** unaware, oblivious **3** reflex, involuntary, automatic
ANT. 1 conscious **2** aware **3** intentional

uncover *v.* discover, expose, disclose, reveal, open, unearth, excavate
ANT. cover

underline *v.* emphasize, draw attention to

undermine *v.* subvert, make less strong, weaken, impair, ruin
ANT. strengthen

understand *v.* **1** comprehend, grasp, see, realize, perceive **2** gather, conclude, hear, learn
ANT. 1 misunderstand, misinterpret

understanding *n.* **1** grasp, comprehension, apprehension, realization, perception, intelligence **2** sympathy, kindness, consideration, compassion **3** agreement, arrangement, bargain

understanding *adj.* sympathetic, kind, considerate, compassionate, patient
ANT. unsympathetic, inconsiderate, cruel

undertake *v.* **1** try, attempt, set about, begin, start, tackle, embark on **2** promise, pledge, guarantee

undertaking *n.* **1** project, enterprise, venture, task, job, interest, affair, matter, concern, engagement, attempt, business, effort, endeavour, endeavor (*N. Am.*) **2** promise, pledge, vow, guarantee

underwrite *v.* guarantee, support, back, finance, fund

undoubted *adj.* sure, certain, indubitable, unquestionable
ANT. doubtful

uneasy *adj.* uncomfortable, awkward, embarrassed, anxious, worried, apprehensive

unemployed *adj.* out of work, jobless, workless, unoccupied

unexpected *adj.* sudden, surprising, startling, unforeseen
ANT. expected

unfold *v.* unfurl, unravel, develop, open

unfortunate *adj.* unlucky, ill-fated, cursed, hapless, miserable, wretched, inauspicious, regrettable, awkward, embarrassing
ANT. fortunate, lucky

unhappy *adj.* miserable, sad, despondent, downcast, dejected, disconsolate, wretched, melancholy
ANT. happy

uniform *n.* outfit, costume

uniform *adj.* 1 regular, constant, invariable, steady, even 2 unchanging, consistent
ANT. changing, variable, varying, diverse, irregular

union *n.* 1 trade union, association, society, guild 2 amalgamation, combination, merger, alliance, coalition, fusion, marriage
ANT. disconnection, separation, divorce, severance, dissociation

unique *adj.* sole, only, single, unmatched, unequalled, unparalleled, incomparable, singular, peculiar, exceptional, rare
ANT. common, universal, everyday, ordinary, familiar

unit *n.* entity, whole, item, machine, system, element, part, component, module

unite *v.* join, add, attach, link, combine, connect, fuse, associate, coalesce, incorporate, consolidate, amalgamate, blend, merge
ANT. separate, divide, disconnect, disintegrate

unity *n.* union, oneness, agreement, junction, uniformity, harmony, singleness, unanimity, concord, conjunction
ANT. separation, disconnection, division, disagreement

universal *adj.* worldwide, general, unlimited, all-reaching, comprehensive, exhaustive
ANT. local

universe *n.* cosmos, galaxy, creation, world

unknown *adj.* strange, unfamiliar, undiscovered, unexplored, unidentified, anonymous, obscure, hidden
ANT. known

unlike *adj.* different, dissimilar, distinct, disparate
ANT. like, similar

unlikely *adj.* improbable, implausible, doubtful, questionable
ANT. likely, probable

unlucky *adj.* unfortunate, unfavourable, unfavorable (*N. Am.*), unsuccessful, adverse, inauspicious, luckless, doomed, cursed
ANT. lucky, fortunate, successful

unnecessary *adj.* needless, uncalled-for, pointless, purposeless, superfluous, redundant
ANT. necessary, essential

unpleasant *adj.* disagreeable, nasty, offensive, annoying, obnoxious, irksome
ANT. pleasant, agreeable

unrest *n.* disquiet, trouble, turmoil, rebellion, discord, worry, anxiety, distress, tension

unusual *adj.* uncommon, unexpected, unfamiliar, remarkable, extraordinary, strange, odd, peculiar
ANT. common, usual, expected, familiar

unwieldy *adj.* cumbersome, awkward, unmanageable, bulky, heavy, large

uphold *v.* maintain, support, sustain, defend, back, endorse

upkeep *n.* maintenance, support, sustenance, subsistence

upright *adj.* 1 erect, perpendicular, vertical 2 honest, just, honourable, honorable (*N. Am.*), conscientious, virtuous, good, faithful, true, trustworthy
ANT. 1 inclined, slanted 2 unprincipled, dishonest, unscrupulous, corrupt, unconscientious

uprising *n.* rebellion, revolt, mutiny, revolution, insurrection

uproar *n.* tumult, disturbance, confusion, bustle, clamour, clamor (*N. Am.*), commotion, turmoil, racket, noise, din
ANT. peace, calm, quiet

upset *adj.* distressed, unhappy, troubled, anxious, worried, disturbed
ANT. calm, happy

upset *v.* 1 distress, trouble, worry, disturb, dismay 2 disrupt, mess up, spoil, confuse 3 overturn, capsize, tip over, topple

up-to-date *adj.* modern, contemporary, new, newest, current
ANT. old-fashioned

urban *adj.* town, city, civic, municipal, metropolitan
ANT. rural

urge *v.* 1 persuade, encourage, spur, provoke, induce 2 advise, recommend, beg, beseech, implore 3 push, force, drive
ANT. 1, 2 deter, dissuade, discourage 3 obstruct

urgent *adj*. pressing, immediate, important, serious, critical, emergency, imperative, momentous, grave
ANT. trivial, insignificant, unimportant

usage *n*. practice, procedure, use, mode, method, manners, behaviour, behavior (*N. Am.*), custom, wont, habit, fashion

use *v*. **1** utilize, employ, exercise, apply, handle, operate, make use of **2** spend, consume, expend, exhaust, use up, waste, squander

use *n*. **1** employment, application, practice, usage, custom, manner, habit **2** advantage, benefit, usefulness, utility, call, need, service, profit, avail

useful *adj*. helpful, good, convenient, valuable, available, advantageous, profitable, serviceable, beneficial, fruitful, suitable, effective, adapted
ANT. useless, profitless, unprofitable, fruitless, unavailing

useless *adj*. vain, futile, profitless, unprofitable, fruitless, ineffective, abortive, unavailing
ANT. useful, helpful, profitable, beneficial

usher *v*. guide, escort, show, conduct

usual *adj*. familiar, frequent, ordinary, everyday, general, normal, regular, prevalent, accustomed, common, customary, habitual, wonted, prevailing, public
ANT. unusual, exceptional, infrequent, extraordinary, strange, uncommon, singular, rare

usually *adv*. generally, normally, commonly, mainly, mostly, in general, as a rule

usurp *v*. arrogate, assume, appropriate, seize, lay hold of, take over

utensil *n*. tool, instrument, implement, appliance, device

utility *n*. profit, expediency, use, usefulness avail, benefit, advantage, service, usableness
ANT. futility, inadequacy, inexpediency, uselessness

utmost *adj*. greatest, furthest, farthest, extreme, remotest, last, most distant, uttermost, greatest

utter[1] *v*. express, voice, articulate, pronounce, say, speak

utter[2] *adj*. absolute, total, complete, thorough, unqualified, out and out

vacant *adj.* **1** empty, void, free, unoccupied, unfilled **2** expressionless, blank, thoughtless, vapid
ANT. **1** occupied, in use, busy

vacation *n.* holiday, rest, break, time off

vaccinate *v.* inoculate, protect, immunize

vague *adj.* indefinite, uncertain, indistinct, ambiguous
ANT. determined, specific, definite, distinct, settled, clear, fixed

vain *adj.* **1** futile, useless, idle, hollow, useless, trivial, unimportant, abortive **2** proud, conceited, arrogant, boastful, big-headed
ANT. **1** fruitful **2** modest

valiant *adj.* brave, bold, courageous, intrepid, valorous, heroic, gallant, chivalrous, daring, dauntless, fearless, redoubtable, undaunted, stout-hearted
ANT. timid, cowardly, fearful, timorous

valid *adj.* **1** sensible, reasonable, logical, sound, convincing, powerful, well-founded **2** genuine, real, authentic, lawful, legal

valley *n.* vale, glen, dale, dell

valuable *adj.* **1** beneficial, important, worthy **2** costly, expensive, precious, high-priced
ANT. **1** worthless **2** cheap

value *n.* **1** worth, merit, utility, desirability, importance, signification, power, gain **2** price, cost, valuation, equivalent

value *v.* **1** appreciate, prize, treasure, esteem, respect, regard **2** evaluate, be worth, rate, appraise, estimate

vanish *v.* disappear, fade, pass away, dissolve, melt away
ANT. appear, approach, arise

vanity *n.* pride, conceit, egoism, self-sufficiency, unreality, worthlessness, emptiness, hollowness, triviality, futility, insubstantiality, falsity, show, ostentation
ANT. modesty, humility, self-distrust

vanquish *v.* conquer, overcome, subdue, defeat, subjugate, overthrow, foil, discomfit, quell
ANT. yield, fail

vapid *adj.* dead, spiritless, flat, tasteless, stale, tame, insipid, dull, unanimated
ANT. pungent

vapour, vapor (*N. Am.*) *n.* fog, mist, fume, steam, reek, exhalation, smoke

variable *adj.* changeable, fickle, inconstant, mutable, shifting, unsteady, vacillating, wavering, fluctuating, versatile, capricious
ANT. unchanging, immutable, constant, firm, unwavering, steady, invariable, unalterable

variance *n.* variation, dissension, disagreement, discord, difference, discrepancy, estrangement, alteration, strife
ANT. harmony, agreement, reconciliation

variation *n.* modification, alteration, change, diversity, vicissitude, variety, deviation, mutation, departure, difference, discrepancy
ANT. fixity, harmony, uniformity

variegated *adj.* streaked, dappled, parti-coloured, diversified, varied, chequered, checkered (*N. Am.*), mottled

variety *n.* diversity, change, difference, assortment, multifariousness, medley, miscellany, multiplicity, class, kind, sort

various *adj.* different, diverse, several, manifold, sundry, diversified

varnish *v.* gloss, lacquer, glaze over, cover, embellish

vary *v.* alter, change, modify, alternate, diversify, variegate, differ, deviate, depart, be diverse, transform, metamorphose
ANT. conform, stereotype, harmonize

vast *adj.* huge, immense, great, mighty, spacious, transcendent, measureless, boundless, colossal, enormous, stupendous, prodigious, gigantic, monstrous, remarkable, extraordinary
ANT. small, limited, moderate, narrow

vault[1] *v.* jump, spring, bound, leap, tumble, turn

vault[2] *n.* **1** grave, tomb, sepulchre, sepulcher (*N. Am.*) **2** strongroom, safe

vaunt *v.* boast, brag, display, show off, flourish, parade
ANT. hide, conceal

veer *v.* shift, turn, change, vacillate
ANT. stay, persist, remain

vegetate *v.* sprout, grow, germinate
ANT. decay, fade

vehemence *n.* impetuosity, violence, fury, frenzy, ardour, ardor (*N. Am.*), fervour, fervor (*N. Am.*), fervency, warmth, zeal, enthusiasm, passion, force, intensity
ANT. passivity, inertia, indifference, unconcern, apathy, inattention

vehement *adj.* passionate, raging, hot, ardent, fervid, burning, eager, violent, impetuous, furious, urgent, mighty, forcible, powerful, enthusiastic
ANT. impassive, indifferent, weak, feeble, mild, controlled, subdued, cold, passionless

vehicle *n.* **1** transport, conveyance, car, lorry, van **2** means, agency, medium, instrument

veil *n.* screen, cloak, cover, shroud, mask

veil *v.* cover, hide, conceal, screen, mask, shroud, envelop
ANT. unveil, expose, disclose, strip, denude, make manifest

velocity *n.* rapidity, speed, swiftness, fleetness
ANT. inactivity

vengeance *n.* revenge, retaliation, punishment, retribution
ANT. forgiveness, pardon, indulgence, amnesty, remission, absolution

venom *n.* **1** virus, poison **2** spite, malice, malignity, hate, ill will, maliciousness, rancour, rancor (*N. Am.*), grudge, bitterness, acrimony
ANT. **1** medicine, remedy **2** benevolence, kindness, good will

venomous *adj.* **1** poisonous, malignant, noxious **2** spiteful, malicious, hateful, bitter
ANT. **1** remedial **2** kind, compassionate, genial

vent *v.* discharge, release, let out, express, utter

vent *n.* outlet, escape, emission, discharge, opening, hole, passage

ventilate *v.* freshen, air, refresh, aerate, cool

venture *n.* adventure, enterprise, undertaking, experiment, chance, risk, hazard, speculation, accident, contingency

venture *v.* dare, adventure, hazard, chance, risk, jeopardize, imperil

veracity *n.* honesty, truthfulness, reality, candour, candor (*N. Am.*), truth, ingenuousness, frankness
ANT. deception, duplicity, falsehood

verbal *adj.* spoken, oral, vocal, unwritten, unrecorded
ANT. written, recorded, documentary

verbose *adj.* wordy, long-winded, diffuse, prosy, tedious, prolix
ANT. brief, terse, concise, succinct, curt, laconic

verdict *n.* decision, judgment, opinion, pronouncement, finding, sentence

verge *n.* edge, margin, border, limit, boundary, rim, brim, confine
ANT. centre, center (*N. Am.*), midst, heart

verge *v.* tend, incline, slope, lean, border, approach, approximate

verify *v.* prove, confirm, authenticate, affirm, correct, establish, corroborate, attest, substantiate
ANT. misrepresent, subvert

veritable *adj.* actual, real, genuine, true, positive, absolute

versatile *adj.* adaptable, variable, many-sided, flexible

versed *adj.* experienced, familiar, studied, practised, practiced (*N. Am.*), skilled, acquainted, conversant, proficient
ANT. unskilled, ignorant, untaught, uninitiated

version *n.* account, description, translation, rendering, interpretation, reading

vertical *adj.* perpendicular, upright
ANT. slanting, sloping

very *adj.* extremely, considerably, greatly, highly, really, remarkably, exceedingly

vessel *n.* 1 ship, boat, craft 2 container, receptacle

vestige *n.* trace, mark, footstep, track, sign, remains, trail, token, remnant, record

veto *v.* prohibit, forbid, deny
ANT. pass, approve, assent to

vex *v.* annoy, irritate, worry, distress, trouble, perplex, bother, fret, offend, provoke, affront, disturb, agitate, disquiet, afflict, tease, weary
ANT. please, soothe, quiet, allay

vibrate *v.* tremble, shake, swing, oscillate, fluctuate, quiver, waver, undulate, quake
ANT. rest, be still

vice¹ *n.* evil, corruption, defect, error, blemish, imperfection, immorality, depravity, wickedness, crime, sin, fault, iniquity
ANT. virtue, goodness, perfection, righteousness

vice² *adj.* deputy, substitute, assistant

vicinity *n.* neighbourhood, neighborhood (*N. Am.*), nearness, proximity, propinquity
ANT. distance, remoteness

vicious *adj.* 1 wicked, evil, corrupt, depraved 2 cruel, dangerous, savage, brutal
ANT. 1 virtuous, pure, good 2 kind

victim *n.* sufferer, prey, sacrifice, martyr, scapegoat, dupe, target

victimize *v.* mistreat, discriminate against, bully, pick on, exploit, fool, cheat, swindle

victorious *adj.* conquering, triumphant, winning, successful, boastful, vanquishing, subduing, prevailing, overcoming, mastering, subjugating
ANT. defeated, humiliated, beaten

victory *n.* success, conquest, supremacy, triumph, achievement, mastery
ANT. defeat, disaster, overthrow, retreat, rout, failure

view *n.* 1 sight, vision, look, survey, inspection 2 scene, prospect, vista, perspective 3 opinion, thought, belief, conception, judgment 4 object, aim purpose, design

view *v.* see, look at, survey, examine, inspect, explore, consider, contemplate, regard, scan, witness, study, reflect upon, behold
ANT. ignore, overlook, neglect, miss

viewpoint *n.* point of view, belief, opinion, thought, attitude, standpoint

vigilant *adj.* alert, watchful, awake, careful, on the alert, on the lookout, wary, wakeful, wide-awake, sleepless, cautious, circumspect
ANT. negligent, thoughtless, unwary, oblivious, drowsy, inattentive, careless

vigorous *adj.* forcible, energetic, powerful, spirited, lively, strong, lusty, robust
ANT. feeble, weak, impotent, incapacitated, inactive, debilitated, powerless, enervated

vile *adj.* low, base, worthless, objectionable, disgusting, revolting, offensive, despicable, mean, depraved, impure, sinful, wicked, bad, dishonourable, dishonorable (*N. Am.*), ignoble, degraded sordid, infamous, low-minded
ANT. noble, exalted, pleasing

villain *n.* scoundrel, rascal, scamp, ruffian, rogue, brute, knave

vindicate *v.* defend, justify, prove, uphold, claim, substantiate, support, advocate, assert, protest, pronounce, declare

vindictive *adj.* revengeful, unforgiving, implacable, spiteful, unrelenting, malicious
ANT. forgiving, generous, merciful, long-suffering, magnanimous

violate *v.* break, infringe, abuse, transgress, interrupt, dishonour, dishonor (*N. Am.*), outrage, profane
ANT. respect, honour, honor (*N. Am.*)

violent *adj.* **1** powerful, strong, forceful, forcible, intense, passionate **2** savage, brutal, cruel, fierce, wild
ANT. **1** mild, gentle **2** kind, gentle

virile *adj.* masculine, manly, strong, robust, vigorous

virtual *adj.* potential, possible, implicit, indirect
ANT. stated, direct, definite, expressed, explicit

virtually *adv.* almost, nearly, practically, all but, in effect, to all intents and purposes

virtue *n.* **1** goodness, morality, uprightness, rectitude, probity, righteousness, integrity, purity, virginity, chastity, honour, honor (*N. Am.*), worthiness, honesty, truth, duty, virtuousness, faithfulness, justice **2** value, merit, excellence, advantage, benefit, worth
ANT. **1** badness, corruption, impurity, depravity, wickedness, dishonesty **2** disadvantage

virulent *adj.* bitter, malevolent, acrimonious, hostile
ANT. mild, bland

visible *adj.* perceptible, noticeable, apparent, open, conspicuous, obvious, manifest, evident, clear, plain, observable, palpable, discernible
ANT. invisible, unseen, imperceptible, concealed, microscopic, indiscernible

vision *n.* **1** sight, eyesight **2** apparition, creation, phantom, fancy, fantasy, spectre, specter (*N. Am.*), appearance, chimera, illusion **3** foresight, farsightedness, wisdom, prudence, anticipation

visionary *n.* idealist, romantic, dreamer, prophet

visit *v.* call on, drop in, look in on

visit *n.* call, stop, stay

visitor *n.* guest, caller, newcomer

vital *adj.* **1** important, necessary, essential, critical, crucial, key, indispensable, paramount **2** living, alive, animate, mortal
ANT. **1** unimportant, immaterial **2** dead, lifeless

vitiate *v.* impair, contaminate, annul, spoil, void, destroy, injure, taint, invalidate

vivacious *adj.* brisk, lively, spirited, cheerful, merry, sprightly, animated, sportive, light-hearted
ANT. inanimate, dead, lifeless, spiritless, heavy, inert

vivid *adj.* clear, lucid, striking, active, lively, quick, fresh, intense, animated, bright, strong, spirited, sprightly, brilliant, lustrous, radiant, glowing, sunny
ANT. dull, opaque, lurid, obscure, cloudy, dark, colourless, colorless (*N. Am.*), dim, pale, wan, dusky

vocal *adj.* **1** verbal, spoken, oral, uttered **2** outspoken, frank, direct, forthright

vocation *n.* business, profession, employment, calling, occupation, trade, career, function, mission, office

vogue *n.* style, custom, way, use, fashion, practice, usage, mode

voice *n.* sound, utterance, language, words, speech, judgment, expression
ANT. silence, muteness, inarticulation

void *adj.* **1** invalid, meaningless, useless, worthless, vain, unreal, imaginary, unsubstantial **2** empty, vacant, unoccupied, unused, unfilled, devoid, wanting, ineffectual, destitute, lacking
ANT. **1** valid, operative, good **2** occupied, filled

volatile *adj.* changeable, fickle, inconstant, flighty, whimsical, capricious, unstable, unsteady, reckless
ANT. fixed, steady, established, determined, solid, settled

volition *n.* will, choice, preference, determination, purpose, discretion, free will, election, deliberation
ANT. necessity, force, predestination, fate, coercion, foreordination

volume *n.* **1** book, work, tome **2** dimension, mass, capacity, bulk, size, quantity, amount

voluntary *adj.* spontaneous, willing, free, impulsive, unconstrained, deliberate, intentional, optional, gratuitous, by choice, discretionary
ANT. coerced, forced, compelled, involuntary, compulsory, necessitated, constrained

volunteer *v.* offer, act freely, proffer, tender, present, bestow

voluptuous *adj.* sensual, sensuous, luxurious, pleasurable, self-indulgent, extravagant
ANT. self-sacrificing, abstinent, ascetic, self-denying, austere

vomit *v.* be sick, bring up, spew, puke (*informal*), throw up (*informal*)

voracious *adj.* hungry, greedy, rapacious, eager, ravenous, gluttonous

vote *n.* 1 ballot, election, referendum, choice 2 suffrage, franchise, say

vote *v.* choose, elect, appoint, opt for, go for

vouch *v.* promise, warrant, guarantee, declare, affirm, attest, support, assure

voucher *n.* token, certificate, receipt, coupon, document

vow *v.* promise, pledge, swear, assert, declare

vow *n.* promise, pledge, oath, word

voyage *n.* trip, journey, cruise, tour

vulgar *adj.* crude, rude, unrefined, boorish, low, coarse, base, bad-mannered
ANT. refined, polite, cultivated

vulnerable *adj.* defenceless, defenseless (*N. Am.*)susceptible, weak, tender, exposed, assailable, liable, subject
ANT. impregnable, unassailable, unexposed, defended

wad *n.* pack, bundle, mass, ball

waft *v.* drift, float, puff

wage *v.* carry out, conduct, make, pursue

wager *v.* bet, gamble

wager *n.* bet, stake, gamble

wages *n. pl.* salary, earnings, reward, emolument, stipend, allowance, remuneration, pay, compensation

wail *v.* cry, weep, mourn, lament

wait *v.* 1 stay, delay, stop, abide, remain, linger, rest, tarry 2 expect, look for, watch, await
ANT. 1 hurry, speed

waiter *n.* steward, stewardess, attendant, servant, maid

waive *v.* relinquish, forbear, refuse, forgo, throw away, cast off, reject, desert, abandon, remit, quit, cancel, drop, surrender, renounce
ANT. enforce, claim

wake *v.* awaken, waken, rouse, arouse, stir, excite, reanimate, revive
ANT. sleep, soothe, hush, tranquillize

walk *v.* step, stride, march, stalk, tramp, plod, trudge, tread, stroll, amble, saunter, move on foot, proceed
ANT. stop, stand still, drive

wall *n.* divider, fence, screen, partition

wallow *v.* grovel, revel, delight, splash, roll

wan *adj.* pale, sickly, languid, pallid, ashen, colourless, colorless (*N. Am.*), cadaverous, bloodless
ANT. bright, rosy

wander *v.* 1 roam, rove, ramble, stroll, range, turn aside 2 deviate, diverge, err, go astray, veer, swerve, digress
ANT. 1 remain, stay, settle, rest, stop

wane *v.* decrease, decline, fail, sink, fade, ebb, pine, droop, deteriorate, contract, recede
ANT. wax, increase, grow, improve, expand, develop, advance

want *v.* desire, like, wish, crave, need, require

want *n.* destitution, poverty, need, lack, deficiency, shortness, insufficiency, scantiness, defect, failure, dearth, indigence, absence, scarcity
ANT. sufficiency, provision, abundance, adequacy

war *n.* conflict, strife, battle, combat, hostilities

war *v.* fight, battle, combat, contend

ward *n.* 1 division, district 2 child, foster child, dependant, orphan, minor 3 watch, guardianship, guard, defence, defense (*N. Am.*), protection, custody

warden *n.* keeper, guard, guardian, custodian, protector, steward

warehouse *n.* depository, store, storehouse, depot

warfare *n.* hostilities, war, contest, struggle, campaign, battle, skirmish, engagement, strife, discord
ANT. peace, truce, armistice, reconciliation

warlike *adj.* belligerent, inimical, unfriendly, military, martial, hostile, soldierly, bellicose
ANT. peaceful, friendly, amicable

warm *adj.* 1 heated, lukewarm, hot 2 sunny, mild, genial, pleasant, hot 3 ardent, zealous, fervent, earnest, eager, enthusiastic, hearty 4 friendly, kind, cordial, sympathetic, tender, affable, amicable
ANT. 1 cool, cold 2 cold 3 unconcerned, frigid, apathetic, chilling 4 unkind, unfriendly

warmth *n.* 1 heat, intensity, glow 2 friendliness, cordiality, enthusiasm, ardour, ardor (*N. Am.*), zeal, interest
ANT. 1 coldness, coolness 2 unfriendliness, indifference

warn *v.* make aware, notify, admonish, caution, advise, mention to, inform, dissuade, deter, alarm
ANT. encourage, persuade, hearten

warning *n.* caution, admonition, advice, intimation

warrant *n.* guarantee, security, authorization, sanction, pledge, voucher

warrant *v.* secure, guarantee, support, justify, sanction, assure, declare, empower, approve, authorize
ANT. invalidate, nullify, cancel, make void

warrior *n.* soldier, fighter, combatant

wary *adj.* watchful, cautious, vigilant, prudent, discreet, heedful, thoughtful, careful, guarded, circumspect, chary
ANT. unsuspecting, unwary, incautious, negligent, heedless, inattentive

wash *v.* clean, cleanse, wet, scrub, rub, moisten, bathe, rinse
ANT. dirty, soil, stain, pollute, defile, contaminate

waste *v.* **1** squander, dissipate, lavish, misspend **2** wear away, impair, use up, consume, spend, dwindle, damage, injure, decay, ruin, devastate, destroy
ANT. **1** economize, hoard, accumulate, treasure, husband, protect **2** restore, renovate, repair, renew

waste *n.* **1** squandering, devastation, loss, decrease, consumption, expenditure, extravagance, prodigality, diminution, dissipation, destruction, havoc, desolation, ravage **2** rubbish, refuse, trash, garbage, effluent
ANT. **1** saving, accumulation, frugality, economy, thrift, hoard, store

wasteful *adj.* destructive, ruinous, lavish, prodigal, profuse, extravagant, careless
ANT. careful, economical, frugal, protective

watch *v.* **1** look at, view, see, observe, notice **2** take care of, look after, mind, guard, tend, protect **3** pay attention, keep watch, keep guard, look out

watchful *adj.* vigilant, awake, attentive, wary, cautious, observant, circumspect, wakeful, heedful
ANT. unobservant, careless, heedless, inattentive, unwary, incautious, remiss

wave *v.* move, show, shake, flap, gesture, signal, flourish, brandish

wave *n.* ripple, undulation, breaker, roller, swell, surge

waver *v.* reel, totter, vacillate, fluctuate, hesitate, deliberate, be undetermined, alternate, be perplexed
ANT. decide, choose, settle, determine, be steadfast

way *n.* **1** manner, method, mode, fashion, approach, technique, style, means, scheme, device, plan, practice, habit, custom, wont **2** path, road, street, route, track, alley, avenue, channel, course, highway, pathway, lane, passage, thoroughfare

wayward *adj.* disobedient, headstrong, perverse, wilful, obstinate, stubborn, unruly, contrary, froward
ANT. amenable, docile, manageable, compliant, obedient

weak *adj.* **1** feeble, infirm, delicate, fragile, sickly, exhausted, unable, deficient, pliant, frail, debilitated, unsound, invalid, fragile, delicate, tender **2** irresolute, undecided, wavering **3** faint, low, muffled, dim, imperceptible **4** insipid, tasteless, thin, diluted, watery
ANT. **1** strong, sturdy, vigorous, hardy, robust, powerful **2** decided, resolute **3** strong, bold

weaken *v.* depress, impair, reduce, lower, sap, dilute, attenuate, debilitate, enfeeble, enervate
ANT. strengthen, empower, invigorate, confirm, corroborate, substantiate

wealth *n.* riches, affluence, prosperity, opulence, abundance, plenty, fortune, treasure, money, funds, cash, property, estate
ANT. poverty, scarcity, indigence, lack, want, need

wealthy *adj.* rich, prosperous, affluent, well-to-do, opulent, moneyed, loaded (*informal*)

wear *v.* be dressed in, have on, don

weary *adj.* tired, exhausted, fatigued, jaded, spent, dead beat (*informal*), tired out

weave *v.* entwine, plait, braid, interlace, compose, fabricate
ANT. disentangle, unravel, untwist, untwine

wed *v.* marry, espouse, unite
ANT. divorce, separate

wedding *n.* marriage, nuptials, espousal
ANT. divorce, celibacy

weep *v.* cry, sob, bewail, bemoan, shed tears, lament, complain
ANT. laugh, smile

weigh *v.* **1** be heavy, measure **2** burden, oppress, weigh down **3** consider, reflect, ponder, deliberate

weight *n.* **1** heaviness, pressure, burden, ponderousness, gravity, load, power **2** importance, significance, influence, consequence, moment, efficacy, impressiveness
ANT. **1** lightness **2** insignificance, triviality

weighty *adj.* important, serious, significant, heavy, ponderous, burdensome, onerous
ANT. slight, unimportant, easy, light, frivolous

weird *adj.* odd, strange, peculiar, unnatural, eerie, uncanny
ANT. ordinary, normal

welcome *n.* greeting, salutation, reception
ANT. farewell, adieu, goodbye, leave-taking

welcome *v.* greet, receive, meet, salute, hail

welcome *adj.* pleasant, pleasing, acceptable, agreeable, gratifying, free
ANT. unwelcome, unpleasant, disagreeable, unacceptable

welfare *n.* prosperity, happiness, well-being, good, advantage, benefit, profit, enjoyment, success
ANT. adversity, misfortune, failure, ill luck, unhappiness

well *adj.* healthy, fit, hale, sound
ANT. ill, unwell, poorly, diseased, sickly

well *adv.* **1** satisfactorily, adequately, fully, thoroughly, abundantly, rightly, skilfully, skillfully (*N. Am.*) **2** personally, closely, intimately
ANT. **1** imperfectly, improperly, badly **2** superficially

well-known *adj.* famous, celebrated, renowned, recognized, distinguished, eminent, noted
ANT. unknown, obscure

wet *adj.* damp, moist, drenched, soaked, rainy, humid
ANT. dry, parched

wet *v.* dampen, moisten, drench, soak
ANT. dry

wharf *n.* dock, pier, quay, jetty

wheedle *v.* cajole, flatter, entice, coax, inveigle, fawn upon

whimper *v.* cry, sob, moan, complain, whine

whimsical *adj.* capricious, fanciful, queer, strange, freakish, quaint, fantastic
ANT. staid, serious, sober, matter-of-fact, steady, sedate

whine *v.* cry, whimper, moan, complain, grumble, whinge (*informal*)

whip *v.* **1** beat, thrash, flog, scourge **2** stir, provoke, drive

whip *n.* scourge, lash, birch, cane

whirl *v.* spin, twirl, turn, rotate, revolve, reel, pivot

whisper *v.* speak softly, sigh, murmur, mumble, breathe

whisper *n.* undertone, sigh, murmur

whistle *v.* warble, trill, pipe, signal

whistle *n.* warbling, trill, piping

white *adj.* snowy, pale, pallid, unblemished, pure, grey, gray (*N. Am.*), hoary
ANT. black, dark, coal-like, dismal, gloomy, sullen, foreboding, impure, sullied

whole *adj.* all, total, complete, entire, undivided, unbroken, undamaged, unimpaired, integral, sound, perfect, faultless, strong, well, healthy
ANT. partial, imperfect, unsound, ill, divided

wholesome *adj.* healthy, nourishing, nutritious, salubrious, salutary, strengthening, invigorating, beneficial, good, fresh, sound
ANT. detrimental, hurtful, pernicious, noxious

wholly *adv.* entirely, completely, perfectly, totally, fully, altogether, utterly
ANT. partially, imperfectly, incompletely, separately, part

wicked *adj.* bad, evil, unjust, sinful, criminal, guilty, immoral, ungodly, profane, unrighteous, atrocious, unholy, vicious, heinous, iniquitous, depraved, unprincipled, irreverent, vile, outrageous, monstrous, villainous
ANT. good, righteous, just, godly, virtuous, fair, honorable, upright

wide *adj.* broad, spacious, vast, extensive, comprehensive, liberal, distant, far, ample, expanded
ANT. narrow, contracted, confined, cramped, constricted, limited

wield *v.* flourish, brandish, manipulate, handle, control

wild *adj.* **1** untamed, uncultivated, undomesticated, ferocious **2** savage, uncivilized, primitive **3** violent, turbulent, furious, stormy, rough **4** disorderly, crazy, ungoverned, unruly, uncontrolled, unrestrained **5** foolish, reckless, rash, crazy, silly, impromptu
ANT. **1** tame, domesticated, cultivated **2** civilized **3** calm **4** polite, gentle, refined **5** rational, reasonable, sensible

wilful, willful (*N. Am.*) *adj.* obstinate, perverse, stubborn, refractory, self-willed, headstrong, wayward
ANT. concessive, compliant, amenable, obedient, docile, manageable

will *v.* wish, desire, incline to have, choose, decide, determine, decree

will *n.* **1** resolution, decision, self-reliance, force, inclination, pleasure, disposition **2** choice, determination, preference, volition, decree, desire, command, purpose, control, order, direction
ANT. **1** indecision, vacillation, indifference

willing *adj.* enthusiastic, eager, prepared, inclined, ready, complying, disposed, minded, desirous
ANT. unwilling, loath, disinclined, reluctant, averse, backward

wilt *v.* droop, sag, languish, wither, shrivel

win *v.* gain, get, obtain, earn, acquire, achieve, succeed, accomplish, be victorious, conquer
ANT. lose, fail, miss, forfeit, be deprived

wind[1] *n.* breeze, air, gust, puff, flurry, gale, hurricane

wind[2] *v.* coil, twine, wreathe, twist, turn, weave, enfold, encircle
ANT. straighten, unravel, untwist

winding *adj.* twisting, circuitous, bending, curving, meandering, serpentine, sinuous
ANT. straight, direct, undeviating, unswerving

wing *n.* branch, arm, section, extension, faction

wink *v.* blink, twinkle, flash

winsome *adj.* charming, attractive, alluring, pleasing, bewitching, fascinating, delightful, lovely, captivating, prepossessing, enchanting
ANT. repulsive, unpleasant, repellent, disagreeable, offensive, repugnant, revolting, disgusting

wipe *v.* clean, rub, sponge, mop, brush, dust

wipe out destroy, devastate, remove, eradicate

wire *n.* cable, filament, line

wisdom *n.* judgment, prudence, reason, understanding, sense, skill, sagacity, attainment, discernment, depth, discretion, foresight, learning, reasonableness, knowledge, insight, judiciousness, erudition, enlightenment
ANT. folly, imbecility, stupidity, foolishness, idiocy, imprudence, indiscretion, misjudgment, silliness, senselessness

wise *adj.* knowing, erudite, wary, learned, sagacious, sage, sensible, deep, discerning, profound, judicious, discreet, skilled, intelligent, rational
ANT. senseless, idiotic, irrational, nonsensical, imprudent, irrational, indiscreet

wish *v.* **1** desire, want, long for, hanker after **2** ask, bid
ANT. **1** dislike, hate

wit *n*. **1** humour, humor (*N. Am.*), satire, sarcasm, irony, burlesque, facetiousness, drollery, waggery, jocularity, sparkle, repartee, joke, playfulness, fun, witticism, pleasantry, banter, jest **2** intellect, mind, understanding, sense, intelligence **3** comic, comedian, humorist, wag

witch *n*. sorcerer, sorceress, enchanter, enchantress, magician, necromancer

witchcraft *n*. sorcery, enchantment, magic, necromancy, incantation, charm, spell

withdraw *v*. take back, draw back, remove, recede, depart, recall, retire
ANT. advance, enter, give

withdrawn *adj*. introverted, shy, reserved, retiring, quiet
ANT. extrovert, outgoing

wither *v*. shrivel, shrink, droop, wilt, fade, weaken
ANT. flourish, thrive, grow

withhold *v*. hold back, keep back, restrain, impede, hamper, retain, suppress, check, rein in, inhibit
ANT. release, let go, give

withstand *v*. oppose, resist, confront, thwart, combat, prevent, contradict
ANT. concede, grant, submit, yield, acquiesce

witness *n*. **1** eye-witness, observer, deponent, corroborator, spectator, onlooker **2** attestation, testimony, evidence, proof

witty *adj*. amusing, humorous, satirical, acute, sharp, smart, facetious, keen, ironical
ANT. dull, stupid, serious, tedious

wizard *n*. sorcerer, enchanter, magician, necromancer

wobble *v*. shake, sway, reel, rock, tremble, quake

woe *n*. grief, sorrow, misery, sadness, unhappiness, disconsolateness, tribulation, melancholy, agony, depression
ANT. joy, delight, pleasure, enjoyment, bliss

woman *n*. female, lady, girl

womanhood *n*. **1** maturity, femininity **2** women, womankind

wonder *v*. **1** ask oneself, question, think about, ponder, be curious **2** marvel, be surprised, be amazed, be astonished

wonder *n*. **1** surprise, astonishment, admiration, amazement, awe, bewilderment, curiosity **2** miracle, prodigy, marvel, portent, phenomenon, sight, rarity, spectacle

wonderful *adj*. amazing, astonishing, marvellous, marvelous (*N. Am.*), surprising, extraordinary, remarkable, strange, incredible, startling, awesome
ANT. ordinary, familiar, expected, usual

woo *v*. court, pursue

wood *n*. forest, grove, thicket, spinney, copse, woodland

word *n*. **1** term, expression, utterance, phrase **2** account, message, statement, declaration, affirmation, promise **3** speech, talk, language, discourse

word *v*. express, phrase, utter

work *n*. **1** exertion, activity, effort, toil **2** business, duty, occupation, job, employment, labour, labor (*N. Am.*) **3** output, product, fabric, production, performance, manufacture **4** act, deed, service, result, effect, achievement, feat

work *v*. **1** exert oneself, labour, labor (*N. Am.*), be engaged, toil **2** operate, act, perform, run

work out 1 solve, calculate, figure out **2** happen, progress, pan out **3** arrange, plan, devise **4** exercise, train, practise, practice (*N. Am.*)

worker *n*. labourer, laborer (*N. Am.*), employee, artisan, mechanic. engineer, operator, operative, craftsman, craftswoman
ANT. employer

workmanship *n*. handicraft, execution, skill, art, handiwork

world *n*. earth, universe, creation, globe, cosmos, planet, nature

worldly *adj*. mundane, terrestrial, earthly, ordinary, secular, temporal, human, common
ANT. spiritual, heavenly

worry *v*. **1** be anxious, fret **2** bother, trouble, disturb, annoy, harass, distress, plague

worry *n.* care, anxiety, concern, solicitude, torment, vexation, trouble, annoyance, plague, disquiet, perplexity, fear, apprehension, uneasiness, misgiving

worsen *v.* deteriorate, degenerate, get worse
ANT. improve

worship *n.* reverence, respect, honour, honor (*N. Am.*), adoration, submission
ANT. detestation, hatred, abhorrence, loathing, disgust

worship *v.* adore, honour, honor (*N. Am.*), exalt, reverence, revere, idolize, respect, defer, venerate, deify
ANT. detest, hate, abhor

worth *n.* **1** merit, excellence, importance, virtue, character, worthiness, integrity **2** value, price, rate, cost, equivalence
ANT. **1** worthlessness **2** cheapness

worthless *adj.* undeserving, useless, valueless, insignificant, unprofitable, ineffective
ANT. valuable, useful

worthy *adj.* valuable, deserving, worthwhile, estimable, virtuous, suitable, adapted, exemplary, upright, righteous, honest
ANT. worthless, valueless, unsuitable

wound *v.* hurt, injure, damage, harm, cut, stab, rend, lacerate, pain, annoy, mortify, offend
ANT. heal, cure, remedy, soothe

wound *n.* injury, damage, harm, hurt, cut, stabbing, laceration

wrap *v.* wind, fold, cover, enclose, envelop, enfold, surround, involve, conceal, hide
ANT. unfold, lay bare, reveal, develop, expose

wrath *n.* anger, rage, fury, ire, resentment, passion, exasperation, indignation
ANT. calmness, control, restraint, composure, placidity

wreath *n.* garland, chaplet, festoon, crown, diadem

wreck *v.* ruin, damage, destroy, demolish

wreck *n.* ruins, remains, rubbish, wreckage, debris, havoc, destruction, ruin, desolation, demolition, shipwreck
ANT. preservation, conservation

wrench *v.* pull, twist, wrest, force, strain, jerk, tug, sprain
ANT. straighten

wrestle *v.* grapple, fight, scuffle, struggle

wretched *adj.* **1** miserable, pitiful, calamitous, afflicted, unhappy, awful, comfortless, distressed **2** awful, shocking, deplorable, atrocious, depressing, sad, contemptible
ANT. **1** happy, successful **2** good

wriggle *v.* twist, worm, squirm, wiggle, writhe

wrinkle *n.* line, furrow, crease, fold, pucker, ridge

wrinkle *v.* crease, furrow, fold, pucker

write *v.* put down, record, compose

writer *n.* author, creator, poet, compiler, editor

writhe *v.* twist, turn, squirm

wrong *adj.* **1** mistaken, erroneous, incorrect, inaccurate, false **2** bad, immoral, illegal, evil, wicked **3** inappropriate, unsuitable, improper, out of place
ANT. **1** right, correct, accurate **2** good, legal, moral **3** suitable, appropriate

wry *adj.* dry, ironic, witty

yank *v.* pull, tug, jerk

yard *n.* square, court, courtyard, enclosure, quadrangle

yarn *n.* **1** fibre, fiber (*N. Am.*), thread **2** story, tale, anecdote

yawn *v.* open wide, gape

yearly *adj.* annual, each year, every year, year by year, per annum

yearn *v.* long, want, desire, be eager, covet, crave, hanker
ANT. hate, loathe, revolt, recoil, shudder at, despise

yell *v.* cry, shriek, scream, holler

yell *n.* cry, shriek, scream

yield *v.* **1** produce, afford, bear, render, furnish **2** relinquish, give in, let go, forgo, resign, surrender, concede, allow, grant, submit, succumb, accede, acquiesce, comply, consent, agree

yield *n.* produce, output, harvest, crops

young *adj.* youthful, boyish, girlish, childlike, juvenile, immature, inexperienced, innocent, ignorant
ANT. old, mature, adult, experienced

youth *n.* **1** adolescence, childhood, teenage years, young adulthood, youthfulness, juvenility, minority **2** boy, lad, youngster
ANT. **1** age, maturity

zeal *n.* ardour, ardor (*N. Am.*), eagerness, earnestness, fervour, fervor (*N. Am.*), enthusiasm, energy, feeling, devotion, intensity, passion, spirit
ANT. apathy, indifference, coldness

zealous *adj.* ardent, earnest, enthusiastic, fervid, eager, steadfast, keen, fervent, devoted, prompt, ready, fiery, passionate
ANT. lukewarm, indifferent, cold, apathetic

zero *n.* nought, naught, cipher, nothing

zest *n.* savour, savor (*N. Am.*), taste, smack, flavour, flavor (*N. Am.*), appetizer, pleasure, gusto, enjoyment, relish, enhancement

zone *n.* area, region, district, section

zoom *v.* speed, rush, tear, fly, race